TERROR IN MY SOUL

Terror in My Soul

*Communist
Autobiographies
on Trial*

IGAL HALFIN

HARVARD UNIVERSITY PRESS

Cambridge, Massachusetts

London, England · 2003

Library of Congress Cataloging-in-Publication Data

Halfin, Igal.
Terror in my soul: Communist autobiographies on trial / Igal Halfin.
p. cm.
Includes bibliographical references and index.
ISBN 0-674-01032-9 (alk. paper)
1. Soviet Union—Politics and government—1936–1953.
2. Language and languages—Political aspects.
3. Vsesoëìznaëì kommunisticheskaëì partiëì (bol'shevikov)—Purges.
4. Political purges—Soviet Union.
5. Soviet Union—Politics and government—1917–1936.
I. Title: Communist autobiographies on trial.   II. Title.

DK267.H35 2003
335.43'01—dc21   2002191959

ПАПЕ И МАМЕ

Contents

Preface

When I started working on this book the Cold War was hot, and research on Communism was considered a prestigious academic pursuit. The 1990s changed all that. As the Soviet Union disintegrated, Western democrats felt vindicated, and Communism ceased to pose an intellectual challenge. But are things really that simple? Do we genuinely understand what made Communism so appealing to so many, both the intellectual and the man on the street, for nearly a century? Communism remains with us because the dream it articulates and the dangers this dream harbors are still very real. Although the answers Communists gave to the question of identity are different from ours, the way they formulated the question definitely is not. The link between science, self-discovery, and salvation as they saw it is key to our understanding and experience of modernity.

To study the Communist work on the self we must open ourselves to the possibility that people mean what they say even when their language is ideological through and through, that they can strive to change themselves rather than just alter the reality around them to fit their interests. Instead of seeing in 1917 a chance to satisfy their old wishes, many citizens of the young Soviet republic were eager to revolutionize their souls. Everyone who is open to the possibility that people do not think, feel, and hope the same way everywhere, that the human self, and not only the human environment, is a historical construct, will be struck by the scope and persistence of the Bolshevik work on the self. The creation of the New Man, more than economic advancement or social amelioration, appears to have been the ultimate goal of the Russian Revolution.

Delving into the study of the Bolshevik soul, I quickly realized that my discipline, history, constricted me. Literary specialists, anthropologists, semioticians, and philosophers were more inclined to recognize my questions as pertinent. They led me to entertain the possibility that men and women are not just creators of history but also its products, and that language, the medium that molds them and the stuff historical documentation is made of, should be examined carefully. It is time for us to read what is actually written in the lines of the Communist text, not only what is between them.

Challenging the traditional approach of my discipline, I must acknowledge an intellectual debt to many people who are not historians. First, I want to thank Boris Uspenskii, a semiotician who may not remember me, but whose interdisciplinary approach impressed me tremendously as a graduate student in New York. Uspenskii's careful reconstruction of the world of belief of Russians in the sixteenth through eighteenth centuries convinced me that, if we are to understand political events and historical change in the twentieth century, we must undertake the same task with regard to Communists. Eric Naiman and Katerina Clark proved that historical insight and theoretically minded research do not contradict each other. I also thank Steven Kotkin, an open-minded and courageous historian who taught so many of us not to be afraid to think in new ways and to ask questions even when we are not certain we have the answers. "Us" refers here to my colleagues, who are also my friends, Anna Fishzon, Jochen Hellbeck, Peter Holquist, and Laurie Manchester. Not only did I learn a lot from them; I would not have been able to complete this work without their encouragement and camaraderie. During my research in Russia I was helped by Taisiia Pavlovna Bondarevskaia, Vladimir Ivanovich Shishkin, and Boris Ivanovich Kolonitskii. Their warmth reminded me that I was studying a living culture and not some ancient society.

Although my work in Israel deprived me of regular contacts with experts in the field of early Soviet history, it offered me an intellectual context that forced me to think broadly. In this country, ideas, history, and the New Man are not mere academic clichés, but the very stuff life is made of, and, for better or for worse, language and intellectual activity cannot be dismissed as inconsequential. As I completed my project in Tel Aviv, I benefited from numerous conversations with Hanan Yoran, a truly interdisciplinary scholar, and my wonderful office mate, Michael Zakim, who profoundly enhanced my appreciation of culture. I also want to thank my teachers Gabriel Gorodetsky and Nurit Schleifman, who encouraged my interest in Russian history.

Maia Rigas read many early drafts of this manuscript. Her comments and suggestions were extremely important. So was the help of my perfectionist editor, Sam Gilbert. Zvi Razi provided me with much-needed advice about how to make the quantitative material in this book an aid to the reader rather than a hindrance. Joyce Seltzer provided invaluable criticisms of the final draft. If this book is reasonably sized and occasionally lucid, it is in many ways as a result of her help. Finally, I must thank Deena Leventer and Tali Nevo, who turned the Russian Institute at Tel Aviv University into my second home and who looked into my chapters more times than I can count.

TERROR IN MY SOUL

Introduction

This is a book about good and evil, the fundamental moral traits of man as the Communists understood them. This is also a book about Party trials and ordeals, about the self-doubt that was ubiquitous in Soviet society, and about the potential for violence inherent in Communist discourse. In contrast to Marxism's explicit perception of itself as wholly scientific, *Terror in My Soul* argues that Communist discourse, when read against the grain, was suffused with ethics. Soviet scholars and Soviet politicians discussed the characteristics of the New Man, the proud, selfless citizen of that classless society presumed to be in the making since 1917. Protracted and animated debates about how to construe the interaction between mind and body—debates that concerned the self-interested drives of the individual and his consciousness—underlined the tensions between value-free Marxist science and the hypermoralistic, millenarian undercurrents also present in Soviet Marxism.

The manichean aspects of the official discourse asserted themselves with violent force during the Great Purge of 1935–1938. By the mid-1930s, after two decades of building the classless society, political behavior was assumed to be governed by moral motivations irreducible to objective facts such as class origins or environmental influences. Once guilt was thus shifted from the body of the accused to his mind, once it was relocated from what was perceived to be the locus of man's nature to what was perceived to be the locus of his moral self, his intentions—and not just his actions—were criminalized. For the first time, individuals were held responsible for their alleged crimes, and Communists were put to death in great numbers.

In contrast to the commonplace explanation of the Great Purge as an

1

unprecedented breakdown of all moral behavior, the Stalinist auto-da-fé rested on an ethical system. The Communist eschatology by which a classless society would be realized only when evil souls were removed from the proletariat established the ideological matrix within which grand-scale violence could make moral sense. Anatolii Lunacharskii, the commissar of education, was clear in rooting the discourse of equality and justice and the discourse of purity and death in the same widely shared Communist moral quest—the desire to bring humanity to moral perfection. "We cannot introduce humanistic principles all at once," this prominent Party theoretician explained. "First we have to annihilate our enemies."[1] Humanism and legal executions were two aspects of the same millenarian project of creating a New Man—the division of the Bolshevik vanguard into the worthy and the unworthy.

Communists insisted that the omnipresent counterrevolutionary plot had to be foiled and that violence was a legitimate way to do so. Selfish or career interests could not be the sole motives for the actions of Stalinist zealots. While "the imagination and the spiritual strength of Shakespeare's evildoers stopped at a dozen corpses," Aleksandr Solzhenitsyn astutely observes, "because they had no ideology," no such limits were known to Party activists.[2] It would have been very difficult for the Stalinist leadership to embark on a systematic elimination of so many prominent revolutionaries, in such a cold-blooded and calculated manner, had not all agreed that the ostensibly good part of society had the mandate to serve as an executioner entitled to eliminate its ostensibly wicked underside.

In the years 1935–1938 the great Moscow Show Trials destroyed the top echelon of Party leadership while a large number of less-dramatized trials resulted in the death of hundreds of thousands of Communists. Individuals confessed to crimes they had not committed, denounced all that was dear to them—family and friends included—but were nonetheless executed in the cellars of the NKVD. Historians have long struggled to come to terms with the flood of denunciations, the mass psychosis that turned Soviet society into a war of all against all. The *mobile perpetuum* of mutual incriminations, of perpetrators becoming victims and back again, all at remarkable speed, is baffling. It is unclear whether the wide-scale executions were intended to be a public spectacle designed to whip the population into compliance, or a secret cleansing procedure that sought to eliminate Stalin's political enemies. Some death sentences were widely publicized; the stenograms of the Moscow Show Trials, for example, were translated into a number of languages and published in large editions by the Ministry of

Foreign Affairs. In other cases, however, family members had to wait for up to half a century before discovering that loved ones had been summarily tried and shot.[3]

What is no less puzzling is that in contrast to this randomness, the thick dossiers containing the material used to convict the condemned—diaries, autobiographies, interrogation protocols, and endless confessions—were carefully preserved. The Great Purge produced death on a mass scale, but one less analogous to Nazi-style industrial killing than to inquisition-style punishments of crimes of the soul. Party members perished in the hundreds of thousands, but they perished as individuals, not as numbers.

Scholars still debate the actual number of those who lost their lives during the Great Purge, and which groups were most severely affected. But what made this phenomenon so appalling was not just the sheer numbers. The collectivization of Soviet agriculture (1929–1933) and certainly the civil war (1918–1921) had witnessed even worse atrocities.[4] The Great Purge was fundamentally different because its violence was aimed at Communists themselves. Ever mindful of the prediction by Pierre Vergniaud, the great French revolutionary orator, that the Revolution would devour its own children, Lenin warned his disciples, "Let no blood flow between you."[5] At first the Party heeded Lenin's injunction. The Politburo strongly objected to the request of the GPU—the Soviet secret police, later renamed NKVD—to sentence the indomitable Oppositionist Martemian Riutin to death in 1932.[6] Not long after, however, the taboo against executions of Party members was broken.

Following the assassination of Sergei Kirov, the head of the Leningrad Party organization, in December 1934, and particularly in the wake of the 1936 Moscow Show Trial, Communists began disappearing from the Party's membership rolls.[7] An open season on Party leadership had begun. Of the 1,996 delegates elected to the Seventeenth Party Congress in 1934, 1,108 were eventually arrested and 848 executed. Ninety-eight of the 139 Central Committee members and candidates elected were eventually killed.[8] According to one observer, throughout these years Party members slept in their clothes in expectation of imminent arrest.[9] A contemporary joke conveyed the popular sense that the Great Purge was directed primarily against Communists: "The NKVD bangs on the door of an apartment in Leningrad in 1937. A terrified voice from inside asks, 'Who is there?' 'NKVD, open up!' comes the reply. 'No, no, you've got the wrong apartment. The Communists live upstairs!'"[10]

The fact that the Communist revolutionary elite turned against itself

with such single-minded purpose, becoming an accomplice in its own destruction, defies simple explanation. If the slaughter on the battlefields of
the civil war, the elimination of the membership of rival parties, and the
starvation of recalcitrant peasants are, however inhumane, explicable as attempts to eliminate the avowed enemies of the regime, the same cannot be
said regarding the destruction of Party cadres. Because it is impossible to
equate intra-Party violence from the late 1930s as a campaign against
"real," rationally explicable foes, the following pages focus on the Great
Purge only and not on terror in general, on the Communist Party and not
on the Soviet population at large, for it was among Party members that
Bolshevik eschatology found its ultimate expression.

What accounts for the nearly complete lack of resistance among high-
ranking Party members who knew they faced probable death? Why, the
whole world wondered, did most of the accused prove willing to assist in
their own prosecution? Communists put their heads into Stalin's mouth,
in the words of Nikolai Bukharin, "knowing for sure that one day he will
gobble us up."[11] Scenes of Communists facing their executioners and cry-
ing out in their last moments, "Long Live the Party! Long Live Comrade
Stalin!" must surely have been surrealistic, not to say macabre.[12] Less a state
policy than a state of mind, at least as far as Communist victims were concerned, Party terror was the result of a never-ending interrogation of the
self. On April 14, 1935, Grigori Zinoviev wrote: "I look into the portraits of
the Politburo members and say: Dear ones, look inside me! Can't you see
that I am no longer an enemy, that I am with you body and soul?" Two
years later, Bukharin longed for "an instrument that would allow you to
penetrate my tortured soul." Both leaders were overwhelmed by fear that
they would be castigated as incapable of resisting counterrevolutionary
temptation.[13]

Were Party members coerced into "speaking Bolshevik," as Steven Kotkin puts it, or were they saying what they were saying of their own accord?[14]
In this context, the relation between the subject and his language remains a
significant theoretical problem. Although scholars are undoubtedly correct
in arguing that Marxist ideology is indispensable to understanding the
Great Purge, the approach here diverges from those of traditional histories
of the period in some very important respects. The "totalitarian thesis" lo-
cates the subject in opposition to Communist ideology.[15] According to
Leszhek Kolakowski, "in the context of repression, the omnipotent state on
one side confronted the lone citizen on the other." The object of the Soviet

system, he argues, was the destruction of all forms of communal life save for those imposed by and closely controlled by the state, "so that individuals are isolated from one another and become mere instruments in the hands of the state."[16] Yet one may question the customary assumption that Communists were capable of a high degree of discrimination between their "true self" and their "public performance." Rather than pursue a personal agenda outside the Communist system of meaning, the individual may have provided a voice for the official discourse. This was an outcome not only of a process of coercion but also one of cooptation, which drew the subject to self-destruction. Individuals identified, partially or entirely, willingly or reluctantly, with the models proposed by the Party. They engaged in Communist "self-fashioning," thus turning the messianic aspirations of the state into their own intimate affair.

But if Communists terrorized themselves, why, having realized they were being victimized by their own actions, did they not simply stop? This key question exposes the most noticeable weakness of the totalitarian interpretation of the Great Purge: its implicit intentionalism. The intentionalist argument advances a historical explanation that unfolds in terms of mental causation. Stalinist zealots must first have conceived certain ideas, which they then acted upon in order to realize. Yet in studying Communist discourse—its system of coding and the matrix of its rules—it becomes clear how the lack of conscious intent can shape human action. Communists themselves would undoubtedly have renounced the eschatological ideas I assign to them here, decrying moralistic notions such as "good" and "evil" as religious superstitions that had nothing to do with their own scientific worldview. But what historical actors actually wanted and what they expected to happen are not at issue here. Although it is widely assumed that a subject controls what he says by knowing what he means, I suggest, by contrast, that what is often said of the economic and social activity of man can also be said of language: namely, that Communist discourse had unintended consequences. Neither the producers nor the consumers of this discourse could have fully known the implications of what they were saying and doing.

This study of how the official discourse—the language and ritual of the Communist Party in the 1920s and the 1930s—was appropriated by the rank and file has little to say about high politics and the decision-making process within the Bolshevik elite. It is the Party rather than this or that Soviet leader that concerns me, what exactly the Party communicated and how its message was appropriated. In this respect, discourse analysis allows us to study the plurality intrinsic in any discourse in a way that studies of totalitarian ideology and its leading proponents do not. The following pages examine not only the official Soviet ideological monolith but also its fissures and contradictions. The Party discourse was polyvalent enough to allow for a number of readings, interpretations, and subversions by contemporary actors, some intentional, some inadvertent.

Communists ended up committing bloody deeds they hardly expected would follow from the lofty principles they thought shaped their project. The dream of universal emancipation spun out of control precisely because those who dreamed of "human perfectibility" or "classless society" never imagined that a vision so perfect, so utopian, could embrace slaughter and systematic persecution. But once entrenched in the tissue of power, messianic dreams that structured the Communist discourse and provided it a frame of moral reference that set standards of conformity could not be easily curbed, even when some of their horrific implications asserted themselves with a vengeance.

1

Good and Evil
in Communism

The Communist hermeneutics of the soul—the complex ritual of words and deeds that permitted the Party to determine who was worthy to belong to the brotherhood of the elect—stands at the heart of the dynamic that led to the Great Purge.[1] Enacted immediately after the Bolsheviks seized power, the Communist hermeneutics of the soul was embodied in a wide gamut of interpretative practices, among which interrogations, purges, comrade trials, and campaigns of self-criticism were the most prominent. Hermeneutics refers here to the way in which the words the individual used in accounting for his thoughts and desires were taken as a clue to or symptom of some vaster reality—his inner moral disposition—which became his ultimate truth.

The hermeneutics of the soul emerged as a manifest, objectively verifiable way of distinguishing true revolutionaries from impostors. The Party had to take the stories comrades told about themselves as evidence of their otherwise hidden moral character. Because self-introspection was ineluctably linked with self-narration, autobiographies, their syntax, their meaning, and the ways in which they were publicly interrogated became a crucial component of the Communist hermeneutics of the soul. Composing their own detailed life stories, each comrade had to understand where he came from, what had brought him into the Party, and what his duties were toward the movement. Without understanding both the moral criteria and the scientific justifications underlying certain readings of Communist autobiography, it is impossible to understand how wide-scale massacres could take place in a country laying claim to the legacy of the Enlightenment.

During the momentous reconfiguration of political and social identities brought about by the revolution, industrialization, collectivization (1928–1934), and, finally, the Great Purge, individuals were relocated within new sets of discursive relations.[2] The new self was exposed, made nameable and describable; the Bolsheviks could define, delineate, and, in a sense, recreate their universe by speaking about themselves in a particular way. The creation of a New Man, equipped with a brand-new identity, was the key to the Communist emancipatory project.[3] Maxim Gorky, the famous proletarian novelist, noted in 1917 that "the new structure of political life demands from us a new structure of the soul."[4] Nadezhda Krupskaia, Lenin's wife and a Party theorist in her own right, concurred few years later that "Yes, if we want to build a new social order . . . we have to create a totally new type of human being."[5] At the peak of the Great Purge, Il'ia Erenburg, another renowned Soviet writer, was proud to be able to recognize the results: "Although we may have borrowed the model for a tractor from the United States, our tractor driver is certainly a man the world has never seen before."[6]

Just beneath the thin layer of Marxist dogma, the Communist notion of the self existed in a contested zone of exchange between various, sometimes very diverse, psychological notions. Visions of the New Man were advanced by Party moralists, sociologists, sexologists, literary critics, and other avid participants in the Communist ethical laboratory—all aspiring to the status of scientists of the revolutionary soul. Schematically put, the Communist self was uniquely articulated within a hybrid of modern science of the psyche and messianic spirituality. Uniting Marxist theoretical insight into the workings of the human mind and self-interrogation typical of the ascetic tradition, Communists were urged to seek new, scientific means of reaching the essence deep within. Only when the dialectic of inner and outer selves was resolved would the new, self-transparent individual be ready to be judged by a proper hermeneutical court as to whether he was worthy to enter the Communist paradise. Hence the Great Purge and its courts.

Recognizing the centrality of the hermeneutics of the soul in the everyday life of the Party compels a reevaluation of the issue of individual guilt during the trials of the Great Purge. Commonly, a "soulless" Communism, with its emphasis on the "science of objective truth," is contrasted with the spirituality of the Christian tradition, which held individual intentions in high regard. Communists were obsessed with history, so the familiar argument goes, because they understood history to be an "objective" and "deindividualized" process. The verdict of the ultimate laws of the universe was expected to take precedence over the conscience of the historical actors. In this interpretation, revolutionary justice disregarded subjective intentions oriented to the verdict of the final tribunal of history. Prominent historians and philosophers writing in the 1950s claimed that Communism had little to say about traditional ethical issues like guilt, that Communism discarded individual moral responsibility. "Despite the fact that their intentions may be subjectively good," maintained the Polish writer Czeslaw Milosz, the guilt of the victims of the Communist regimes had an "objective character." According to Milosz, whereas Christianity was based on a concept of "individual merit of guilt," the New Faith was based on "historical merit and guilt."[7]

To the extent that the Communists had an ethics at all, agreed the German-Jewish philosopher Hannah Arendt, their ethics constituted a major break in the history of Western thought. The twin concepts of objective enemies and historical necessity, "so all-important for purges and show-trials in the Bolshevik world," were unique Communist inventions entirely unknown even during the French Revolution. "Robespierre's terror of virtue was terrible enough, but it was not directed against people who, even from the viewpoint of the revolutionary ruler, were innocent."[8] The Hungarian-Jewish writer Arthur Koestler observed as early as the 1930s that the Party invented "new rules of ethics," based on responsibility toward historical truth. Only "who is objectively in the right," Koestler argued, mattered to the Communists. Whereas the "liberal ethics of fair play" questioned whether one had acted from good faith, to the Communists this question was supposedly of no interest. In Koestler's scenario, Communists threw overboard the old Western moral code that punished intentions and not consequences in favor of what he called "consequent logic." That the convicted may have been honest, well-meaning, and loyal Communists was entirely irrelevant.[9]

However, the centrality of the moral-psychological discourse in Communism calls into question this position. The Stalinist regime preserved much of Western civilization's concern with the truth judged according to the state of the soul. According to Marx, there was nothing in the objective development of capitalism that could alert men to their messianic role. Left to their own devices, the alienated and stupefied workers became cogs in the vast capitalist machine. Convinced that a history left to develop deterministically would only have deepened human bondage, Marx arrayed himself in the robes of a gnostic prophet who miraculously saves humanity by awakening workers' souls to the gospel of truth. This moment represents the transcendent element in Marxism. Had the source of the revolutionary consciousness been immanent in history, the genesis of Marxist ideology would have been transformed into a simple cause, an event inserted in the deterministic chain of events and utterly inadequate to bring about a messianic awakening and emancipation. Indeed, Communism did not believe in an entirely autonomous human agent, but Stalin's inquisitors attributed an important role to the individual as a liberating force. The Communist concern with the subjective response to the revolutionary message cannot be dismissed.

Given that counterrevolution was considered to be more a state of mind than a course of action, it is hardly surprising that the civil-war concept of "revolutionary illegality" explicitly included criminal acts that were meditated and not just committed.[10] The distinction between intent to commit a crime and the crime itself was dispensed with. Rather, the GPU distinguished between crimes perpetrated with "evil intent" *(zloi umesel)* and crimes that could not be thus characterized. The state prosecutor, Nikolai Krylenko, told a meeting of the soviet executive committee in July 1923 that "we consider as counterrevolutionary those acts which the perpetrator knew full well undermined the Revolution."[11] Without a proper appreciation of the Communist notion of guilt by intent it is impossible to understand why confessions played such an important role in Soviet jurisprudence.[12] What, we may ask, prompted Krylenko to propose that judges be allowed to skip the judicial inquiry entirely in cases in which the accused had confessed? Why did Andrei Vyshinskii, the general prosecutor during the years of the Great Purge, regard confession, "however obtained, as in itself sufficient grounds for a conviction"? Even if we assume that the writing of confessions was coerced from the high-ranking leaders accused during the great Show Trials for propaganda reasons, it remains unclear why elaborate confessions were also extorted from lower-echelon comrades, about whom the Soviet public never heard much.[13] The injunction to extract confessions does not make much sense unless we take seriously the concern with the self.

The workings of the Communist courts of conscience show that individual guilt was subjective. The accused had to bear witness against themselves because only they were privy to their inner truth. When Viacheslav Molotov chided Nikolai Bukharin for attempting a hunger strike in 1937,

Bukharin justified himself by saying that this had not been his "subjective intention."[14] Eventually Bukharin was cajoled into convicting himself: "I do not want to minimize my guilt," he stated at his 1938 trial; "I want to aggravate it. This is not my defense, it is my self-accusation."[15] Stalin's vow in 1937 to destroy "anyone who by his actions or thoughts—yes, even thoughts!—encroaches on the unity of the Soviet state" should also alert us to the fact that movements of the soul mattered a great deal.[16]

Only a subtle application of the hermeneutics of the soul induced a Party tribunal to distinguish an inexperienced doubter from a counterrevolutionary heretic. "Doubt" *(somnenie)* and "heresy" *(inakomyslie)* were two different subjective states, not easily distinguishable through external, objective indices. Doubt signified a lapse of Party consciousness, quickly dispersed with the aid of proper indoctrination. Heresy, on the other hand, was hopeless. It was a basic presupposition of the Party purge and testimony to the importance of subjectivity in Communism that comrades were expected to recant sincerely. A doubter had nothing to conceal. He might have vacillated for a while, but once the Party congress came to a decision, his incertitude evaporated without a trace. But there was always the other possibility, that a comrade was a counterrevolutionary in disguise. Such an individual had plenty to hide; feigning obedience before the congress, he was actually a "double-dealer" *(dvurushnik)*—an epithet that was attached to many of the victims of the Great Purge.

Communist Eschatology

Starting at the beginning of time with man living in harmony with man, continuing with man's fall and the emergence of a class society, and concluding this grand epic with the promise of salvation at the end of time, Marx's story of humankind is a unique articulation of time and narrative. The onset of Communism was to be a radical disjuncture in human history, its consummation and end. It is an "eschatology" in that the human soul moves through time from the darkness of capitalism to the light of Communism. The Marxist narrative was articulated around two mythical events: "Original Expropriation"—the beginning of history, which introduced exploitation of man by man—and "Expropriation of the Expropriators," which terminated history by terminating class struggle. The former event resonates with the Christian notion of the Fall, the latter with the advent of the messiah. Both eschatological metaframeworks share interchangeable plot structures: similar agents drove plots forward, and similar metaphors and figures were used to characterize historical events. Leonard Wessell argues convincingly that the rhythm of the development of class entities was also the rhythm of a "salvational drama," and that Marxist class categories derived their intelligibility from the mythoreligious story they related.[17] Inserting new, scientific terms into the traditional eschatological lexicon, Communism substituted "comrades" for "faithful," "classless society" for "paradise" and the "proletariat," the epitome of laboring humanity, solely endowed with a universalist perspective on the world, for the "class messiah." The proletariat was to express itself fully in the "Revolution," the conclusive event in the epic of man's self-alienation and return into himself.

Distinct though the Christian and the Communist narratives are from each other, eschatology seems to be at work in both. Such a homology between the Marxist and the Christian historical narratives does not imply an interpretation of Communism as a surrogate religion. Hannah Arendt pointed to the weakness of such an interpretation when she ridiculed "the widespread conviction that Communism is a new religion, notwithstanding its avowed atheism, because it fulfills socially, psychologically, and 'emotionally' the same function traditional religion fulfills in the free world. The concern of the social sciences does not lie in what Bolshevism as ideology or as a form of government is, nor in what its spokesmen have to say for themselves . . . Their concern is only with functions, and whatever fulfills the same function can, according to this view, be called the same. It is as though I had the right to call the heel of my shoe a hammer because I, like most women, use it to drive nails into the wall."[18] Reducing twentieth-century ideologies to mobilization mechanisms, the approach deplored by Arendt remains indifferent to political discourse, thus leaving out of sight precisely what makes Communism unique and historically significant.

The Communist historical metanarrative structured universal time as an odyssey of proletarian consciousness. Marx articulated the relation between historical man and an ideal New Man through his use of the terms "proletarians" and "Communists." As long as capitalism existed, the two sides of the same messianic coin remained distinct: while the proletariat stood for self-alienated humanity, Communists were the bearers of the proletariat's genuine spirit, the agent striving to realize the proletariat's salvational potential. The Revolution could not occur without the active intervention of the Communist Party, the agent that brought about mass conversion to Marxism. Both human and divine, a real institution and an incarnated idea, the Party had to be infallible. Any challenge to the validity of the laws of history it embodied was scientifically obstructive and ethically repugnant. Alongside its constructive role (the enlightenment of the proletariat as to its true self) the Party had a destructive role. It was a redemptive force bent on eradicating all that had been real in the bourgeois world so that the New Man could realize himself. Oriented toward the future, the Communist eschatological sensibility viewed contemporary humanity not as a value in itself but as raw material from which an aesthetically perfect man had to be sculpted.[19]

The Communist conception of the Party had little in common with the liberal notion of a party. The Party was a messianic order, not a pragmatic political organization formed to represent a concrete constituency. Whereas for liberals a "party" mediates between citizen and state, for Communists the "Party" mediates between the proletarian soul, buried under false appearances (man as "subject to the tsar," man as "citizen," etc.), and its emancipation. The Party could not compromise with society on the level of shared interests, nor even govern according to its own private interests, because, as Alan Besançon pointed out, it existed only "in the fiction of the total dedication of its own private interests to the common interest ... called Communism."[20] What was at stake in the activity of the Party was the proletariat's historical task, not its mundane needs and interests. "It is not a question," wrote Marx, "of what this or that proletarian, or the whole proletariat, at the moment, regards as its aim. It is a question of what the proletariat is, and what, in accordance with its being, it will historically be compelled to do."[21]

On its way to final victory, the Party encountered many obstacles. Evil was a leading actor in the Communist historical drama. Filled with crises, history, for Marx, was propelled by "revolutions" rather than "evolutions," because counterrevolutionary machinations ensured that there could be no seamless historical development. A historical impediment, the very force that slowed emancipation, evil made emancipation morally meaningful. A manichean view of the universe penetrated the Communist discourse, albeit in a somewhat displaced form. How else should we understand a Bolshevik leaflet from the time of the civil war: "You have the choice between two very different armies waging two very different wars. One is the holy war of workers for freedom and socialism, the other is a wicked war of capitalists for bondage and servitude."[22] The division of universal economy into capitalist and socialist had to lead to an all-out struggle between two cultural universes, Bukharin reasoned. "One of these universes will have to perish!"[23]

Far from dispensing with the division of human souls into good and evil, Communism endowed this tradition with the status of a thoroughly scientific observation. The Communist conceptual architectonics was full of black-and-white oppositions: proletariat versus bourgeoisie, revolution versus counterrevolution, progress versus reaction, knowledge versus ignorance, consciousness versus interests, health versus degeneracy, and production versus wrecking.[24] What is most significant is not the moral dualism itself (similar bipolar visions can be found in other ideological formations) but the concept of historical progression, leading through ever-changing antitheses to the teleological goal—the elimination of evil and the creation of classless society.[25]

The notion of evil was a familiar one in the Communist conception of the universe.[26] The Party insistently and repetitively identified a panoply of adversaries scheming against the proletariat. Every beginning Communist publicist knew he could easily go back and forth between "bourgeois imperialists," "Social Democratic traitors," "kulaks," "wreckers," "spies" and "Oppositionists." Counterrevolutionaries were variously described in the Soviet press as "baleful" *(pogannye)* and "pernicious" *(vrednye)*. The name of the wicked changed over time, and some of these incarnations were more important during the early years of the Soviet power, while others came into prominence in the 1940s and 1950s: "wicked ones" *(negodiai)* populated the Bolshevik universe during the 1920s and "evilmongers" *(zloumyshlenniki)* during the 1930s; Tomskii talked in 1933 about "melodramatic wrongdoers" *(melodramaticheskie zlodei)*.[27] During the Great Fatherland War (1941–1945) the Red Army security forces executed the most "malevolent" *(zlostnye)* of the deserters. And in February 1953 the secret police informed Stalin that it had been merciless toward "Jewish nationalists," whom it regarded as "especially malicious [*zlobnye*] enemies."[28]

Since morality permitted the active choice of good, it had also to allow for the active choice of evil. What Communism enjoined was the ultimate moral faculty—will *(volia)*.[29] It was this faculty that moved humans away from necessity and compulsion and into the realm of freedom, enabling them to say "yes" or "no" to the Party. The choice between willingness and

unwillingness determined, in the final account, the political stance an individual took. Communism was supposed to be achieved when enough
disciples of Lenin chose to embrace it—not when a blind and mindless
historical process had run its course. Before one could become a good
Communist, one's divided will had to be healed. Every Communist had to
submit to the Party line not only externally but also internally, by getting
rid of "vacillations" *(kolebaniia)* or "waverings" *(shataniia)*. Communists
worthy of the name were "strong willed" *(volevye)*, "disciplined" *(distsi-
plinirovannye)*, "energetic" *(energichnye)*, and "goal oriented" *(tseleu-
stremlennye)*. "Determination" *(reshitel'nost')* and "cold-bloodedness"
(khladnokrovie) were key virtues. Revolutionary pseudonyms like "Stalin"
(made of steel) and "Kamenev" (made of stone) as well as Dzerhzinskii's
nickname, "Iron Felix," suggested this ideal, resolute character. Conversely,
as Bukharin pointed out, "the might of the proletarian state found its expression not only in the fact that it smashed the counterrevolutionary
bands, but also in the fact that it disintegrated its enemies from within,
that it disorganized the Will of its enemies."[30]

It is of course possible to explain the division of society into good and
evil under the Soviet regime as the result not so much of Marxism as such
but of Russia. The Russian culture is often characterized in terms of its pre-
dilection to a sharply polarized view of the world and black-and-white
descriptions of moral conduct. According to Iurii Lotman's and Boris
Uspenskii's classic study, the life of the medieval believer in the West admitted three types of behavior: "the unconditionally sinful, the unconditionally holy, and the neutral, which permits eternal salvation after some
sort of purgative trial. In the real life of the medieval West a wide area of
neutral behavior thus became possible." By contrast, "the Russian medieval
system was constructed on the accentuated duality . . . Intermediate neutral spheres were not envisaged. Behavior in earthly life could, correspondingly, be either sinful or holy."[31] Fascinating as this analysis may be, when
applied to the Soviet context it tends to get hopelessly intertwined with
problematic Marxist apologetics. Claims about the uniqueness of Russia
(themselves usually related to arguments concerning its supposed "backwardness") invoking the argument that Bolshevism was somehow a purely
"Eastern phenomenon" have little or nothing to do with Marxism proper.
Viewing Stalinism as a stream of thought that failed to shake off the manichean cultural baggage of Russia trivializes the Great Purge. Such an in-

terpretation explains away the messianic outbursts in twentieth-century Russian history as irrelevant to the Marxist science and thus ignores the connection between Enlightenment and terror.[32]

Bolshevism and the Encounter between Eschatology and Modernity

While preserving certain Christian components, Marxism transformed other traditional beliefs and practices beyond recognition. Jacob Talmon, one of the founders of the totalitarian school in historiography, has shown that it was the eighteenth-century idea of the natural order as an attainable, indeed inevitable goal that engendered a political attitude hitherto unknown. Whereas previous messianic movements had always broken away from society, the modern revolutionary movements were very much of this world, "acting on society in order to attain salvation in society." In uniting absolute claims with temporal references, secular messianism aimed not at salvation in the beyond but at happiness on earth and at the social transformation of this world and of the individuals inhabiting it.[33]

Attention to the messianic aspects of the Communist discourse opens a way toward a reconceptualization of continuity and change in Russian history. The old continuity, the one that emphasized the preservation into the 1930s of the repressive practices of the Russian state, may be replaced by a new discontinuity, triggered by the introduction of modern state practices designed to recreate the self. And inversely, the old discontinuity that posited the replacement of Christian dogma with the Western rational and scientific worldview is replaced by a new continuity concerned with the preservation in Russia of some traditional eschatological concerns. Sharing with the church the promise of a just and harmonious society, the revolutionary experiment eroded the socially and politically passive attitudes of post-Petrine, Orthodox Christianity, which had deemphasized human agency by declaring attempts to build heaven on earth heretical. Militant and iconoclastic, Marxism presented social activism as a prerequisite of this-worldly salvation and in so doing promoted a radical break with the conservative Russian intellectual tradition. Communism became the medium through which Western activist and interventionist politics, geared toward social improvement and progress, was introduced into Russia.

Striding dramatically onto the historical stage in 1917, the Bolsheviks claimed to be for the tsarist empire what Marxists were for the entire

world. Claiming a monopoly on theoretical orthodoxy, the Bolsheviks believed that Russia would play a leading role in the drama of universal redemption. "The Russian Revolution," wrote Stalin, "is the nodal point of
the world revolution. The fundamental questions of the Russian revolution
are the fundamental questions of the world revolution."[34] Having renamed
themselves the Communist Party, the Bolsheviks stressed that they, the sole
legitimate heirs of Marx, were "the only truly revolutionary proletarian
party in Russia."[35]

Once in power, the Bolsheviks turned social engineering into scientific
know-how, much as a sculptor operating on marble (the body politic) dis-
cards the excess and extracts the statute he wants (classless society). The
Bolsheviks ventured to delineate the boundaries of socialist society and to
homogenize its fabric, using in the process cutting-edge tools of sociological analysis. In so doing, they imported to Russia the conception of politics
as a system of government ruling not territories but populations and individual selves.[36] Data collection under the Party's auspices became an important tool, securing the integrity of the healthy and beautiful body politic and eliminating bourgeois "microbes." The detailed questionnaires and
workbooks; the 1926, 1937, and 1939 censuses; and the mid-1930s grand-
scale passport campaign not only produced statistical compilations that
divided the population into discrete "elements" with specific, qualitative
traits, but also provided the state with invaluable biographical information
that allowed it to judge individuals.[37]

The Bolshevik state provided the practitioners of the hermeneutics of
the soul with the sites from which they could launch their discourse. These
sites included the Party apparatus, the newspaper, the judiciary, and the
Communist Academy. A system of rules was initiated whenever a certain
theoretical object was to be transformed (e.g., the self), a certain new
concept was to appear (e.g., the "degenerate," the "Oppositionist," the
"wrecker"), a certain strategy was to be modified (e.g., the shift from edu-
cating to isolating and eventually annihilating). Objects, concepts, and
strategies did not arise in isolated environments. Only the interactions between diverse Bolshevik institutions and practices permitted the creation
of workable types of good and evil selves. Here we have to take into account (1) the relation between the authority of a Party hermeneut and
the authority of the medicopsychological expert; (2) the relation between
the filter formed by GPU-NKVD investigation and the filter formed by the
Party archive—a vast documentary field that included questionnaires, au-

tobiographies, and interrogation protocols; and (3) the relation between rituals structuring the life of the Party cell (a place of systematic and coded observation of the individual) and NKVD court procedure. Forms of treatment and punishment, from a therapeutic dispatch to the factory to confinement in a labor camp—a space where those who could be redeemed through labor were separated from those who were incorrigibly evil—all need to be examined. Without detailed procedures for the interactions between various discursive sites, changes could not be transcribed from one domain to another, new strategies (e.g., execution by firing squad) could not be designed to accommodate new objects (e.g., the "irredeemable counterrevolutionaries").

While it is quite possible that many Communist practices were part and parcel of modernity as such, the Bolsheviks were certainly innovative in the degree to which their project demarcated the human self. Until then the tsar's largely passive servants, the Soviet subjects, were compelled by the new regime to become masters of their own destiny.[38] It was perhaps the introduction of this peculiar, post-Reformation form of secularized Christianity that made the Bolshevik Party so effective. The new regime called for the removal of all mediation between the objective and the subjective, the citizen and the community, so that the conscience of the individual and the messianic goals of the state naturally coincided.[39]

The Good Self, the Wicked Self

Not everyone deserved membership in the brotherhood of the elect. Only worthy comrades, those who contributed, body and soul, to the victory of Communism, deserved that right. Michael Walzer's discussion of participatory rights in the Puritan commonwealth is instructive here: "The congregation would not include all the residents of the parish . . . That would make godliness a matter of geography, said the ministers, and turn the church into 'an inn to receive whoever cometh.' Instead, participation depended on behavior and behavior presumably upon Will." Puritans demanded the careful testing of all who wished to enter into the parish commonwealth and claimed the right "to exclude even neighbors and kinsfolk from the communion in order to maintain a clear distinction between the godly—who lived in pious and sober order—and the sinners—who 'rioted' in uncleanness."[40] Communist membership was equally a question of pure will and intent. Elaborate admission procedures encapsulated the spiritual meaning the Bolsheviks attributed to participation in the broth-erhood of the elect. Suitability for membership was largely determined by the applicant's ability, first, to present a cogent claim to have reached the light of Communism, and then successfully to uphold this claim in the face of possible counternarratives.

Communist autobiographies were the standard by which entrance into the brotherhood of the elect was determined and a daily means of control over the self. By spotlighting the poetical structure of these documents we can see how Party applicants told the story of who they were, how their stories varied according to the identities of their narrators and their audi-ences, and how the rules for the construction of the Communist self inter-acted with wider Bolshevik practices. Because these applicants to the Party modeled their narratives on descriptions of spiritual growth, telling their lives up to the moment of "rebirth," the Communist autobiography dein-dividualized lives. Details could be pruned, embellished, or ignored in or-der to fit the author into the Communist literary conventions and write him into the Soviet order.[41]

Communist autobiography is presented in this study as a locus of dis-course rather than a reflection of a self. Autobiography does not only ex-press the self; it creates it. The self examined here does not necessarily ex-haust the self-understanding of contemporaries. Soviet citizens may well have had alternative forms of self-identification. We should not be sur-prised then that Soviet refugees who found their way to the West after the Second World War venerated "personal autonomy" and "freedom of con-science," proving to be highly adept at liberal self-presentation. Such a rapid transformation of identity does not present a problem, since a his-torical subject can articulate itself along a number of language axes and take part in a plurality of identity games. The point is that as long as indi-viduals lived in the Communist system, they could ignore the Communist discourse, including the discourse that engaged their private sphere, only on pain of becoming outcasts.

What were the historical roots of the Communist self? Scholars who tie the rise of the autobiography as a genre of self-presentation to the dissemi-nation of the modern notion of the self point out that the word "autobiog-raphy," coined in England, came into currency only in the first decade of the nineteenth century.[42] In Russian, "autobiography" (*avtobiografiia*) was apparently first used in an 1817 letter from Aleksander Turgenev to Petr Viazemskii.[43] It has been shown, however, that much older literary genres such as "confessions" or "memoirs" closely resemble what came to be known as autobiography. Indeed, it is difficult to establish in what sense the Communist self was indebted to an ancient tradition and in what sense its characteristics were modern.

The Communist revelation of the revolutionary prophecy in the "theater of the individual spirit," where one experiences a prophetic enactment of the final, redemptive historical events, is clearly a notion with Christian roots. Augustine was probably the first to describe in detail the sustained struggle between "two Wills"—the subjective equivalent of the forces of Christ and the Antichrist—culminating in a spiritual armageddon in the Milanese garden. At the moment of the final triumph of the good will, grace was manifest, Augustine's old being annihilated, and his new self born: "Dying unto death and living into life" (*Confessions*, book VIII). In elaborating the psychohistorical parallelism, Augustine established the Christian paradigm of the interior life. Concurrently he created the notion of subjective time and the enduring literary genre that attempted to capture this time, a genre that existed in the Communist discourse and may be indebted to the founder of the Western church.[44]

The Communist rejection of Christianity's ascetic relation to the self—a relation that depended on the repeated renunciation of the self—was, however, a significant transformation. The Christian believer was reluctant to articulate a firm allegiance to a positive self, for there was no truth about the self that could not be used by the devil to tempt the believer into a prideful mutiny against God. Consequently, Augustine's true self was manifest in self-mortification and self-sacrifice. Communism, in contrast, promoted the development of a positive self. Communists, too, peeled away layers of themselves in repeated rituals of self-criticism, but they were confident that the result was personal improvement, that their true self was a subject to cultivate and cherish. To be sure, the continual conflict within one's soul between the grace of God and the lures of the devil adumbrated the Communist struggle between proletarian justice and bourgeois temptation, but Christianity's final judgment was superseded by scientific evaluation in the here and now. Instead of resolving ethical problems in the light of divine authority, Communists preferred to link ethical problems to scientific investigation, an activity that affirmed humanity's maturity and autonomy. While the Christian self was morose and pessimistic, the Communist self was optimistic and forward-looking.[45]

Thus, while the Christian proto-autobiographer engaged in a personal dialogue with God, the modern autobiographer was busy conversing with himself. Rousseau was perhaps the first to locate the source of wholeness, which Augustine found only in God, within his own self. "I long for the time," he wrote, "when I shall be myself, at one with myself, no longer torn in two, when I myself shall suffice for my own happiness."[46] Conversion to Christianity was sent to Augustine by the grace of God, but Rousseau, and the Communist subject following him, reinvented themselves through the supreme effort of their own will. Modernity abandoned the Christian, bifurcated self, one part learning to get by in this world, the other preparing for the beyond. From a candidate for salvation in the beyond, the soul turned into a self called upon to immerse itself in this world.

Instead of asking who they were meant to be and what was their true place in the universe, the moderns began asking themselves who they wanted to become and what they wanted to be known for. Identity became malleable—a project, not a given. If in shedding his old self and taking another the Christian convert assumed a self already molded for him by tradition, the Communist autobiographer not only fitted himself into a new mold but also designed this mold. In this reading the Communist autobiography should be situated in the context of the modern subject that takes itself as an object of its own creation. The explosion of autobiographical writing in the Soviet Union should be related to the wide dissemination of a conception of the self as autonomous, expressive, and hoping to achieve wholeness in the here and now. It appears that the traditional and the modern features of the Communist autobiographical narratives are as inseparable as the Christian and the scientific components of the contemporary moral universe.

The Revolution was clearly granted a spiritual interpretation defined not only by the objective course of events but also by the growth of individual selves. An intricate relationship formed between the Communist eschatological narrative and the autobiographer's endeavor to show that he had traversed the same route within his soul. Vladimir Maiakovskii's obsession with incessantly refashioning himself, with purging all of the evil within himself, was such that his only enduring identity was a living project:

> I purify myself to be like Lenin
> So that I can float
> Further along the Revolutionary stream.[47]

In the final account, there was no simple test for discerning the locus of the exploiter and the exploited; no class had a clear monopoly of either. The discrimination cut into the very substance of the Party, as it cut into the inner being of a man himself. The key categories "one of us" and "one of them" could prove meaningless: within, that which is of the bourgeoisie is to be repudiated; and outside, that which is of the proletarian is to be acknowledged. A study of Stalinist diaries demonstrates that Communists were desperate to establish whether they had truly recreated themselves and so constantly put themselves on trial. Most diarists felt they were as yet neither saved nor condemned. In the early 1930s Stepan Podlubnyi wrote in his diary: "Right now I am a person in the middle, belonging neither to one side, nor to the other, but quite capable of sliding to either. Though the odds are already good that the positive side will take over, a touch of the negative is still left in me. How devilishly it torments me!"[48]

Defining the ideal self, the Communist autobiography tells us something about what made a subject into an "incorrigible evilmonger" *(neispravimyi zlostnik)*. For sins that preceded his conversion the autobiographer blamed mental darkness. For sins that postdated his conversion, however, this option vanished. Given the golden rule of the eschatological narrative that advance toward the light had to be unidirectional and that illumination promised rectification, it was impossible to explain how a conscious individual could reject the truth. Violation of the Party line could mean in this case nothing but the premeditated rejection of the Revolution. Conscious injury to the revolutionary enterprise could be perpetrated only by a trusted comrade who turned unexpectedly jealous and hostile. Such an intimate enemy had to be placed beyond the pale. The teaching of the earliest Christian churches was similar in that it did not allow those who committed serious sins after baptism "to renew . . . unto repentance" (Hebrews 6:4–6).[49] In his rebellion against God, the angel-turned-devil Lucifer acted not out of ignorance but out of malice. His treason was deliberate, making terrible use of the freedom God had bestowed upon him. Since Lucifer's rebellion could not be justified as an error, it had to be construed as the epitome of wickedness. Communists who betrayed the Party in full consciousness—Oppositionists, first and foremost—had likewise to be perverse. A wicked act done out of free will cannot be explained (when we explain we deduce from previous causes and therefore render an act predetermined, not free)—it can only be characterized in ethical terms as "evil."

The two classic eschatological stories, Lucifer's defiance of God and Trotsky's treachery, functioned similarly as paradigmatic tales describing the genesis of evil. Comrades gone bad occupied a unique position in

Soviet society. No longer members of the brotherhood of the elect, they could not claim an ordinary status either. Never perceived as having simply reverted to an unconscious state—since the process of enlightenment could not be reversed—they were portrayed as deliberate counterrevolutionaries. Traitors to the Party could not be counted among the politically uncommitted "swamp" *(boloto)*.[50] While non-Communists did not embrace proletarian consciousness, they had the potential to do so; traitorous Communists, by contrast, rejected proletarian consciousness. Forever branded, they were assigned their own separate category—"the formers," not simply non-Communists but, as it were, inverted Communists.

The Party condemned no soul without a trial. In order to expose his moral core, every individual had to be brought into the spotlight. Yet no amount of enlightenment could reform the one who chose evil. Fond of the old saying "You can lead a horse to water, but you can't make him drink," Communists believed that alongside the uninitiated who had to be taught reason there was another category of people—those who would never be converted. A prerevolutionary leaflet argued: "Against unconscious comrades who are shrouded in darkness our weapon must be enlightenment. But against conscious traitors, the hired hands who model themselves after Judas, words are powerless. Here action is mandatory! Not waiting for divine retribution, we have to engrave the signs of our own, human retribution on the faces and the backs of these damned traitors!"[51] It was with such wicked souls in mind that Aleksandr Kosarev, the head of the Komsomol in the 1930s, observed that "there is an enemy that would not relinquish its position willingly and that can be removed only through . . . political isolation, and, when needed, physical annihilation."[52] Guilt depended on whether injury had been done "willfully" *(po vole)* or out of "character weakness" *(po slabosti kharaktera)*. In their autobiographies erring comrades claimed that their mistakes had been made out of "political naiveté" *(nezrelost')*, "ideological idiocy" *(ideologicheskoe nevezhestvo)*, "lack of knowledge," "ideological shortsightedness" *(blizorukost')*, or "political thoughtlessness" *(nedomyslie)*, but not out of premeditated evil. For that, Bukharin admitted shortly before his own execution, "there was no excuse."[53]

What does all that say about the Communist moral outlook? Was Communism an open, forgiving, universalist creed or a vindictive and punishing particularist one? Scholars who see it as universalist point to its general appeal: the founders of Communism posited that anyone could assume the proletarian perspective and be redeemed. Scholars who believe otherwise prefer to highlight the identification of the Communist gospel with a single class.

Ultimately, the issue hinges on the relation between class and ethics. Marxist class theory may be seen as an attempt to recast as a scientific challenge a key moral question that Christianity had left unresolved: How would one respond to the salvational call? Marxism, argue those who stress Communist particularism, prided itself on the discovery of a key regularity: proletarians tend to embrace Communism; bourgeois tend to reject it. However, their universalist opponents respond that this presentation is misleading: Communism never maintained that class affiliation and ethical disposition always went hand in hand. L. Lebedinskii, a Bolshevik literary critic, argued in 1927 that "it is quite possible that a particular worker will be a carrier of a typically petit-bourgeois ideology and, inversely, that an offspring of a nonproletarian class will adopt proletarian psychology."[54] Stalin himself maintained that "all classes can potentially be integrated into Communist society."[55] The general secretary urged members of the Military Council in June 1937 to judge individuals by their deeds and not by their class: "General criteria, wholly accurate when describing classes, are totally inapplicable to individuals. When we speak of nobles' hostility to the laboring people, we mean the nobility as a class . . . But that does not mean that certain individuals who are from the nobility, like Lenin, cannot serve the working class . . . Engels was the son of a factory owner—also a nonproletarian element, if you will. Marxism is not a biological science, but a sociological one."[56] At first glance, it is surprising to find Stalin, then in the midst of his search for the internal enemy, stressing that class could be transcended. But this universalism melted into thin air as soon as Stalin came to deal not with unconscious human conglomerates—classes—but with discrete individuals who had chosen evil. Universal conversion, so went Stalin's core assumption, was impossible because conversion to Communism was constantly competing with, and taking place parallel to, conversion to counterrevolution.

In Communism, the tension between universalism and particularism was conceptually irreducible. While the boundary between the proletariat and the bourgeoisie was permeable (hence universalism), the boundary between good and evil was not (hence particularism). It was a truism that a bourgeois could convert to Communism, but it was equally true that some workers refused to live up to their messianic potential and had therefore to be excluded from the body politic. At the First Moscow Show Trial the accused Mrachkovskii noted: "Let everybody remember that not only a general, not only a prince or a nobleman can become a counterrevolutionary; workers or those who spring from the working class, like myself, can also become counterrevolutionaries."[57] Party historians marshaled a long list of workers who had turned out to be hopelessly wicked: worker-Mensheviks, worker-Oppositionists, and, in the most extreme cases, agents provocateurs. A secret letter the Politburo circulated after Sergei Kirov's assassination raised this issue explicitly: "It might appear strange and perverse that the role of the agent of terror, the last resort of the dying bourgeois classes, was assumed by individuals who came from within us . . . But is it not the case that Malinovskii was a scion of the working class? Was this agent provocateur not a former member of the Bolshevik fraction in 1913?"[58]

This basic duality can be recast as a dialogue within Communism between two conceptions of darkness. Until an individual was shown the light, the Party could not be sure whether his political wavering had been caused by ignorance and "dark consciousness" (temnoe soznanie), in which case he had to be shown the way, or by "wicked will" (zlaia volia), in which case he had to be annihilated. To an extent, Communism followed the Neoplatonic tradition, which understood darkness as a lack of good, an absence of universalist perspective. The Greek philosophers did not distinguish between simple failure to be good and positive wickedness; to be in the dark was to lack virtue. But Communism also inherited the Judeo-Christian conception of darkness as the will's surrender to temptation by the adversary. Insofar as it held fast to the view of political life as a journey in which counterrevolutionary plots were bound to crop up, Communism acknowledged darkness as an active eschatological obstruction, the wicked voice within the soul.

Degeneration Anxieties

Eschatological time reckoning is crucial to the understanding of permutations in the Communist diagnosis of the soul. Thus, it is imperative to examine the workings of Party courts of conscience historically. The black and white features of the Stalinist discourse of the self were not a perennial characteristic of the Bolshevik discourse, but an outcome of a specific evolution. Unless we know how comrades' souls were interrogated in the early years of the regime we will not be in a position to appreciate the crucial changes in these practices, changes that made the Great Purge into what it was. This requires a focus on the time of the New Economic Policy (NEP), pursued from the end of the civil war to the onset of Stalin's Revolution from Above in 1928.[59]

On the most mundane level, the NEP, launched by a slew of decrees that followed the Tenth Party Congress (1921), represented a decentralized and quasiliberal method of economic organization. Faced with insurmountable economic difficulties at the conclusion of the civil war, risking starvation in the countryside and rebellion in the cities, the Bolsheviks were forced to retreat from stern anticapitalist measures and to permit a certain resurgence of private entrepreneurship in the country. But the NEP had wider ramifications regarding the purity of the Party. Concessions to the bourgeoisie, Lenin explained, had to come at a cost: "Alien classes encircled the proletariat, fragmented it, and imbued the proletariat with petit-bourgeois weakness of character."[60] The Bolshevik leadership feared that "the waves of the philistine element threaten to overturn our ship."[61]

Before the Revolution, proletarian purity had ostensibly distinguished the Bolsheviks from rival political parties. "In 1917 our organization was made up primarily of workers from the bench," a nostalgic Party spokesman writing in the NEP era recalled. "The number of intelligentsia and employees in our midst, by contrast with the Mensheviks and the Socialist-Revolutionaries, was very low."[62] It was the transformation from party militant to party triumphant that seriously "polluted" the ranks of the Bolsheviks. Now Communist historians were dividing the history of the Party into three periods. First was the underground epoch, when only committed revolutionaries joined the movement. A second, more ambivalent period coincided roughly with the civil war; the worse things looked for the Reds, the more heroic and virtuous those who joined their embattled ranks.[63] With the coming of peace and the introduction of the NEP, a third and least satisfying period commenced: legions of "petit-bourgeois hangers-on" now coveted the mantle of the Communist. "We cannot exclude the possibility," the Party stated in 1921, "that some join the Party with the intention of ruining it from within." In order to exclude as many "carriers of the bacillus of degeneration" as possible, the Tenth Party Congress created "stumbling blocks" on the road to membership.[64] Bearing witness to the 1920s obsession with counteracting bourgeois contamination, Afanasii Selishchev, a Soviet language theorist, noted that the Party described itself as "monolithic," "unassailable," and "iron-clad." Banners stated: "The value of unity has to dwell in the soul of every Bolshevik!" "Long live the unity of the iron-clad Leninist ranks!"[65]

There was a widespread Communist phobia that the revolutionary spirit was threatened with a general decline. Etymologically, "degeneration" meant debasement, fall from a previous state of perfection or, within the specific NEP discourse, lapse of consciousness. "Degeneration"—used to describe the propensity of the proletariat to contract diseases that could not be described as either physical or moral, but had to be characterized as a hybrid of both—was widely used because it could account for many anxieties regarding the health of the body politic: the revival of capitalism supposedly threw Soviet society backward into an era of unfettered economic competition associated with the animalistic state of human existence.

However concerned some were about the malign influence of the NEP, the Party declared that there was no threat of traducing the significance of the 1917 Revolution. History had already entered its final phase; the NEP was a "gateway" to Communism, a pivot linking the time of bondage to the time of freedom. This had to be a time of profound eschatological significance, a time of probation and final discrimination between the wheat and the tares, and so the Party invested all its energy in making this last effort to change the hearts of men. The intense social engineering to which Soviet society submitted was premised on the view that the body politic had entered something like a purgatorium. Ranking individuals along a continuum of graded purity, the Party divided the body politic into the proletarians who had supposedly reached the light of Communism, the petit-bourgeois swamp located someplace along the road to salvation, and the class aliens who had yet to set out on the road toward the light. The metaphors employed by Bolshevik columnists alluded to the eschatological roots of this tripartite division: "On the one flank, leaning toward the 'sinners,' we have the worthless, alien elements, the bribetakers, the careerists, the drunkards, the conceited and supercilious fools, and such-like scum. On the other flank, leaning toward the 'saints,' we have real Communists, the heroes of the battlefield, the dedicated builders of Communism in the rear. The two flanks are locked in battle over the middle—regular comrades who are neither very good nor very evil."[66] To prevail, the Party had to rely on the "good Communists, our righteous men (pravedniki)."[67]

This view of the body politic had a direct impact on Bolshevik self-fashioning. Communist autobiographers had to select from a menu of social identities, some closer to the dark side of the class spectrum, others closer to the bright side. But once a stock role was assumed, it not only structured self-evaluation and organized behavior but also fixed the way in which the author was perceived by his contemporaries. From the point of view of the Communist autobiography, all class identities were legitimate starting points on the voyage toward the light, but each required a different approach. The writer closer to the proletariat had less work to do on himself; he could write a brief, uneventful autobiography. But the writer closer to the bourgeoisie had to repudiate his identity and narrate at great length his self-transformation into a Communist. Regardless of one's position along the spectrum of purity, conversion was an element intrinsic to the poetics of the Communist autobiography, serving as a bridge between a particularist frame of mind and a universalist consciousness. "Peasants," "members of the intelligentsia," and even "workers" were summoned to rewrite their individual selves in the Communist key. Party poetics outlined the paths members of each class had to follow to supraclass individualism.

The dissemination of the Communist gospel throughout the universities was the starting point of the Bolshevik project of revolutionizing the human psyche. Bolshevized during the civil war, the Soviet institution of higher learning functioned in the 1920s as a meeting place between the proletariat and its consciousness. The bulk of the material for this study comes from the records kept by Party cells in tertiary institutions in Petrograd (Leningrad), Tomsk, and Smolensk. Petrograd was a former capital, an educational center second only to Moscow; Tomsk was the "Siberian Athens"; and Smolensk was a typical agricultural backwater. While the Proletarian Dictatorship had faith in the revolutionary consciousness of Petrograd students, it routinely expressed anxiety regarding the "peasant" constituency of Tomsk and Smolensk. In addition, the regions differed politically: Leningrad was the "cradle of the Revolution" and a bastion of the new regime, while Tomsk was a former White territory. But even Petrograd was not without its problems: the city had a history of Menshevik sympathies from before the Revolution, and in the 1920s its Communist contingent tended to be "Oppositionist." Although comparison of Party norms in the three cities tells us something about the differences between the industrial north and the agricultural east and west, revolutionary discourse ultimately went a long way toward flattening regional idiosyncrasies.

In the Communist cosmology, students were an anomalous social category. Although the autonomy of all bodies was undermined by Bolshevik medical theory, students' bodies were construed as sources of greater dangers, and everyday practices in the universities were sites of intensive surveillance and intervention. According to Pavel Sakulin, a contemporary sociologist, students were undecided souls: "During the years of study, everything brews in their minds. A student has yet to acquire the knowledge of good and evil . . . If collectivism has a chance to take hold, now is the best time."[68] But many in the Party believed that students were not its ideal raw material. Whereas in worker-Communists consciousness could be initially dormant, eventually developing through the influence of industrial labor, "individualistic" and "decadent" university life was unlikely to generate a Communist consciousness. A paradox ensued: on the one hand, students were placed in a highly questionable institution from the point of view of Bolshevik class analysis; on the other, those among them who wished to become members of the brotherhood of the elect had to present a particularly enhanced Communist consciousness.

"Student youth" was considered by Bolshevik moralists a high-risk category for degeneration. Separated from the healthy industrial environment before their consciousness was fully developed, exposed to the lifestyle of the reclusive academic intelligentsia, they tended to succumb to "individualism," "philistinism," and "hypertrophy of the mind." The fact that academic Party cells, more than any other sector of the Party, had supported Trotsky worsened students' reputation; their dormitories were perceived as breeding grounds for political deviation. Even as Communists described intellectual activity as an indispensable path to salvation, they perceived mental labor as a dangerous competitor to manual labor: excessive study threatened to corrupt workers' identity and turn them into lascivious and weak-willed bourgeois.

Above all, the Bolsheviks viewed the university as the locus of perverse sexuality. Perhaps the most obvious symptom of degeneration, immoderate sexual activity was said to divert precious energies away from productive labor, exhausting the student's young and frail body and plunging him or her back into the abyss of an unconscious existence. Increasingly, experts of the time held that it was sexual misbehavior that brought students into the Oppositionist camp. With the body thus politicized, ideological deviation turned into an object of sexological discourse. Flagrant sexuality signified to Party politicians the animalistic, antisocial side of man—a major obstacle along the eschatological path.

The bourgeois forces that overwhelmed the universities found their corollary in the "animalistic" drives obstructing students from within. Vladimir Bonch-Bruevich, a Bolshevik publicist and close collaborator of Lenin's, urged: "It is finally time to rid ourselves of this ancient serpent-seducer which we must really beat over the head, because this is in fact the very flesh that weighs us down."[69] (Indeed, the Marxist corporeal notion of "class interests" can be traced to Plato's "body" or the Christian "weak and tempting flesh.") Communists, experts argued in the 1920s, had to learn how to control not only nature outside (economic competition) but also nature within (instincts). Only Communism as a conscious, scientific organization of human affairs had the wherewithal to "teach man to get hold of his feelings and elevate instincts to the highest levels of consciousness."[70]

Informed by a rich body of moralistic literature, a number of mid-1920s Soviet lowbrow novels set in the university milieu grappled with the opposition between narrow interest and universalist consciousness. The Bolshevik cultural establishment insisted that literature was an important vehicle of the revolutionary enterprise, able not only to reflect reality but also to shape it. An interpretive discussion sprang up between revolutionary literature and everyday Bolshevik practices, ritualized public readings providing a dramatic structure through which the Communist ethos was hammered out. Through detailed sketches of continent and sexually perverse protagonists, the Bolshevik literati offered their readers the archetypes of good and evil students. These novels as well as the contemporaneous sociological and sexological treatises that explored the sexuality of the Party's "new guard" reveal how the Bolshevik ethics was framing questions and delineating issues.

While contemporary scientists, fully committed to the betterment of the human species, evaluated the moral qualities of the population, Communist leaders, deeply immersed in the scientific ethos of their time, borrowed from the science of their day to buttress the Party's hermeneutics of the soul. Whatever the disagreements among them, the basic commonality of concerns shared by the various professional and political groups operating in the Soviet Union of the 1920s and the 1930s opened up a discursive space in which the debate on the Communist self could unfold. Proletarian writers, Party theoreticians, Marxist natural scientists, psychologists, and sexologists—an affiliation of ethical experts designated with the umbrella term "Bolshevik moralists"—all cooperated in filling the outline of the New Man with detail and content.

The Opposition as the Paradigm of Evil

Oppositionism—understood by contemporaries as deliberate disobedience of the Party line—was the paragon of evil in the Communist discourse.[71] Oppositionism is in focus here not as a political movement but as a mental predicament.[72] What is at issue is not so much how political battles in the Party unfolded but the evolution of the soul-judging framework that gave meaning to the gradual demonization of Oppositionism. Throughout the history of Bolshevism, certain positions were ensconced as proletarian orthodoxy while other positions were excluded and designated as heterodox. As a highly respected member of the Politburo, Lev Trotsky dismissed Aleksandr Shliapnikov and Sergei Medvedev in 1920 as "the so-called Workers' Opposition" only to find the same pejorative applied to himself three years later.[73] Widely recognized as two pillars of the orthodox triumvirate who fought against the now arch-Oppositionist Trotsky during the Thirteenth Party Congress (1924), Lev Kamenev and Grigori Zinoviev had also been turned into Oppositionists by the time the Fourteenth Party Congress convened (1925). Among all these shifting political labels, no matter how loosely an Oppositionist identity was constructed, Oppositionism was turned into a character trait.

"Oppositionism" was very anomalous from the point of view of the Communist believer. Messianic truth, according to the Party doctrine, was supposed to speak in a single voice. Since there was only one path to the light, and only one platform indicating that course, it followed that in any of the so-called Party Discussions—the official deliberating periods that preceded a Party congress—one of the disputants had to be somehow "in opposition" to the proletarian truth and, as such, a source of dissension and pollution in the Bolshevik camp. Communists were unanimous in the opinion that the positions rejected by the Party congress had to be anathematized. Lenin had maintained that even the constant splintering of the Party was not too high a price to pay for the preservation of doctrinal truth: "Unity is a great thing and a great slogan, but our cause requires the unity of Marxists, not the unity of Marxists alongside the enemies and distorters of Marxism."[74] And Zinoviev, already an Oppositionist leader at the time, concurred: "There can be only one Marxism and therefore only one Party."[75]

Given this set of premises, the ideological apparatus of the Party had to put in extra hours to explain how dissent could originate within a Communist soul. By examining how the Opposition was diagnosed by the official hermeneutical discourse, one can fully appreciate the sophisticated theoretical apparatus Communists deployed in order to make sense of the origins and meaning of heterodoxy inside the movement. The imperative of explaining the etiology of heterodox political thinking engendered a

whole series of systems of knowledge psychologizing and pathologizing errant behavior. As official appraisal of the Opposition shifted, diagnosis of
the heterodox soul changed as well. Was Oppositionism caused by an absence (of consciousness) or by a presence (of evil will)? Should the Party
"cure" Oppositionists or denounce them, purge and deprive them of civil
rights?

In the early 1920s the diagnosis of Oppositionism was still relatively
mild. The Ninth Party Conference (1920) stipulated that "repression of
comrades who espouse heterodox opinions [*inakomyslie*] on certain issues is impermissible." At this early date, Oppositionism had not been
essentialized; a comrade could be allowed to hold heterodox opinions on
some issues and orthodox opinions on others.[76] Treating the Opposition as
a "psychological crisis," Lenin encouraged the Party "to apply to them a
carefully individualized approach, a sort of healing treatment . . . We
should do all we can to reassure the members of the so-called Opposition,
to explain the matter to them in a comradely way, to give them advice and
counsel."[77] The diagnosis of Oppositionism as a form of psychological degeneration refrained from framing Oppositionists as irredeemably evil. Although they had been suddenly swayed by NEP petit-bourgeois influences,
they could be brought back into the fold by a good dose of enlightenment
and persuasion. This is why in the 1920s the line of defense that blamed
the diseased body for having temporarily dislodged the mind from its supremacy was a popular and legitimate way out for many repentant Oppositionists. But in the late 1920s circumstances changed. Far from being
innocuous and well-meaning comrades who temporarily lost their way,
Oppositionists were now proclaimed dangerous counterrevolutionaries—
a "malevolent pseudocommunity" in the words of Robert Tucker. The Opposition's most menacing feature was its alleged condemnation of the Central Committee majority in the name of the very doctrinal principles on
which the latter's legitimacy rested. Through the lure of a pseudo-Party,
the Opposition supposedly threatened a diabolical dispossession of Communism and assumption of control over innocent proletarian souls.

Gradually but inexorably the Opposition was assimilated into the ste-
reotype of the wicked enemy, along with the kulaks and the bourgeoisie,
with whom they rapidly became identified in rhetoric and invective.[78] Such
a change in diagnosis naturally entailed a change in remedy. Rigorous in
theory, the persecution of the Opposition remained fairly intermittent in

practice until the Fifteenth Party Congress (December 1927), when a comprehensive apparatus of persecution was worked out. At that time the earlier practice of admonishing and censoring Oppositionists was replaced with purge, exile, and sometimes even incarceration. Thus it was during the Discussion with the United Opposition that the GPU—an organization that was defined as the "Party's sword in the struggle against the counterrevolution"—was extensively used against Trotskyists for the first time.

The persecution of the Opposition reached its zenith in the mid to late 1930s, just as the economic situation in the country was improving (according to Naum Jasny, 1934–1936 marked "the three 'good' years" in which there was a vast increase in industrial production").[79] Following closely the logic of Bolshevik eschatological time-reckoning, it is possible to get some inkling as to why murderous events unfolded when they did. While the key redemptive event in human history had already taken place in 1917, the granting of a brief respite to the bourgeoisie had left the process far from complete. But once the collectivization and industrialization campaigns of the First Five-Year Plan (1927–1931) had rendered bourgeois elements wholly superfluous it was time to intensify the drive toward social and individual purity. The closer to completion the revolutionary process seemed, the higher was the pitch of messianic zeal.

A watershed in Soviet history, Stalin's constitution declared in 1936 that "the foundation for classless society has already been laid" and that "a second phase of development of the Soviet State has begun."[80] Contemporaries understood this to mean that the end of history was imminent. The imperative to weed out elements likely to be a liability during the upcoming universal war—the pinnacle of the eschatological epic and its most demanding hour—also intensified the hunt for enemies. "Our adversaries," Stalin explained, "plan to strike not during peace but during war."[81] Stalinist eschatological diagnosis was paradoxical inasmuch as it interpreted the late 1930s both as a time of unrivaled purity in Soviet society and as the time of the last stand of the counterrevolution against Soviet society, a short but terrible reign of violence preceding the triumph of universal peace.

Although the Communist vision of historical time was deterministic, it rejected the notion of incremental progression. The final showdown between the exploiters and the exploited, between the bourgeoisie and proletariat, corresponded to the Judeo-Christian belief in a final battle between Christ and the Antichrist in the concluding epoch of history. Stalin repeatedly declared that peaceful evolution was impossible because the enemy was intensifying with every step the Soviet Union took toward Communism: "The further we move, the more successful we become, the more enraged the remains of the defeated exploiting classes will become. They will take the most extreme measures, harming the Soviet state and attempting the most desperate means, the last resort of the doomed."[82]

During the Great Purge, the Party invested great effort in terminating the struggle over the future. Official ideologues stated that history had reached a state of a closure, and that a perfect society had essentially been consummated. Given this unusually strong eschatological presupposition, individual identities had to be fixed once and for all. Messianic languages have this peculiar feature: at some point they claim to have realized what they have promised. At such times these languages bear particularly tangible effects, not in the sense of truly living up to their expectations but in the sense of bringing their expectations to bear in a remarkably powerful way.

As things came to a head in 1936 and 1937, the severity of the purges increased dramatically.[83] The wheat now lay separated from the tares, and the time had finally come to reveal the true nature of every individual. Aleksandr Afinogenov, a prominent Soviet playwright, described the Great Purge in his diary as "the Final Judgment and the verdict of the Revolution, a time when so many people turned out to be different from what we had thought them to be."[84] The Party now believed that an individual was either absolutely good, in which case the recent purification of the class landscape inspired him to purify his soul, or radically evil, in which case he clung to his bourgeois spirit. Brought to the threshold of a moment of great decision, the individual's will appeared as either revolutionary and creative, or counterrevolutionary and destructive.

Individuals were now denied any additional time for refashioning their souls. No longer attributed to external circumstances, Oppositionism came to be explained in terms of a fundamental quality of the soul. In the early days, when a will could still be "forged" or "tempered," Party schools had taught "gymnastics of the will"; now will was pronounced "an innate trait" (prirodania cherta). Once described as "weak-willed individuals" (bezvol'nye), too irresolute to put the Communist truth they had intellectually accepted into practice, Oppositionists metamorphosed into intransigent, "self-willed" (svoevolnyi) heretics, "innate rogues" (vrozhdennye negodiai).[85] Describing his puzzlement that the civil war hero Marshal

Mikhail Tukhachevskii had been charged with Trotskyism, Soviet general Aleksandr Gorbatov "finally accepted the answer most common in those days: 'No matter how you feed a wolf, it will always look toward the forest.'" As far as Gorbatov was concerned, it was as pointless to attempt to rehabilitate Tukhachevskii as to try to domesticate a wild beast.[86]

The Moscow trials of 1936–1938 persuaded contemporaries that seemingly quite normal persons were capable of the most terrible deeds. Moreover, the enemy did all this on a superhuman scale, accomplishing the most titanically destructive feats by will power alone. The fact that before 1935 Oppositionists had been kept within society or, in the worst-case scenario, given over to the sprawling system of "corrective work," and that now they were shot in droves, points to the growing identification of ideological heterodoxy with wicked consciousness. This worked both ways: while Oppositionism was rendered synonymous with counterrevolution, counterrevolution became another word for the Opposition.

The existence of terrorist Oppositionist centers was, of course, a figment of the NKVD's imagination. But the need to assign a specific guilt to individual Oppositionists, even when an elaborate work of fabrication had to be carried out, suggests all the more strongly that Oppositionism functioned as a key ideological concept designating premeditated evil. Sarkis Sarkisov, a Central Committee candidate in the 1930s, maintained that "all the gangsters with Party cards in their pockets come from Trotsky's club— old scions and new progeny."[87] "Oppositionism" became a label that ensured the annihilation of its carrier. "'Trotskyism' has become a collective noun referring to everything that has to be destroyed."[88] It is not at all the case that Stalinist victims were exclusively or even predominantly Oppositionists. Prosopographical studies have shown that, despite allegations, many victims of the Great Purge had no real links to any Opposition.[89] Yet interest in factual accuracy should not preclude an appreciation of the very real effects of the Communist perception of things, however phantasmagoric. Whether members of the Opposition or not, victims of the Great Purge died as Oppositionists.

In what was perceived as a sublime eschatological irony, the Opposition's constant changing of masks inadvertently strengthened the hermeneutical acumen of the Party. With each new peak in Communist consciousness, both the Party's own history (the history of the good) and the history of the Opposition (the history of evil) were freshly reinterpreted. In May 1937 Stalin suggested to the editors of the definitive Party history a periodization scheme "based on the Bolshevik struggle against anti-Bolshevik currents and factions."[90] The Party proclaimed that it had finally come to understand that the Opposition had not suddenly, overnight, become counterrevolutionary. Rather, it had never been anything else. Retroactive diagnostics pronounced that all the participants in the various Oppositions were well-coordinated members of the same clandestine counterrevolutionary organization, which had existed since prerevolutionary times. The procrustean bed of Oppositionism proved able to accommodate strange bedfellows. For example, in 1932 Stalin characterized the "Union of Marxist-Leninists" not only as a "counterrevolutionary group" but also as both the continuation and the consummation of all previous "struggles against the Leninist line in the Party . . . waged by Menshevism, Anarcho-Syndicalism, counterrevolutionary Trotskyism, the kulak-oriented Right Oppositionists and the cowardly Rightist-Leftists Bloc."[91]

The Stalinist leadership now maintained that all the disagreements within the Oppositionist camp were feigned, craftily enacted to confuse the Party. Nikolai Ezhov discovered that the former Leftists and the former Rightists were "two interconnected prongs" of a long-standing conspiracy. Already in 1918, he argued, Trotsky and Bukharin "had plotted to murder Lenin and Stalin and overthrow the Soviet government." Bukharin had allegedly stood behind the attempt on Lenin's life by Fanny Kaplan in 1918, while Trotsky had been deeply involved with the German espionage agencies operating in the Soviet Union since 1921. In the updated version of events, both the Left and the Right Oppositions "had from the start been subversive movements motivated by criminal anti-Soviet aims rather than genuine Oppositionist convictions."[92] No more accurate analysis of this discourse can be offered than that of the writer for the émigré Menshevik press who stated that "Trotsky is forced into the role of the tempting demon, a Satan who holds in his hands the reins of all conspiracies."[93]

"No longer a working-class political movement, as it was seven to eight years ago, Trotskyism," according to Stalin, "had become the name for a shameless band of wreckers and saboteurs" who "sold their body and soul to the fascists."[94] While Krylenko believed that "Trotsky will enter history as the monstrous blend in a single person of all the lowest and most ignoble crimes . . . human imagination can bring to mind," Anastas Mikoian denied that Trotskyists were human at all: "Trotsky gave birth to a new type of man—a monster disguised as a person."[95] "Everything dark, sinister and criminal," the contemporary Soviet press observed, "all the human scum, all the dregs of society gather at the sound of Trotsky's cry, ready for ignoble and sordid deeds."[96]

Hermeneutics—now an art of exposing Oppositionists—was a demanding métier. The main Party organ stated: "Our Leninist-Stalinist Party demands that every Communist should be able to identify, mercilessly and promptly . . . all Trotskyist-Zinovievists, no matter how cunning the mask they have contrived."[97] The talent of "recognizing" the danger early became a precious token of advanced consciousness. Questionnaires distributed among Communists who served in the Red Army in 1939 and 1940 asked: "What actions have you taken against the Oppositionists during the Discussions of 1921, 1923–24, and 1925–27?"[98] Vyshinskii stated in June 1937: "Of course, it is impossible to recognize a spy by his appearance. In fact, it is altogether difficult to write some kind of recipe valid for all, on how to identify a cleverly masked enemy."[99] A high-ranking Party functionary "waved his hand in despair" a month earlier. "Who can I work with? One has to be a King Solomon to tell a decent human being from a fascist crony."[100] Nikita Khrushchev admitted: "With each enemy Stalin was unmasking I was thinking to myself, 'Oh! He is so perspicacious! He recognizes the enemy right away!' And me? Around me there were so many enemies who got arrested. I was hanging out with them every day without noticing anything!"[101]

Hermeneutical failure constituted a grave offense that could easily turn a judge into an criminal. Postyshev's "original sin" (pervorodnyi grekh), according to Lazar' Kaganovich, was that he "could not separate a friend from a foe. If in Kiev Postyshev counted foes among friends, in Kuibyshev he did the reverse."[102] At the peak of the Great Purge Ezhov noted that there were Communists who "could recognize wreckers" and there were Communists who "simply could not be taught to do so."[103]

Shifts in hermeneutical theory and practice were reflected in the Soviet penal policy. In the early years of the regime, when all souls were still potentially corrigible, sentencing was regarded as a prelude to spiritual healing. "When the court has to deal with a habitual criminal," The ABC of Communism stated, "isolation from society is enforced, but in such a way as to give the offender many opportunities for moral regeneration."[104] Accepting mitigating circumstances like hunger or deprivation, the 1922 Criminal Code reflected the prevailing wisdom that a petit-bourgeois environment could lead comrades astray.[105] Amnesty was applied to class aliens whose good production records proved that they had overcome the vestiges of bourgeois upbringing in their souls: "kulaks could be rehabilitated after five years of hard labor; those who worked in the gold and platinum mines would be cured after three years."[106]

Healing powers were attributed to labor because it was seen as an ennobling experience that linked man with his essence as *Homo laborantus*. Leopol'd Averbakh, a Soviet writer trying to capture the amazing transformations in the minds of men wrought by Stalin's Revolution, claimed that he had hard empirical evidence to buttress this philosophical supposition: "As early as a few months after the prisoners had arrived in the camps, you could not recognize the men. They are possessed by a fever of industrial activity; they begin to operate and manage thriftily; they go in for cultural achievements."[107] Gorky praised those who "remolded themselves though hard labor on the Belomor Canal," and Genrikh Iagoda claimed that "labor breathes a new soul into people."[108] "Work without Beauty and Art is Barbarism," stated huge posters hung in the central squares of the labor camps, and the inmates were depicted as enthusiastically embracing labor's redemptive potential.[109] "By their own initiative and volition," prisoners called for lengthening the working day to twelve and even fifteen hours and wished to cancel all days off. Barred from working, they were reportedly "so saddened" that prison authorities could actually use the threat of removing a prisoner from the workforce to exert a "moral influence."[110]

It is remarkable that in the early 1930s even Oppositionists could be cured through such means. Addressing a row of Zinovievists accused of alleged complicity in Kirov's assassination, one NKVD chief said in 1935, "You are the enemies of the people! You have just committed an atrocious crime. But despite all this you are now being given the chance to atone for your crimes . . . You must redeem yourselves by heavy work."[111] Enlightenment complemented hard labor. Zenaida Nemtsova, an imprisoned old Bolshevik, recalled that in the early 1930s "library access was free. 'Study,' the wards were telling us. 'Check the originals. Revisit Marx and Lenin. Work on yourselves. Maybe this way you will be able to order your mind.'"[112]

There is no denying that draconian measures against the "incorrigible counterrevolutionaries" were enforced throughout the years under consideration. Stalin's statement that the theft of socialist property was a "counterrevolutionary outrage," and the corresponding Law of August 7, 1932, which condemned such thieves to death, cannot go unnoticed. What is important, however, is that the Law of August 7 explicitly distinguished two categories of criminals: those who deserved the death penalty (open enemies of the regime) and those for whom ten years of imprisonment was an adequate punishment ("toilers" who could cite "extenuating circumstances"). This preserved the crucial distinction between unconscious and conscious offense. A Politburo resolution from February 1933 directed that the courts separate out the cases of petty theft "committed out of need and lack of consciousness" and apply to them the rather mild article 162 of the penal code. The accused were thus granted a chance to be saved by labor.[113]

But things changed dramatically once guilt became intrinsic to the soul. When the terms "crime" and "punishment" made their way back into Soviet jurisprudence in 1936, what was restored was the concept of legal responsibility itself.[114] Now that the line between "mistake" and "treason" had been erased, Oppositionists were obliged to account personally for their sins. "The individual takes part in the shaping of his own character," the gospel of Soviet psychology stated, "and he himself is answerable for that character."[115] The Soviet legal establishment was quickly brought into line with the new anthropology. Vyshinskii unmasked a leading legal specialist, Evsei Shirvindt, as a "Rightist Opportunist" who "had smuggled into the Code of 1924 the counterrevolutionary belief in the possibility of correcting all men." Shirvindt's real and alleged abettors were speedily removed from all branches of the judicial system.[116]

The innocence and naiveté characteristic of Rousseau's "noble savage" were no longer in vogue. "Talks about conscious sabotage are everywhere," the academician Vladimir Vernadskii wrote in his diary.[117] Vyshinskii's secret directive dated November 1936 ordered all prosecutors to review cases of economic sabotage to uncover "elements of counterrevolutionary wrecking." One highly placed economic manager noted: "Before, we thought that explosions at the oil refineries resulted from neglect. But recently the accused have confessed that they were planned."[118] When he sent Professor N. Gel'perin to Kemerovo in February 1937 to investigate breakdowns in the local industrial operations, Sergo Ordzhonikidze, the commissar of heavy industry, told him, "Remember, your main task is to distinguish inadvertent mistakes from wrecking."[119] Molotov insisted that what appeared at first sight to be a petty crime might ultimately be revealed to be a counterrevolutionary act. Many convictions for "criminal negligence" (article 111—unintentional crime) were overturned in favor of "wrecking" (article 58—deliberate crime).[120]

When it was determined that the enemies of the Soviet power were "premeditated criminals," the death penalty replaced incarceration in labor camps. Whereas before only a handful of Communists had been executed, from October 1, 1936, to September 30, 1938, the Military Collegium of the Supreme Court, to take one example, sentenced 30,514 individuals to death; only 5,643 were sent to labor camps.[121] It was a sign of the times that even minors had to take responsibility for their actions. By the terms of the decree of April 7, 1935, children over twelve years of age, who had formerly been exempt from the death penalty and dispatched to juvenile correction camps, were now to be tried under the general penal code. Every penal measure, including execution, was applicable to them.[122]

Retroactive sentences abounded.[123] Ezhov fumed that nine out of the eighty-six members of the "particularly virulent Smirnov group" convicted in 1933 were released almost immediately and that the punishment of another sixteen was soon commuted. "Since I began running things in the NKVD," Ezhov added, "we have dealt very strictly with those who were formerly censured. Everyone who was not entirely sincere regarding his Oppositionism will be arrested."[124] On September 29, 1936, the Politburo resolved that prominent Oppositionists, including those already in labor camps, had to be retried: "When we deal with the Trotskyist-Zinovievist scoundrels, it is essential not to leave out . . . those whom we have already finished investigating and who were exiled earlier.[125] Nearly every Communist who had ever been accused of Oppositionism, even in the mildest of terms, was now beyond the pale. Only when the Opposition was exterminated "without any mercy," Party spokesmen explained, could "the Soviet land move rapidly along the Stalinist route."[126]

The Soviet jurisprudence rejected the principle of Roman law that no one can be tried twice for the same offense *(non bis in idem)*.[127] Many Oppositionists who had been sentenced to five-to-ten-year prison terms were retried and condemned to death starting in September 1936. From the standpoint of Communist jurisprudence, double jeopardy made perfect sense: the Party had a right to review verdicts because its growing consciousness provided it with new insights into old crimes.[128] While erring Communists could hardly hope to appeal their sentences, the state had great latitude in revisiting the sentencing process. The speed with which the Oppositionists' fortunes changed during the late 1930s points to the dramatic shift in the nature of the guilt attributed to them.[129]

Communist justice was now restructured along a binary principle. What had been in the 1920s an elaborate technique designed to establish one's distance from the light gave way to a much simpler procedure for separating "us" and "them." The hermeneutics of the soul became simple and extremely repetitive—simple because truth lay now on the surface, repetitive because there were two and only two types of individual, good and evil.

As a result of the proclaimed end of social strife within the Soviet Union and the ascendancy of the issue of individual response to the Communist calling, class analysis, the alpha and omega of Marxism, became basically irrelevant. With the end of history in sight, class position, the starting point of the journey toward the light, turned out to be little more than an index of the individual's subjective moral properties; it no longer predicted moral choice, only registered it after the fact. During the Great Purge autobiography lost its sociological mooring. Among the most conspicuous omissions in the political debates of the late 1930s is the subject of social origins, now largely irrelevant to the appraisal of Communist autobiographies. On the one hand, the Politburo allowed the children of kulaks to obtain passports and granted class aliens "equal opportunities in education and employment"; on the other hand, it characterized those who insisted upon resisting the triumphal march of Communism not as "class aliens" but as "enemies of the people."[130]

Behind the story of universal salvation, with its built-in element of development, Stalinist inquisitors unearthed a frozen picture of the human soul. The interest in individuals' life trajectories persisted; however, it stemmed now from the belief that only the study of one's conduct over time could unmask one's hidden moral kernel. From stories of self-transformation, autobiographies turned into stories of self-discovery. Because good and evil were parts of the soul's ontology, their end could be foretold. Communism (and here again the parallel with Christianity leaps to mind) always equivocated between free choice and predestination, never quite transcending the contradiction between the view of evil as an innate trait, and the view of evil as something freely chosen; but during the Great Purge the former position became noticeably stronger.

The Great Purge was possible because of the Communist desire to pursue moral goals through scientific means. What Christianity strictly relegated to the realm of the mysterious will, Communism attempted to transport into the realm of hard evidence. Augustine's notion of the unpredictable working of grace led him to deny the possibility of determining a person's real worth on the basis of his actions in this world. A man cannot be sure even of himself, Augustine once wrote; how much less of another! "Therefore do not pronounce judgement before the time, before the Lord comes, who will bring to light the things now hidden in darkness and will disclose the purposes of the heart" (1 Corinthians 4:5). Christian eschatological reservation had enormous implications that became especially obvious when the belief in the Last Judgment was invoked to restrain moral zealots and to suspend excesses of human judgment in the present ("Judge not, that you be not judged"; Matthew 7:1, Luke 6:37).[131] Communists, however, wanted nothing to do with this sort of moral skepticism. Whereas the traditional Russian state had regarded many things as matters for God alone, the Bolshevik hermeneutical establishment recognized no such limitations. N. Belov, an obscure Soviet professor, was confident that he could penetrate the most intimate secrets of existence: "Seated in the first row of the theater of knowledge, the man of science can observe universal mysteries directly. Able to penetrate the internal mechanism of human behavior, he is pleased by his ability to understand the mainsprings of action."[132] The privacy of the human soul, what Talmon calls "the salt of freedom," was violated by intrusive messiahs who arrogated to themselves a power once held as divine monopoly, that of recreating men and women.[133] The Great Purge was the child of the encounter between eschatology and modernity. Their combination proved lethal.

2

A Voyage toward the Light

Every student who wanted to become a Party member had to submit an autobiography. In addition to cover letters and questionnaires, the personnel files kept by the primary Party cells at the university contained a considerable number of handwritten autobiographies, one to five pages in length. These were unquestionably the centerpieces of the Party application dossier. Autobiographies allowed students to rewrite their selves, Communist style. A well-executed autobiography testified to its author's Communist world outlook and contributed greatly to convincing authorities that he was worthy of induction. Foreshortened and intensified by their authors to maximum effect, many of the turbulent and intense beliefs of the revolutionary era emerge from these documents.

In the act of autobiographical composition, the barrier between narrated self and narrating self was broken. The perception of the self not just as an author but also as a product obviates the need to establish the veracity of the autobiographical content, its correspondence to the life it purports to describe. While the Communist autobiography may be problematic in terms of what individuals really were, it tells us something about what they hoped to become.[1] There need not have been a problematic fusion of identity and discourse, according to which the autobiographer's discourse expresses, more or less accurately, his real, authentic self. While every Communist autobiography discloses a particular dimension of the self, none articulates a complete portrait. At the other extreme, one does not have to postulate an equally problematic radical separation between identity and discourse against which an author is constantly dissimulating. The forces that shaped the New Man did not operate from top to bottom (the approach of the totalitarian school) or from bottom to top (reflecting the revisionist emphasis on social support and resistance), but constituted a field of play delimited by a set of Communist beliefs and practices. Each autobiography tells us something about the way in which authors assimilated, manipulated, and challenged the officially prescribed identity blueprint.[2]

Since my concern is with the "epistemological context" in which the Communist self was produced, the analysis below is instructive only regarding the subject as the text constitutes him. Just as the notion of an act is that of a moment in an autobiography, so the autobiographer is not a real historical actor but the protagonist abstracted from an autobiography. Still, a certain disjuncture has to be posited between the way the author is presented and the way he wanted to appear; otherwise the autobiography will be repeated, not analyzed. My understanding of how a text produces meaning leads me to emphasize a symptomatic reading—what is sometimes called "reading against the grain"—that interprets omissions, distortions, and insinuations. Trying to pin down the narratological strategy employed by an author is interesting because a Communist autobiography seems always to reveal certain slippages in identity. The intention behind students' self-fashioning was always subverted, because the rules of poetics could not be manipulated without taking some decisions out of the hands of the storyteller.[3]

There was no shortage of blueprints for would-be autobiographies. Through political rallies, lectures, wall newspapers, and "evenings of reminiscences," Soviet students were exposed to stylized revolutionary lives, moral tales instructing the students in the Communist virtue. The Party constantly cited Old Bolsheviks and the fallen heroes of the civil war as examples of men who had lived pure and blameless lives worthy of emulation.[4] A Communist publicist named Fil'shinskii wrote in 1924 that "explicit directives were not always given as to how the Party applicant was supposed to write his autobiography. Many were written spontaneously." On occasion, however, students were given hints about what sort of text was acceptable. Students at Sverdlov University were enjoined to think about the following in constructing their autobiographies:

(1) General background. (2) The social and financial status of my parents. (3) The modes of thought and opinions of the elder members of my family. (4) In what kind of atmosphere did I spend my childhood?; Was it happy or joyless? (5) Studies. (6) Profession, occupation, secondary job.[5]

The Communist autobiography was much more than a random collection of statements about the applicant's past. And the truth-value of the text was something more than the truth or falsity of a heap of assertions taken separately. The difficulty with logical conjunction is that it produces that blandest of narratives, the chronicle. The only ordering relation a chronicle knows, the "and then . . . and then . . . and then . . . ," cannot do justice to the Communist autobiographical narrative, which claims truth not merely for "each of its individual statements taken distributively, but for the complex form of the narrative itself."[6] Rather than providing a detailed individual chronicle, the student-autobiographer carefully selected and ordered a set of events from his past, typically presenting a complex narrative.

Spiritual development was the crux of the Communist autobiography. Facts and events mentioned by student Party applicants were significant not in themselves but as indicators of the presence or absence of consciousness. Fil'shinskii's scheme continued thus:

(7) What were the especially important moments and events in my life? (8) How was my worldview [*mirosozertsanie*] formed: gradually, in a checkered way, or under the impact of a spiritual break? (9) When and how had I become a revolutionary and a Communist? What had been the influence of my milieu, close friends, books and important events? (10) When and how had I extricated myself from religious superstitions? (11) Were there any clashes with members of my family because of differences in convictions? (12) What was the extent of my participation in the civil war?

Clearly the point was not an exhaustive tally of facts but the applicant's conversion to Communism, its timetable and its instigators. Applicants who limited their narrative to dry facts, no matter how accurate, were rejected; they were unable to comprehend the meaning of their life experience.

The autobiography of Bubnov, a student from Leningrad State University, is a masterful case of Communist self-presentation.[7] At the outset one learns that Bubnov, born in 1896 and a "member of the intelligentsia" by social position, had worked as a journalist and was able to read French, German, and Georgian. His replies to the personal data questionnaire indicate that Bubnov's parents were "peasants," but his social background was not discussed at any length. The autobiographer moved at once to the account of his education: "When I studied at the Vologda *realschule,* I was granted a tuition waiver." Dissociating himself from the rich peasant children, Bubnov was eager to convey his impecunious origins. "The war began soon after I graduated . . . I was at a loss as to what to do with myself and, bowing to the proposal of the military authorities, I enrolled in the Vladimir Military School. Thus I became a corporal."

By suggesting that his career choice was forced on him, Bubnov was attempting to empty it of all meaning. No less significant were the additional reasons he cited for enrolling in the tsarist army: "an excess of youthful energies and a desire to gain personal autonomy." The implication is clear: independence from reactionary parents, albeit through a totally misguided mechanism, is to be understood as the result of an instinctual drive to distance himself from his background and to begin his search for true consciousness. And thus Bubnov became an officer in the old army and, as such, an oppressor of the international proletariat. No wonder he hastened to note that his promotion "due to the death of all commissioned officers in the course of the war" was a matter of happenstance.

The telos of Bubnov's development emerges gradually. At the start his Bolshevism was limping—his revolutionary consciousness was held hostage by the world in which he dwelt. But when the First World War—referred to by Bubnov as "the imperialist war"—developed into the Revolution, a path to enlightenment opened up. And so the "false patriotism, inculcated in me by the tsarist school," came to be contrasted with the joy Bubnov felt as the army of Nicholas II came apart. Projecting this Leninist interpretation of the war (referred to as "defeatism") back onto his former self, and ignoring the ideological incompatibility of the Bolshevik desire to turn the "imperialist war" into "civil war" with his own chauvinist career as an officer in the tsarist army, Bubnov the autobiographer was clearly anticipating the future.

Bubnov had described his earlier outlook only to disavow it immediately. The existence side by side of two Bubnovs—patriot (Bubnov in 1914) and defeatist (Bubnov in 1926)—becomes possible as the protagonist's subjective reality is bifurcated into two levels: phenomenal and ephemeral patriotism vis-à-vis essential and enduring defeatism. Based on the distinction between essence and appearance, Marxist analysis served as Bubnov's objective vantage point, and from there "false consciousness" could be diagnosed as such. Without knowing what particular transgressions he had committed by joining the tsarist army, he would not have known what to recant.

Had the autobiography concluded with Bubnov fighting in the ranks of the tsarist army, the insertion of a Communist rationale into the description of a set of choices far from doctrinaire would have been absurd and doomed. But no story is judged before its completion. By collapsing time and inserting intimations of the future into the present, Bubnov was betting that his later deeds would absolve his youthful blunders.

The story continues. We learn that Bubnov was injured, demobilized, and sent to "recover from a head wound in a military hospital." This period of recuperation allowed Bubnov to skip the otherwise obligatory autobiographical chapters organized around the themes "Me and the February Revolution" and "Me and November 1917"; literally unconscious, he saw none of these momentous events firsthand. The crucial omission was acceptable; those who were recovering from serious injuries were somehow superior to unforgivable cases of petit-bourgeois vacillation and absenteeism.

When the autobiography resumed, taking the reader to 1918, Bubnov reemerged as a delegate to the First Congress of Peasant Poor Committees in Petrograd. The wound he had suffered—and it was, after all, a head wound—clearly worked miracles on his soul. Upon recovery, Bubnov was performing only good Bolshevik deeds: organizing a workers' cooperative for the improvement of agricultural equipment, serving as its delegate to the VSNKh (supreme economic planning agency), and, most important, joining the Red Army. At the time of writing, Bubnov was a member of a workers' education section and a prolific contributor to Communist journals such as *Village Poor* and *Red Star*. His recent activities proved that he was in full possession of Communist consciousness. Contributing little to an already perfected political mind, those actions were important only in corroborating the autobiographer's claim to be a loyal Bolshevik. Strictly speaking, their mention was superfluous, included only to appease a skeptic who sought to make sure that Bubnov had indeed converted and that his conversion had taken place when he claimed.

What Bubnov accomplished in his autobiography was, to use Hayden White's terminology, "a displacement of the facts onto the ground of literary fictions." The autobiographer brought to bear a "process of transcodation," in which the events of his life, originally recorded as chronicle, were retranscribed in literary code.[8] To dismiss the analysis of the organizational principle of Bubnov's autobiography as a quixotic curiosity, an inquiry into, as it were, the text's embellishments, is to miss completely the

Communist notion of the self.[9] The poetics of an autobiography is not an-
cillary, not just part of the presentation or simply an aesthetic response to
an ideological dictate that could be specified in other terms. Bubnov's autobiography is interesting precisely for its tropes and figures of thought,
without which the author would not have been able to turn the real events
of his life into a narrative and transform them from a chronicle into a
story.

What made an autobiography into a Communist autobiography was
the careful separation of the morally meaningful—which the text highlighted—and the morally neutral—which was trivial and thus had to be
left out. Moral inquiries usually take a narrative form. "Orientation in
moral space," Charles Taylor maintains, "turns out to be similar to orientation in physical space. We know where we are through a mixture of recognition of landmarks before us and a sense of how we have traveled to get
there."[10] Their moral quality made Communist autobiographies resemble
the stories of the Old Testament. The ancient historian Josephus explained
that "the main lesson to be learned from history is that men who conform
to the will of God, and do not venture to transgress laws that have been ex-
cellently laid down, prosper in all things beyond belief; whereas, in proportion as they depart from the strict observance of these laws . . . things they
strive to do end in irretrievable disasters."[11] What Josephus said of the
biblical heroes can be applied to Communist autobiographies; both sets
of narratives went beyond a motley compilation of individual exploits
to form a larger whole, united by the idea of moral judgment. Whatever
precipitated the awakening of the Communist autobiographer was right;
whatever obstructed it was wrong. Instead of charting all the peaks and
troughs of his past, Bubnov dedicated space only to the events that enhanced his ability to distinguish between the proletarian and the bourgeois (the touchstone words Bubnov used were "conscious" and "unconscious").

Having crossed the ontological gap between the here and now and the
eternal proletarian consciousness, the Communist autobiographer fell out
of time. A comparison of Bubnov's autobiography with Augustine's *Confessions* may be revealing in this regard. The first nine chapters of the
Christian classic consist of a narrative that describes the protagonist's sins
prior to seeing God. As soon as Augustine attains the light, however, the
diachronic dimension of his memoirs disappears; the succeeding chapters
are metaphysical, lacking any temporal dimension.[12] Likewise, Bubnov

gave very little space to specific life events that took place after his conversion; his life as a Communist had transcended narrative.

The manner in which the Communist autobiographer contrasted his subjective states before and after conversion also suggested that his spiritual itinerary had been accomplished. Before he had been unhappy with himself, impatient and restless, had always been reaching for something just beyond his grasp; now the convert was "radiant" (*svetlyi*) and "calm" (*spokoinyi*). His "even" (*rovnoe*) keel evinced Bubnov's inner mastery. Balance arose from the equanimity with which the autobiographer faced both past and future, a past from which, no matter how checkered the course, an emancipatory trajectory could be described and a future that held the Revolution's final victory.

Bubnov began his autobiography by implying that his class position no longer mattered. He was calling on the Party to recognize that since his spiritual evolution was essentially complete, the starting point for his voyage to the light did not matter all that much. Here the autobiographer had been inspired by the Central Committee's statement from July 1923: "It is absolutely intolerable that after admission to the Party a comrade who has proved equal to all the trials and ordeals he has faced would continue to face distrust on account of his social origins . . . A decisive struggle must be waged against every attempt, even the slightest, to create an atmosphere in which comrades are divided into the group of those who enjoy full membership rights and the group of those who do not."[13] In 1925 the Party Secretariat reckoned it a logical correlate that the "transfer of a Party member from one sort of work to another cannot alter his social position."[14]

Communist Confessions, Communist Conversions

Recanting Communist sins, those anti-Party acts that the applicant had come to regret resembled nothing so much as confession. Indeed, it is striking that despite the fact that in writing autobiographies Party applicants affirmed their new selves, their narratives usually took the form of apologies, and were laced with numerous statements of bitter self-criticism.[15] Only he whose autobiography hid nothing, who had "spoken from his heart," was accepted. To confess usually means to admit, to acknowledge improper actions fully, to "speak fully about the trial of self under the active guidance of the interior conscience."[16] In the Russian language, "to confess"—*soznat'sia*—conveys the additional sense of attaining self-transparency and consciousness. Such expressions used by students as "accept my purehearted testimony [*chistoserdechnye zaverenia*]" and "I sincerely and self-critically admit and condemn my political mistakes/sins" typify confessional motifs in the autobiographies.

Communist poetics borrowed directly from Christian models of self-narrativization. The literary critic George Gusdorf was among the first to call attention to the affinity between the modern, Western autobiography and the traditional confession. Both genres tell their stories as the soul's drive for moral perfection: "Confession takes on the character of an avowal of values and a recognition of self by the self. Under the guise of presenting myself as I was, I exercise a sort of right to recover possession of my existence now and later."[17] In writing their autobiographies, student Party applicants had to move their refractions on the prerequisites for conscious awareness back to the event itself. The Party applicant could not indulge in a passive contemplation of his private being; he had to set out to discover himself through the recollection of his life. This may seem paradoxical when one considers that what was at stake in the Communist confession was not so much the recreation of the writer's past as the interpretation of his present. But so long as the consciousness of the autobiographer-confessor directed the narrative, it appeared incontestable that he had also directed his life.

Authors who had achieved class consciousness often seemed to feel estranged from their imperfect pasts. When Trotsky sat down to write his autobiography, he found it difficult to imagine how his petit-bourgeois Jewish childhood could have had anything to do with his Communist adulthood. Barely recognizing himself in his younger form, he could not bring himself to use the first person singular for those passages. "In writing this memoir," Trotsky admitted, "I felt that I was describing not my own childhood but an ancient journey in a faraway country. I even tried to write about myself in the third person singular."[18]

Such difficulties beset all those who set out to write their confessions. They were obliged to recognize themselves in the (unconscious) other they had once been, own up to the faults of this other, and at the same time maintain a sense of a radical break with that resolutely superseded former self. The Communist autobiography was the record of values overcoming error. Repentance entailed the assimilation of past sins, both by the narrator's consciousness of them as sins and by the assumption of responsibility for resistance to the Party.

Communists had to tell and retell their life stories with a particular emphasis on wrongs committed in the past. Each Communist had a duty to know who he used to be, to acknowledge faults, to recognize past temptations, and, when necessary, to bear public witness against himself. Transparency was equated with virtue, opacity with evil. "Gossip," Lenin explained, "loves darkness and anonymity."[19] This was how the Soviet official press described a counterrevolutionary meeting: "They are speaking slowly, under their breath . . . It is impossible to hear their conversation. If you get close to them, they will immediately become silent with suspicion and stare frigidly straight at you."[20] The insistence that hiding negative information was worse than the sin itself indicates that it was the health of the Communist's interior self, not his external behavior, that was primarily monitored through the rituals associated with Party admission. Why is autobiographical self-narration able to assume this purifying role? The difference between good and evil thoughts, Foucault maintains, "is that evil thoughts cannot be expressed without difficulty, for evil is hidden and unstated."[21] By praising some actions and condemning others, Communists reestablished the cosmological difference between light and exorcised darkness and evil. Verbal articulation was the key, carrying with it the mark of truth.

What might be called the "Communist conversion" was the centerpiece of the autobiographical narrative.[22] Although its specific formulations varied, conversion both capped the story of the birth of the corrected self and presented its moral lesson. In conversion, according to the classic definition of William James, a hitherto divided self became "unified and consciously right, superior and happy, in consequence of its firmer hold upon doctrinal realities."[23] The Party applicant shed his old bourgeois self and embraced the new Communist truth. Party applicants referred to the experience of conversion both by isolated words such as "transformation" *(prevrashchenie)*, "transition" *(perekhod)*, or "remolding" *(perekovka)*; and by longer expressions such as "spiritual break" *(dushevnyi perelom)*, "reversal in worldview" *(mirovozrencheskii povorot)*, or "alteration of political beliefs." "Under the influence of events," a typical autobiography would announce, "I, so and so, have radically changed my views. I have departed from class alien ideas and have embraced the Bolshevik position."[24]

While the element of confession was essential to the Communist autobiography in that it provided the self with a sense of continuity, the element of conversion was equally important. Those who had been converted had experienced the contradictory yet complementary sense of a radical rapture in their spiritual evolution. Since one could not disclose his inner self without, in a sense, renouncing it, Communist autobiographical self-revelation meant the refusal of the self and a sort of self-destruction.[25] Jean Starobinski insists that those who had failed to experience a rebirth might as well not write an autobiography: "If such a change had not affected the life of the narrator, he could merely depict himself once and for all, and new developments would be treated as external historical events." Ultimately, Starobinski explains, "it is the internal transformation of the individual that furnishes a subject for the autobiographical discourse in which 'I' is both subject and object . . . The personal mark—the first person of the 'I'—remains constant. But it is an ambiguous constancy, since the narrator writing today differed from his earlier self."[26] The moment of conversion supplied the autobiographical plot with closure: the unconverted state of the soul at the beginning of an autobiography bespoke a certain basic flaw in the nature of things; a reversal, whether in the soul of the autobiographer or in the structure of external reality, brought about a conversion that was usually coupled with a realization that the new configuration had somehow been implicit in all previous configurations.[27]

While conversion to Communism was certainly a natural event, it also had mythical overtones. Suffused with mystical symbolism, Communist conversion rituals underscored the boundary between the impure, petitbourgeois society and the brotherhood of the elect. They sharply dramatized the discontinuity between the world the student was leaving and the world he was entering. Indeed, the rituals of Party admission may be counted among the classic rites of passage. When he enrolled in the Party, the student shed his individualistic self, died as a rank-and-file citizen, and was reborn as a member of the brotherhood of the elect.[28]

Often the break with the bourgeois past was sharp, as when Bubnov experienced a revelation that transformed him from a tsarist officer into a Bolshevik. In William James's classic typology, this type of conversion is known as a "crisis conversion." Alternatively, the break might have been presented as gradual, a natural outcome of an incremental process, as was the case with those who presented themselves as proto-Bolsheviks almost from birth. For them, the road to Bolshevism was seamless and their conversion little more than the formal registration of the political inclinations they had always held. William James referred to such a process as "lysis conversion," a conversion that "develops" or "concludes."[29] Whereas the crisis converts flung mud at the denigrated, and now abandoned, image of the self, the lysis converts minimized such self-flagellation, providing instead a consistently positive portrait of the author-convert. If we try to see things from an eschatological perspective, however, the importance of James's dichotomic typology diminishes somewhat. When life had involved tremendous disturbances, ups and downs, regresses and advances, losses and victories, a Communist had to find a way to combine dramatic transformation with continuous development.

Intrinsic to the interpretative framework Marx had borrowed from Hegel was the same dichotomy of continuity and rupture (contained by transcendence) the autobiography needed. Developing "dialectically," the Communist life could now make sense of the two periods divided by conversion: the converted self was a "transcended version" of the former, unconscious self; the two were at once identical and radically distinct. When the tensions in the autobiographer's existence reached a boiling point, conversion brought about a qualitative leap in his soul. Since continuity and break were tightly woven together in such dialectical narratives, it was a matter of poetical choice whether it was the continuity of individual biography that was stressed (thus conforming to the "lysis conversion" formula) or the obstacles that had to be overcome in heroic leaps (coming closer to the "crisis conversion" formula).

Socialist Realism—a Communist literary genre in gestation as early as the 1920s—would appear to have been specially designed to highlight the break that conversion effected in the autobiographer. The realistic was to the heroic literary style as the preconversion part of an autobiography was to the postconversion part. Socialist Realism should not be confused with what is generally called Realism. Anything but gloomy, the upbeat heroism of the 1920s literature had little to do with the humdrum, gray tone of the nineteenth-century Realist novel. What Communist literary theory called "Heroic Realism" was, according to the art historian Igor Golomstock, an attempt to construct an ideal world, "purged of old-fashioned (bourgeois) nuances in mood and permeated instead by a single powerful emotion— stern zeal, radiant exultation, heroic resistance, a world where nature appeared only in the form of a building site or the scene of combat."[30]

In the nineteenth-century context, the Realist self is a self that is controlled by its social and physical environment. In Rudolf Bultmann's formulation, such a self is shaped "only by historical, economic and social conditions, by his milieu, and that not only with regard to his fate, but also with regard to his thoughts, volition, and morality. All this is at bottom nothing but fate, and man himself is not a stable and constant person. What is constant is only his bodily nature, with its impulses and passions and its striving for earthly welfare."

Such matters had to be treated in the Party applicant's initial depiction of the "formative influence of his milieu." At this stage, the narrative was informed by Marxist materialistic determinism; the autobiographer described the unpleasant but necessary starting point of his story as an unfortunate state of mind resulting from an adverse environment. To substantiate his claim, the autobiographer employed Realist tropes, creating the impression that the self renounced responsibility for the actions attributed to it. Typically, he was "floating" *(dreifovat')* or "carried by the stream" *(plyt' po techeniiu)*.

While emphasizing consciousness and action, the Communist autobiography also had a strongly pronounced Romantic side. According to Romanticism, to cite Bultmann again, humans are able to change the world: "Man is not seen as qualified by his past. The future is thought of as being at the disposal of man."[31] The Romantic individual has the power to improve and even to perfect humanity through an act of will.

A split between "what is" and "what ought to be" was the quintessence of the Communist autobiography.[32] And when the writer crossed the border and entered the land of "what ought to be," the Romantic side of Social Realism always asserted itself. Then the author extricated himself from bourgeois influences and asserted his revolutionary will. At the moment of conversion the autobiographer was supposed to penetrate to the secret of reality. The understanding that his environment was a social construct and not a natural given released him from what had been the reality of that environment, and he thereby became capable of changing it. We have seen that the crux of Bubnov's text resided in the contrast between volunteering for the working-class army—a self-motivated and conscious act that led to conversion—and enrolling reluctantly in the ranks of the tsarist army, "out of nothing better to do." Before his conversion, Bubnov was passive and sinful; immediately thereafter he became active and pure. His ability to act as a conscious Romantic hero was contingent upon the appearance of an active self eager to mold reality in the Communist image.

It was a crucial feature of the poetics of the Communist autobiography that the description of conversion involved a shift from the Realist to the Romantic literary style. While a break in the life of the writer prompts the reader to look for changes in narrative style, the narrative's shift from a Realist to a Romantic poetics helps us locate that pivotal moment in the life story, a moment the autobiographer sometimes underemphasized for fear of overdoing the contrast between his present purity and his past sins. The moment of conversion is not dictated solely by the contents of the life; the rupture in the applicant's life was less a contingent event than a poetical necessity. The very notion of the autobiographer's journey, in itself and without any necessary recourse to objective reality, necessitated a transition from Realism to Romanticism.

The earlier the conversion of the protagonist to Bolshevik defeatism, the sooner the Romantic tropes made their appearance. The autobiography of a Leningrad Communist University student named Shumilov centered on revolutionary defeatism, much as Bubnov's did.[33] Wretched living conditions precipitated the autobiographer's conversion. Born into the household of an impoverished village priest, Shumilov labeled himself a "poor peasant" and construed his early life as an apprenticeship to opposing the old order. Bubnov's boyhood in a wealthy peasant household had produced nothing but conformism. In contest, Shumilov, born in Karaksh in Kazan Province in 1892, spent his childhood in a village environment as part of a family of seventeen. "Only shortly before the war did my parents break away from grandfather's household and establish a household of their own." Shumilov's style is dry and realistic, as in this: "Having become accustomed to agricultural labor at a young age, at the age of twelve I already knew how to handle a plow."

Shumilov's eschatological journey started very early in his life. The autobiographer took great care to point out that he was not an illiterate peasant. "I was sent to school at the age of six and a half." Shumilov traced his independent thinking back to his school years. "Because of my naughty nature, the teacher called me intransigent," implying that seeds of Bolshevik steadfastness had been planted in him already during his youth. In 1906 "I was expelled from the church school in Cheboksary, which came as a punishment for my participation in a student strike." Shumilov made himself out to have been a Bolshevik of sorts from very early on, quite capable of resisting his environment while still a teenager; he explicitly identified his school years as crucial to his revolutionary development: "The institute passed on to me nothing but a proclivity to struggle against my environment and a desire to damn once and for all religious-spiritual-moralistic edification." In all likelihood, the word "proclivity" (*povadka*) was used here to connote animalistic behavior. Describing himself at this stage as instinctually but not yet consciously revolutionary, Shumilov employed Realist tropes. The autobiographer stated that "the recollection of my adolescence made me sad for many years," but hastened to add, "I did not lose spirit." An early rebel, Shumilov was also an early romantic.

Expelled from school, Shumilov returned to his village for the sake of reviving "everyday life and agricultural work." There he "subdued" his zeal for a time. Still, he was independent enough to break away from his backward father, "who was selfish by nature, and often took me to task for my irreverence to authority"; apparently father viewed son as "almost a lost soul." Shumilov's mother was his "sole defender." Renouncing religious education—another sign of arrival at the Communist consciousness—Shumilov did not completely neglect his studies, which would have precluded his attainment of Bolshevik consciousness. "My motto was to learn at all costs." He graduated from a pedagogical institute, but life gave him "no chance to become a teacher." In 1913 Shumilov was drafted into the tsarist army, where he served until August 1914.

At first, much like Bubnov, Shumilov was subdued in the face of military discipline: "My will and my mind were taken into alien hands. Everyone who was in the old army knows how severe and inhuman it was. Soldiering immediately suppressed my youthful impulses." Like Bubnov, Shumilov mentioned his "youthful impulses," but the function of this phrase differed in the two narratives. Bubnov's natural impulses were selfish and reactionary, the impulses of a member of the intelligentsia, and they served to explain his collaboration with the reactionary camp. Shumilov's natural impulses, since he had allegedly been born into a poor peasant household, were, on the contrary, proletarian. Their "suppression" by the tsarist army, not their "expression," came to explain Shumilov's participation in the imperialist war. Bubnov the soldier had to experience a radical change of values before joining the Bolsheviks; Shumilov the soldier was a slightly misguided radical who from very early on rebelled against the tsarist army. The autobiographer's reference to the start of the war—"the manslaughter has begun"—has the same anachronistically defeatist tone we have encountered in Bubnov's autobiography. Shumilov depicted himself back in 1914 as cannon fodder for tsarist imperialism. "Even before we completed drill we found ourselves on the East Prussian front. During our advance, they shot at me as if I were a rabbit."

A prisoner of war after only a month on the front, Shumilov begun an accelerated ideological transformation. With deep roots in physical labor, and steeped in secular education, he turned against the war much faster than did Bubnov, who, after all, was promoted to the rank of officer. "In the face of the adversity I experienced, this period of my life was a landmark in my spiritual revival," Shumilov averred. While held by the Germans in Bessarabia,

> I passed through an ordeal and experienced a spiritual rebirth. The camp, and the many prisoners from all of the allied powers, exercised a profound influence on both my Will and my mind . . . As early as my second year of captivity I experienced the revelation of the essence of Being. Until that point, I had been a believer, but now I lost my faith in religion, which I saw to be foolish. In the camp, I read plenty of illegal literature. Marxist books were sent to us from Switzerland. Some said Lenin himself sent them.

Shumilov boasted that he attained a Communist consciousness "in spite of cold and hunger [*kholod i golod*]." Here he clearly styled himself after the extraordinary warrior of the Russian epic tales—the mythical knight (*bogatyr'*) who frequently and effortlessly "goes through fire and blood," demonstrating his superiority to destructive natural forces.[34]

Indeed, thenceforth the presence of Romantic conventions in the autobiography became unmistakable: Shumilov recounted, for example, a series of marvelous escapades to show that he was a Bolshevik who acted on reality rather than being molded by it. The autobiographer's metamorphosis would become complete after a stay of five and a half months in infirmaries and another two years with Bavarian peasants, whom Shumilov described as "these hard-working laborers, who meshed in my mind with Bavarian mountains and towers."

If for Bubnov the civil war was the key transformative experience, for Shumilov, who had got a head start, the spiritual turning point had already occurred during the First World War. By 1917 Shumilov was prepared to join the Revolution. In his words, "when the Russian Revolution erupted, our dreams—to be free, to go to a now liberated Russia—came true."

Another autobiographer, Anfalov, a student at Leningrad Communist University, was a revolutionary almost from birth. A model of conscious resistance to the imperialist war, Anfalov could claim Bolshevik credentials superior to Shumilov's, and certainly to Bubnov's. Once he had mentioned his birth into a peasant family in 1896 Vologda Province, this petitioner was very chary of other details about his childhood and adolescence. All we learn is that Anfalov graduated from a one-year *zemstvo* school and worked in his father's household until 1915. Sent in February 1917 to the front, he took an active antiwar stance, and in March 1917 joined the ranks of the Bolshevik Social Democratic Party, where he was admitted to the cell of the sixteenth special regiment. Since it amounted to finding and embracing the party that expressed the views he had always held, Anfalov's conversion followed naturally from those stages in his life that preceded it.

Anfalov converted early. While Bubnov fought in the ranks of the imperial army and Shumilov marked time in German captivity, this autobiographer was already consciously executing the directives of the Bolshevik Party. A good defeatist, Anfalov subverted the war effort of the Provisional Government:

> At the behest of our cell, I engaged in agitation against Kerenshchina among the soldiers of my regiment. Kerenskii insisted upon the military offensive, and the officers corps supported him. I distributed Bolshevik leaflets and our newspaper, *The Truth of the Trenches*. Later I took an active role in conducting the elections of the commanders and the organization of regiment and company soldier committees.

Spirited and bustling with activity, Anfalov described himself in the Romantic key almost throughout his account. His antiwar agitation made Anfalov so popular among the soldiers that they enthusiastically elected him to the company's committee. Later he was sent to participate in the Army Congress in Dvinsk. Having grown accustomed to Anfalov's unending parade of exploits, the reader is hardly surprised to learn that the autobiographer credited himself with helping demobilize the old army, with working on behalf of the provincial executive committee, and with assisting in creating the Red Army.[35]

Autobiographers Interrogated

Without the context of an eschatological narrative, the regulations that guided the operation of the cells of the Communist Party make little sense. Every narrative enacts a structure that corresponds with the community's basic values: just as the Homeric epic produced ancient aristocratic "heroes" who were potent protagonists of a magnificent saga, and as the Sophoclean tragedy gave birth to "citizens" who defended their values in the public arena of the polis, so the Communist tale of universal emancipation created "comrades" in the omniconscious "brotherhood of the elect" (*izbrannye*).[36] Admission to the Party was viewed by no one as mundane and routine. Certainly it was not a rote mechanism for filling the ranks of the nascent Soviet bureaucracy. No matter how technically skilled an applicant might be, the Party would not hesitate to reject his application if it became a question of protecting the "purity [*chistota*] of the Communist ranks."

Whether they read their life stories aloud or presented them to the Party cell in written form, applicants were obliged to enter into a dialogue with their audience of judges. The two sides were pressed into a dynamic relationship structured by the fundamental premise that the conversion of one individual was meaningless outside a collective conversion. Normally considered one of the more private genres, autobiography became public because of the nature of the application process. Autobiographical interrogation was a ritualized procedure designed to evaluate the consciousness of the applicant. A certain presentation of the self could always be "unmasked" and rejected as "phony" *(nepravdivaia).*[37]

It is possible, of course, to dismiss the battle over the interpretation of autobiography as a thinly concealed power struggle having little to do with the lofty ideals that supposedly motivated them. In this interpretation, debates over the personal qualities of this or that student were couched in eschatological language because of political anxieties. But since personality clashes and competition for spoils exist in all social organizations, preoccupation with ulterior motives is not likely to deepen our insight into the specifics of the Communist experience. A close look at how identity battles were waged and how personal ambitions were justified to the outside world—and possibly to the historical actors themselves—ultimately tell us most about the politics of Communist identity.

It was not human nature, with its petty personal interests, but the ideological critique of "private life" that made the examination of the Communist autobiography so momentous an issue. The distinction between the public and the private spheres itself, according to the sacred official dogma, was nothing but a fetish produced by the bourgeoisie. By dissolving society into atoms, Soviet class analysts argued, capitalism erected the myth of the individual in his private domain. This mythologizing concealed on otherwise obvious truth—that production, the basis of all social life, was in fact a collective and not an individual endeavor.

According to Marx the "conscious absorption of society by the individual, the free recognition by each individual of himself as bearer of the community, is the way in which man rediscovers and returns to himself."[38] Inspired by this analysis, the critic Sergei Tretiakov condemned any celebration of personal privacy: "Everything known as 'private affairs' or 'personal interest' should come under the control of the collective. Each member of the collective has to see himself as a tool, necessary to the collective, which must be looked after in the interests of everyone."[39] Since the life of the individual did not concern him alone but affected all members of the Communist brotherhood, it was a matter of principle, the Party declared, that private affairs had to be open to public scrutiny. Mikhail Prishvin's diary dwells on the effects of this ethos: "Nothing is beyond us any longer, everything has become our business. Huge efforts are thrown these days into the eradication of the private, so that the worker will look for happiness only in the public. Constantly visible, social X rays rendering him absolutely transparent, the worker can no longer hide by retreating into the private sphere."[40]

In pleading his case, the applicant had to contend with very strict requirements of truth, dogma, and canon. The smallest lie or omission, immediately apparent to his reader or listener, could destroy all chance of admission and stain the Party applicant forever. Ideally, the applicant's encounter with the Party cell was to resemble a legal confession. He was put under oath and forced to give a solemn promise that his "testimony" (the Russian *pokazaniia* has the same juridical connotation) would contain only the truth. When examining the public interrogation of the Communist autobiography, it is crucial to notice who was speaking and when. Who, among the individuals present at a Party meeting, was accorded the right to use the Communist language and with what authority? What voice was the applicant accorded, and how did he exploit his right to speak the last word?

Hermeneutical diagnosis could not be dissociated from the statutorily defined individuals and institutions who had the authority to claim that they spoke the truth. The hermeneutics of the soul involved not only criteria of competence and knowledge but also the existence of the Party statute, ideological texts, ethical imperatives, and procedural norms. The division of roles within the cell, hierarchical subordination based on function and Party seniority, and the exchange of information concerning the applicant with the state representatives, GPU, and the judiciary all played a role in determining what happened at a Party meeting.

Construed as omniscient and omnipotent, the audience for a Communist autobiography was supposed to strip all coverings from the autobiographer's consciousness and find out whether a conversion had been sincere or convenient. This was the main task facing the members of the cell who discussed the autobiography of Klein, a student at the Tomsk Technological Institute, on November 23, 1925.[41] Time and again, the discussion of Klein's credentials came back to the period of the civil war. The stand taken by the applicant at that time was crucial. If during the NEP individuals stood to benefit from expressing Communist sympathies, neither their actions nor their statements could be taken at face value. Their relation to the Soviet power during the civil war became a litmus test of political orientation. Siberia had been occupied by the Whites from 1918 to 1920, so Bolshevik sympathizers there had been a brave group. The buro of the Party cell, its managing body, would have been impressed had Klein applied for Party membership at that time. Once it transpired that Klein had not, the buro became determined to understand why he had failed to help the Party during its greatest ordeal:

Q: Why had you not applied then?
A: Because I could not tell left from right and regarded myself as unprepared to enter the ranks of the Party.
Q: Your sister is a major underground worker. How could you fail to learn about things from her?
A: I was drafted during the imperialist war, and was a prisoner of war. I returned home in 1917 and departed to study in 1920. [Thus I was barely in touch with her.]
Q: What party did your sister belong to?
A: As far as I know, in 1917 she was a Social Democrat.

Klein declared that he had lacked any political consciousness in 1919, the year that tested ideological loyalties in Siberia. But many remained unpersuaded. Since the trajectory of Klein's political evolution was in doubt, someone suggested from the floor, "Let us have his Tomsk study bench peers say what they make of Klein." Whereas one such individual, Mal'gin, evaluated Klein's past record favorably ("Klein consistently followed our strategy regarding the professoriate, studied well, and quickly graduated"), Epifanov advanced a succinct but well-thought-out denunciation: "Taking into account Klein's mature age and his sister's own activities, I cannot accept that he knew nothing. Klein belongs to the category of people who want to put us on trial. 'If Soviet Power prevails I will join it, otherwise I remain clean,' they say to themselves." Epifanov emphasized that he had nothing against Klein's personality. "Actually, he is charming. Still, we have to reject his application." In this scenario, Klein had not applied to the Party during the civil war because he had sympathized with its enemies, not because he had been unaware of the truth of Communism.

Klein's best friend, Goliakov, then came to his rescue: "People like Klein can unite with the Party only after climbing many stairs." One could hardly expect someone with his background to become a Communist overnight. Fixing 1919 as an early stage in Klein's eschatological journey and thus scaling back the applicant's political consciousness at the time, Goliakov attempted to rehabilitate his political identity. Klein's defenders recognized that their protégé was eschatologically retarded by comparison with real workers, but they still thought it best to accept him: "Epifanov is mistaken. We cannot expect Klein to have applied to the Party right away. Since he had not received the education available at a production site, how could he find out about the Party? . . . More recently, through his work for our public organizations, Klein has proved to be sound in his convictions."

The seesaw of opinion took another swing with comrade Popko: "Back then the Party needed activists, especially those with proper education. Yet Klein did not join the Party. Furthermore, concerning his spiritual evolution, I think he was obviously already developed before he began studying." The reference to "spirit" (dukh) went to the crux of the issue. Ultimately, the cell had to pronounce not on Klein's actions, which were open to opposing interpretations, but on his consciousness. Popko did not reject the application outright, but he believed that before he could be admitted Klein must be purified and made ready for Party membership in the factory: "He should go into production, prove himself, and apply to the Party there."

But others were determined to do Klein in once and for all. One of his numerous detractors, Gavrilov, pulled out a trump card: "I dimly recall that Klein handed in a Party application questionnaire back in 1920." If verified, this act would have condemned Klein for adjusting his Communist sympathies to the vicissitudes of the political situation. Worse, Klein's failure to mention that he had already applied to the Party could be seen as proof that he had tailored his autobiography to suit his current needs. In this case, the description of recent conversion to Communism would have been given the lie, and its writer would have been irrevocably discredited.

Recognizing the danger, Klein hastened to respond to the latter charge: "Yes, I did try to apply then, but the district committee procrastinated, and I was automatically rejected."

To judge by the clamor from the bench, many comrades were not satisfied with this justification: "Why is that not [mentioned] in your questionnaire?" Klein answered that "there is no paragraph for that." This explanation was clearly not satisfactory: "And what about 'comments'?!" "I did not notice it," was all Klein could say in reply.

One Communist articulated what many by now suspected: "I think Klein did not take a Party card in 1920 because the situation was tense. I remember that in those days many tore up their cards and left the Party." The discussion had gone on far too long, and the chairman thought it time to put an end to it. Klein used his right to a final word to reiterate that he had not concealed anything in his questionnaire, and that his recommenders knew about his 1920 application to the Party. Although the final vote was in Klein's favor (fifty-nine for, twenty-three against; thirty-one abstained), his admission was vetoed by the district committee. The suspicion that Klein was not a true convert could not be dispelled.[42]

In the universities, Party applications were processed painfully slowly. Marked on the candidate's questionnaire, the resolution of the cell's buro —"to accept" or "to decline"—was only a recommendation. The ultimate decision, to be made by the general meeting of the Party cell, could take quite a bit of additional time, since a quorum (usually two-thirds of the cell's membership) had to be present to give the verdict a binding force. And the procedure did not end there: stamped with the seal of the cell, the applicant's personal file and all the "accompanying materials" (which normally included application forms, recommendations, denunciations, excerpts from the debates of the buro and the cell on the merits of the candidate, and an indication of the number of voters for and against the candidate as well as abstentions) were moved up to the district committee and, in the case of third-category applicants (i.e., nonproletarians), the provincial committee. Most of the authority in matters of Party personnel was vested in these bodies, which had the power to ratify or reverse the original decision. Students could wait up to four years, from the moment they applied to the Party, until they became Communists.[43]

The class category to which a successful student was assigned was recorded on his Party card, which in turn determined the length of time that had to elapse before he became a full Party member. The 1922 Party statute recognized three membership categories: "workers and peasants who were Red Army veterans"; "peasants and handicraftsmen"; and "others" (*prochie,* including white-collar employees, professionals, artisans, etc.). Students occupied the lower echelons of this class hierarchy. "Vania, do you know what social category we are relegated to?" one student quizzed another in a contemporary short story: "To 'others,' along with all the riff-raff!"[44] Students who were relegated to the second category could apply for transfer to full Party membership after one year of probation. The least fortunate students, who found themselves in third category (the majority), had to wait an additional year before they could do so.[45]

The "Party quarantine" was treated as a period required to permit "the neophytes to be properly tested." Without reaching the very end of his intellectual odyssey, no student could become a full Party member. Having been put "on trial"—the Russian for "trial" *(iskus; ispytanie)* has the same connotations of a religious ordeal that it once had in English—successful applicants were officially designated Party candidates. A statute issued by the Central Committee's organizational department stated that "Party candidacy is not a 'reformatory battalion,' but a time during which the Party examines the personal qualities of the applicant." Concomitantly, the probation period was supposed to be used by a near-Communist to complete his self-purification—an observation that brings us back to the concept of the Party admissions procedure as rite of passage. In the rite of passage, anthropologists tell us, the preparation of the initiate is a "transitional" or "liminal" phase, involving a symbolic retrogression into chaos. Similarly, if the student was to be created anew, he needed time to annihilate the old within him first. Helping the Party to assess whether he was ready, the candidate himself was supposed to engage in prolonged introspection, double-checking his suitability to become a member of the Communist commonwealth. "I tortured myself over this question [*pytal sebia*]," a self-doubting Party candidate would routinely say, wondering whether "I am strong enough in my Communist convictions."[46]

Some Conversion Narratives

The rituals of Party admissions moved between two poles: particularism and universalism. The noticeable preoccupation with the class of Party applicants points to the strong particularist dimension in Communism. Only proletarians could demand a place in the brotherhood of the elect; all others were obliged to speak in dulcet tones. At the same time, however, the Communist autobiography was used as a class-transcending vehicle. In fact, at times universalism became a dominant concern in admissions: whenever a complete conversion to Communism was proven, class origins became subsidiary.[47] Even children of the disenfranchised could enroll, provided they publicly renounced their "reactionary" parents and demonstrated their own commitment to the proletarian movement. "Our Party organization is open to each and every one [*vsem i kazhdomu*]," Grigorii Evdokimov, a trade-union activist, stated at the Twelfth Party Congress.[48] Such inclusiveness, however, did not extend to conscious, mature individuals who had deliberately made what the Bolsheviks considered unforgivable political choices. It was not class affiliation but will that determined who belonged to the brotherhood of the elect and who did not. It was here that Communist particularism really asserted itself; the Party gates were locked shut before the wicked ones.

In the daily life of the brotherhood of the elect, class took the form of a ritual of words and deeds that had to be performed faultlessly by the students who wished to join the Party. And conversely, when they pronounced on the Party applicant's social identity, the various microstructures of power operating both within and outside the university were in fact determining his or her suitability for membership. Although students could disagree with this or that aspect of the official admissions policy, they were obliged to appeal in the name of class. The difficulty of determining who was a proletarian during the 1920s is well-known: "class origins" and "current occupation" were equally relevant. But these were not just taxonomic obstacles. Rather, the issue was the relation between class and consciousness as posited by Marxist eschatology. Class identity was an index of the student's readiness to fulfill his historical role: years of work in production could not make a student into a proletarian if his consciousness was not that of a member of a class-redeemer.

While the demands of the genre ensured that autobiographies ended fairly uniformly, with a conversion to Communism, their beginnings could vary. The path to perfection was directly influenced by the social position the autobiographer ascribed to himself. Any point of departure was imperfect by necessity; indeed, all the student autobiographers considered below reported that they had begun life as individualistic intellectuals, possessive peasants, or unconscious workers. Hardly aberrations, such poor beginnings were necessary to the Communist eschatological narrative, since a progression toward the light made sense only if the Party applicant emerged from the darkness.

How the Communist autobiographer chose to start his story was a question of paramount importance: after all, individuals from different milieus fought against different illusions and temptations and traveled their own, unique roads to consciousness. At the end of the autobiography, the applicant underwent a rebirth into a new identity. From a particularist, interest-driven class actor he turned into a universalist proletarian, a member of the only class that could transcend all classes. This new identity preserved its former class identity as a sublimated identity, reborn through Communist knowledge. From the vantage point of the reformed, conscious self, the autobiographer proceeded to remember and represent himself to himself as he was during the earlier stages of his development. The rigidly formalized demands of the Communist autobiography assisted him in recollecting and reliving his past as a peasant or a bourgeois. Comprehending his class-driven past, the autobiographer could move into the Communist future. The 1920 "Uniform Party Card" divided the population into the categories "worker," "peasant," and "nonproletarian" ("employee" or "intelligentsia").[49] The social position that students reported at the outset of their autobiography (and in the personal data questionnaires that accompanied it) shaped their self-fashioning.

The Party was convinced that the working class was the only class fit to shoulder the enormous tasks of human emancipation. This faith was not based on the sheer number of workers—in fact they were relatively few, compared with the peasants. But according to the Communist eschatological reasoning, the fewer the workers were, the more magnificent was their messianic prowess.[50] Workers were said to possess remarkable epistemological acuity. Separation from the means of production turned them into the first unselfish class that history had ever known. "Since they exploited no one," Aleksander Bogdanov pointed out, "workers were the only class capable of discovering the interconnectedness of the various facets of social relations."[51]

Before writing a word, the worker student who wished to apply for Party membership had earned the respectful attention of the Party admission commission; he had class on his side. But class was not enough, and consciousness was far from irrelevant. So, like every other student who applied, the worker student had to write an autobiography. These narratives

were a peculiar version of the growth-of-consciousness narrative. They allowed that working-class capacity for universalism might have been repressed or nullified by the negative influence of their environment, but by
the time of the Revolution, or the civil war at the latest, it inevitably burst
forth, uniting the protagonist with the general movement of his class. The
worker-autobiography posited that when a worker enrolled in the Party of
the proletariat he actualized his inborn class potential.

Almost a paradigm in this genre is the very succinct autobiography submitted by Petrov in his application to the Party cell at the Leningrad Engineering Institute in January 1925: "The son of a worker, I come from a
truly proletarian family. My proletarian parents were the children of landless peasants from Saratov Province. My older brother has been a Communist since 1904, and my younger brother and sister are members of the
Komsomol. My wish to enter the Party is motivated by my social origins
and my conviction that the Party is the true representative of the interests
of my class."[52] An irreproachable worker like Petrov presented himself as
conventionally hale and hearty, his stride sprightly and assured.

Few student applicants, however, could legitimately lay claim to such
spotless pedigrees. Key to workers' conversion was the impact of the city
and of its productivist environment on their psyche. Kutuzov's autobiography from 1921 was written by a young man from Smolensk Province, notorious for its peasant preponderance. Although peasants were respectable,
and although the Bolsheviks conceded that the young working class of
Russia had its roots in the village, it was as important to avoid bucolic nostalgia as it was to suggest that all along one had been a proto-proletarian.
Those who recalled the village too fondly might be seen as either Mensheviks, whose ranks had supposedly been filled by immature and disoriented
parts of the working class, or even as a Socialist Revolutionaries or Anarchists—petit-bourgeois parties with reputedly agrarian constituencies.
Kutuzov portrayed himself as a student at the Technological Institute wavering between the city and the country.[53] The opening is classic: "As soon
as he completed his military service, my father became a worker at the
metal shop of a Briansk factory." In 1905 the elder Kutuzov was fired as a
result of a strike and had to become a conductor on the Riazan-Ural railway. But soon he "returned to the factory and recommenced work in the
metal shop."

The autobiographer spared no pains in conveying his out-and-out proletarian background. Although the seeds of Communist consciousness had been planted in his soul early, its progress was not straightforward. Troubles started when the family moved to the countryside and became deproletarianized. "After the death of some relatives, we inherited a house and a garden in the village. We moved from the city only to find that we could do nothing but till the land . . . We struggled to set our lives on a steady footings and got a nag." Adding that "from morning to evening I helped our poor horse plow the field," the autobiographer was invoking Il'ia Repin's classic theme of poor Russian peasants serving as draft animals. While the family had given up industrial labor, crushing physical toil was still part of daily life, Kutuzov emphasized—so much so that "my father could not take agricultural life and died in 1918, his strength completely sapped." The young protagonist left the village and headed north.

What is crucial here is the link the narrative makes between the protagonist's movement back and forth between the city and the village and the vicissitudes of his political outlook. While Kutuzov's childhood and a Briansk factory primary school inculcated in him some working-class values, the retreat into the stultifying agricultural milieu, combined with a prolonged stay in British-occupied Archangelsk, retarded his revolutionary development. As a declassed village youngster, Kutuzov started behaving like a typical fence-sitter:

Even after enlisting in the Red Army I vacillated for quite some time between political movements. In particular, I was drawn to Anarchism, enticed by this doctrine's attempt to mediate bourgeois freedoms and proletarian demands for equality. I borrowed Anarchist brochures and was fascinated by their speculation about the future organization of society. My body and soul were fully dedicated to the supreme and bright future Anarchism promised.

For a while, Kutuzov confessed, he had been imbued with a "peasant penchant for unrestrained freedom [krest'ianskaia volia]"; this deviation was the unfortunate consequence of his move to the village. But the return to the city opened Kutuzov's eyes. "In Moscow I went to the Anarchist club to listen to debates. I particularly remember the speech given by a famous anarchist named Passe. Except for pretty phrases, anarchists had nothing to say . . . The deeper I penetrated into anarchist and Communist tactics, the more drawn I was to the latter. Finally, and without a second thought, I embraced Bolshevism." As his suppressed proletarian self at last broke through, Kutuzov became a Communist.

According to simplest definition, "proletarians" were manual laborers who owned no means of production. But the Bolsheviks feared that the country in which they lived was not sufficiently proletarian, and was not likely to become a classless society in the foreseeable future. Since the majority of the population in the Soviet Union of the 1920s had to be described as "peasants," some wondered whether "peasants" could be described as some sort of "proletarians."[54] After all, peasants were regarded as the proletariat's revolutionary allies. Little distinguished workers who sold their labor in the cities from landless "agricultural laborers" *(batraki)* who did the same in the countryside. Such arguments produced a compound definition of "proletarians"; it seemed that poor peasants, and not only industrial workers, deserved the honorable title.

Dubrovskaia, a student at the Leningrad Engineering Institute, explored the narrative of peasant spiritual growth to the fullest.[55] Writing in the mid-1920s, this autobiographer emphasized the connections between a poor peasant background and a Communist consciousness. The facts of her family's status were flatly enunciated at the opening. "In 1900 I was born to a very poor peasant family in a village in Orel Province. My family has been living in that village for three generations. In the time of Nicholas our belongings were few: one *desiatina* of land, a shabby house, a cow, and a few chickens." It was immediately clear that the family's hardships were the result of the horrendous exploitation of the poor peasantry before the Revolution. "We never bought a horse, since at harvest time we hired ourselves out to the rich peasants and gentry, who were as plentiful as mushrooms after the rain in our province. Often we would harvest the clergy's land in return for no more than two bales of hay and bread that was not even enough for our family of six souls. During the winter we spun and sold all of our cloth to others." By contrasting herself with her wealthy exploiters, Dubrovskaia styled herself as an impoverished peasant.

In raising the issue of consciousness, Dubrovskaia soon moved beyond her peasant class origins per se. The next paragraph of the autobiography brilliantly evoked a whole gamut of Bolshevik assumptions regarding the darkness of the peasant mind:

My two teachers in the parish school were a drunkard and a priest who would talk only of Kievan relics. Gradually I came to doubt what the priest was saying, and in August 1917 I persuaded my mother to let me make the pilgrimage to Kiev and see with my own eyes whether there really is flesh that does not rot. I plagued everyone in the village with questions about how such a thing was possible, but no one could say a thing. My brother, who was politically minded—he organized peasant uprisings and often sat in the county jail—said to me: "Tell them the priest is a liar" . . . When I got to Kiev, I discovered that all the relics are made of garbage—wax, metal, cotton wool, and woodshavings.

It was impressed upon the reader that Dubrovskaia's early life had been shrouded in Orthodoxy and other kinds of "peasant credulity." But she had challenged these "peasant notions" thanks to the guidance of her brother, a revolutionary and, as such, a conscious peasant. "I listened to him carefully and once borrowed his copy of the *Underground Russia*." Dubrovskaia confessed to have "understood little" but noted that she had liked very much the work of Sofiia Perovskaia, a prominent leader of the People's Will movement, which this journal carried. Eventually she converted to the Bolshevik cause and embarked on revolutionary activity. Although she remained in Kiev with her relatives and became an apprentice in a shop owned by the Whites, this was only a cover. The autobiographer participated in clandestine gatherings, agitated for an eight-hour working day, and suffered persecutions all along. Because of her ability to read and to write she was elected as a delegate to the soviet. Transferred a bit later to Odessa, Dubrovskaia "worked with peasants in the field, conducted antireligious propaganda, and told the peasants that relics were made out of garbage and that the priests had deceived them." Having attained the light, she hastened to bring it to her fellow peasants.

The conclusion of the autobiography was generic. Dubrovskaia reviewed her family's acceptance of the Revolution: "Now my parents lead a decent existence. They have a house, a calf, a cow, a few sheep, and more land because Soviet power has given them some. My brother is a Komsomol member and so is my sister. My husband is in the Party." The brief report on her present life was carefully encoded. The description of the household's economic condition—"not too poor"—contrasted well with the prerevolutionary period. Prosperity was out of the question, of course. The last thing Dubrovskaia needed was to become a kulak. But she did want to convey the message that the Revolution had benefited the poor household by bringing equality to the village. The entire Dubrovskaia household was identified with the Bolshevik regime. Reciprocally, the Bolshevik regime identified Dubrovskaia as "one of us." For what other reason would she be sent to a workers' faculty "upon recommendation of none other than the Party itself"? Upon proclamation of her unity with the Revolution, Dubrovskaia expressed an expectation of finding her natural place in the Party.

Would-be members of the Communist Party were granted a certain degree of leeway in their self-depictions. At times, even students from admittedly petit-bourgeois backgrounds were permitted to make themselves into good proletarians by showing that they had assumed the Communist worldview. This plasticity of identity, however, was not boundless. Politically, a student had to be a tabula rasa; if he had ever manifested a formed consciousness, it had to be a Communist one.

In this respect the position of the intelligentsia was peculiar. Seldom politically naive, the attitude of this class to the Communist mission tended to be described in highly charged terms. Before the Revolution, Lenin had articulated the relation between the terms "working class" and "intelligentsia." The former was a virtuous and morally good but self-alienated humanity, men reduced to cogs in the great machine of capitalist production; the latter was the bearer of the genuine spirit in man, the agency that strove to realize the capacities of the working class by setting the working class free. But by the 1920s members of the intelligentsia who wished to join the Party were viewed with supreme suspicion.

Offering a variety of strategies regarding the narrative presentation of their life experience, the autobiography allowed intelligentsia Communists to inject proletarian spirit into a nonproletarian framework. Bolsheviks believed that a typical member of the intelligentsia came from the urban petite bourgeoisie (meshchanstvo). In an intelligentsia autobiography, interaction with the proletarian milieu and revolutionary activity drove the protagonist toward the comprehension of class relations, gradually relieving him of his petit-bourgeois character traits. Alternatively, intelligentsia autobiographies could be composed according to the conversion crisis model, describing a story of miraculous transformation. But in these cases, an intelligentsia narrator tended to claim that deep within his soul a proletarian ember lay hidden, glowing beneath the cinders. Once blown into a flame, it kindled a conflagration that destroyed such intelligentsia vices as passivity, cowardice, opportunism, utilitarianism, and the tendency to make corrupt bargains with the enemies of the proletariat.

The intelligentsia autobiographers paid much more attention to the phenomenological aspects of their conversion than worker or peasant autobiographers. Incessantly self-reflective, they documented every movement of their soul, revealed every inner spring of their intentions, and described every inch of their personal growth in cerebral terms. Cut off from active life, students who called themselves intelligentsia had to keep their narratives logical because rational deliberation and theoretical insight were the only impetus that was accepted as a force that could convince them to embrace the Party.

The autobiographical genre was perfectly suited to flesh out the subtleties of intelligentsia conversion. Composed in 1925, the autobiography of a Leningrad State University student named Andronov presented the arduous process through which a petit-bourgeois individualist evolved into a conscious proletarian.[56] In full accord with the genre, Andronov supplemented factual biographical details with a detailed account of how they had shaped his soul. He needed to set down a narrative because only that literary form enabled him to emphasize duly the changes in his spiritual outlook.

The autobiography opened with Andronov's confession that his family background was less than perfect:

> I was born in 1903. My father was an employee of the Old Regime, the assistant director of a railway station . . . I did not know him, and he played no role in my life. He died when I was four years of age. My mother says he was a drunkard and a loser, that he beat me with no mercy and took bribes. Starting with the terminal illness of my father, I lived among strangers, since mother had no time or means to raise me . . . She lived in Vitebsk, but kept a shop in Petersburg . . . I lived with my grandmother and with family acquaintances.

At this stage, Andronov could not have been further away from the proletariat. But the reader was urged to be patient—the autobiographer was young, and so was the Revolution.

Before beginning his studies at the Vitebsk gymnasium, Andronov rejoined his mother. The text had to confront the nature of her economic activity, to which the protagonist was strongly exposed: "At first we were very poor, no one knew my mother, hardly any orders came in. Then things improved, mother expanded her business, took female apprentices, and opened one other shop, which she staffed with her helpers. Mother's business, she herself and the surrounding atmosphere at the time, I recall, were typically artisan. Yet they were marked not by a tendency toward capitalist enrichment [*obrastaniie*], but rather by the opposite tendency of proletarianization." The autobiographer's analysis of his family's economic activity had nothing to do with his self-understanding as a youngster. Instead, the economy of the household was assessed from the hindsight of the mature Andronov who had absorbed Karl Marx's theory. It was from this perspective that the family's "tendency of economic development" was carefully evaluated:

> Mother's family became impoverished and scattered. Grandmother's shop was bursting at the seams. Mother's sister became a maid in Petersburg. One of my mother's brothers became a vagabond. The other worked in a factory. During the Revolution he was a Communist, occupied important posts, and died at the civilian front. Further development of capitalism would surely have plunged my mother too into the ranks of the proletariat.

Good Marxist that he was, Andronov knew that the influence of his mother's economic life on his thinking had to be examined: "The unique conditions of her craft—piecework according to concrete orders—both facilitated my mother's proletarianization and hampered it. It also brought the family into contact with female customers, which naturally bred in us a petit-bourgeois consciousness." Why would the writer have chosen to emphasize the retrograde aspects of his urban background? Presumably, he hoped to make his own progressive orientation all the more remarkable for having resisted the temptations of the surroundings into which he was thrust. Contact with the intelligentsia could be beneficial. In this regard, Andronov mentioned the time he had spent living with a highly educated family that took care of him shortly after his father died: "As I recall, I spent a particularly long stretch of time in the rich intelligentsia family of an engineer. This environment must have left an imprint on me." Unlike the artisans with whom he had rubbed shoulders earlier, these members of the intelligentsia at least cared to develop their consciousness somewhat.

Soon Andronov was sent to the gymnasium. This was a mixed blessing. Studies tended to intensify the petit-bourgeois individualism of the protagonist:

> Mother saw to it that I received a proper education, hoping that I would "become somebody" [*vyidu v liudi*]. In the gymnasium I was in the same class with the children of petty clerks, village priests, and Jews who

taunted me as a "tailor's son." This led me to have a certain contempt for
human beings . . . and to distance myself from social life . . . In general,
the gymnasium gave me very few positive values and encouraged only individualism, renunciation of society, and the desire to live solely in order
to study. I still have much of this individualism entrenched in me even
now, but I want with all my heart to exorcise it.

The autobiographer described his years in Vitebsk (1919–1921) as a "period of major work on my personal development and widening of my intellectual horizons." Andronov read literary works extensively, wrote, and
earned money by tutoring. He met "all kinds of people and argued about
urgent issues, among them Communism." Skillfully, the autobiographer
sketched a portrait of himself as a member of the Russian, pre-Marxist,
traditional intelligentsia. At this stage of his life, he was consumed by
heated intellectual debates: "My convictions were very close to those of the
Tolstoyans; I somehow managed to combine them with the philosophy of
imitators of symbolism. The image of myself talking a lot about nonresistance recurs. No one could budge me from my position, although sometimes I was able to change the opinions of my opponents." With a good
dose of irony, Andronov resuscitated his long-overcome, arrogant intelligentsia self, a self convinced he had arrived at the eternal truth.

Under such circumstances, who could be surprised that Andronov had
missed the importance of 1917? In the questionnaire Andronov admitted
flat out that "I took no active part in the Revolution." What else was to be
expected from the pacifist intelligentsia that loved to talk endlessly but
do little? "The Revolution exploded. I saw it, talked about it a great deal,
but failed to understand its meaning . . . I read no political literature, and
the individuals around me were incapable of presenting an articulated
Marxist system. Doubts abounded, but no one could show me a Communist path to their resolution." As a true member of the intelligentsia, Andronov could experience events only intellectually. There was not even the
smallest bit of proletarian instinct in his soul. Yet to surrender his hope
that the bourgeoisie could be shorn of its exploitativeness he continued to
believe in a class compromise.

In 1921 Andronov entered the Petrograd Herzen Pedagogical Institute.
Upon arrival in the old capital, he dove into the activities of the local literary circles. For example, the autobiographer took a leading part in the
republication of Nikolai Nekrasov's collected works. Nekrasov's elegies

to the poor peasant had made him one of the Bolsheviks' favorite writers of the nineteenth century. His work on this publishing event managed to gain the writer a position somewhere along the line between Tolstoyism and Bolshevism. Eventually Andronov realized that he had to join forces with the Revolution and sever his contacts with the literary world, "which smacks of intellectualism and the cult of individuality." He transferred to Leningrad State University and volunteered to teach a course on the economics of the Soviet Union at the Institute of Technology and Electronics. Andronov proudly stated that having no formal education in these matters, he had been able to master them on his own. Clearly, not all of the intelligentsia's attributes were liabilities.

During those years Andronov attended many student gatherings. The healthy proletarian environment left its mark on his soul: "Not a trace remained of my Tolstoyism. The creed of nonresistance became as distasteful to my mind as the ignoble Menshevik sweet talk." While the "malevolent social tone" of his effeminate, infantile intelligentsia milieu turned many away from the light, Andronov was happy to report he was redeemed by the vibrant atmosphere around him: "Though I clung to old philosophical tenets, I had begun to think about Communism and the historical importance of our Revolution." As the aesthete became the activist, Andronov was clearly on the right track. "Gradually I became a fellow traveler, though with one important difference: fellow travelers know everything and yet remain fellow travelers, no more and no less, whereas I knew then only little and was politically completely illiterate." The outlines of a proletarian self-consciousness were already visible at the end of the narrator's road. The fellow travelers, who had to remain a part of the old intelligentsia, went as far along their particular eschatological journey as they could, but they were forbidden from seeing the promised land. Though for the time being he was hardly more advanced in his thinking, Andronov had the impetus to continue on.

It was the mastery of proletarian theory that made Andronov's conversion imminent. "I forced myself to read Marx thoroughly. These readings brought about my first mental upheaval. The shaky philosophical constructions that I had embraced fell like a house of cards." The moment of conversion itself, however, still lay ahead. "If theoretical doubts disappeared, personal ones remained. The essence of my vocation, books and ideas I was imbibing—all these had so deformed [*iskoverkali*] me that little remained of my initial proletarian base except an unconscious hunch that the downtrodden on earth had a moral right." Although the autobiographer confessed that he was still somewhat polluted by "my environment," and that "very little of my self abstained from wallowing in the intelligentsia's morass [*intelligenshchina*]," the abundance of pejoratives in his prose indicated the approaching apotheosis of Andronov's proletarian self.

Lenin's death completed Andronov's transcendence of his intelligentsia identity. "The crucial thing that allowed me to overcome my doubts was this departure. The Revolution became a necessity not only in my mind but in my heart as well." In the Communist economy of pure souls, Andronov's soul would fill the vacuum left by the death of the most saintly of all Communists. His conversion already behind him, Andronov had not rushed to the Party as a typical hanger-on would have done. Beset by nagging fears that he might be unworthy, he devoted the following year to self-examination, attempting to determine whether he could become a loyal Communist. In his quest for his true self, the autobiographer read extensively and worked with working-class students. His willingness to compare himself with the salt of the proletarian university helped him to conduct a final examination of his "class inclinations."

Once he was satisfied that he was ready, Andronov swore to remain dedicated to the Revolution even if the Party turned him down. He expressed bitter regret that the chance to join the Bolshevik underground had been denied him forever, since that would have constituted the very best proof of his inner gold. Yet, Andronov intoned, his cerebral past was worth something if the Party put it to the proper use. The autobiographer concluded that the intelligentsia could donate its knowledge to the proletariat. "I am not dross in need of a lot of refinement. The Party can expect me to contribute to its goal from my first steps. My opportunity is not yet completely lost, although a lot of time has been wasted. At present I feel I am still young enough." But he feared that should the Party fail to embrace him, he might relapse into a petit-bourgeois consciousness.

When it made class a starting point rather than an end point, the Communist autobiography suggested that a nonproletarian background was not the end of the world. Lenin's comment that "we accept gladly anyone who wants to help us whatever is his past, and whatever labels he carries . . . for such fresh inductees help us secure our victory" brought out the universalist potential present in Communism.[57] Insofar as access was limited to proletarians, Party membership was exclusivist. But what, exactly, was a proletarian? In the Communist understanding "proletarians" were all those who adopted the Party's perspective, becoming in this way proletarians in spirit. This subtle point was not lost on Bertrand Russell, who visited Soviet Russia in 1920. "When a Communist . . . speaks of the proletariat he means the word in a Pickwickian sense. He includes people by no means proletarian who have the right opinion, and he excludes such wage-earners as have not the right opinions."[58] In fact, the Party excluded no one on the basis of his class origins alone.

Autobiographies written by "class aliens"—a category far worse than intelligentsia—suggest some of the scenarios that enabled even them to become worthy of the Communist brotherhood. The Tomsk Technological Institute student Berman, for example, became a Party member despite "socially incriminating material against him."[59] Difficulties had arisen as a result of Berman's wealthy background, and the Tomsk district committee rescinded the cell's original decision to enroll this student upon discovering that "Berman's family owned a spacious house in Chita." At this point, Berman pleaded that the Party pay attention to the part of his life that he, Berman, had been directly responsible for, and ignore his socioeconomic roots. Candidly admitting that his parents were petit bourgeoisie, he pointed out that "since the age of seventeen I myself have worked as a hired laborer, a teacher, and a cattle procurer." More important, Berman was able to prove that his political development corresponded to his gradual proletarianization. Starting as a member of a Zionist organization (1916), he progressed in a few years to become a Red Army sapper. Incarcerated at one point by Aleksandr Kolchak (the White Army general who ruled Siberia during the civil war), the autobiographer presented the six weeks he had spent in a White jail as his conversion experience.

The members of the cell were clearly satisfied with the political profile of this student. "When Berman requested my recommendation I asked him about his social origins," admitted one of the applicant's recommenders. "Upon hearing that he was a merchant's son I thought to myself that he was alien to us. On second thought, however, having taken into consideration the four years Berman had dedicated to revolutionary work, I decided to shoulder the responsibility of supporting his Party candidacy." The cell upheld its previous decision and voted overwhelmingly in Berman's favor. The only dissenting vote came from a comrade who clarified that "I too have no reservations regarding Berman the individual. Since I do not know the applicant well, I felt obliged to vote against him on account of his alien class origin."

When she applied to become a member of the same Party cell, Bukhareva also found her alien class background a serious liability.[60] Yet the source of her trouble was not purely that she was a clergyman's daughter but that her spiritual break with her family was apparently incomplete. She began quite well. "The applicant gave exhaustive answers to all queries regarding her social origins." Although a certain Solonikin voiced some reservations, declaring that "Bukhareva cannot join the Party because our party is the party of the proletariat," this argument in itself did not sway the cell, particularly as the secretary of the institute's Komsomol organization testified that Bukhareva was a conscientious Komsomol member with an adequate social physiognomy and political consciousness.

It was a certain Dereviagin who tipped the scales against her: "Although Bukhareva was in the Komsomol from 1919 to 1921 she continued to live with her family." This meant that Bukhareva's three years in the Komsomol coincided with cohabitation with her clerical father and that they should therefore be crossed out. Bukhareva's clergy origins would not have precluded her becoming a Communist provided she convincingly showed efforts to overcome them. The trouble with her application was that many in the cell interpreted her participation in the Komsomol as a utilitarian step, the evidence being Bukhareva's inability to renounce her parents. Although the case was resolved in Bukhareva's favor, in all likelihood the vote was too close to be ratified by the district committee (sixteen were in favor of Bukhareva's admission, ten against; three abstained).

Narratological Obstacles

Within the Communist brotherhood, class distinctions were to disappear. Prefiguring that blissful state, all students, even those born in the most retrograde of homes to the most conservative families, were invited to reinvent their selves and become true Communist converts. Provided good will was there, so the Bolshevik assumption went, anybody could find a way to the light.

The autobiographies of former "socialists" (read: Bundists, Mensheviks, Socialist Revolutionaries, or SRs, and members of a slew of smaller proletariat-oriented parties) had always been regarded as a category unto itself, however. Many such memoirs can be found in the Party archives covering the early 1920s: by 1921 socialists who had converted to Communism during the civil war (each such defection from a non-Bolshevik party was an-

nounced in the local press) accounted for 5.7 percent of Party membership. Official policies involved a shrewd combination of stick and carrot
toward socialists, ultimately yielding the dissolution of their party organizations on Soviet territory.

After the civil war active membership in non-Bolshevik parties was
criminalized: the 1922 trial of the SR leaders was only the most publicized
of the antisocialist maneuvers. In October of the same year the government interned "activists from defunct political parties that had competed
with the Bolsheviks." (At this time the government refrained from identifying members of socialist parties with counterrevolutionaries: camp ad-
ministrators distinguished between "counterrevolutionaries" [*kontr-y*], a
category that included former members in the "rightist parties" [Kadets
included]; and "politicals" [*politicheskie*], which meant Anarchists, Mensheviks, and Socialist Revolutionaries.)

The proceedings and resolutions of the National Congress of Socialist
Revolutionary Rank and File Members, convened in Moscow in March
1923, were typical of the steps taken by socialist organizations in Russia to
dismantle their own apparatus. Convened by the Ural SR organization and
clearly working under official auspices, this congress called on "all those
who are loyal to the revolutionary traditions to endorse the Bolshevik platform." With the declaration that "our party has fully degenerated . . . and
has disappeared from the historical stage," the congress urged the creation
of a "united front with the Communists . . . Former members of the SR
central committee and of other émigré groups no longer have the right to
speak on behalf of the SRs or of any other socialist grouping. Our so-called
leaders are shameless pretenders."[61] Declaring that the SR Party should
henceforth be considered "dissolved," the SR congress made an appeal to
the members of the Twelfth Party Congress (then under way): "could it
perhaps accept some nine hundred of our most experienced activists into
the Bolshevik Party"? In response the Central Committee created local
commissions to evaluate former SRs who "expressed full solidarity with
Communism and promised to sever all ties to their mother party."[62] Stalin
hastened to point out that the end of the Mensheviks was already in sight
as well. "In addition to the request from the SR congress that we open our
gates to its membership, you must have heard that so Menshevik a bastion
as Georgia is crumbling. The flight of two thousand Georgian Mensheviks
(one-fifth of the total number) from their party attests to the decay of rival
parties . . . along the entire front."[63]

Yet it was not that easy for a former Menshevik or SR to cross the lines, as the Bolsheviks were very distrustful. To be sure, the Party expected the mature citizen, who was capable of making sensible political decisions, to join the brotherhood of the elect. Failure to enroll had to be a mistake: generally the offender was ignorant of the Communist message. Cases of intentional, self-conscious nonenrollment, such as happened when individuals chose Menshevik or Socialist-Revolutionary allegiance over the Bolshevik one, were, however, politically criminal.

This meant that very different criteria could be brought to bear on seemingly similar misdemeanors—in this case, nonenrollment in the Leninist ranks. The motive, more than the act, was what counted. We have seen above that a "tainted past" *(podmochennoe proshloe)* could be excused—this points toward a universalist tendency in Communism, a tendency to embrace individuals who transcended their bourgeois origins. But those who avoided involvement in the movement deliberately were pronounced "irredeemable" *(neispravimye)* and, in most cases, excommunicated. Communism's particularist dimension comes to the fore here, a dimension that has little to do with the Party's suspicion of class aliens per se. The Party was eager to exclude, but it excluded not categories of people but particular souls, souls that had denied the Party while fully aware what was at stake.

Whereas an endorsement of the bourgeoisie was an ill-defined notion that could be variously interpreted, open adherence to a non-Bolshevik party was a compromising biographical detail less easily remedied. The Bolshevik leadership noted at the end of the civil war that "too many recent Party recruits come from the defeated parties, a number of which had been dissolved by 1921." Concerned that "we have absorbed a colossal number of people who formerly belonged to other parties, many of them hangers-on [*primazavshiesia*]," Ivar Smilga warned the Tenth Party Congress that the battle against "opportunistic tendencies" should not be regarded as complete.[64] "Doubtless, the vast majority of the Mensheviks and SRs came to us with the sincere intention of becoming true Communists. But just as certainly it is not enough just to transfer from one party to another to shed completely the ideological baggage accumulated over years." Efim Ignatov, a leading Oppositionist, shared Smilga's reservations: "After we squashed the Left SRs and other petit-bourgeois parties . . . their members begun pouring into our ranks, hoping to exploit some ambiguities in our system."[65]

Why did Communist inclusivism tolerate the socially alien while it broke down when faced with the politically alien? The life stories of erstwhile Bundists, Mensheviks, and Social Revolutionaries undermined the Communist conversion narrative. According to what may be described as "the jealousy motif"—an important aspect of the Communist conversion discourse—these individuals had already been, as it were, ideologically deflowered, or, in the official parlance, "initiated into politics" (*priobshchilis' k politike*). The heart of the problem was that the agency of this initiation was not the Bolshevik Party but some other political organization. Since in the case of the "have-beens" a premeditated, intentional decision to participate in a rival party had to be assumed, such applicants had a hard time describing their past as innocent. Thus the Bolshevik press contrasted two kinds of intelligentsia that streamed into the Party: "the Menshevik or the Socialist-Revolutionary intelligentsia and the intelligentsia that is raw in the political sense." The terms in which the contrast was set up suggested that former members of alien parties were not "raw" but "molded" (*oformlennye*) or "ripe" (*zrelye*), that is, already endowed with a developed, and erroneous, political consciousness.[66] He who had formed a party alliance must have done so, it was reckoned, with a certain awareness of the political scene. Presumably, he had preferred a nonproletarian party, and all parties except the Bolshevik one were considered petit bourgeois by definition. These applicants could not claim to have arrived at Communism gradually, to have become increasingly more aware of their proletarian class identity. To make matters worse, the Party statute stipulated that in the case of the politically criminal, proletarian social position had to be absolutely disregarded.

"Have-beens" had to portray their misguided former affiliation as aberrant, a temporary inclination toward counterrevolutionary consciousness that they now regretted. "While I was knocked off course for a time [*sbit'sia s puti*]," such a Party applicant usually claimed, "I eventually found a way out of the ideological quagmire [*ideologicheskaia rasputitsa*]" and "climbed back onto the correct road." Only a proletarian milieu could help so besmirched a wanderer back to that road, and from that point he might, if lucky, recommence his odyssey.

Few dared to try to conceal their embarrassing pasts completely. More frequently, Party applicants only played down the importance of their non-Bolshevik affiliations. In his 1921 autobiography, a Smolensk Institute student named Treivas offered a defense for his membership in the Bund.[67]

He simply minimized the difference between the Bund and Bolshevism to the point of obliteration: the Bund, in this scenario, was simply a Jewish forerunner of Bolshevism. "I was born in 1897 in a Jewish settlement [*mestechko*] by the name of Onikitshakh, in Rovno Province," the autobiographer opened. "Need chased my father from home. He emigrated to London, where, after a long period of unemployment, he managed to find work as an unskilled laborer in a factory. Mother's illness forced father to return. Lacking any skills or sources of income, my parents opened a shop with the help of our relatives."

Of course, by opening this store Treivas' family had exhibited unmistakable bourgeois inclinations. But Treivas' narrative relied on the impact of capitalism on his native area: "Economic life in the Jewish settlement flourished. A factory for the production of felt boots opened, a second factory shortly followed suit, then a third one. Yesterday's patriarchal Jewish settlement turned industrial. In 1905 it had a substantial worker population in comparison to the surroundings. Industrial unrest and revolution came with it." These socioeconomic developments shaped Treivas' consciousness, and he was converted to the revolutionary cause as early as 1905. The autobiographer was not sparing in details:

> Although I was a child, the 1905–06 revolution left an indelible mark on me. My eldest brother, then a member of the Bund, was swept up in the revolutionary movement. I had to live through many terrifying scenes: police raids, endless searches of the apartment, the arrest of my brother, and finally the appearance in 1915 of a detachment of one of the penitentiary expeditions. The dragoons pillaged our apartment and beat my father in front of my eyes for refusing to turn in my brother. I saw how soldiers clobbered workers with their rifle butts after the demonstrations had already dispersed, I saw the parade of bound revolutionaries sitting on manure carts, and I had to bear my brother's flight from the country. All that doubtless sunk deep into my very young mind and inspired a profound hatred of the existing regime. I was revolutionized.

This was a rare thing indeed: a Communist autobiography describing a conversion to something other than Bolshevism, namely Bundism. Had Treivas become a revolutionary before 1903, his transformation into a Bundist would not have seemed strange. But since his conversion had taken place after the appearance of Bolshevism, the narrator was presented with a narratological obstacle: he had made the wrong political choice.

Ever careful, Treivas did not mention the Bund with reference to himself, only with reference to his brother; nor did he get into the details of his enrollment in the Bund or the specifics of his activities there. Instead, he discussed the revolutionary tendency of his youth in general, ignoring the differences between Bundism and Bolshevism.

> I read newspapers and devoured the socialist literature, supplied to me by comrade Segal, a worker and old revolutionary. These books escaped the gendarmes' inspections thanks to this binder's resourcefulness. Segal used to stick pages from the *sidur* and other prayer books in the front of every book. Persuaded from conversations with me that I was a revolutionary by disposition, he divulged to me that a revolutionary circle, comprising a few workers who had been activists in the 1905 revolution, held meetings in Onikitshakh. A few days later I was drawn into the work of the circle.

Milking his imperfect conversion for all he could, Treivas claimed for himself a fully articulated proletarian consciousness very early in life. This is how he described his encounter, while still a child, with Jewish education: "At the age of six, I was sent to a patriarchal school [*kheder*]. At first I was praised for my abilities and diligence, then later I was despised for my criticism of everything ancient that had receded irretrievably into the past, for example, the school and its head, the rabbi . . . Until the beginning of the imperialist war I attended high school in a provincial city where the administration picked on me." Proving again how conscious he had become, Treivas expressed in this passage classic ambivalence toward his tsarist education.

Even at that tender age, Treivas had begun to perceive the world around him through a revolutionary lens. Whereas Bubnov criticized the First World War only from the hindsight of the 1920s and Anfalov had become disillusioned only after enlisting in the tsarist army, their contemporary Treivas had condemned the war as it was raging and, unlike the other two autobiographers, had the commendable presence of mind to dodge tsarist military service altogether. In a sense, this was the trade-off for being a veteran Bundist: although as a Bundist-turned-Bolshevik Treivas was always suspected of political opportunism, he could—on the basis of his fundamental assumption that Bundism and Bolshevism were essentially the same—claim to be a proto-Bolshevik.

During the war, Treivas joined a conspiratorial political organization.

Classic landmarks of a revolutionary vita followed. Now an old hand, Treivas proselytized among workers, inspiring them to political action:

> By the spring of 1915, our circle had grown into a full-fledged organization. I enthusiastically assumed responsibility for teaching workers the basics of politics. We used to meet in the winter, on Friday evenings, in the small hut of a poor peasant, and discuss burning questions by the light of a single candle . . . During the short period that this group existed, we organized two economic shutdowns and a political strike on April 18—May 1 according to the new calendar. Shortly thereafter, a letter I had written detailing plans for our political actions was discovered in the possession of comrade Iankel', and the resulting searches forced me to leave town . . . My family also left after retreating Cossacks attacked Jews. Workers who had nothing to do with our activity were incarcerated.

The autobiographer styled himself and his Bundist collaborators as revolutionary martyrs. Deliverance had to await the February Revolution, "when the arrested workers were finally released." In the meanwhile, Treivas occupied himself with the Jewish relief committees.

Hiding out from tsarist recruitment officers, continued the narrator, "I witnessed the February and October Revolutions in the small town of Koroshetsk." The text did not attach the usual cathartic importance to these events. The tone was commemorative, but not quite enthusiastic. For a politically conscious individual, the 1917 revolutions were certainly long awaited and fulfilling, but they could not be subjectively transformative events.

As it was, between the lines the narrator could not resist intimating that he had enjoyed quite a career as an activist in the Bund. "When the Bund decided to merge with the Bolshevik Party"—referring to the All-Russian Special Conference of the Bund (March 5–12, 1921), which resolved on unification with the Communists—"I followed suit."[68] These organizational steps were narrated with exceptional terseness to emphasize that for him this was a "nonevent." Any other treatment of the subject would have worked against the autobiographer, highlighting the change in his party affiliation and framing him as a "have-been." By implying that the change in the name of the party to which he belonged was of no significance, Treivas stuck to his implicit assumption that the Bund was a forerunner of the Bolshevik Party. Moreover, the decision to incorporate the Bund into Bolshevik Party certainly had not been made by Treivas the individual; it could therefore shed no light on the protagonist's own political consciousness. Divested of any ideological significance, it was a pragmatic step taken by the Bund as a whole and reflecting the tactical expediency of abolishing the Jewish branch of the Bolshevik Party.

What to do with former Bundists who wanted to join the Bolshevik ranks? Matvei Shkiriatov, on the board of the Central Control Commission, noted in 1922 that this was "a touchy question . . . We have to be especially careful here—the Bund has been around for quite a while." The applications of Bundists for Party membership did not just come in sporadically. In the Ukraine, for example, entire local branches joined the Bolsheviks. Shkiriatov spoke of the search for a criterion that would separate those inductees who were "useful to us from those who are not. Paying no attention to the reputation an applicant enjoyed with his former party, we focused on comparing the level of activity in the former party with the level of activity subsequent to enrollment in our ranks . . . If one did not help educate the masses, the sword of Damocles descended on one."[69] Treivas, who had worked as "a political instructor" during the civil war, reaching the eminent position of secretary of the Smolensk Bund committee must have been active enough even by the strictest of Shkiriatov's criteria.

In the early 1920s the Bolshevik Central Committee considered a transition from a policy of "noncooperation" with the Bund to an effort to eliminate all "alienation" and "animosity" between Communists and Bundists.[70] Treivas' language lay different emphases. For him, the Bund and the Bolshevik Party had always upheld the same ideals, and the former had preserved its organizational independence only to position itself better for the task of converting the Jewish population to Communism. Propaganda had been adapted to the conditions at the Jewish pale of settlement, a Yiddish revolutionary press had been set up, and so forth. In fact the two groups were not so far apart, and Treivas had a good chance of having a successful career as a Communist in the 1920s.[71]

Though certainly imperfect, perhaps even erstwhile Bundists like Treivas could be fully reformed. Dissolving itself into Bolshevism, the Bund offered no eschatological alternative to Communism. A 1921 stipulation made it clear that the Party acknowledged the Bund as its precursor: all Bundists could enroll in the Party provided they did so immediately. The zero hour of former Bundists' Party membership was established as April 1, 1920—the date of the merger. Former affiliation with the Bund was favorably mentioned on the Bolshevik Party card.[72]

The Bund had only a past. It had been officially (and practically) swallowed up by the Bolsheviks. By contrast, Socialist Revolutionaries and the Mensheviks, with their vociferous émigré organizations and, until at least the mid-1920s, a slew of underground publications within Soviet Russia, were a much more serious threat. The Bolsheviks were less inclined to construe former affiliation with these "petit-bourgeois parties" as a natural prelude to conversion. When they mentioned the Bund, history textbooks focused on its unification with the Party in 1920; when Menshevism was discussed, its split from Bolshevism in 1903 got most of the attention.

A number of canonical Bolshevik autobiographies published during the 1920s taught Party applicants how to remember old revolutionary disputes. The blueprint was rather simple: the truly revolutionary Bolshevik political identity hatched out from a larger and quite nebulous revolutionary movement, leaving outdated and inferior ideological currents far behind. "After long meditation over the writings by Marx and Engels," Evgenii Preobrazhenskii's autobiography stated, "I decided that the populist outlook was untenable and unscientific, and that only Marxism could show me the correct path." This watershed in Preobrazhenskii's intellectual development did not fail to produce "certain practical consequences." While previously Preobrazhenskii "had distributed to students not only Social Democratic literature . . . but also Socialist Revolutionary literature," after his conversion he could no longer do so because he "had become a Social Democrat."[73]

Nikolai Skrypnik, the leader of the Ukrainian Bolsheviks, also confessed to somewhat eclectic political interests at the beginning of his political career. "In 1902 . . . the comrades closest to me in the Party were Uritsky, Dzerzhinsky, Lalayants [all future Bolsheviks], as well as some future Mensheviks and SRs, including Tserateli, Budilovich, and Khovrin." But as soon as Skrypnik read Lenin, his political identity took its proper shape. Thereafter, wherever he went Skrypnik set up independent Social Democratic party organizations. In Saratov, where the local party committee was following a "very indeterminate line," he brought about "the final split of the SDs from the 'Union of the SDs and SRs,'" and in Ekaterinburg he was successful in "winning over" most of the workers' circles from the SRs.[74]

Celebrated autobiographies such as these could also provide tips to Party applicants about how to present their improper former political affiliations. A youthful flirtation with the Socialist Revolutionaries could not easily be portrayed as proto-Bolshevism, so Smirnov, a student at Leningrad State University, could afford only an indirect and quite casual refer-

ence: "Before the Revolution, my brother was affiliated with one of the political parties; I think it was the SRs." Only the use of the first person plural
in Smirnov's subsequent recollection of how the tsar's repressive tactics
"set us against the government" gave away the narrator's own affiliation
with this party. Perhaps in order to fend off the suggestion of a causal linkage of SR retrograde revolutionism with the backwardness of the village,
Smirnov said little about his peasant roots.

His response to the February Revolution was the autobiography's nodal
point: "Before the Revolution, my brother, a pupil in an artisanal board-
ing school, used to shiver in fear [of tsarist gendarmes]. When the Revolution broke out we all jumped for joy." Both Socialist Revolutionaries and
Bolsheviks had celebrated the coming of the February Revolution, and
Smirnov got as much mileage out of this as he could. This did not keep
him from acknowledging the distinction between his former impulsive SR
radicalism and his present-day conscious Communism: "At the time I understood precious little of what was going on, of course" (the offhand "of
course" was inserted to register that siding with the SRs had been a mistake). "I experienced only those waves that shook the entire population."
Only later, in 1920, "having begun to find my way in politics, did I befriend
the members of the Bolshevik Executive Committee and organize with
them a Komsomol cell." Having matured, physically and politically, Smirnov was now requesting admission to the only true revolutionary party.[75]

Students with stained organizational pasts who wanted absolution for
their sins had somehow to weave their lapse into the standard growth-of-
consciousness narrative. Just as the published autobiographies of celebrated revolutionaries provided the models for applicants of how that task
was to be accomplished, so one may speak of antimodels, autobiographies
whose authors insisted on violating every rule. Katiugin, a student at the
Tomsk Technological Institute, was a total and pitiful failure.[76] Informed in
December 1927 by the district committee that he had been rejected because of his past association with Bundists and Socialist Revolutionaries,
Katiugin simply could not understand the fuss. A revolutionary of long
standing, all the autobiographer cared about was that "right now I am
completely out of political work." The Revolution, he blurted out, could
not wait! He mixed up party identities, glossing over not only the differences between the various "petit-bourgeois" parties but even the differences between them and the Bolsheviks.

One by one, Katiugin broke all the fundamental rules of Communist

self-presentation. Adding crime to injury, the autobiography Katiugin submitted must be read to be believed.

> As an active revolutionary I regard myself, in a sense, as a Bolshevik. I fled
> the tsar's army and first worked in the Bund party. Before 1905 I was
> forced to move from place to place. Afterward our task was to battle the
> bourgeoisie and the autocracy. In 1905 I became an SR. In the Nikolaevsk
> Jail I talked with Lev Davidovich [Trotsky] about the struggle against the
> intelligentsia that we both knew lay in the future.

The words "our task" suggest that before 1917 all revolutionaries were
united. Never mind that Katiugin never quite put on a Bolshevik uniform.
If this carefree narration was not detrimental enough to Katiugin's case,
the boastful suggestion that he had been chummy with the long-discred-
ited Oppositionist leader dug his grave for him.

Bewildered by Katiugin's convoluted narrative—it remained unclear to
what parties he had belonged and in what sequence—the buro asked the
applicant whether he had "any clearcut political convictions" and, if so,
how he explained his "frequent changes of party affiliation." Katiugin came
close to dismissing the question as irrelevant: "We workers believed that
the disagreements among the parties were transient and subsidiary. Once,
when I went into exile along with some Mensheviks, we all shed tears when
we had to part. I fixated on only one task—to topple the autocracy." When
a pogrom was expected, Katiugin was sent from Gomel to a Jewish settlement to do some agitation. "At the time, you could meet someone on the
street, salute him with liberation slogans [svobodnoe slovo], and, the next
thing you knew, you had bonded and were working shoulder to shoulder."

Defiantly or naively, Katiugin dismissed the importance of former party
affiliation altogether. He saw no harm in having befriended Socialist Revolutionaries, Mensheviks or any other revolutionaries. In what was probably
his biggest blunder, Katiugin did not bother to establish connections between his own beliefs and activities and Bolshevism for any of the stages of
his long revolutionary career. "I did not rise during the April days," he un-
abashedly admitted, "because I was anxious about the possible results—I
doubted the strength of the working class during the Revolution." Skepticism toward working-class consciousness in 1917 completed Katiugin's
self-portrayal as a conciliator, not a Bolshevik. Having violated basic ta-
boos of Communist political narratology, the applicant left the cell no
choice but "to approve the previous negative decision of the regional Party
committee."

The naiveté of Katiugin's self-fashioning becomes obvious when one considers the repentance formula advanced by Kononov, a Petrograd worker nominated in 1923 by the "Central Buro of the Former SR Party" to explain why huge numbers of Socialist Revolutionaries were defecting from their party: "What brought us to this point? Why are we renouncing [*otkazyvaemsia*] the party with which we have been associated for decades? . . . The time has come for us to say 'Enough! No more acting as accomplices in crimes against the Revolution!' Although many of us experienced spiritual tribulations over the following years, we got to the point where we can openly say 'Yes, we hereby break with the past.'"[77]

A similar narrative was built into the questionnaire the Bolsheviks designed to be filled out by former Mensheviks and SRs. The phrasing and the ordering of material indicated how their autobiographies had to be constructed (and what was missing from Katiugin's self-presentation). The questions already contained their own answers: a firm hand led the one-time Menshevik or SR along, drawing out the nature of his former allegiance, on account of the motives that brought him so low, then inducing the painstaking narration of gradual disillusionment with petit-bourgeois politics and finally the resolution of self-doubts and a climactic Bolshevik conversion.

The sequence of answers had to amount to a narrative of spiritual transformation, so the questionnaire provided signposts in the form of questions:

1. When did you start sympathizing with the Mensheviks/SRs?
2. How old were you at the time?
3. When did you enter the Menshevik/SR party, and what work did you do there?
4. What pushed you away from Mensheviks/SRs in 1917?
5. What appeared to you to be the best plank in the Menshevik/SR program and tactics?
6. Did you entertain any doubts regarding the tactics of the Mensheviks/SRs? On what issue did you disagree most with the Bolsheviks?
7. When and in response to what influence did your opinions start to change?
8. Did you discuss your doubts with the Menshevik/SR leaders, and what did they tell you?
9. What particular issues did the most to erode your support of the Mensheviks/SRs? Was it (a) democracy and dictatorship; (b) the

end of the imperialist war; (c) civil war; (d) War Communism; (e) terror; (f) national problems; (g) the NEP; (h) the intelligentsia; (i) war discipline in the Bolshevik Party?[78]

A veritable procrustean bed, these questionnaires forced Party applicants to twist their autobiographies beyond measure. Imagine how someone like Burevich, a student at the Tomsk State University, would have writhed in filling out the questionnaire; he had been a Spiridonovist and a sometime member of the Left SR party committee, an activist on the Tomsk SR organization from February 1918 to February 1920, later a Maximalist, later still a Communist, and finally a workers' Oppositionist purged from the Bolshevik ranks in 1921.[79]

Students were not to question the basic structure of the questionnaire's narrative. The Bolshevik truth was one, and the road to attain it was one as well. What Katiugin and his like failed to grasp was that the historical reality both presupposed and reproduced in these questionnaires did not focus on the overlap between Menshevik, SR, and Bolshevik political activities but rather on the divergences. The official narrative demanded that the Party applicant find the right track, see through Menshevik and SR petit-bourgeois ploys, and realize that only the Bolshevik platform was right.

Solar Eclipse or Evil Will?

Communists who had left the Party by choice could not easily gain readmission. They were, in fact, far worse off than the group of erstwhile members of non-Bolshevik political parties. Politically mature, students who disobeyed the Party line had done so in cold blood. Only an apostate would refuse to recant when made aware of the counterrevolutionary significance of his political stance. The Twelfth Party Congress instructed local organizations not to accept any second-timers.[80] Although this resolution was later repealed, the strong bias against lapsed Communists in admissions persisted, and "formers" (*byvshie*) had to accomplish great things to atone for their departures. Readmission of every single "former" had to be sanctioned by the provincial Party committee.[81]

What, if anything, could a "former" do to be pardoned? The 1923 readmission request sent to the Omsk Medical Institute by a student named Shangin-Berezovskii was an attempt to clear his Party name and to show that his departure did not reveal a thing about his true self.[82] "I am the son of a migrant peasant," the text opened. "Having completed a course of studies in the second-degree teachers' school in 1912, I was sent by my backward [*temnyi*], fanatical father to a seminary in Ufa Province." Things began to look good as Shangin-Berezovskii described his youthful determination to release himself from the spell of religion:

> I lost faith in the holiness of the church early in life. I had no wish to become a priest, since that would mean hoodwinking the simple people. Against the will of my parents, I did not enroll in the ministerial course but went to Omsk and entered a school for medical assistants in 1912. I applied myself to the natural sciences and completely dissociated myself from the church. For this my father cursed me.

The narrator laboriously set up the contrast between the starting point of his eschatological journey—a family shrouded in superstition—and the self-transparency the future held in store for him. Working in his favor were the similarities between the autobiographer and Turgenev's Bazarov, a priest's son who, like Shangin-Berezovskii, renounced religion for science and in the process became an ur-revolutionary in the mind of the Russian radicals.

No amount of shrewd poetic maneuvering could, however, dissipate the cloud that hung over the autobiographer. For how could one convert twice to the same truth? Before he grappled with this issue, the narrator softened the reader up some more. "In 1914 I was given away into the army ['*otdan v soldaty*']"—a passive construction that highlighted Shangin-Berezovskii's lack of consciousness and explains why the outbreak of the Revolution caught him unprepared:

> At the time I was politically immature and could not correctly assess the February Revolution. Like all the others, I was happy that the tsarist tyranny had come to an end. Little did I imagine that behind the pretty banners of February lurked the bared teeth of the bourgeoisie and the policies of the parties of social betrayal. These were the black forces of Kolchak, and they opened my eyes. Only in the fall of 1918 did I really come to understand the meaning of February and October 1917; to my shame and dismay, such meaning had earlier eluded me.

Describing here what must have been his true conversion, Shangin-Berezovskii presented himself as a zealous revolutionary who yearned to be united with the Bolsheviks: "I tried to contact underground organizations, but they are secretive and conspiratorial by nature, and I could not reach them." Tragically, Shangin-Berezovskii was coerced into signing up with the enemy. "In the spring of 1919, I was mobilized by Kolchak as a medical assistant." But the autobiographer's soul was clearly elsewhere: his short stint with the Whites did not embarrass Shangin-Berezovskii; at the first opportunity he declared his true convictions and joined the Party (December 1919). "When the Reds came to Omsk I took up arms to help them to chase out the retreating enemy."

Why, then, the second application to the Party? Only in the coda to his autobiography did Shangin-Berezovskii briefly relate the circumstances that had expelled him from the brotherhood of the elect the year after his admission. The text here is brief, almost perfunctory: "Poor health drove me back to the countryside. There I was attacked by an anarchist gang and had to flee. All my documents were lost. When I returned to the city the first thing I did was to reapply. It was only externally that I detached myself from the Party. Spiritually, I was always linked to it and lived to see its goals realized." So, he had never betrayed Communism deep down. His abandonment of the proletarian vanguard had been caused by circumstances beyond his control.

Shangin-Berezovskii realized he would not be condemned for his youth. A journey toward the light could include moments of opaqueness, and these the Party had already forgiven him; the distance the autobiographer's consciousness traversed only added pathos to his conversion. But desertion—and Shangin-Berezovskii feared that his retreat to the village and the mysterious loss of Party documents could be interpreted as precisely that—could not be justified by an imperfect political knowledge. His conversion was already behind him, so Shangin-Berezovskii was obliged to insist that it was not his consciousness that had driven him from the Party.

Although someone who had once been removed from the Party rolls faced a difficult task in reapplying for membership, the odds were not insurmountable. In composing a life story that would successfully reinstate him, a repentant traitor had one and only one narratological strategy in his poetic arsenal—the solar-eclipse line of defense. The term "solar eclipse" encompasses a set of rhetorical devices deployed by errant Communists: after all, even a perfect mind could be overcome by a physical malady. Such a mind was just like the sun—a classic symbol of consciousness in Soviet poetics and iconography—being temporarily obscured by the moon. The solar-eclipse line of defense had a double merit: it allowed repentant Communists to suggest that their lapse had been ephemeral—the sun re-emerges after the eclipse just as the consciousness of lapsed Communists resurges once they are cured—and it described a physical, not a spiritual predicament—the moon as the symbol of the body that obstructs the mind. Precisely because it was the site of instinct, somatic processes, and irrationality, the body was thought to be reformable.

Shangin-Berezovskii's only chance for redemption was to make the solar-eclipse metaphor a foundation of his defense. For a brief period, so the argument went, a physical malady could overcome the mind, prompting a loyal comrade whose mind (the spiritual, the self-transparent) was overshadowed by his body (the physical, the opaque) to act like a traitor. In the jerking puppet that abandoned the Party, the reader was asked to recognize Shangin-Berezovskii's flesh. The strings were pulled by delusion. He was possessed. For a moment, the Party member was simply a place where something like a mental disease, with its own determinants and its own logic, settled in and took command. Somewhat like a madman who was no longer in possession of himself, Shangin-Berezovskii became a blind instrument of a counterrevolutionary behavior, not its author. A quick remedy had to be administered to return him to the full possession of his wits. Introducing into the Communist notion of guilt something similar to a plea of insanity, known to the Communists from the "bourgeois law," the solar-eclipse line of defense allowed for the concept of limited responsibility.[83]

The one who wished to explain his betrayal not in terms of his consciousness and will, which were expected to be pure at all times, had to blame his corruptible body. Former Communists reapplying for Party admission freely improvised on the solar-eclipse apologia structure to explain the sudden darkening of their consciousness. Nazarenko, a teacher in the Leningrad State University workers' faculty and a Party member of three years' standing, had committed grave crimes: he had been married in a church and, adding insult to injury, had submitted, on his own initiative, a request to be relieved of the responsibilities of a Communist.[84] By 1922 Nazarenko had again had a change of heart, and explained: "True, I made many mistakes . . . Perhaps I am a weak Party member, but I am by no means a counterrevolutionary one. What happened . . . happened to me at the moment of a most acute nervous breakdown: my problems are rooted in my physiology!"[85] Bodily weakness had triggered mental collapse.

When the defendant's credibility was extremely low, his supporters might invoke the solar-eclipse line of defense on his behalf. Bordelov, a student at the Smolensk Technological Institute, was nearly purged in 1921 when it turned out that he had disappeared during the crucial stages of the civil war and had to be listed as "someone who left the ranks" *(vybyvshii)*. At the last minute, one of his benefactors intervened to offer an ingenious solution: what had really happened was that "depression engulfed Bordelov when Deninkin, Kolchak, and the Poles made their advances." Bordelov, in this scenario, escaped blame because it was not a loss of faith but a genuine concern for the fate of the Revolution that had triggered a psychological breakdown.[86]

But over time the solar-eclipse defense became somewhat threadbare from frequent use, and those who tried to exploit it risked the ire of Party boards. The publicist Kisilev maintained in the pages of the official press that "it is generally known that during moments of danger many Communists abandoned the Party under all sorts of pretexts. Many who fell 'very ill' and had to leave the front crawled back into camp as soon as the crisis faded. We should not retain comrades with weak health . . . Would it not be better to let them convalesce outside our ranks?"[87]

Those admitted to the Party had been judged infallible. Eclipses of consciousness aside, claims to have unwittingly abandoned the Party were not an option once one had undergone conversion. Deliberate betrayals were the work of people entirely overtaken by counterrevolutionary consciousness. Far from simply reverting to an unconscious state, a Communist who apostasized became evil incarnate. The Party construed the betrayal of its dogma as no less demonic than Lucifer's revolt. Those who rebelled against the Party were cast down. The image of Lucifer sheds crucial light on the Bolshevik theory of action. The Bolsheviks posited that human behavior could be explained in two radically different ways: as causally determined or as an expression of free will. Was a given individual a free being responsible for his actions, or was he an ignorant creature governed by his own instincts?

To establish that one's actions were wrong was relatively easy; in fact, every violation of the Party line fell within that category. The more complicated question was to find the reason for such a violation: Was it a physical breakdown, or was it a token of a wicked intention? In the former case one acted like an automaton and had to be restrained, corrected, enlightened; in the latter case one acted in full self-awareness and had to be mercilessly punished. Conceiving of the Bolshevik actor as free and aiming at the public good, the Party had also to conceive of his opposite: a wicked but equally free actor aiming to retard human emancipation. Here a totally wicked actor, be it Lucifer or Trotsky, came in handy.

The Party expected its initiates, by virtue of their lofty consciousness, to see through everything and everyone, themselves included. A comrade who violated Party policy, who openly rejected the authority of the Party organs, had to be absolutely evil. Recall that Lucifer and the angels who were cast down with him became a category unto themselves, neither humans nor gods, neither pure spirits nor wild animals. According to Augustine, "evil angels" *(maligni angeli)* retained "not only life but with it some of the attributes of their earlier state, reason in particular."[88] The emphasis on reason here is crucial: Communist traitors were likewise regarded as very dangerous precisely because they were conscious of what they were doing. No longer members of the Communist brotherhood, these evil creatures could seldom simply revert to being Party "sympathizers"—the group located between rank-and-file citizens and the Communists elect. That was not their place. Their place lay beneath all other places; they were cast into the hell of Communism.

3

The Bolshevik Discourse
on the Psyche

The poetical structure of the student autobiography tells us something about the growth of the proletarian self as the Party perceived it. But the conceptual underpinnings of the Communist hermeneutic were considerably more complex. Much more than a set of Enlightenment clichés, the metaphors the Party used referring to mental states rested upon a sophisticated body of sociological and psychological theory. The lexicon that described human interiority and the art of its decoding formed a multilayered system of signs, a system that has been periodically reconstituted in the Communist official discourse.

The basic theme animating the Marxist eschatology—the good/evil contrareity—governed scholarly writings just as much as it did Party protocols. What distinguished the Soviet psychological literature was that it attempted to account precisely for the vocabulary it used. Thus the Bolshevik moralists invested mightily in the work of translation from religious metaphors into the language of hard science that lay at the core of the secularization process the new regime presided over.

The issues discussed in this chapter map out the forces that, according to the Bolsheviks, challenged the self. Full consciousness was pronounced a delicate and precious state of being, easily susceptible to breakdowns. The contemporary scholarly literature has bequeathed a picturesque catalogue of human weaknesses coupled with their proper remedies. Experts' deliberations usually took the form of an attempt to arrive at a sort of a map of the Communist self—a catalogue of the paths to degeneration and the paths that could return one to the main road.

The Bolshevik transcription of the body/mind problem informed much of the Communist therapeutics. Those wrongheaded actions that Communist hermeneutics associated with bodily breakdowns were, in principle, treatable. In this rosy-hued scenario, the corporeal forces that beclouded consciousness could be forced to set the mind free and the eschatological journey could be resumed. By contrast, if it was the mind itself that was guilty, if one simply refused to embrace the Communist message, the individual in question was pronounced incorrigible. While the theory of degeneration, which was in vogue in the 1920s, paralleled the medicalization of the Communist view of the self, allowing for the possibility of a remedy, the later resurgent emphasis on consciousness made healing impossible. Once understood as expressions of evil nature, ill intentions could not be reformed, only punished. In the last account, culpability—that is, the degree of responsibility a subject could bear for his actions—depended on how pure and "self-transparent"—in other words, how autonomous—the self was perceived to be.

How the Party conceptualized the human soul was essential to its notions of a "counterrevolutionary." Any acts of political insubordination and the psychological origins of Oppositionism are our underlying themes. The imperative of explaining the etiology of heterodox political thinking engendered a whole series of systems of knowledge that pathologized errant behavior. In determining to what extent an Oppositionist was responsible for his actions, much had to be said about his "negative character dispositions," acquired or hereditary.

We have already seen how the Party treated students whose consciousness was found lacking. Now we shall see how the various treatments employed were scientifically justified. What is important in the "scientificalness" *(nauchnost')* of these studies is not so much their objective validity by today's standards as their source of legitimization during the period under review. Obscure allusions to backwardness, temporary insanity, or personal crisis emerge as more or less concrete references to a rich and established body of modern theory. Indeed, science was a crucial tool in the hands of the Communist hermeneuts of the soul: it was in the name of this body of theory and practice that they pronounced who was injurious to the brotherhood of the elect and who was not, what defense pleas had to be rejected as groundless, and what defense pleas were justifiable.

What follows is not a comprehensive history of the Bolshevik sociology and psychology or an inquiry into the interplay between science and society. Rather, the object of the present investigation is the place where Marxist theory and Party discourse met.[1] While some attention will be paid to sets of theoretical concepts, their origins and interdependence, it is even more pertinent to examine here their patent incompatibility, reciprocal alteration, and displacement. We need to know according to what criteria the manifestly contradictory statements were linked and made somehow to cohere. Without clarifying why statements about comrades' "health," "consciousness," and "degeneration" recurred in highly heterogeneous discourses, and how these concepts were taken up into new, "materialist" theoretical structures, we will find it hard to understand how Communist hermeneutics deployed them.

Preoccupations with the purity and consciousness of the Bolshevik self did not change over the decade and a half under investigation (1921–1937), however much the understanding of these concepts changed. This was also the case with the agencies that enforced official values in tertiary institutions, the Party and Komsomol, the scholarly community, and student organizations. Although it never threatened the supremacy of the Communist ideology, the scientific discourse was not immutable. The relative weight of the various components in the complex relations between institutions, practices, and signs that constituted this discourse evolved over time. Two changes can be identified in the discursive configuration. The first occurred in the late 1920s, when the Party directed its demands toward an active, assertive subject capable of implementing the First Five-Year Plan. The second change took place in the mid to late 1930s, when the Party demanded that the Soviet self be declared perfect.

Not all the components of the Bolshevik discourse evolved with the same speed. In revolutionary Russia the pace of political development was exceptionally fast, much faster that the pace at which the scientific practice could transform itself. The stock of scientific notions Soviet scientists were armed with remained more or less constant. Various conceptions of the self coexisted and competed with one another, sometimes within the writings of a single scholar. What made the difference was the fact that the Party required a certain emphasis on the self at one time, and another emphasis a few years later, thereby urging scholars to reaccentuate certain aspects of their theorizing while playing down others. Consequently, theoretical positions were stretched and made compatible with the political demands of the hour.

The Communist scholarly debate was a debate with a predetermined political direction. Participants had to be attentive to Party demands, taking into account important political decisions. The primacy of politics was an essential characteristic of the scientific discourse: salvational in their orientation, Soviet scientists saw no meaning in their work outside the revolutionary project. For most of them, politics was a source of expression, not of coercion. Most Party leaders, as good Marxists, identified strongly with the scholarly endeavor. Many scientists were politically involved, and a good number were Party members. Besides, the Party did not possess the will or the ability to exercise full control over scholarly research. It was content to limit itself to supervision, delivering important arbitration when scientists, deadlocked in their furious debates, approached it for help. Much as the Party liked to pronounce on various subjects, it never went against the entire scholarly community. Issues had to be marked as problematic by the scientists themselves before the Party intervened and made a judgment.

"Degeneration" in Science and Literature

When the Bolshevik leadership spoke of troublesome students who rallied against the Party line, they were describing an illness, a malady tainting the lifeblood of Russian Communism. What is at issue is not the general phenomenon of student Opposition—the contestation of Party policy in the university cells was, in itself, a familiar phenomenon—but the ways in which the Bolshevik discourse framed Oppositionism. The Party diagnosis of student errors has a fascinating history of its own, and it is this history, a medicopsychological history of sorts, rather than the institutional-political history of the Opposition, that will occupy us below.

The official view of the nature and wellsprings of student deviance developed gradually over the 1920s. Early in the decade the Party leadership had attributed students' resistance to the lamentable persistence of nonproletarian attitudes. The remedy to the supposed resurgence of the White, bourgeois element within the universities was an intensive proletarianization of the student body. But the success of the Opposition in the universities in the winter of 1923–24 shattered the premises of this diagnosis. It had become evident that it was the Bolshevik Party cells themselves, not a scattering of retrograde non-Party student organizations, that stood in open defiance of the Party line. That many wayward students were offspring of the working class rendered their support of a "petit-bourgeois Trotskyism" all the more anomalous.

A widespread explanation of how Communist students could slide into heterodoxy was that they suffered from degeneration. The notion of degeneration had historically been employed to explain the human propensity to contract not only physical but also moral diseases—and the official discourse understood Oppositionism as a moral collapse. The Latin root of "degeneration" means "a fall from the genus of the stock" and often refers to the debasement of some person of "good or noble stock." This etymology comes quite close to the general sense of what the Bolshevik moralists sought to convey—that the consciousness of those Party members who supported the Opposition was in decline. Ultimately, the "degeneration" diagnosis had the marvelous quality of explaining the treason of proletarian-born students by arguing for a "lapse" *(padenie)*—a deterioration in character that had rendered them incapable of recognizing the truth.

The sources of the Bolshevik ideas on degeneration lay in late nineteenth-century European thought. The term owed its wide circulation to the writings of Bénédict-Auguste Morel, a nineteenth-century French psychologist, who transcribed the Christian notion of the Fall into modern, scientific language. According to Morel, the social problems of our modern age were the outcome of "hereditary degeneracy."[2] The idea that humans could degenerate went hand in hand with racial theories.

Darwinism was principally responsible for the adoption of the theory of degeneration by social theorists. In his venture into social science, Darwin drew on the example of the decline of the Greek and Spanish civilizations to urge his readers "to remember that progress is no invariable rule. [Degeneration] has too often occurred in the history of the world."[3] With a bit of stretching, class theory yielded similar notions of decline. Marx himself showed the way when, toward the end of his life, he attempted to assimilate social and biological processes. "My standpoint," Marx wrote in 1867, is that "from which the evolution of the economic formation of society is viewed as a process of natural history . . . Society is no solid crystal but an organism capable of change, and is constantly changing." From here the road to a full deployment of the concept of degeneration was short: "When society is undergoing a silent revolution," he had written a few years earlier, "the classes and the races, too weak to master the new conditions of life, must give way." When Marx had to account for the economic backwardness of the African continent, he stated that "the common Negro type is only a degenerate form of a much higher one." Speaking at Marx's funeral, Engels drew an analogy between Darwin's discovery of "the law of the development of organic nature" and Marx's own discovery of "the law of development of human history."[4] This analogy inspired Engels to widen the meaning of degeneration so that it "no longer occurred at the racial level, but at the level of societal analysis."[5]

Engels deepened the Marxist theory of degeneration by making it more specific and applying it to the decaying European social order. In his view, degeneration was an important component of a paradigm through which the crisis of capitalism could be described. Originally, Engels argued, capitalism had been progressive. Having exhausted itself toward the end of the nineteenth century, however, this social order had entered a "retrogressive state" and had degenerated. One economic crisis had succeeded another until, during an era of unbridled struggle for existence, capitalism had forced humanity back into a primitive, animalistic state. Engels admitted that it had been Darwin who had convinced him "that nothing discredits modern bourgeois development so much as the fact that it has not yet got beyond the economic forms of the animal world."[6] He pronounced capitalism irredeemable and its perpetuation extremely dangerous. Humanity had to rediscover itself, to find a way to reemerge from its savage predicament. Engels' allies in the Social Democratic camp unanimously declared that only conscious organization of labor could overcome degeneration: "At every step we are reminded that we by no means rule over nature like a conqueror over a foreign people, like someone standing outside nature— but that we, with flesh, blood and brain, belong to nature, and exist in its midst, and that all our mastery of it consists in the fact that we have the advantage over all other creatures of being able to learn its laws and apply them correctly."[7] August Babel, another famous German Marxist, stated that only under socialism would every individual have an opportunity for an "untrammeled development." Guaranteeing such progress, something like Darwinian social engineering was to be "consciously and expediently applied to all human beings." Enrico Ferri, an Italian Social Democrat, likewise highlighted the importance of Social Darwinism—"a natural continuation and completion of biological Darwinism." Ferri saw Social Darwinism as destined to correct the ill effects of capitalist social selection, which was, in his view, too natural: "[Under socialism] in truth the result of the struggle for existence will be the survival of the best and this for the very reason that in a wholesome environment the victory is won by the healthiest individuals."[8]

The Bolsheviks adapted these arguments to the conditions of NEP Russia.[9] Capitalism, they claimed, had indeed been superseded in 1917. A full proletarian consciousness had been achieved for the first time in history, and for a moment the proletariat had appeared in its grandeur, self-aware and self-transparent. Alas, the exhaustion of their vital energies during the bloody battles and the deprivations of the civil war had thrown many proletarians back into the state of nature. At the Ninth Party Conference (1920) Lenin noted that "some comrades suffer from so much fatigue that they have become hysterical." Mikhail Tomskii concurred: "the atmosphere in which we work today is indeed nervous, unhealthy . . . The cream of our human material has exhausted itself."[10]

Fear of decline in workers' mental capacities was especially visible in the writings of Soviet eugenicists.[11] The eugenics movement, which was concerned with engineering a biologically superior human being, was one of the main avenues through which the notion of degeneration was assimilated into Bolshevism. The paragon of Soviet eugenics *(evgenika)*, Nikolai Kol'tsov, contended in the early 1920s that the Revolution had exhausted the proletariat's vital capacities and brought about a decline in the revolutionary genetic pool. Most workers died young, leaving no progeny, and the next generation was consequently replete with "inert individuals." The workers' race degenerated, losing its creative powers, and found itself far removed from the progress of humanity.[12] Iurii Filipchenko, another eugenicist, suggested in 1922 that "mental laborers gave eugenics a thought if they wished to avoid possible anomalies in matters of complexion, physical power, temperament."[13] The Bolsheviks had to be on the alert to prevent the total degeneration of the Revolution, particularly in the face of the New Economic Policy, which regrettably encouraged men to return to a condition of bestial, unthinking economic competition.[14]

What had all that to do with Marxism? Were not race and class contradictory notions, the former stressing "nature" and seeking explanations of human behavior in the animal kingdom, the latter emphasizing instead "nurture" and pointing to culture as the key? It soon became clear that these methodological differences could be reconciled. As the natural sciences became the dominant scientific paradigm, the concept of degeneration took on a wide metaphorical sense and was commonly applied to the social domain. The eugenicists' frequent employment of the notion of "race" did not stand in the way of its intellectual exchange with Bolshevism, since the concepts of race and class could be used synonymously. The commissar of culture, Anatolii Lunacharskii, for example, suggested that "class" and "species" *(vid)* might be interchangeable terms, and went on to draw a parallel between social progress and biological progress.[15]

The somewhat cleaned-up notion of degeneration was the one utilized in the Soviet Union. Reserving the physiological term proper *(degeneratsiia)* to clinical analysis, the Bolsheviks deployed milder terms—"decay" *(razlozhenie)* or "decadence" *(upadochnichestvo)*—when referring to Party members' ideological decline. Still, it did not always prove possible to resist brooding over the consequences of Oppositionism in the language of the clinic. When the official Party press likened Oppositionist students to Communist perverts *(vyrodki, pererozhdentsy)*, its resort to the racial-physiological connotations of degeneration was all too evident.[16]

Taking the notion of degeneration from Engels' scientific naturalism and from the eugenics movement, the Bolsheviks spoke of a decline in consciousness. Although it grew out of formidable intellectual sources, the Bolshevik idea of degeneration developed some unique components. It had a specific patient—the proletariat; it was applicable in only a specific time and for a specific period—for the duration of the NEP; and it proposed specific remedies.[17] The diagnosis of student Oppositionism as a sort of degeneration may be seen as a scientific rendering of the metaphor of the solar eclipse, which Communists had been using to explain their political lapses. It was argued that if the Enlightenment had elevated humanity, the fall from full, proletarian consciousness signified the degeneration of humanity. According to the Bolsheviks, the exhaustion of the proletariat in the Revolution, coupled with the partial reinstatement of capitalism in 1921, had induced just such a fall.

The generality of degeneration theory, and its tendency to collapse biological and social causes, allowed the official discourse to pass freely from cases of individual degeneracy to degeneration as a collective problem. Positing a malleable human nature, Marxist experts concluded that proletarian degeneration resulted from interaction with an unhealthy class environment. Exposure to the lifestyle and the beliefs of the petit-bourgeois university milieu supposedly caused students' "embourgeoisement" and their return to prerevolutionary habits and attitudes. A pernicious old-regime academic culture imprinted itself on the proletariat, allegedly inducing "hypertrophy of the mind" and concomitant "individualism," "sexual excess," and "political deviationism." These inexorably produced proletarian despair, disillusionment with the Revolution, and, finally, suicide.[18] Although each pathology of student life invited the intervention of Party and medical specialists who brought a specific field of knowledge to bear on it, the official discourse made regular connections between them. The various expressions of the students' decline turned out to be so hopelessly confounded with one another and with the issue of Oppositionism that their treatments were in practice virtually interchangeable.

Many specialists related degeneration to urbanism, hypothesizing that student pathologies had resulted from an "aborted transition to city life." To be sure, Communism was normally associated with enthusiasm for the urban environment. Indeed, class theorists usually described the city as a "healthy place," since it was the venue that created conscious proletarians. "We love the city," wrote the worker-poet Pavel Bessal'ko, "because it unites us, because it teaches us to rebel, because it beats the parochialism of the peasant out of us."[19] Yet there was an antiurbanist current in the Bolshevik discourse as well. Outside the industrial sphere the city presented many dangers. In this regard Bolshevism was consistent with a widespread Rousseauian paradigm that presented the city as the site of the contamination of "idyllic" life through the imposition of artificial, unnatural institutions.

The widespread contrast between the city and the garden, not entirely alien to early twentieth-century Marxism, evoked something like the image of the Fall, and transformed the city into the "icon of the rejection of redemption, of Abraham's failure in Sodom and Gomorrah, of the Jerusalem of Herod."[20] In the encounter with the city, the young had the most to lose. Publicists repeatedly made the argument that young students, especially those who came from the countryside, were deeply susceptible to the adverse influence of the decadent urban milieu. The fact that students were separated from the rejuvenating and relatively healthy environment of the factories at an early age, before their proletarian consciousness had been fully forged, increased the likelihood of degeneration.

The Bolsheviks identified the urban landscape with perverse sexuality— undoubtedly the clearest and the gravest expression of student degeneration. The city streets conveyed the message that sexual mores lost their mooring in the "natural" realm of procreative activity.[21] In the Communist rendition of this phobia, sexual excess in the sprawling cities was a channeling of precious energies away from social work. It led to irreparable exhaustion among students and, inevitably, impotence, both sexual and political.

Two different formulations of the university as a site of degeneration were offered, depending on whether the emphasis was sociological or physiological. According to the one, the university was dangerous because it immersed proletarians in a petit-bourgeois environment. According to the other, the university artificially separated mental and manual labor, both firmly united at the factory, and induced a "bodily exhaustion." Communist sexology, which was enjoying a boom, provided the link between the social and the physiological sets of phenomena; sex was regarded as both a cultural and a natural behavior, an environmentally determined activity and a bodily function at one and the same time.

The link between the university and health brought the issue of the sexual behavior of young proletarians under a spotlight. Marxist theory was corrected to include not only social but also biological factors. As early as 1884 Engels had claimed that the "determining factor in history" was of a "twofold character," the "production of the means of existence" on the one hand, and on the other "the propagation of the species."[22] By relating questions of the proletarian "means of production" (sredstva proizvodstva) to questions of the proletarian "means of reproduction" (sredstva vozproizvodstva), Communist social sciences united the eugenicist's interest in sexuality and the Marxist's interest in class struggle. Within the framework of this new synthesis, the squandering of sexual resources by the proletariat weakened its productive capacity and ultimately reduced its chances to prevail against its enemies.

Sexuality had become a key arena for class struggle in the Bolshevik moralistic discourse. If it was to be victorious, the proletariat had to remain united. But the sexual drive often operated in the opposite direction, encouraging antisocial, individualistic drives. According to one definition, "a good revolutionary of the transitional period" was a proletarian who put "loyalty to his class" before the "satisfaction of his instincts."[23] Under normal conditions, bourgeois sexuality was no match for proletarian sexuality. The former was individualistic and morbid, the latter collectivist and healthy. The bourgeoisie was eulogized in the language of a sexologist: "The psychosocial stability of this declining class has been undermined. We see that the socioeconomic demise of the bourgeois classes finds a biological and a psychophysiological expression." Unfortunately, experts claimed, the conditions of the transitional period complicated this equation. Many of the workers sent to universities degenerated and no longer matched the ideal, proletarian sexual type: "Degenerating biologically and creatively, they became reflexologically depraved. Individualist worker-students placed themselves outside the socialist construction, outside the course of the Revolution, outside life itself."[24]

Contemporary Soviet literature captured many of these themes. Degeneracy and the dangers of the city appeared often in stories that centered on the life of the academic Party cells, as in Sergei Malashkin's novel *Moonlight from the Right Side,* published in installments a prominent student journal in 1926; and Lev Gumilevskii's novel *Dog Alley,* originally published by the author himself in Moscow the following year.[25] Even a cursory look shows that these works had much in common: both represented the universities as the cradle of proletarian degeneration, both featured sexually depraved Communist students as their main protagonists, and both touched on Oppositionism (Gumilevskii only indirectly). Malashkin's and Gumilevskii's novels received a great deal of attention from contemporaries because they not only bore on the Bolshevik laboratory of the New Man but also dared to discuss the recently revealed difficulties in the social experiment. All Bolsheviks agreed that the New Man could never come to life unless all dangerous detours and dead ends were carefully avoided. In providing a manual of Communist psychology and a map of the mines on the road to salvation the two novelists in question were facilitating prophylactic measures that, they hoped, could eventually save young Communist souls.

The literary production of the 1920s in the Soviet Union was closely tied to the enterprise of the engineering of souls. According to the Bolsheviks, literature was to play a significant role in the creation of a classless society. It was not, however, entirely clear what that role should be. The critical reviews of Malashkin and Gumilevskii bore on a larger controversy in the contemporary literary establishment: Should Soviet literature reflect reality or construct it? "Literature is the barometer of reality," argued those who adhered to the former position. The proliferation of novels that dealt with the breakdowns in university life, they argued, was symptomatic of student maladies. One critic believed that "Malashkin's work shows a deep understanding not only of student life itself but also of the milieu from which students come," and therefore deserved to be carefully studied.[26] Other critics claimed that descriptions of decadence and depravity were completely blown out of proportion. Taras Kostrov, a prominent Komsomol activist, sarcastically noted that in the old days, authors who dwelled on the negative "used to write about philistines to revolutionaries. Now they write about revolutionaries to philistines."[27] I. Bobryshev, too, accused

Malashkin of "decadence. Decadent literature is part of the phenomenon of decadence itself."[28] "We must attack writers like Malashkin and Gumilevskii," Sergei Gusev joined the chorus of condemnation. "They besmirch our youth."[29] Taking offence at these charges, Malashkin claimed that his characters were true to reality: "If you read this thing, you know I did not relish [its description of depravity] . . . I wanted to evoke revulsion toward these people. I thought I had succeeded."[30] Gumilevskii was also upset that so many readers asserted that his novel was libelous. A more careful examination, he claimed, would prove that "I had only followed the instructions Lenin laid down explaining that . . . 'We have to fearlessly admit that evil exists for otherwise we will not be able to embattle it properly.'"[31]

But critics who attacked Malashkin and Gumilevskii claimed that veracity was not the main issue. In their argument the problem with the novelists in question was that they failed to understand that Soviet literature ought to be not descriptive but prescriptive. "A novel should be a conscious manipulation of reality," wrote Viacheslav Polonskii, "not its photographical reproduction."[32] Others agreed that "the trouble with Malashkin's novel is that it does not mobilize the feelings, consciousness, and will of the reader to struggle against decadence. He describes despondent moods but offers no remedies."[33]

Though troubling to contemporaries, a distinction between the reality reflecting and the reality creating aspects of the Bolshevik moralistic discourse was more symptomatic than real. The real and the ideal in the Bolshevik discourse intermeshed because of the contradictory perception of the NEP as, at one and the same time, the period during which the petite bourgeoisie remained to a large extent intact and the period already affected by powerful revolutionary changes. Indeed, both Malashkin and Gumilevskii pointed to the crucial tension in the 1920s between the NEP as a conservative, preserving force associated with the petite bourgeoisie, and Bolshevism as a majestic, creating force associated with the proletariat. With regard to the not-yet-changed reality, the bleak colors of the Realist genre were typically used to portray the retrograde aspects of student life that remained intact. The bright colors of the Romantic genre were reserved for everything that was progressive, all those dreams the Bolsheviks were bringing to life.

Writers in the 1920s were urged to describe only what was or could become real, and readers were invited in turn to experience what they read as an intimate part of their everyday lives. Literary pieces were discussed at the universities in group readings "to magnify their effect."[34] A discussion of Turgenev's *Fathers and Sons* in one of the workers' faculties, for example, opened with "an analysis of the historical and social background of the novel." Then a report was made by one of the students on the "Bazarov type," examined from various angles. The traits of the remaining characters were subsequently presented and evaluated by other students, and finally a public trial of Bazarov was organized.[35] Mock prosecutions of literary heroes were staged alongside "comrade trials" *(tovarishcheskie sudy)*, bringing the nexus between literary production, quasi-legal judgment, and training in hermeneutics of the self into sharp relief.[36] The rationale behind putting the trials of literary protagonists and the trials of the real individuals on the same platform was educational: students had to be enlightened as to the basic principles of Communist jurisprudence and trained in the arts of looking into each other's souls. When a student measured his own personality against the literary protagonists facing trial, he summoned himself to trial.[37]

Ideally, proletarian writers, Soviet scientists, and Bolshevik leaders had complementary agendas. The contemporary critic Ekaterina Troshchenko used the catchall term "Bolshevik moralists" to refer to a wide group of otherwise diverse experts who expressed concern with Communist ethics.[38] Literature was expected to play "the same educational role as the moral sciences."[39] While writers modeled their novels on archetypes provided by scientists, the latter saw literature as a means by which to realize the ideal Communist psyche.[40]

Undergirding the unity of the moralists' notion of a deviant self was a group of rules that enabled the official discourse to mediate the descriptive observations of students' inner life with institutional regulations that laid out strategies of inclusion and exclusion from the brotherhood of the elect as well as therapeutic practice and court procedure. A deviant self was an assortment of hierarchized, related, and more or less interpenetrable signs. The body was seen as a surface that could teach about the student's personality as well as a volume of organs able to influence his political thinking. The student's biography was a tangle of traces that could give away reactivated bourgeois patterns of thought and behavior.

Malashkin and the Decadent Student Milieu

Moonlight from the Right Side opens with a conversation between the narrator and his friend Nikolai. A distraught Nikolai tells Malashkin that his sister, Tania Astrakhova, has recently committed suicide. In answer to the queries regarding her motives, Nikolai offers up Tania's letters and diary. These tell the story of a peasant who joins the Party during the civil war and acts as one of the pillars of the Bolshevik revolution in her native village. Working for the committee of the poor, Tania is active in the redistribution of land, including the requisitioning of her father's extensive property. At the end of the civil war she is sent to Moscow. After a brief interlude during which she works with factory youth in the Komsomol, the young woman is sent by the Party to study at Sverdlov University. There she falls in with the student intelligentsia. Eventually Tania is swallowed up by the decadent environment of the university, loses hope in the future of the Revolution, and succumbs to philistinism and sexual promiscuity. Toward the end of the novel Tania expresses remorse at having lost touch with the earth and with nature and expresses a longing for "the sight of moonlight from the right side," which, as her grandmother had taught her, was a sign of good luck.

Since Malashkin conceived Tania as both a Communist and a daughter of a kulak, the ultimate meaning of Tania's identity remained ambivalent. Did she represent a petit-bourgeois student who, lured by a romantic infatuation with the Revolution, joined the Bolshevik camp during the civil war without ever developing true proletarian consciousness? Or did she represent a toiler led astray by the disorganization the NEP introduced into the proletarian camp? The novel opens with a diagnosis: Tania is a decadent youngster with suicidal tendencies. It proceeds to dwell on her peasant/petit-bourgeois social origins and the part such a background plays in exacerbating the dangerous influences of everyday student life. The cathartic evening party scene, describing Tania's sexual debauchery, brings the theme of ethical decay into sharp relief. It is immediately followed by Tania's self-revelation and resurrection. Throughout the novel, Malashkin counterposes Tania's troubled psychology to the unswerving Communist psychology of Petr, a healthy comrade from Tania's village, her mirror, confessor, and savior.

By making Tania an attempted suicide, Malashkin raised a hotly debated issue: in 1925, 14 percent of deaths among Bolsheviks were self-inflicted.[41] According to some Bolshevik moralists, many youngsters could not cope with the new times and chose to put an early end to their lives. Workers, some of them argued, were not likely to commit suicide unless they just came to the city from the village and were, much like Malashkin's Tania, "not yet fully absorbed by factory life." An alternative explanation, one that

fits the novel's characterization of Tania equally well, posited a "link between suicide and typical intelligentsia self-flagellation [*samobichev-
anie*]."[42] On the whole, the Party expressed an ambivalent attitude toward
suicide. While there was some sympathy for comrades who killed themselves because the civil war had shattered their nerves, the bourgeois elements who allegedly "despaired of the prospects of their class" were openly
scorned as belonging to the garbage bin of history.

Malashkin's narrator tells Nikolai: "We should try to get closer to your
sister, to understand her suicide, an act so surprising and so negative."
Against the backdrop of the battle against "Oppositionist pessimism,"
however, such a call for comprehension, and even mercy, could have been
interpreted as "defeatist." When Karl Radek suggested in his article "Don't
Blame It on the Thermometer" that "suicide attempts should be seen as
symptomatic of the fever engulfing our social organism," his view enraged
the loyalist David Khanin, who portrayed Radek as a Trotskyist who had
capitulated before the difficulties of socialist construction.[43] Wrenching
suicide from the exclusive domain of medicine and transporting it into social theory, some loyalist Bolshevik moralists presented the act of suicide
not only as an "indication of madness," but also as a "counterrevolutionary
act" that destroyed a "potential fighter for proletarian emancipation."[44]
"We do not have the right to die," one moralist argued. "We are obligated
to continue living and struggling for the working class!"[45]

To Aron Sol'ts, a leading specialist on Communist ethics, the suicide of a
young person was a regrettable upshot of the compromises of the NEP:
"We live in an epoch when the nerves of many Communists undergo so
many ordeals that they cannot go on doing what the Party expects . . . Because they had earlier thought 'this is the final effort, and the gates of the
Communist paradise are about to open,' such Communists now feel a great
disillusionment."[46] In the earlier years of War Communism, suicide had
been unthinkable, another moralist agreed. "But the grayness of everyday
life leaves one nothing to live for."[47] Still, self-annihilation under the NEP
could not be compared with the glorious revolutionary self-annihilation of
the days before 1917. "To be sure, underground Bolsheviks committed suicide. But they did so in protest against the surrounding socioeconomic and
psychological conditions. What parallels can possibly be drawn with recent
suicides? Such acts constitute protests against the dictatorship of the proletariat!"[48]

The temporal and spatial organization of Malashkin's narrative relies on the juxtaposition of the Tania of the civil war, a symbol of proletarian purity, with the Tania of the NEP, synonymous with pollution and degeneration. The heroine's notes open with a description of changes in her perception of reality:

> Four years have elapsed since I first came to Moscow. Then, though it was late summer and the corpses of dead animals were everywhere, I seemed to feel snowdrops. Now it is again late summer, the moon is full, and Moscow is the same. Though the dead horses are gone and skeletons are no longer piled on every corner, the odor of snowdrops from four years ago is no longer with me . . . Why has this happened? I have no answer. I don't care.[49]

This striking passage attracted much contemporary attention. Critics explained that Tania's inability to smell snowdrops was not "an emblem of mysticism" but a symbol of the heroine's decadent distance from nature. Instead of struggling with class enemies, outside and within herself, the heroine, much like Trotsky, sank into despair. Throughout the novel she repeats the words "Life has passed me by" (p. 59).

If we heed the contemporary moralists, Tania's key deficiency was her total inability to assert "self-control." Setting out to describe youth's "degeneration syndrome," *Pravda* provided a sort of reader's guide to the novel: "decadence is represented by depravity and dissipation in sex. Pornography, as well as bawdiness, smut, a cult of the anecdote and the bottle in everyday life"—all regarded as consonant phenomena—"abound in such cases."[50] For the most part, the Bolsheviks considered degeneration an attribute of declining classes. Mainstream Soviet sociology argued that the "ruling classes in periods of economic decline, like the elites of ancient Rome and the Far East, were characterized by a particular nervousness, sickness, and sexual depravity."[51] Degeneration supposedly reflected the "bourgeois classes' sense of doom."[52]

But Communist students at Sverdlov University hardly met the definition of decaying classes. Forced to admit that some proletarian youngsters degenerated, Sol'ts regarded this phenomenon as "unforgivable. Rotten individuals may be encountered among idle rich men whose lives are purposeless, among children of nobles and NEPmen, but should be absent from the lives of proletarian youngsters."[53] In grappling with the roots of decadence within the Communist camp, Malashkin set forth three intersecting explanations for Tania's degeneration: her kulak origins, her NEP environment, and her inability to make a smooth transition from work to study.

The NEP was widely construed as a demoralizing epoch. The previous, unequivocally positive moment had been the civil war; the present, problematic moment was the conciliatory social and economic regime established after the Tenth Party Congress. The civil war had produced "revolutionary romantics." It had stirred people's imagination "by imbuing youth with the enchanting desire to squash the class enemy . . . That period inculcated into youth's psychology elements of heroism, revolutionary trust and enthusiasm."[54] Now, in the face of the NEP retreat, this youth experienced an "emotional slump."[55] When Malashkin described the radical alteration in Tania's sense of her Moscow environment he highlighted the disturbing effect the contemporary Party program, with its focus on small, discrete acts, had on young Communists who wanted to be heroes. Youngsters complained: "Our enemy is no longer tangible . . . and the methods of struggle against him are no longer simple and obvious." "Gray details of everyday work," Bolshevik moralists concluded, "do not appeal to young hotheads, who sink into unbelief, vacillation, and doubt."[56] During the dispute over Malashkin's novel in the Krupskaia Academy, speakers contrasted Tania's "revolutionary excitement" with the "dry revolutionary routine" that engulfed the heroine during the NEP. In the civil war period, "when life was collective," interest in personal matters had been set aside; it was no wonder that at that time Tania had been healthy. "But the recently diminishing participation of Communists in public activity has caused her selfishness to resurface."[57]

The "problem of youth" had been in the headlines since 1923, when Trotsky broached the problem of the generational change in the Party. "Only continual interaction between the older generation and the younger," he wrote, "can prevent the old guard from ossifying."[58] Whereas for Trotsky the youth were the guardians of the conscience of the Revolution, a loyalists' article, "On the Question of the Two Generations," saw things in very different light. "Do students really have more 'power of resistance' to the negative influences that surround us? It is more likely that the turmoil and the temptations of the NEP and its ideological 'encirclement' are especially dangerous for the young."[59] Another reason why youth was particularly susceptible to despair was its lack of historical perspective. Had Tania but lived in the time of the tsars, so this argument went, she would have been able to see what a difference the Revolution had made. Unfortunately, "the mass of contemporary youth did not experience autocracy and does not remember the bourgeois regime."[60] The young were often in the wrong. For example, it was the young generation of the German Social Democracy that had followed Bernsteinian revisionism.[61] In the Soviet Union, too, there were "Party subversives," Lunacharskii stated with Trotsky in mind, "cultivated by decadent inclinations among the young."[62]

"Not all Soviet youth has lost hope in the Revolution," a literary journal insisted.[63] "It is the student youth specifically that is decadent," Vladimir Ermilov explained.[64] Tania's brother brings that point home to the narrator: "Tania used to say to me, 'Nikolai, I beg you never to confuse children of specialists and employees . . . with true working-class youth.' And she was right . . . Have you closed your eyes to those who followed Trotsky at the time of the notorious Discussion?" (p. 59). The link between the decline of Tania's Communist consciousness and her sojourn in the university was not missed by Malashkin's readers. "It is not by chance that Malashkin's novel is set at Sverdlov University," participants in the Academy dispute argued. "The author's choice of location is related to the appeal of the Opposition in that institution."[65] Tania had become emblematic of the perils of degeneration. Her story was reportedly taken up by zealous Trotskyist students in Moscow who sang:

> Ochen' iavstvenno vesna
> Priblizhaetsia;
> S pravoi storony luna
> Ukhmyliaetsia.
>
> (The spring is clearly
> nearing;
> The moon on the right
> is grinning.)

Bolshevik moralists agreed that an academic environment was able to separate a young worker from his class. "Students' craving for initiative could turn into individualism, their desire for development into renunciation of Marxism, and their quest for knowledge into vulgar simplificationism."[66] "Youngsters who are moving into the universities today," an official elaborated, "lack productive experience." Alien forces "take over their minds."[67] In this view, it should only have been expected that "remnants of the defeated parties put their wager on the student youth hoping to restore the old bourgeois order."[68] In making youth rather than the working class the barometer of the Party, the Thirteenth Party Conference stated in January 1924, "the Opposition objectively reflects the pressure extended on the proletarian Party by the NEPmen."[69]

Not necessarily Marxist in its origins, the perception of the student milieu as decadent, pessimistic, and depraved was widely shared by the Bolsheviks.[70] As early as 1921, two years before the Discussion with Trotsky, Innokentii Stukov published "a very characteristic document" specifying the issues students in Sverdlov University were interested in, among them (1) the roots of pessimism and suicide, (2) sexual morality and prostitution, (3) the new female, (4) syphilis and abortion.[71] It was hardly fortuitous that Stukov's discussion of the decline of youth mentioned syndicalism and "care-for-nothing academism," two classic sorts of deviation that alluded to students' political untrustworthiness.[72] Other members of the Soviet medical community shared Stukov's pessimistic evaluation of the university milieu. The items in a 1923 Petrograd student questionnaire reflected many of the grim expectations regarding student moods:

Q: How would you describe your character? As (a) morose; (b) quiet; (c) introverted; (d) social; (e) joyful; (f) merry.

Q: What sensations predominate in your life? (a) of the lower kind, instinctual; (b) personal, egotistical; (c) impersonal; (d) spiritual; (e) idealistic.

Q: What is your temper? (a) even; (b) relaxed; (c) fickle; (d) unstable; (e) exultant; (f) low (pessimistic, melancholy, bored); (g) tending to fall under the sway of affect, love of strong sensations, fervor; (h) deprived of self-esteem, disillusioned with life, people, ideals of truth and justice.

Q: From what age and under what circumstances did thoughts of suicide appear? What do you think of them now?

This questionnaire was never distributed because university authorities found its approach "too negative."[73] A provincial moralist who criticized similar documents argued that "clearly drawn up with melancholic and skeptical tsarist students in mind, they erroneously assume the old intelligentsia type to be typical in our universities. Actually contemporary students are happy to have a decent meal and a good pencil and have no use for the sentimentalities the questionnaire assumes." Yet when a question-naire addressing identical concerns was distributed in Perm' it reportedly established that one of five students had attempted suicide.[74]

Indeed, the problem of "despondent moods among students" could not be brushed aside easily. The majority of the Bolshevik moralists insisted that the universities "tend to stand in the way of organic wholeness. An unstable environment always exacerbates the negative traits implanted in students by the unhealthy conditions of their childhood . . . Be they 300 percent peasants, or 400 percent workers, the universities will nonetheless expose weak points in students' personalities."[75] According to one view, "at the universities we find inveterate opposition to public life expressed by those who, by virtue of their individualistic and deeply egotistical nature, find the notion of a public spirit utterly strange, types who reiterate to themselves, 'It is no concern of mine.'"[76] According to another, "the aca-demic setting, by alienating youth from practical work, fuels Opposi-tionism and counterrevolution."[77]

Two actual Sverdlov University students, potential classmates of the fictional Tania, had no doubt that "the seclusion induced by academic pre-occupation, coupled with the imperfect composition of the student body, contributed to Trotsky's success in the university."[78] Martyn Liadov related the onset of degeneration to the corrupting influence of mental labor. "The nonworker minority, coming to the university armed with a strong penchant for thinking solely in the abstract, exerts a deep influence on the rest of our students. To keep up with their studies, worker-students have either to imitate their knowledgeable comrades or be ousted from the uni-versity . . . It might well be that only the elements who manage to trans-form themselves into intelligentsia remain in academic institutions."[79] The implication was ominous: instead of acquiring a proletarian conscious-ness, workers who enrolled at the university tended to lose their class iden-tity. "A worker went to school," Troshchenko stated outright, "is no longer a worker. Detached from the factory, he is declassed."[80] The Sverdlov Uni-versity Party organization concluded that "only organic participation in work beyond the university walls can give a proper and healthy outlet to the students' energy and neutralize the negative effects of a long separation from practical work."[81] "To pull youth back to our side," the Thirteenth Party Congress convened shortly thereafter decided that the Komsomol should assist youngsters who are atomized and "on the brink of losing [their] class identity."[82]

Invoking a spirit from the past, the novel's second scene shifts from Tania's immediate NEP urban environment to her peasant socioeconomic past. Malashkin contrasts Petr, a Communist from a poor peasant family, a background that rendered him immune to all degenerative influences, with Tania, a daughter of a kulak, totally degenerated by the student milieu. The beginning of the scene finds Tania, who narrates this portion, reminiscing nostalgically about more straightforward times: "I sat through the night, thinking about father, grandmother, mother, my village, the Revolution, the muzhiks, Akim . . . I realized how many of the young villagers had gone to the front and paid for the Revolution with their lives. The survivors returned and now defend October's achievements." As Tania, soothed by these memories, falls asleep, Petr, whom she has last seen as a lovesick teenager five years earlier, enters the room. Nikolai, who accompanies Petr, rushes to his sister to ask her why she has gone to sleep on the floor. "Four years have passed since I came to Moscow," she answers, cryptically implying that her denial of the flesh reflects a deep longing for the heroic asceticism of the civil war (pp. 60–62).

Consistently, Malashkin utilizes "left" and "right" to underscore political inclinations. The heroine's exposure to Petr's penetrating Communist gaze is emphasized by the fact that the weight of his body is supported by his "left" arm. Tania, on the other hand, needs the moon to appear on the "right" side. By successfully transforming himself into a proletarian, Petr emerges as an all-around Bolshevik. "During these last five years Petr had undergone very little physical change . . . A peasant lad had become a man of a city. He had not turned, as many others do these days, into a dandy, but had become a fellow . . . who will without a whisper of complaint carry out the tasks with which the Party and the working class entrust him." Tania's old friend, a son of the "poor peasant" Vavila, is a pure, direct type. Everything in Petr expresses sociopolitical prowess. "He had not been broken by the hunger, cold, typhus terrors of the front and hard work he had faced. He had grown even better, hardened" (p. 63).

The contrast between Petr's natural life and Tania's artificial life in the university presents a classic example of the 1920s Bolshevik narrative of inoculation: the proletariat was supposed to build an immune system against the temptations presented by the feeble bourgeoisie the NEP had brought into existence; should the bodily constitution prove too weak, however, the foreign organism took over. When he encountered the NEP, Petr remained a staunch peasant proletarian; the weaker Tania was overwhelmed by her encounter. Petr explains that back in the village peasants had said to him that he did not look any older. "No," Tania responds, "you are as you used to be." Not so Tania—which does not escape Petr's notice. He vows that had he seen her on the street he would not have recognized her. "Remember," Tania explains, "I was not at the front. Since the autumn of 1920 I have been in Moscow, where, you know, life is good [read: luxurious and decadent]." At this point Petr lifts a small book from a shelf, a collection of Aleksandr Blok's poetry, and leafs through it. "How they loved there, struggled, and perished," he says. Returning the book to the shelf, Petr repeats a verse. "I like this line," he says, "but the rest is so-so. I don't think that everything will die" (p. 67).

The lines of the decadent symbolist are clearly designed to evoke the burning subject of "decadence in literature."[83] Blok, and even more Sergei Esenin—a celebrated poet who committed suicide in 1925—described worlds akin to the one in which Tania found herself. By "Eseninshchina" critics meant an "attitude that confines the youngster within the private sphere," an expression of "rotten individualism," "free love," and "degeneration."[84] In the last period of his creativity, Esenin supposedly represented the spiritual, if not the physical, death of "those who cannot walk in step with the new times."[85] Esenin was an emblem of utter despair. Drawing on the idea of the survival of the fittest, the Bolshevik moralists equated oversensitive souls with souls who were unable to endure the hardships of the eschatological journey. "This troubadour of spiritual turmoil hanged himself because he could not bear the grave truth that he had no part in the driving force of our time."[86]

Participants in a Moscow dispute over Malashkin's novel acknowledged that what was said of Esenin applied to Tania: both tried to kill themselves because they could not find resources within to meet the new challenges.[87] Recognizing the allure of a romantic suicide, Vladimir Maiakovskii, another famous early Soviet poet, called on his fellow artists to "make Esenin's suicide uninteresting. Instead of getting caught up in the "'light beauty' of death," he wanted to see the promotion of "a totally different type of beauty. In the face of the trying contrasts produced by the NEP . . . toiling humanity must celebrate the happiness of life, the joys of the difficult march toward Communism ahead." Instead of Esenin's famous "Dying in this life is not new / Living is not new either, of course," Maiakovskii proposed his own poetic maxim, one emphasizing an optimistic, transformative attitude toward life:

> For joy
>   Our planet is poorly equipped
> We have to
>   snatch
>   happiness
>   from future days.
>   In this life
>   To die—this is not difficult.
>   To build a life
>   This is the hard task.[88]

Nikolai Bukharin could not have agreed more. "We need a literature produced by vibrant individuals who are in sync with the pulse of our existence." Unlike the decadent poets whom Tania loves so much, "our writers should be courageous builders who are disgusted with putridity, grave-digging, the tears of the tavern, slovenliness, bumptiousness, and holy feeble-mindedness."[89]

Still, there was a question that Bolshevik literary potentates could not easily sweep under the rug: "If Esenin is the bard of a receding epoch, how did he come to reign in the hearts of much of the Soviet reading public?"[90] Many claimed that a disturbance in village equanimity lay at the root of Esenin's popularity. "This peasant bard," whom a number of Bolshevik critics regarded as the "voice of the kulak," had committed suicide "out of nostalgia for the golden days when a naive peasant religiosity had given peace and internal balance to one's soul." According to others, the problem was not so much with where Esenin had started as with where he had ended up. In this version of his biography, the poet became a declassed, bohemian member of the intelligentsia who talked to his friends of a "little love," "two dozen cigarettes," and "bacchanals leading to a rotten decay."[91]

Both narratives are suggested in the novel. First Malashkin offers a grotesque image of Tania's typically intelligentsia degeneracy. "Rolling her eyes and twisting her lips, Tania asked Petr for a cigarette. Large red spots, the size of handprints, appeared on his cheeks. 'You do not smoke?' Tania began to laugh. 'What kind of man are you then?'" (pp. 67–68). By emphasizing that Petr is looking in disbelief at Tania's lifestyle Malashkin is clearly inviting the reader to share Petr's penetrating gaze at the putrid intelligentsia milieu. Turning to her evaluation of the political situation in her native village, the novelist, however, returns to the peasant theme. Petr, we are told, believes that the Revolution will win over the countryside. Tania, on the other hand, expresses grave reservations regarding the future of the Revolution in the village. "My father is not stupid," Tania avers. "With the instinct of an animal he senses the return to older times! He is right—another small step and we shall return to the old days." "You are mistaken," says Petr, but Tania only blows smoke into his eyes, persevering in her anxiety, typical of Left Oppositionists, regarding the resurgence of the kulak in the village (p. 79).

Class as a Psychological Type

Whereas Petr has developed into a full-blown Communist, Tania has failed to understand the NEP and has been plunged into despair. Given their similar class backgrounds—the fact that "Petr loves the Tania of the old days" underscores the affinity in their primordial class background—it was obvious that crude sociologism did not suffice to show why the former had succeeded where the latter had failed. Tania's lapse in eschatological progress must have had something to do with the hazards of transition to an academic lifestyle. Bolshevik moralists widely regarded the university as a fascinating field for the application of their psychological theories. A. Makarov, a pedagogue and a social scientist, was struck that "nowhere can one convince himself of the psychological validity of Marx's insights better than in comparing one psychological type with another, capturing the peculiar development of each student persona."[92] "If we are to completely re-educate the peasant and working class youth," Lazar' Shatskin, a Komsomol leader, pointed out at the Eleventh Party Congress (1922), "we have to learn how to adjust to their specific psychological features."[93]

Since it was widely accepted that the university exerted the kind of "pressure" that only true proletarians could survive, adaptation to life there was regarded as a testing ground for a student's class persona. The peculiar academic environment, Makarov maintained, operated as a litmus test that separated collectivist students from individualists.

> If students are to become decent Party members, they need a psychological foundation erected in the village or in the factory. Incapable of studying, reading, or drawing in rooms where dozens of individuals are doing

the same, the "delicate," "soft" members of the intelligentsia sink into dissipation. Young workers and peasants, disparaged as "gruff" and "rude" by softies [*beloruchki*], create a solid network of mutual interaction in the universities based on delicate and thoughtful respect of the common need . . . The natural condition of a true proletarian psychology resists the self-indulgence and greed characteristic of exultant, idle talkers from the intelligentsia.[94]

Although in Makarov's eyes true proletarians generally not only resisted the temptations common to the difficult conditions of study, but, quite to the contrary, were "forged" by them into "worthy Communists," breakdowns could occur. "At times a young peasant or worker," one who had reached higher education before having experienced "the full social impact of the workers' community on an individual mind, could exhibit unbridled individualistic traits."[95] Fine-tuning his sociological observations, Makarov introduced age as a factor in the creation of psychological typologies:

We have students from different revolutionary periods. They vary according to the imprint on their psyche of the prewar period, the imperialist war, and the revolutionary years. Psychological makeup depends so much on the years when the young psyche is first formed that one can tell from the first conversation one has with a student that this is one of "the men of 1918–1919," "the men of 1920," or "the men of 1921." Older students exhibit psychological fatigue. For them the world of knowledge is a place of respite, a quiet harbor. At the same time, their struggles taught them how to endure and remain indifferent to the external conditions of life. This is their forte. The younger students, by contrast, had entered adult life when the Revolution had already peaked, during its triumph. Whatever preceded Soviet power had not registered in their psyches. They are better adjusted but also less complex and less rich in experience than the offspring of the revolutionary Sturm und Drang period.[96]

When this scheme was applied to Malashkin's Tania, the reader realized that the heroine took on the worst traits of both generations. Tania was not a seasoned old Bolshevik who, having suffering under the tsars, knew what a difference a Soviet government made, NEP or no NEP. Nor was she quite the well-balanced youngster Makarov talked about, because she could not let go of the promise of the days of civil war enthusiasm and harness herself calmly to the slow socialist construction.

The biographical refraction of class origins was a crucial factor in the development of the student psyche. According to the Bolshevik moralists, "class conflict in the individual psyche is scientifically compelling." The complexity of students' class background gave birth to manifold grueling internal conflicts, "confrontations arising from various psychical make-ups."[97] One contemporary specialist examined "how students spent their childhood and adolescence and whether they go on to sever their ties with their childhood social milieu." This was deemed very important, since "the organism of a child is extremely susceptible to outside impressions. The imprint of the environment forms the youngster's character and evokes his first emotions."[98] Vladimir Antonov-Saratovskii developed a typology featuring three basic proletarian-student types: healthy proletarian elements, less stable elements who lost their grip on the "revolutionary line," and weak personalities who chose the path of least resistance and slid back into capitalism.[99]

Makarov's alternative typology postulated only two generic proletarian-student types: those with a "remarkable capacity for work and a sharklike appetite for knowledge, great powers of endurance, sexual temperance, and self-control"; and those prone to pessimism and whining, whom he called "children of the twilight."[100] Makarov's binary analysis, however, reveals itself on close scrutiny to be more complex: two categories became three as he divided the negative student type into "students on the verge of being lost by the proletariat" and "petit-bourgeois student degenerates." It was not by accident that Makarov's terminology preserved the essentials of the contrasts pointed out by Antonov-Saratovskii. Tripartite typologies were intrinsic to official analysis of the universities; eschatologically minded, the Bolshevik moralists had been looking for positive student types (those saved because they had reached the light of Communism), negative student types (those doomed because they had never embarked on the road toward the light of Communism), and middle student types (those still torn between the two extremes).

Malashkin's heroine clearly belongs to the intermediate type. Malashkin suggests that Tania's frail, undecided class persona succumbed to the pressures of rigorous studies. The demanding academic environment quickly exposed weaknesses in personalities like hers. "For a youngster to survive our system of higher education it is necessary that his class invest his psyche not only with a drive for knowledge but also with a physical and a psychological ability to endure," wrote Makarov.[101] He noted that in coming to an institution of higher education, manual laborers usually faced the reservoir of human knowledge for the first time in their lives. In the case of some proletarians, "the thirst for knowledge is accompanied by a more or less distinct awareness that only knowledge makes one a real master in the society of toilers. With others, the hunger for knowledge operates in its instinctual form."[102]

Either way, the proletarian was "drawn" to the university. Makarov praised higher education as a crucible in which "amidst upheavals and explosions, like in the magical cauldron of a medieval alchemist, the new man of the future is forged, a highly original phenomenon armed with a true proletarian psyche." Believing that the proletarian educational institution "induces a colossal psychological revolution in the soul of the youngster in two or three years and makes him plumb the depths of his psychological being," he suggested that the proletarian encounter with mental labor was dangerously cataclysmic, "a veritable revolution in itself."[103] Another moralist, M. Postnikov, agreed that degeneration among university youth "may reflect the pain of transition from manual to mental labor."[104] According to Troshchenko, the move to the university could easily undermine young proletarians' "fragile psyche."[105] In such a case, "nervous fit follows nervous fit, escalating all the while, rapidly developing into a wild form of insanity."[106]

Although Makarov viewed both workers and peasants as "proletarian students," he insisted that the distinction between these classes remained palpable in the universities. "Distinct economic settings create distinct student psychologies. The peasant who arrived at the university has had almost no previous interaction with the hectic economic activity of the urban everyday. Hence his peculiar psychological rhythm: the beat of his heart is much slower than that of the worker-student; phlegmatic, kind, and somewhat suspicious, he is a slow thinker [*dolgodum*] who needs time to get to the bottom of the person he observes." The worker-student, by contrast, was faster and surer of his conclusions. "His attitude toward people is more straightforward and he is faster in dividing them into friends and foes."[107] Antonov-Saratovskii glorified the worker-student's "strong sense of class pride. 'I am a worker!' he typically reiterates, bespeaking a slightly exaggerated consciousness of self-worth. Possessing a highly developed sense of camaraderie and a sensitive appreciation of the suffering of the working class, he hides these sentiments under a superficial cover of crudeness. In fact, it is safe to say that the worker-student's sensitivity easily supersedes even the sensitivity of the most 'delicate souls' [*tonko chustvuiushchie*] among the intelligentsia." Antonov-Saratovskii maintained that the peasant-student fell a bit short on this score. "While the former perceives things according to the healthy common sense of his class, the latter hopes only that he will not be deceived. The critical stance of the worker-student reflects an objective vantage point, while the vantage point of the peasant student reflects a subjective one."[108]

Since the factory environment was closer than that of the village to the university, Makarov maintained, "worker-student psychologies are easily adaptable to the universities. Peasant-students, on the other hand, have to give up their village habits and get used to the pace of urban life." Alternations in the language of the peasant-student allowed moralists to follow his metamorphosis into real proletarian. "His first essays are written like tales and fables and sometimes like medieval chronicles. In a year and a half his lyrical style disappears, and the quest for a direct and specifically technical terminology becomes evident. In the university, soft-spokenness, simplicity, and fear of abstraction typical of peasants will turn into direct, dry, and precise proletarian speech. A peasant becomes more scientific, more Marxist."[109]

For a time, Tania appeared to have acquired these desired traits. But as her subsequent decline clearly demonstrated, a peasant-student's adjustment to university life was rife with dangers. The slow pace of country life proved incompatible with life in a hectic higher educational institution.[110] Noting that most of the students who killed themselves came directly from the village, Troshchenko dwelt on the special difficulties that rustics encountered in their effort to cope with the transition to the relentless and often cruel academic milieu. "Strain induced by the imperative to cope with a high level of engagement in mental labor, an activity for which they have not been previously trained, creates psychological instability and anxiety and destroys the peasant psyche . . . The individualistic nature of mental labor, the solitude of the struggle with the book, the one-on-one encounter with one's memory, can bring a peasant to the brink of despair."[111] When considering suicidal peasant students, another moralist echoed Troshchenko, "we deal with individuals who undertook the journey toward the proletariat but got lost along the way."[112]

Not all peasants were believed to be innocent, however, and not all peasants elicited so much compassion from Bolshevik moralists. A number of commentators maintained that the causes of Tania's antisocial behavior had to be sought in the negative residue of her village background. Some peasant students were hopeless after all, because deep down they were petit-bourgeois proprietors with a decidedly anarchistic frame of mind.[113] Malashkin's contrast between his two peasant protagonists conveys this point strongly: a son of a poor peasant, Petr was pure enough, whereas Tania succumbed to the kulak streak in her character. According to Makarov, "a church-oriented village mode of thinking, the alien psychology of a village kulak, sometimes got into the heads of peasant youngsters." Even those among them who were inspired by past military-revolutionary experiences were "not immune to vacillation and contradictions."[114]

Some pointed to rural backwardness as the key to Tania's decline. "Could a kulak's daughter sympathize with the experience of a teenaged girl working in a factory for twelve or fourteen hours, a laborer who hated with all her heart the [pre-revolutionary] order?" one reviewer asked. "No! Her class perspective is too limited. Tania must have joined the Komsomol only because she found the Revolution romantic. Convictions had nothing to do with it."[115] Others saw in Tania not so much a trapped but well-meaning peasant or a wicked kulak daughter as a degenerated worker. It was obvious to one Bolshevik moralist that the old petit-bourgeois student traditions could sometimes "percolate" even into the minds of innocent proletarian students.[116] Indeed, in the novel Nikolai tells the narrator that Tania's Oppositionist student environment is not free from workers. "Don't we know of certain workers who support Mensheviks? Yes, we do. There is no difficulty in explaining that, my dear . . . Weakness of class consciousness is conducive to the thriving of Oppositionist banners amidst the most backward and nagging groups of the working class" (p. 56).

Although it was not easy for a Marxist to explain how a worker could go wrong, Makarov was not deterred. "Digging into the degenerate workers' past we usually find the following material: the father is a migrating laborer who did well economically. The child, denied his physical presence, is reared in the big city under the wing of his mother. She loves him tenderly and shields him from the worker milieu." It was this overprotective feminine environment, Makarov believed, "that formed sickly individualism and the habits of a spoiled child. The capacity for diligent daily labor is stamped out, as is will power. Most important, the sense of comradely solidarity disappears, together with any candid and deep love for one's comrades and for the native proletariat. Revolutionary views may remain, but only as a cerebral habit, similar to the psalms that atheists sometimes recite automatically." This type of worker-student, "rarely coming from the factory, was immersed in the completely disoriented social milieu from the beginning of the Revolution."[117] "Once-upon-a-time gifted and strong wards of the working class," wrote another expert, "these individuals held on only so long as extrinsic props existed. As soon as they found themselves outside the network of unmediated ties to the familiar worker milieu, and were deprived of a stable, firm personality, they tacitly succumbed to the temptation of alien social circles."[118]

Malashkin's reviewers alternated between reading Tania's character as predisposed either to a peasant, proprietary frame of mind or to a superficially proletarian outlook, concealing her fundamental lack of faith in Communism with revolutionary rhetorical flourishes. The critic G. Iakubovskii spilled much ink blaming Tania's decadence on "the inheritance of some of the blood of her kulak father."[119] His peer Polonskii, on the other hand, preferred to understand Tania as someone influenced by the urban atmosphere, with its "notorious penchant for self-analysis and obsessive reflexivity."[120] What is crucial is that the student milieu—as far as Bolshevik moralists were concerned a dystopian universe—was seen as uniting the worst of both worlds, dubious peasants and declassed proletarians alike.[121]

Malashkin's typification of his heroine parallels to the letter Makarov's description of the self-divided student. "A sharp collision with the Revolution, part of which anyway was alien to such students, along with recollections of the 'philistine happiness' of their childhood days . . . creates a psychological feebleness, a premature worldweariness, and real bewilderment about which way to turn. The Manfred and Hamlet types oscillate around petit-bourgeois students whose fathers are petty clerks, railroad or chancery employees, or, finally, petty proprietors." The result was a "self-enclosed, weak-willed individualist," incapable of adjusting to new conditions, one who was "exhausted" by the demands of village life or of factory labor. "Carried away by revolutionary banners and a frank, though undependable, thirst for knowledge . . . he is drawn to higher education. Such a type collides with a new environment, its motley crowd of comrades whose class psychology, character traits, and levels of political consciousness differ from his own." The result was disastrous. "Either he shamefully flees . . . or else he sinks into the lumpenproletariat." The NEP had turned these poor souls into "restless, nervous, unbalanced youngsters, not lacking talent but normally lazy, unstable, without practical purpose or life goals."[122]

This student type encompassed a broad spectrum of moral personae, starting with the "average no-good vagabond" *(perekati-pole)* and ending with a highly dangerous social element, a quasi-bandit.[123] Tania herself exemplified the type of student who plummeted toward moral and sociopolitical nihilism, sometimes sinking as low as "petit-bourgeois emotionalism." A student like her—in the view of Antonov-Saratovskii, a "practical anarchist"—displayed "an instinctive, though at times conscious animosity toward communal property as well as a penchant toward individualistic and blind mutiny against any discipline and collectivity, coupled with utter disrespect toward even his closest friends."[124] Makarov's experience had taught him that an anarchist student was "a short-term guest within the walls of a proletarian educational institution." The decline of students like Tania was unavoidable unless she shook her disillusionment so that the "thirst for the book built on the psychological traits developed during the proletarian phase of life" might be allowed to prevail over the habits fostered during the kulak childhood. Tania badly needed the influence of "energetic" and "life-affirming" comrades like Petr to complete the building of her personality and save her "from a state of agitation [*razvinchennost'*]." If left in her emotionally unbalanced state, Tania was bound to find consciousness "inaccessible," her teeth being "too weak to bite into the stone of knowledge."[125]

The NEP and the Problem of the Everyday

The revival of a Russian bourgeoisie and the consequent strains felt by the proletarian soul were at the center of the Bolshevik moralists' lamentation over "NEP realities." Malashkin weaves the motif of contemporary social injustice into the novel's narrative. "As I looked out my window," Tania recalls, "I saw a strange scene. Over a two-hour period a Communist wife tried on eleven dresses, all of different colors and designs. Each time she turned to admire herself in the looking-glass." On a different occasion, Tania saw in the dormitories a fat woman, "looking like a damp white cloud, and, standing beside her, a much taller man . . . kissing her hanging breasts. Looking at this couple, rare species that they are, at this kind of satiated socialism, I could laugh myself to death" (pp. 60, 61). Both diary entries reiterate some typical themes of the day, namely the lamentations of civil war veterans over the high pay given to specialists at the workers' expense, the resurgence of economic stratification, and the country's relapse into a meaningless, petit-bourgeois existence.[126]

Malashkin invokes here what was called at the time the problem of everyday life. The "everyday" *(byt)* was defined by Nikolai Semashko, the head of the People's Commissariat of Public Health, as "the aggregate of habits, customs, beliefs, and, partially, convictions espoused by individuals or collectives."[127] Revolution in the everyday, the overturning of all the premises on which the old society had been based, was an integral part of the Party agenda. By breaking down the foundations of the moral order, the Bolshevik revolutionary discourse was to instigate a reassessment of all values. This kind of radicalism is endemic to revolutionary discourses. Cultural iconoclasm, Bolshevik or any other, must proceed, or the revolution, understood as a project of perpetual and radical change, will be aborted. It follows that the demand for a revolutionary everyday—a relatively stable system of ethical imperatives—involves a contradiction. Endorsement of a given, normative state of things entails the erection of a new moral code and so the termination of the revolutionary process.

The emphasis in revolutionary times on the complete rejection of tradition encouraged a perpetual debate over what might replace normative notions. The Bolsheviks were well aware of the sort of critique Edmund Burke had offered of revolutionary practice. According to Burke, the French Revolution amounted to an infringement of the delicate tissue of social relations. If everything in society was interconnected, the conservative English political theorist argued, any radical break with established tradition totally disrupted human relations. Burke went on to conclude that the violation of long-standing traditions and the abrupt alterations of the social fabric were highly undesirable. The conclusion the Bolsheviks drew from Burke's argument was, however, the opposite: if everything in society is interconnected, then everything in society has to be changed, up to the most minute daily routines. Institutions, laws, habits, beliefs—all had to be revolutionized. The Party therefore argued that the proletarian revolution could not be limited to the political domain. The Soviet state rejected the liberal idea of a separation between everyday life, understood as the apolitical realm of the mundane, and politics. The dichotomy between the political and the apolitical, the public and the private, was, according to the Bolshevik moralists, an effect of the bourgeois social order, concealing the political nature of the everyday with its economic exploitation.[128]

In the final analysis, however, the construction of a socialist everyday in the universities was a task no less political than any other the Party set it-self. Bukharin reformulated Lenin's classic question about the socialist construction—"Who prevails over whom? [*kto, kogo*]"—in relation to the struggle between the bourgeois and the proletarian everyday.[129] "Against all odds, the young generation must break with the old everyday and build a new humanity. What," Bukharin asked rhetorically, "is the meaning of the cultural revolution? A dramatic change in human qualities, habits, feelings, wishes, and in the everyday of man—a revolution that turns him into New Man."[130] That all Bolsheviks concurred that the New Man involved a com-plete rupture with the past does not mean there were no important nu-ances of opinion. During the years of War Communism, most moralists had believed that the New Man was the immediate and natural product of the Revolution. Possibly incomplete at first, the New Man was an instan-taneous child of the Revolution, its enthusiasm, and the spirit of regen-eration it unleashed. Since the realization of the New Man could not be reversed, the proponents of this position believed that no special prescrip-tions or constructive actions on the part of the Party were needed. But in the face of the recent retreat from Communism, more and more moralists reached the conclusion that the New Man was a precocious infant who had to be vigorously defended. They pointed out that old habits die hard and that the path to Communism abounded in obstacles. If the supporters of the first position were confident of the outcome, the more pessimistic adepts of the second position saw breakdowns and regressions at every corner. More intrusive in its basic attitude during the NEP, the Party warned that under the conditions of the bourgeois revival the state had to actively foster revolutionary spirit. Observing that "contradictory ten-dencies are currently locked in a struggle over the proletarian soul," K. Koshevich maintained that "a conscious intervention could be useful in preventing our people from sliding into the bourgeois slump."[131]

The issue of the NEP, many Bolshevik moralists argued, was an issue of cultural hegemony. There were only two basic scenarios: either the Party would maintain control over the commanding heights in the territory of the everyday, or the rising bourgeoisie would conquer them. Moralists be-lieved the Party ought to assume the task of constructing the "new ev-eryday" *(novyi byt)*. "Otherwise, developing spontaneously [*stikhiino*], our everyday would be tainted by the colors of alien classes."[132] But would not the creation of a new everyday spell a return of normative ethics under a different name? Indeed, Evgenii Preobrazhenskii rejected "all immutable ethical imperatives"; and Lenin advanced a utilitarian position on such matters: "Our ethics has to be subjected to the class interests of the proletarian class struggle." Bukharin argued that "what the proletarian needs is not ethics—the essence of ethics is a fetish—but technical rules, rules as simple as the rules that guide a carpenter in constructing a chair. Whatever is expedient from the point of view of the construction of Communism is also imperative."[133]

In recommending a new moral code, Bukharin was aware that he had to contend with the argument that ethics always stands for a veiled class interest. "The rules of behavior to which we adhere are based on our revolutionary goals and not on abstract first principles," he defended himself. "Before, we opposed the norms of the enemy in order to upset his ordinary ways. But now, in the face of the philistine capitalist surroundings, we need norms to attain our own unity [spaika]." In other words, proletarian ethics was a tool of class struggle, not an immutable set of moral imperatives.[134] Aron Zalkind, a Party member who penned numerous scientific brochures, posited that "ethics will disappear only when the class struggle has withered away."[135] The guiding principle for the construction of new, "Komsomol commandments" was that the proletarian ethics had to reflect the proletarian interests. Zalkind did not stop before recasting the biblical decalogue into Bolshevik language:

"THOU SHALT NOT STEAL"—expropriate expropriators;

"THOU SHALT NOT KILL"—unless it is an organized killing of a class enemy by a class following an order of the class state, in which case it is moral;

"HONOR THY FATHER"—respect only a father who stands on the proletarian-revolutionary platform and consciously defends the interests of the proletariat. If all attempts to move your father from mystical, proprietary positions fail, you are morally free to abandon him;

"THOU SHALT NOT COMMIT ADULTERY"—sexual activity is permissible only to the extent that it promotes the growth of collectivist feeling.[136]

The Bolsheviks viewed the struggle for a "new everyday" as a political struggle against a disguised class enemy. "Holding in custody millions of toilers," Stalin maintained in 1924, "the habits and prejudices we inherited from the old society are the most dangerous enemy of socialism."[137] Besides the external enemy, coming from alien social groups, "there is another enemy, the one that sits in our own minds," the Bolshevik press elaborated.[138] What made the everyday of the NEP doubly dangerous was the fact that "it does not march, but creeps in; it does not attack, it surrounds."[139] At every step the moralist G. Bergman encountered revolutionaries armed with Marxist theory, "fearless in battle, steadfast and dedicated, who at the same time cling to an old-regime style of life." This phenomenon could be understood once one acknowledged that political attitudes changed more rapidly than personal habits. "While the political consciousness of a human being, nurtured by a fierce class struggle, develops by leaps and bounds . . . his everyday, residing in the very deep layers of the personal, petty, individual existence, finds itself waiting at the curbstone of history." The everyday moves along only slowly and unwillingly. "The old everyday creates in human consciousness a setting [*ustanovka*] that not only resists new revolutionary ideas and attitudes, but is actually fed by old antirevolutionary and antisocial attitudes." A new society does not emerge at once, Bergman concluded. "Neither does the New Man, who is the product of this society."[140]

The youthfulness of Malashkin's protagonists complicated their transition to the new, proletarian everyday. The first-generation Communists had reformed themselves through actual struggle with a ubiquitous autocracy, Lunacharskii noted. "No wonder that their everyday was characterized by a uniquely pure, natural, vigorous asceticism. Youth nowadays, however, lives under completely different circumstances."[141] Lunacharskii's pessimism was not unusual. Taking up the Leninist theme that "many of our people entered a new society without becoming New Men," moralists elaborated: "Joining hands with the traditional conservative forces, a new NEP petit bourgeoisie impairs the young psyche." The gist of the problem was that the juvenile psyche had absorbed too much of the retrograde, unconscious habits (as opposed to the conscious opinions) of the older generation. Even parents who were theoretically informed had unwittingly passed along to their children old-fashioned beliefs that lay too deep to be completely removed.[142]

For a Bolshevik, the NEP went hand in hand with contamination. In Tania, Malashkin presents the reader with a female student who has failed to work out her attitudes toward private property and lax sexual mores, with which the NEP was associated. "Unfortunately," wrote a literary critic bemoaning Tania's fate, Communist youth "is not separated by a Chinese Wall from decadent youth. Having emerged in a nonproletarian milieu, everyday depravities can be transplanted into the proletarian elements in the Komsomol, the Party, and the student milieu."[143] Emel'ian Iaroslavskii employed a similar metaphor when he fretted that "had it only been possible to build a fence between the proletariat and other classes the bourgeois influence would have been less significant. Alas, these days the proletariat cannot separate itself from the other classes."[144]

Bolshevik moralists agreed that the NEP had spread *meshchanstvo* in the universities. *Meshchanstvo* resists translation because it functioned both as a noun, referring to the petit bourgeoisie, and as an adjective, denoting the philistine mentality the Bolsheviks attributed to that class.[145] Difficult as its rendition is, the term merits a detailed investigation because it goes to the heart of the interface between class as a social notion and class as a psychological notion in the official discourse. Countless Bolshevik moralists addressed the problem of petit-bourgeois philistinism. Thus Kostrov provided a Marxist genealogy of philistinism, a condition widely associated with "an idiotic social life," by tracing it to the alleged "narrow-mindedness of the Russian urban estate." Iaroslavskii defined a philistine as a "petit bourgeois who places his individual, small, artisan or peasant business above the interests of his class."[146]

Generally, the psyche of the small producer was believed to be organized around the dichotomy between the cozy artisan's shop and the threatening (because unknown) chaos of the market. The petit bourgeois was supposedly incapable of merging into the collective because he could not picture himself within a social category. Instead, he could think only of himself. From this perspective society appeared as a myriad of individuals, "a sack of potatoes, so to speak," and nothing more. Enslaved by the market, the philistine was frantically aware of a need to defend his ever-threatened interests against buyers and sellers alike. "This position forces him to believe in the solitary, egotistical, self-seeking 'I' as a first principle. 'Everyone for himself,' he liked to reiterate, 'everyone in himself, everyone an enemy of everyone else.'"[147]

The postulation of the petit bourgeoisie–philistine nexus validated Malashkin's connection between Tania's social environment and her psychological makeup. Philistinism—and here the novelist could rely on many moralist tracts—was a trait of both the peasantry and the intelligentsia, the two components of Tania's class identity. According to Mikhail Reisner, a founding member of the Communist Academy and the Russian Psychoanalytical Society, "philistine heritage is the result of a peasant private ownership, with its stinginess, narrowness, hatred of everything new, and what Marx called 'the idiocy of rural life.'" The intelligentsia milieu, "wherein petit-bourgeois habits were very much alive," was not held to be much better.[148] Because of its intermediary class character, the intelligentsia was as anxious to find a market for its intellectual commodities as were the artisans.[149] Liadov found the roots of what he called "intelligentsia philistinism" in the "medieval alchemist or scholar who used to work in the solitude of his insular laboratory. On guard against anyone who attempts to penetrate the secrets of their creative process, they share secrets with no one and painstakingly conceal the details of their work process, aware that fame and wealth will come only if their discovery is not preempted." This outlook, Liadov concluded, inculcated in the intelligentsia "the philosophy of a selfish individual. The world, he believes, exists to serve him."[150]

The entire scope of student philistinism, individualism, and decadence is brought into sharp focus in the final scene of Malashkin's novel. At the center of the scene is a raucous evening party in Tania's apartment. The guests are "from the petit-bourgeois families of small traders and artisans, a philistine swamp, which is, like a spoiled radish, Red on the top but inside stinking and putrid." The evening party is a gathering of "superfluous men." Throughout the evening, Tania's student friends swear and curse. "Dazed with smoke and drugs, shouting and throwing candy at each another," everyone sings lewd songs and talks about love, the devil, and "animal passions" (pp. 106–107).

Ever element is designed to convey a sense of utmost debauchery and decadence. Women try to jump into Petr's lap; all he does is sweat and search for a door through which to escape. By making his negative heroes almost freakish dancers, Malashkin joined with the widespread Bolshevik view that "while some elements continue to swing their legs, the toiling masses certainly did not take power into their hands in order to indulge in such petit-bourgeois pranks."[151] The Bolshevik moralists associated the fox-trot with "wild passions" and "Fokstrotizm," and "Tangoizm" with "tropical lust." The American anarchist Emma Goldman was told that "dancehalls are gathering places for counter-revolutionaries." As a half-hearted substitute for dancing, some Komsomol organizations actually organized evenings for revolutionary youth, during which men and women marched up and down the dance floor singing revolutionary songs.[152]

Amidst the dancing, pushing, and shoving in Tania's apartment, a young man embraces a woman, who "melted into his arms." "Don't squeeze her too hard!" cries out an onlooker. "Her soul might spew out." Malashkin depicts the ensuing singing as a squalid and blasphemous affair. "Attention." Volod'ka, a Komsomol member, yells and raises his hand. Everyone falls silent, and he starts singing:

> Who will replace the Communists?
> Who will replace the Communists?

Then in unison they sing:

> Members of the Komsomol, my friends
> Members of the Komsomol.

Grinning, Volod'ka continues, conducting with his hands: "'Who will replace members of the Komsomol?' Everyone sings loudly, in phony voices, sounding like the breaking of crockery, 'The Pioneers, my friend / The pioneers'" (pp. 96–97).

The degenerative displacement of the purest by the less and less pure, symptomatic of youth's degeneration, is captured in the mocking song. A contemporary Bolshevik anxiety had it that although Party admissions were strictly monitored, the Komsomol, absorbing the younger generation into the Bolshevik fold, had a more permissive admission policy. The Pioneers even more liberal. It was feared that liberal admissions rendered youth organizations susceptible to petit-bourgeois infiltration.[153]

In principle, the Party regarded the Komsomol as a valuable asset because of its role in preparing the new generation. Many posited the intrinsic superiority of Komsomol students over non-Party students: "the Communist youth who have passed the familiar stages of Komsomol training are objectively ahead of and above the non-Party youth." Troshchenko conjured up "the four-eyed [ochkastyi] studious youngster who lives for his own private interests" and contrasted him with the Komsomol youngster, who was "disciplined and able to set society before his private interests."[154] And yet, despite the privileged position of the Komsomol, degeneration within its ranks was, in the eyes of at least some Bolshevik moralists, undeniable. A provincial student journal stated that "we cannot close our eyes to the fact that the main mass of Communist students, the Party youth, know nothing of the harsh school of the revolutionary years."[155] In the same vein, Party leaders warned that the Komsomol membership was steeped in individualism and continued to be entangled in the old philistine everyday.[156]

The fact that Oppositionism was in vogue in the university Komsomol organizations did precious little to enhance their status. Alarmed officials noted in the aftermath of the 1924 Discussion with Trotsky that more than half of the 5,000 Komsomol members sent on to higher education came from nonproletarian families.[157] The problem of Komsomol "pollution" (*zagriaznenie*) loomed large in the debates over Malashkin's novel. "What the author described," one disputant maintained, "is the Komsomol swamp, which kills all collectivism . . . and sucks Tania in."[158] One of the novel's reviewers wondered, "What is described in the novel? A Komsomol or a brothel? Who is the heroine? A Komsomol member or a prostitute?"[159]

The Komsomol was on the verge of becoming a philistine organization. Behind the veneer of phony happiness the philistine youngsters concealed fear and despair. The syndicalist-turned-Bolshevik thinker Iuda Grossman-Roshchin contended that their personalities were manic-depressive. "A rosy optimism, even an ultrarevolutionary one, disorganizes the will to fill cracks in the construction of socialist reality . . . Cross out illusions, and the optimist will become a decadent pessimist. No wonder: groups hostile to the working class are no longer subjects of History . . . Creating many illusions in the nonproletarian milieu, the NEP means that a bourgeois can eat well, enjoy a jazz band. But since he has no access to political power, these illusions are rapidly dwindling."[160]

Mood swings between optimism and pessimism, experts agreed, were endemic to declassed Komsomol students. Since the petit bourgeoisie is torn between the desire to climb to the heights of the upper bourgeoisie and the fear of plummeting into the depths of the proletariat, "it cultivates a duplicitous, perennially vacillating attitude." While the bourgeois of the upper regions "is strong and confident, like the capital that gives birth to him, the petit bourgeois is as weak and unstable as his workshop or vending stand. On occasion, the petit bourgeois can be very assertive, aggressively defending his interests. But self-pity is a no less common expression of his sentiment." It was as if, realizing that history was passing it by, the petit bourgeoisie had begun to bewail its eschatological redundancy. "It was not uncommon for the petit bourgeois to sink into pessimism, despair, and, the nadir of such moods, a sense of 'universal sorrow.' No social class produced an ideology of lamentation and joylessness like that of the petit bourgeoisie." Succinctly put, the argument was that petit-bourgeois individualism has two poles: "on the one end anguish and melancholy as a result of a desecrated and solitary individuality, and on the other the alluring lights of a monstrous superman."[161]

Expressing this dualistic attitude toward life, Malahskin's readers concluded, petit-bourgeois students embraced either the Right deviation, with its "inclination toward a lifestyle adorned by pink and light-blue curtains," or the Left deviation, with its infantile radicalism, which "negated love and feelings."[162] Tania's character was typical of the petit bourgeois who put on revolutionary airs. Taken in by the destructive aspects of the civil war and "wavering between absolute freedom and complete enslavement," such heroines were, in Reisner's contention, "attracted both to anarchy and chaos and to limitless despotism." Tania's petit-bourgeois background explained the vicissitudes and contradictions in her behavior and the behavior of her friends. "During 1917 the possibility of destruction enraptures the petit bourgeois. Like an ignoble freed slave, they take revenge against property, upon which they depended only yesterday." But when peace came, the attitude of such types underwent a dramatic change. The well-dressed and carefully groomed students were perfect examples of "those who never lose sight of the small proprietor in themselves, who rob and accumulate and pile up, preparing for the future."[163] One observer came away with the impression that the NEP had made many petit-bourgeois youngsters "feel that they were once again in their element. Their belly full, they now proclaim that 'We too contributed to the Revolution.'" At the same time, "a terrible supposition crosses their obtuse mind," that they are not what they used to be. "They look around to find a mirror that will reflect Communist faces, but see instead only the mugs of philistinism."[164]

A perfect example of this type is a figure who occupies center stage at Tania's evening party, Isaika "The Alien" (Chuzachok), a youngster ready to sacrifice the future "for a moment of pleasure."[165] A creature of deep contradictions, Isaika is "eager to cover his wretched nudity. In the name of Nietzsche and the superman, he stole from the Revolution its garments and piled up useless ideas about unrestrained sex."[166] The Bolsheviks were in agreement that following the Revolution attitudes toward sex and relations between the sexes had to change.[167] This had been a fundamental tenet of the Russian revolutionary movement at least since Nikolai Chernyshevskii. But in what way? Diametrically opposite views of "the sexual revolution" could be presented as Bolshevik with equal conviction. Since moralists concurred that sexual mores were the turf on which the battle for the youth's new everyday was to be won or lost, Isaika's advocacy of sexual license had to be unmasked as revolutionary only in appearance. Early in the evening Isaika launches into a long diatribe that amounts to a call for sexual promiscuity: "Some say that the new love is unethical. But don't we know that it appears thus only from the bourgeois standpoint? We have imbibed the notion of the old love, based on the property instinct, and cannot rid ourselves of it. The new love is a free tie based on economic independence and on an organic attraction between individuals of different sexes." When Zinka retorts with "Liar, such love never happens," and "females are human too," Isaika dismisses her with a few disparaging remarks. The bourgeois love, he declares, "an economic transaction no more," should be replaced with the proletarian "free love. There must be no coercion in a beautiful and free love consciously preserved only as long as the mutual need exists . . . As soon as harmony breaks down and dissonance ensues, the link has to be severed" (pp. 90–91). Although Isaika makes his plea for sexual freedom and the abandonment of bourgeois sexual ethics in the name of a radically new everyday, Malashkin suggests that this freethinker remains very much a closet philistine.

To reinforce his point, Malashkin attires Isaika in the very best NEP fashion, in "dress shoes and gray and white checked socks and a good suit." For the Party, plain dress indicated a proletarian identity; richness and luxury in dress unfailingly signaled alien classes. Isaika's clothes obviously have nothing to do with the "ascetic dress that civil war heroes could be recognized by."[168] He violates such admonitions as "Communists should dress so as not to arouse the indignation of workers."[169] A direct linkage was made between class and aesthetics.[170] Isaika's petit-bourgeois dress provides a warning to readers to take Isaika's professed antiphilistinism with a grain of salt. Not a proletarian but a member of the intelligentsia, not a supporter of the Party line but an Oppositionist, Isaika engages in obvious fraud: just as petit-bourgeois students advanced Trotskyism in the guise of Leninism, he advances sexual degeneration, pretending it is sexual liberation.

Isaika's sexual manifesto echoes that of the onetime doyen of feminist revolutionaries, Alexandra Kollontai. The heroine of one of her early novels, the Komsomol girl Zhenia, took lovers according to her moods. She used to declare she was pregnant but unaware who fathered her child, nor did she care about it. Zhenia lives out Kollontai's vision of sex as something as free and simple as drinking a glass of water.[171] Kollontai's views on sex were undergoing harsh Bolshevik criticism in the mid-1920s, however. "Zhenia is a member of the intelligentsia through and through," wrote Zalkind. "We should not be surprised that when female workers are introduced to this literary persona they are disgusted by her."[172] Also targeting Kollontai, Iaroslavskii stated that "her view of sex is at once antisocial and non-Marxist." In fact, hers was a philistine-intelligentsia view. "Sexual life involves not only the natural but also the cultural."[173] The publication of Klara Zetkin's reminiscences of Lenin in 1925 completed the delegitimation of free love. Kollontai's theory reminded Lenin of a cheep, bourgeois "brothel. Our youth went crazy over Kollontai's equation of sexual intercourse with drinking a glass of water," he reportedly remarked. "Of course, thirst requires satisfaction. But will a normal person stoop to lying on the ground and drinking from a puddle? . . . The recent interest in sexual issues is primitive rubbish, an obsession of the intelligentsia and the adjacent social layers."[174]

Fearing that free love was still widespread among students, Liadov historicized the sexual drive. Sexual promiscuity, he argued, was not a biological given but a recent bourgeois perversity.

> During a very long historical period humans copulated only once a year, as animals do. At such times a free female chose for herself the future father of her child. Only in a relatively late period, when a woman became a slave taken by another tribe as part of the spoils of war, did completely new relations take root . . . When a society of commodities emerged and accumulation of private property began, women became property ready to satisfy the lust of their masters at any moment. It was in the harem, a place where robbers kept their women, that the art of taking pleasure from sex developed . . . There the female was first trained in "sensibilities" that no longer served for procreation but for the satisfaction of sexual desires . . . Because of the ease with which sexual excitation was satisfied by an obedient female an insatiable sexual drive was cultivated in the male as well . . . A normal human, a human of the future society, will return to nature and require normal procreative instincts.

With the advent of a fully proletarian society, Liadov concluded, "the beautiful sexual instinct will be relieved of all the additional burdens heaped upon it by historical development, which turned it into an aim in itself." No longer "the source of calamity" it had been for Tania and other Communist students, it would be the wellspring of "the highest pleasure."[175]

Time and again, Bolshevik moralists warned proletarian students against the wholesale rejection of bourgeois sexual temperance. The young were urged not to turn the notion of petit-bourgeois philistinism into an excuse for failure to assimilate the cultural benefits acquired by humanity in the process of its development.[176] Besides, philistinism appeared in unexpected places. Ultraleftist rejection of culture as such, for example, was a sort of philistinism, doubly dangerous because it was passing itself off as its antipode. One Bolshevik moralist maintained that "a philistine is recognized not by his attitude to a necktie or a gramophone but by his attitude to a comrade, to public work, to society."[177] A fellow moralist begged his readers not to confuse philistinism as an "ideology" with philistinism as a "lifestyle"—even though they considered their nihilism a courageous "struggle with petit-bourgeois philistinism," many "anarchists of the everyday" remained thoroughgoing philistines themselves. As one commentator explained, "calls for sexual anarchism are a foreign ideology, cultivated by declassed elements. This ideology flourishes where the reek of death and decomposition of the social fabric of bourgeois society are strong."[178]

The increased preoccupation with sexual mores in the late 1920s was a part of a larger process of infiltration of official ideology into private life. The Soviet discourse eroticized issues related to everyday life in order to eventually politicize them more effectively. Lines of penetration were deployed as the Bolsheviks sought to use pleasure to increase their control over the youth. When one Komsomol member demands in a script for a trial of "Free Love," "Should the government interfere?" voices in the crowd respond, "The government interferes!"[179] Literature and criticism were yoked to this task, reinforcing each other. A pattern emerged: novelists' sexual excesses triggered an outburst of critical letters from their readers, the issues being vented in excruciating detail during public disputes (in turn themselves published). "It would be more than naive to claim that questions of sexual relations do not penetrate Pioneer circles," Gusev noted. "And the task of the directors of the Pioneer movement is not at all to prevent that penetration . . . What is important is that such questions penetrate the Pioneer environment not as psychological but as public questions."[180] Whatever side one identified with, one examined the depravity of student youth using almost identical terminology. Sexual mores, being the topic of repeated discussion for a sustained period, had the effect of destroying the autonomy of sexual life.[181]

Jewish identity was regarded as a typical source of students' sexual excess. As a typical petit bourgeois, the Jew allegedly set himself against the proletarian collective, all the while adorning his selfishness with sweet words about absolute freedom. One of the revelers at Tania's party tells Isaika, "You speak so smoothly that your accent vanishes." Laughing and turning to Rakhil', Andriushka, another decadent student, asks: "He has lost his nationality completely. Ain't I right?" In response, Rakhil' only "exposed her small teeth." Malashkin here reveals Isaika (Isaac) and Rakhil' (Rachel) as Jews. Small proprietors who organized their economic activity around the household and lived apart from the rest of society, Jews were often described as individualist, pseudoradical, and megalomaniacal. Isaika "The Alien" is clearly conceived as an outsider. Overdetermining Isaika's nickname, the novelist renders him alien to the body politic along notional as well as ideological lines. The two meanings of Isaika's otherness are, of course, inseparable. It was the type of economic activity Jews engaged in at the pale of settlement that supposedly rendered their national character philistine.[182]

As a typical Jewish Communist, Isaika combines physical degeneration with its ideological manifestation, Oppositionism. The following passage from the novel makes this clear: "Isaika bounces his leg, bows so that his curls swing in the air, and says, 'I am international, that is why I am well versed not only in love but in politics too. In the city of Poltava they call me "Little Trotsky"'" (p. 92). Here Malashkin provides further hints about Isaika's Jewish roots by alluding to the allegation that the Jewish Party intelligentsia supported Trotsky's dissent on account of his racial background.[183] During a street fight in Leningrad that led to the death of a student who expressed some sympathy toward Trotsky, the attacking gang members egged each other on with "This Judas, Trotsky, sold our Lenin!"[184]

Malashkin characterizes Isaika, like many stereotyped Jewish figures, as "petty." He is "narrow chicken-shouldered" and his face "long and thin"; Jews allegedly had small bodies. In describing Isaika as slight and weakly, and his behavior as compulsive, Malashkin draws on the contemporary medicalized image of the Jew. "When Isaika speaks he licks the inside of his mouth with the tip of his tongue, tosses back his hair, and starts flexing his leg" (p. 93). According to the scientific discourse of the time, the Jew was the symbol of primitive and perverse behavior, whose contribution to world history belonged to the distant past. Jews existed in the twentieth century only as a degenerate species.[185] Once Communist hermeneutics put intention before action and substituted a juridical typology of crimes with a typology of criminals, special attention was paid to the anatomy of a deviant body. A number of Soviet physiognomists accepted Cesare Lombroso's argument that attention to bodies would deliver the sciences of men from "idealism" of the classical schools.[186] Physiognomism and phrenology, which attempted to locate signs of internal intellectual and moral states on the body's surfaces, particularly on the head and the face, promised to make student dispositions—the elusive, largely invisible object of the hermeneutical discourse—intelligible.[187]

In his physical portrait of Isaika, Malashkin elaborates many of these themes. The weak body indicates deviance and possible derangement. The decadent features are a sort of a physical inscription of Trotskyism. To leave no doubts about Isaika's degenerate state, Malashkin describes his dancing as "hilarious. As he labors to stay in time, Isaika looks like a grasshopper, or an emaciated goat up on its legs, forced to jump up and down. His left hand is still while his right hand moves convulsively" (p. 92). There were experts who explained that "convulsive grimaces popularly known under the name of 'ticks' often follow excessive sexuality."[188] However, Bolshevik moralists could not help but treat such notions with a degree of wariness. The Marxist theory of the plasticity of human nature made the idea of an innate connection between physical and moral deformity problematic. In the nature/nurture debate, no Bolshevik could ascribe everything to nature. At least in part, Isaika's degeneration had to be blamed on his class environment and not on his thyroid gland.

Be that as it may, Isaika's "wild abandon," "nervousness," and "frequent changes of mood" had to be considered unmistakable features of sexual degeneration.[189] Contemporary medics discovered numerous symptoms of this predicament, among them "tics," "anomalies of sensory function," "moral depravity," "imbecility," and "sexual irritability."[190] One expert distinguished between "somatic" and "psychic" signs of degeneration. The former category included "impotence" and "nervous weakness"; the latter included "instability of mood," "hedonism," "a contempt for life," and "suicidal inclinations."[191] In his ceaseless exultations, Isaika squanders all the energy given him by nature. Appropriately, Malashkin completes the physical typification of his antihero by making him sexually impotent. Isaika elliptically states, "As far as sex goes . . . I studied it." Aleshka interrupts with "You mean, in practice?" Shurka then bursts out laughing and asks our heroine: "Tania, what do you say? He is completely impotent, is he not?" (pp. 92–95). Here again Malashkin's Isaika is true to the Bolshevik conception of his race. Thus sexual sensations were thought to appear among Jews very early in life, causing young Jews to be quite virile. But over time Jews lost out to gentile Russians. Jewish energies were quickly spent, while adult Russians got to enjoy a healthy and intense sexual drive.[192]

"The Revolution cannot accept orgies!" exclaimed one expert.[193] Swollen sexual appetites had destroyed the students' sense of a collective and had pushed them into degeneracy. "The truly revolutionary disappears when love swells too much," wrote Zalkind. In a proletarian society, it was necessary that students be "attracted to the collective more than to their sexual partner."[194] It was precisely in these terms that one reviewer of Malashkin's novel explained the hyperindividualism of Tania's friends: "the channeling of social energy away from social problems and into individual physiological pleasures transfers the emphasis from class to the individual and brings on pessimism combined with sexual depravity."[195]

When Malashkin juxtaposes Isaika's speech on the merits of free love with an orgy, he invokes a cliché regarding student debauchery. Men seat themselves on women's laps, "punching holes in their transparent dresses." Ol'ga and Rakhil' approach Tania to ask whether they should initiate an "Athenian night." Rakhil' wants to sample some drugs. Excited by the thought of the drug, the decadent Jewish body of this lascivious student, clearly the feminine counterpart of Isaika, is lustfully "shaking" (pp. 97, 93). Only Petr does not enter into things. Asked for his opinion on Isaika's speech, he expresses amazement at its vulgarity.

The lessons of history confirmed what Malashkin was implying, namely that association with the academic intelligentsia could have a degrading influence on sexual conduct. Zalkind urged readers to recall how, after social forces were suppressed in the reactionary period of 1907–1912, "the intelligentsia youth plunged into sexual pleasures, organized orgies, consumed pornographic literature, and was besotted by romances of various kinds."[196] The implications of this analysis with respect to the NEP university milieu were obvious. The Bolshevik moralists believed that "the sexual problem became the most burning aspect of the students' everyday life."[197] Youngsters were torn away from the realities of factory labor and needed plenty of "artificial stimulants" and "sexual narcotics."[198] A basic axiom of the Bolshevik sociology was that "the greater one's distance from reality, the more unreal one's sexual fantasies." That the university atmosphere promoted an overflow of sensual excitation was proved by a number of studies demonstrating that working-class students were more sexually active than workers who remained in production. Malashkin leaves no doubt that the way the petit-bourgeois Isaika experiences sex and the way the peasant-proletarian Petr experiences sex are not the same. Here the novelist relies on sexological research establishing that "workers engage in the sexual act in the most affectionate manner, the representatives of the petit bourgeoisie with the most composure. The former are more direct, the latter partially spoiled." Furthermore, physical dissatisfaction resulting from the sexual act was found to be most widespread among petit-bourgeois students and least among the worker-students. Sexologists noted the sense of shame engulfing petit-bourgeois students after sex and contrasted it with the pleasant sensations during sex that were most commonly reported by worker-students.[199]

Overall, Soviet physiologists believed peasant sexuality to be natural and thus the closest to normality. Empirical data were marshaled to buttress the claim that sexual overexcitability emerged first in students drawn from urban areas, particularly the petit bourgeoisie. The sexual-sensitivity threshold of peasants, by contrast, was said to be the highest. Sexologists explained those findings in terms of "the hard labor in the country," which had the effect of curbing premature sexual activity. Peasant sexuality was healthy also because peasants were led into their earliest sexual experiences not by the sexual drive nurtured in the recesses of their organisms but by outside stimulations, such as "observation of the natural copulations in the animal kingdom."[200] Despite the antidotes provided by their healthy childhood, it still remained true that some peasant-students were led astray by the decadent urban mores. A female peasant-student with a background identical with Tania's reminisced that "a change from the countryside to the city, where customs are different . . . forced me to conceal the residue of the village in my personality. In the big city people jeer at sexual innocence and at ignorance of what every ten-year-old city dweller knows. The city's dust and dirt, its moral depravity, prevented me from becoming what they call here 'ascetic.'"[201]

Tania's Spiritual Awakening

Was Tania one of the lost youth? Did Malashkin mean to present her as doomed? Tania's sexual mores are purposely left unclear. The sight of a "huge lanky fellow kissing a fat woman" unleashes an inner conflict in her.

"It was only one lanky fellow that kissed her, no?" "And were you not kissed by six lanky fellows in one night?" "Yes, you were," one voice answers. The other voice, still alive in me, clamors, "You have been kissed, grabbed, and sullied endlessly. Your life, run down amidst sound and fury.'" (P. 72)

The dialogue between Tania's inner voices captures the polyphony of her sociopolitical soul. On a different plane, it also echoes the larger struggles inside the body politic: whereas the declassed peasant identity within her has made Tania promiscuous, the influence of the civil war has made her chaste. In her present state the heroine's fall from grace is abundantly clear. "Listening to these two voices inside me, I closed my eyes and tried to recall the last seven years, so that they rush by me with incredible speed, carrying me . . . Now, I lie in squalor . . . My senses are dull. I do not smell the night as I did in my youth." In falling "off of the wings of time," Tania has wandered from the path to Communism (p. 105). The NEP, itself a deviation from the straight path of socialist construction, has led her astray.

It is Petr, the novel's unambiguously positive figure, who passes judgment on the evening's bacchanal. As the other guests are carried away by sensuality, Petr sits still on the couch, leaning as usual on his left arm. He averts his eyes from the debauchery, casting his gaze instead on a table covered with books, obviously the room's locus of political consciousness. In the middle of the dance, Tania finds herself pressed against Petr, who is reading. To enable the two to talk, Malashkin empties the scene. Shurka, realizing that Tania has slipped out of the mood, yells: "'Everyone out! The Athenian night will continue at my place.' 'Bravo! Bravo!' guys yell back and pour out into the corridor" (p. 100). While Tania begins cleaning up the room, Petr reprimands her:

Why did you have to invite me here? So that I might smell them stink like decomposing corpses? . . . As if it wasn't troubling enough that our Komsomol is full of men and women marked by philistine, bad inclinations, idleness, the refusal to improve themselves and rise to be good Bolsheviks, to fill the thinning ranks of the old Party guard, I've met tonight people more repulsive than any I've met in my work.   (P. 101)

Indeed, in the crucial party scene Malashkin clearly strives to diagnose the various "abscesses and ulcers" in the Party. Zalkind's entire catalogue of fallen Communists is present in the novel: (1) the "Frondeurs" *(frondery)*, who work actively in the Party without having adjusted to the new conditions of life under the NEP, all the time busily scheming against colleagues; (2) the "ailing" *(boleiushchie)*, who direct their unused emotions inward, effecting a "flight into illness"; (3) the "sexualists" *(seksualisty)*, who channel emotions toward a "sexual breakthrough," substituting for the hatred of political enemies a thirst for sexual possession; (4) the "splashers" *(vypleskivateli)*, who direct their emotions into artificial stimulations; (5) the "predators" *(khishchniki)*, who egotize their emotions, directing them toward careerism and material success in life; and (6) those Party members in whom one can observe an emotional chaos and a gradual fading of energies.[202] Petr asks, "Tell me, where did you dig up such creatures? These promiscuous fellows, and the even more obscene females, are they all Communists?!" (p. 106).

Ashamed and embarrassed, Tania has no answers. Tacitly, Malashkin begins to draw a distinction between Tania, the fallen Communist who might still be saved, and her hopeless friends. "How could you join them?" Petr asks her. "How could you enter their society?" Tania and "these scoundrels from the Komsomol" are not the same after all. The heroine promises to dance with Petr alone, this time properly dressed. Clearly, she is on the brink of recovery. Before changing clothes in her cramped quarters, Tania covers Petr's eyes with a towel. As she dresses, she looks through the window "and sees that the moon was brilliantly lit on its right side. What luck! Forgetting herself, she stares out the window until Petr interrupts her with the words 'May I open my eyes?'" Malashkin emphasizes that "these simple words shocked Tania." Symbolizing the heroine's imminent return to the fold of Bolshevism is Petr's call for Tania to open her own eyes. Evoking the conversion motif, Malashkin shifts voices, transcribing Tania's inner thoughts in the first person singular. "I realized how difficult it was to open my eyes and see the depth and beauty of life. I sank into thought once again. Then, suddenly, I heard words of terrific simplicity: 'Closing his own eyes he opened ours.'" Lenin's eyes, the eyes of the proletarian leader who has just died, "struck me like lightning piercing the darkness." The moon, thus far a symbol of Tania's darkened mind, is now transformed into a symbol of enlightenment. "Its light makes objects, particularly the mirror, painfully clear" (pp. 103–104). Tania becomes self-transparent.

"Wait!" says Tania; "I want to turn myself inside out." The stage is set for Tania's confession: "The first years of my work will remain forever in my mind as something pure and wonderful. I will never forget how we sent to the front about forty poor peasant volunteers—that uplift, that sense of confidence, that belief in yourself and in victory over the tsarist generals" (pp. 107–109). As long as Tania talks about the civil war, her face beams.

But as the autobiography progresses it becomes more and more opaque, gradually approaching a plaster mask. Recapitulating Malashkin's main theme, the link between the university environment and degeneration, Tania continues: "but then, in 1923 I was recalled from the industrial region and attached to a university cell, where another type of youth was present, not at all like the peasant, let alone the industrial one." Tania found herself engaged in a lopsided battle with Trotskyist degenerates. "After one impetuous meeting where I was the sole defender of the Leninist guard, the cell resolved to purge me as 'an alien element.' The district committee reinstated me as a Party member. But that did not save me from the milieu I found myself in" (pp. 110–111).

Here, near the conclusion of the novel, Malashkin takes a giant step toward redeeming his heroine from her social origins. Tania was honest with the Party. "I never concealed my origins," she tells Petr, "and always wrote in the questionnaires that I was a daughter of a rich kulak and a trader" (p. 109). Those who wanted to purge her, by contrast, had lied in their questionnaires. For Tania, Trotskyism proves to have been an alien influence that obscured her consciousness, but not a political position that she consciously embraced. The edifying perspective of a converted Communist is not to be lost on the reader. In the words of one critic, "Petr knew Tania could be purified at once."[203] Petr tells her, "All you have spoken of are trifles. I see even deeper into your soul and am convinced that it is healthy. It is just that you have not bathed for a while and so much alien mud remains stuck to your skin." He recommends the "transparency of cold water," a necessity if Tania is to regain her Bolshevik class consciousness. Petr, Malashkin informs his readers, is well suited to serve as Tania's confessor. "Human life was as clear to him as if it was something placed on an outstretched palm" (p. 104). Touched by a true Communist, Tania regains her original consciousness. "Petr and Tania smiled at each other, and Tania became aware of the odor of the black soil and of the first snowdrops." As she regains her lost sensitivity to nature, the heroine realizes that her real inner nature is proletarian, not bourgeois.

The inevitable marriage of Petr and Tania, a true union of proletarian souls, has nothing to do with carnal attraction. Tania exclaims, "We never thought 'You are male,' and 'I am female,' though we used to lie together to warm our bodies" (pp. 108–109). A good proletarian marriage was based on the joining of consciousness, not of bodies. As one expert pointed out, often a "husband-revolutionary manages to infect his wife's psychology with a burning fire, turning her into a zealous public worker as well. Consuming enormous amounts of energy, such revolutionary fervor would weaken the sex drives without doing away with spousal sexual life all together."[204]

The novel's happy ending is not straightforward, however. Instead, the story concludes with a "death as transfiguration" motif. The version of Tania's narrative given to the narrator to read leads him to conclude that the heroine committed suicide after setting down the last entry in her diary. Only months later, when he runs into Tania's brother, Nikolai, at a professional conference, does the narrator discover that Tania is alive after all and has rejoined her husband only two weeks earlier. "'You mean, Petr?'" asks the narrator surprised. "Yes," Nikolai answers. "He barely recognized her. She had become healthier and younger looking. He was overjoyed to see her." Nikolai explains that Tania had just come back from the north where she had been "working in a forest, skiing, hunting—in short, living a virgin's life. Now she has come back to her husband and says she wants to go back to work" (p. 121).

Many critics took exception to the novel's ending. "Why did Malashkin send Tania to the forest instead of the factory?" one of them asked. "Would the heroine not have been reborn by interacting with our industrial proletariat? . . . To be sure, nature has the power to relax, yet in the absence of adequate social conditions nature cannot save anyone."[205] Two other critics insisted that the "youth's path to salvation lies not in a retreat away from the human environment and into the forest but, on the contrary, in a juncture with the life of the class."[206] It took the scientific expertise of Zalkind to provide the motivating logic beneath the novel's resolution. "The organism," he explained, "drained by sexual overwork, has to be given back its natural powers and drives." What was needed was not an "expiring breath absorbed in amorous contemplation, nor a chest stuck out to impress sexual competitors, but natural and pure fresh air unpolluted by sexual absurdities."[207] Having absorbed far too much academic pollution, Tania required some sort of natural purification to regain herself.

There were two contrasting images of nature dominant in early Soviet culture: nature as the garden of harmony, and nature as an arena where one struggled with elemental forces. In Malashkin's novel, nature indeed symbolizes both the path to a harmonious society and the enemy that obstructs harmony. Nature is both the source of Tania's health and purification (the nature inside the heroine, her revolutionary instincts) and Tania's chief antagonist, the controlling metaphor that links the various forces threatening her consciousness (the nature outside the heroine, the NEP, and the animalistic competition that went with it).[208] The fact that Tania was able, by extricating herself from the bestial capitalist competition around her, to regain her capacity to "smell the earth" proved that she was proletarian after all.[209]

CHAPTER

CHAPTER

4

From a Weak Body
to an Omnipotent Mind

- What form will sexuality take in the future society? Should we recognize a pure, Platonic love? Is love a temporary or a lasting emotion? Will Communism be a time of monogamy or polygamy? Is polygamy a sign of the degeneration of the working class?
- What should we do with the knowledge that monogamous marriage separates us from the collective but that polygamous marriage is abnormal from a physiological point of view?
- Explain your view that the one who forms sexual relations for the sake of pleasure alone is an individualist. Do you know how hard it is to think about class reproduction during sexual intercourse? Trying to enjoy an evening party while at the same time thinking about class made me feel I was going nuts.
- Which is right, free love or abstinence? If abstinence leads to the degeneration of the working class, should we assign a norm for sexual activity? What should be its minimum and maximum?
- Are you aware that a human being is intellectually rich only when his sexual organs are highly developed? When sexual hormones fill the organism the brain is aroused. If it is true that unused sexual energy applies itself elsewhere, why did I never see the limbs of the abstinent individual grow stronger?[1]

Love, lust, and sex clearly provoked a great deal of curiosity among students, who raised these questions during a discussion that took place at Irkutsk State University in November 1924. When Lev Gumilevskii's *Dog Alley* is examined alongside Malashkin's *Moonlight from the Right Side,* the richness of the Bolshevik moralistic discourse and the complexity of the scientific theories involved become apparent. To be sure, both novels had much in common: their resemblance was not lost on contemporaries, who described the protagonists—civil war heroes who, having become lost for a while in the decadent university milieu, eventually recognized the folly of dissipation and were miraculously saved—as "twin souls."[2] However, despite similarities in plot, characterization, and moral, there were important differences in the ways in which student degeneration was conceptualized.

The implicit dialogue between the two novels reflects the intricate process of negotiations concerning the shape of the Communist self. The uniformity of Communist terminology veiled significant pluralities of meaning. The alpha and omega of the Marxist method—"materialism"—was a case in point. Although both novelists professed to be "materialist," this catchall term concealed more that it revealed; "materialism" could stand either for the interpretation of phenomena in terms of the underlying objective conditions of production (the sociological explanation) or for the reduction of all human thought and sensation to bodily processes (the physiological explanation). If for Malashkin materialism indicated the primacy of action or practice (the real) over contemplation (the ideal), for Gumilevskii materialism meant a reduction of the mind to matter. Embracing the sociological interpretation of materialism, Malashkin was inspired by the early nineteenth-century thought of Hegel, Feuerbach, and the British political economists, as appropriated by the young Marx. The physiological theoretical framework, on the other hand, reflected the incorporation of scientific naturalism into late nineteenth-century Marxism. According to the naturalist branch of Marxist theory, drawn on by Gumilevskii, sociology was incapable of giving all the answers. While sociology questioned "human aims," one contemporary noted, "it could not do without biology that asks what techniques humans possessed to attain those aims."[3] Sociological studies, wrote another, lost sight of the real human being, with his "natural," "innate inclinations," turning him into a mere "tabula rasa for society to write on."[4] Critics pointed to the naturalist sources of Gumilevskii's novel. Its very title was an obvious allusion to the "animalistic origins of the human instincts," wrote one of them; another declared that it read like a "treatise in zoology."[5]

The divergences between the terms of analysis deployed in the novels are consistent enough to suggest that the two novelists abided by fairly distinct analytic frameworks. Malashkin objected to crass reductionism insofar as his Marxism established qualitative differences between mental states. His was a somewhat voluntaristic theoretical framework, wherein "revolutions" in human psyche, that is, qualitative leaps from one level of psychic organization to the next, were possible. Gumilevskii's quite different brand of Marxism operated in terms of quantity alone and attempted to demonstrate the materialistic/energetic unity of essence behind seemingly different phenomena.[6] For Gumilevskii, a human being was a sandwich of tissues and a bundle of nerves. He was in line with the hard-core determinists, who believed that the New Man would evolve gradually thanks to a scientific manipulation of the human body.

Identical terms connoted very different things. Whereas for Malashkin the New Man was a highly spiritual creature, for Gumilevskii the New Man was a sort of biological Superman. Whereas in Malashkin's novel "pollution" meant contamination by alien ideology, in Gumilevskii's novel the same term stood for the infiltration of the body by malignant substances. Whereas social pathology meant to Malashkin a contamination by class aliens, to Gumilevskii it indicated a biological aberration and physical degeneration. Malashkin understood "young growth" (*molodniak*—in its original sense, a veterinary description of young stallions between the ages of one and three) as a sociological term for an age cohort. For Gumilevskii, on the other hand, this was a physiological notion, denoting adolescent bodies in a biological process of growth.

In Malashkin's usage, class meant a conglomerate of agents with the same relationship to the means of production. In Gumilevskii's terminology, class stood for an aggregate of individuals with similar innate properties. Whereas for Malashkin nature was spiritless and only history had meaning, for Gumilevskii history was a limiting case of natural, biological struggles; he would surely have dismissed Malashkin's talk of overcoming human "alienation" *(otchuzhdenie)* in the natural world. Finally, there was the all-important concept of "consciousness" *(soznanie):* in Malashkin's theoretical framework it denoted the subject's self-awareness, in Gumilevskii's a unique quality of an object that stems from the object's sophisticated material organization.[7] To be sure, the different meanings outlined above are not so distinct each time they occur. Yet the consistent ambiguity in the theoretical vocabulary that emerges when the language of the two novels is juxtaposed suggests the persistence of conflicting intellectual traditions in Bolshevik discourse.

The divergent conceptual schemes employed by Malashkin and Gumilevskii led to different explanations for student degeneration. For Malashkin, "intellectual environment" was dangerous because it connoted intelligentsia individualism, isolation from the collective of producers,
antisocialism, and despair. For Gumilevskii "mental labor" was equally
hazardous, but for quite different reasons. He believed that an excess of
thought overstrained the brain and precipitated a physical decline of its
nervous tissues. Again, the difference clearly arose from the authors' respective emphases on sociology and natural science.[8]

For Malashkin, "degeneration" was a sociological term referring to the
proletariat's downward slide toward a bourgeois lifestyle. In Gumilevskii's
mind, the same term stood for a medical concept denoting the disintegration of an individual's mental capacities and his decline into madness. In
the first case, the proletarian standard was articulated on the level of the
social, the worker's relation to his class. In the second case, the proletarian
standard was physiological, the health of the proletarian body. As one
might expect, the explanations for why a certain medicine was prescribed
for a certain condition were different. While Malashkin and Gumilevskii
both championed factory labor as an antidote to unrestrained sexuality,
the former did so because he believed that sexuality was an individualistic
mode of behavior that could be negated through the social effects of work,
whereas the latter thought of work in terms of the proletarian metabolism
and as a requisite for sexual sublimation.

The Communist psychological theory was a body of thought not entirely consistent with itself. Key terms were kept vague enough to allow for
significant disagreements that could give rise to different techniques of the
hermeneutics of the soul. "Marxism" was an unavoidable catchword; one
could debate its meaning, but one had to invoke it. Yet it was precisely its
ability to conceal theoretical tensions under the aegis of a common Marxism that gave Soviet science its inclusive flavor. Proponents of various
and often mutually exclusive theories exploited this potential to reinterpret
the tenets of the Bolshevik moralistic discourse to their liking; this was
permissible as long as they claimed to be speaking in the name of true
Marxism.

In the final account, more united than separated the theoretical apparatus underpinning the two novels. The complementarity of these appa-
ratuses allowed the two novelists to be active participants in the same moralist discourse.

Khokhorin: A Free Man or a Slave of His Body?

The main hero of *Dog Alley* is a young Communist student named Khokhorin—the son of a worker and civil war veteran who serves as a Party cell representative on the board of an unspecified university on the Volga. Khokhorin, like many other students of his ilk, is a compulsive sensualist. Indeed, the question of sexual permissiveness animates the novel, which often reads like a Bolshevik combination of lowbrow erotic fiction with a didactic lesson in corruption and sexual dissolution. At the outset, Khokhorin is seduced by Vera Volkova, a "new woman" with an open sexual attitude. Inflamed by Vera's talk about "infatuation" and "desire" and anticipating the forthcoming sexual act as the "satisfaction of basic human needs," the lascivious Khokhorin hurriedly undresses. Surprisingly turned off by the fact that Khokhorin dispenses with all emotional overtures, Vera chases him from her apartment, ominously located in Dog Alley. The symbolic significance of "alley" in the title of the novel, one critic explained, "is that it is not a straight street." Thus it denotes deviation from the main proletarian road. "We have to know how we got there and how we want to get out," he explained, a knowledge that Trotskyist students desperately needed.[9]

The story is laced with titillating detail. Usually, the reader is told, Khokhorin indulges in carnal delights with libertine women who emulate Kollontai's "free-loving" heroines. His recent sexual defeats have hurt "Khokhorin's masculine pride." Bobrokov, a peasant-student, tries in vain to persuade Khokhorin to try sexual abstinence. When Khokhorin is rejected by yet another student, Babkova, he turns to the services of a prostitute. Shortly after this sexual encounter he comes to believe that he has contracted syphilis. This belief, however, only fuels his lust, and his entire outlook begins to deteriorate. Visiting a factory, ostensibly to begin work in political enlightenment, all Khokhorin does is inspect the working-class females in the hope of finding a new sexual partner. In the meantime, Khokhorin's passion for Vera does not fade. As the story unfolds, the genesis of Vera's predatory sexuality finds its explanation. In flashback the reader learns of Vera's involvement in a passionate love affair with Burov, a celebrated university lecturer in microbiology. Pregnancy and an abortion, however, destroy Vera's belief in her love for Burov and catapult her into a long series of meaningless sexual adventures. The remainder of Burov's life story is similarly grim. His single-minded pursuit of Vera's body to the neglect of all professional duties leads the university authorities to realize that he has lost all control of himself.

The drama concludes with a meeting between Vera and Khokhorin. Khokhorin's passion has laid him low; he has become a real degenerate. When he tells Vera that she should expect to be infected with syphilis, they come to blows, and Vera falls dead. Believing he has killed Vera, Khokhorin shoots himself in the stomach. The ensuing investigation, however, reveals that it was not Khokhorin but Burov who killed Vera, by firing at her from a hiding spot. Having eluded the Yalta police, Burov commits suicide. Medical science, the symbol of modernity and enlightenment, shows that Khokhorin's syphilis was only a false alarm. Khokhorin recuperates from his wound and goes to Siberia to work, eventually continuing his studies at Tomsk University.

Gumilevskii's novel can be read as an attempt to understand why students were prone to Oppositionism. The explanation provided is that excessive mental labor tended to augment the sexual drive, rapidly waste the energies of the young organism, and bring about political indifference. This was considered to be a typical vice of the intelligentsia. Yet Gumilevskii avoided the wholesale condemnation of thinking. The problem was not mental labor as such—how could it be, when consciousness, so dear to Marxists, was a mental activity through and through?—but its separation from manual labor. The key to health was "energetic harmony" in the organism, a balance between mental and physical expenditure. "The nervous system is a most complicated and sensitive mechanism for the satisfaction of both spiritual and physical needs," argued Doctor Faingol'd. "All our bodily organs must be connected into one harmonious whole."[10] Speaking at the Socialist Academy in 1921, Aleksandr Bogdanov sought a reliable device "to measure energy investment in mental labor as compared with manual labor" so that the Bolshevik scientists would be able to fine-tune the operation of the human machine.[11] In his belief that the release of bodily energies had to be controlled and rationalized, Gumilevskii and his fellow Marxist scientists harked back to notions of equilibrium, which have a long tradition in the history of Western medical thought.

Resonating with the scientific debate over the manual labor / mental labor problem raging in contemporary Soviet theoretical journals, *Dog Alley* is a record of the process through which Marxist eschatology and the equally Marxist materialism negotiated their respective positions on the body-mind question. Whereas Malashkin's sociology was considered too abstract by many of the Soviet scientific community, Gumilevskii's hyper-naturalism was even less acceptable to Party ideologues. Exemplifying the intellectual evolution of Marxian psychology in the 1920s, Khokhorin undergoes a long journey of suffering before coming to understand how a real proletarian ought to live. At first, infected at the university with "intelligentsia depravity," Khokhorin takes the Revolution for a triumph of the sexual drive, a wild libidinous release that swept everything from its path. He comes under the sway of a crude materialism that has reduced all human phenomena to the physiology of the body, ultimately denying the mind any importance. The bulk of the ensuing narrative consists of a chain of dialogues between Khokhorin and fellow students, in the course of which his vulgar naturalism is overturned. The calamities he experiences teach Khokhorin to respect the mental side in man. While Gumilevskii was clearly fond of naturalism, he professed an awareness of the impasse at which it arrived. If freedom of the will was to be given its due, Khokhorin had to retract a good number of his reductionist ideas.[12]

Gumilevskii came to agree with Malashkin that neither work nor thought, taken in isolation, could produce the New Man. Petr and Korolev, the characters with whom the two novelists identified, are model Communists precisely because they are healthy workers and thinkers at one and the same time. Having undertaken difficult theoretical work, Gumilevskii, through the medium of his protagonist, Korolev, managed to accommodate, within the Marxist physiological language, "will," "personality," "love," and similar mentalist notions heretofore dismissed as "bourgeois" and "idealist." The physiological reduction of quality to quantity—a tendency that threatened to subvert the belief in the New Man as a qualitatively new and final creature—was arrested, and "consciousness" was proclaimed an irreducible notion. But while Malashkin was of the opinion that "consciousness" gave students the ability to emerge from their isolationism and to mend their relations with the working class, Gumilevskii was more interested in the capacity of "consciousness" to enable students to gain control over their bodies and heal their degenerated constitutions. In the first case, consciousness came close to being a universalist spirit; in the second, to a physical function. Gumilevskii set the mind on a par with the other bodily parts, an organ with a unique role in the organism but without a unique essence that would allow it to transcend the organism.

The Liberation of Instincts

The need to transform the language of naturalism becomes clear only at the end of the novel. But first let us trace the gradual unfolding of the story and its message. The novel opens on a streetcar, where Vera is seducing Khokhorin. The counterpart of Isaika the alien, Khokhordin proudly explains that "love is a repulsive word. We do not acknowledge any such thing!" Desperately in need of a release after Vera has refused him, he loses his usual composure and becomes obsessed with sex. "All this is the natural result of his need for a woman, not satisfied that evening in a normal way," he thinks, "shrugging his shoulders, proud of the remarkable clarity of his perspective."[13]

The motif of Khokhorin's sexual promiscuity is elaborated further in the following scene. A chess tournament is under way, and the student club is buzzing. The sound of athletes exercising in the nearby gym can be heard. But the healthy combination of manual labor (symbolized by sports) and mental labor (symbolized by the game of chess) does not occupy the mind of Khokhorin, who is hungry for sex. Desperate, Khokhorin sits down next to his classmate, Babkova, pulls away her notebook, as if trying to deprive Babkova of her consciousness, and giggles: "I need to relieve myself. Will you come with me to the surgery room. . . . There is a cot out there." Babkova blushes and looks straight into Khokhorin's eyes: "Khokhorin, are you out of your mind? . . . Had you not lost all control, you would not have such needs! Go to hell!" Babkova offers a clue to what Khokhorin will be taken to task for: antisocial attitudes, obsessiveness, and lack of self-control. But at this early stage the still self-assured Khokhorin only looks at Babkova with disdain. What he believed to be a comprehensive and well-thought-out perspective—and, even more, a materialist one— Babkova sees as ridiculous. "She appears to him pitiful, cowardly, stupid" (pp. 36–38).

Sexologists claimed that Khokhorin's attitudes toward sex were symptomatic of students' attraction to naturalism and physiologism. "Gumilevskii's hero," claimed one sexologist, "relegates love to the realm of 'romanticism.' He acknowledges only naked physiology. Instincts have to be satisfied since they are natural: Hungry?—Eat! Attracted to a woman?— Have her!"[14] The writer Kornei Chukovskii saw many Khokhorins around him. "Men are happy where such things as cards, races, wine, and women exist," he confided to his diary in 1922. "Everyone is expressing his zoological and physiological self."[15]

A study by sexologist I. Gel'man concurred that students "remain restless prisoners in the dark kingdom of instinct." Notes made by students on the margins of Gel'man's sex questionnaires show them to have been quite close to Khokhorin in their thinking:

> I acknowledge no limits in sexual life. I have intercourse almost every week, and if the opportunity arises, I do it every day, every hour, as long as my energy holds out.
>
> Love is something I do not recognize. Excitement is all that I am after.
>
> I abstain from sex only when female objects are not available. When that happens, I blame the women, who try to outwit nature—which is impossible.
>
> Since we think sexual intercourse is a natural need and a law of nature, and as we build nurseries for its products, why don't we open houses of free love? Do not think I have brothels in mind. I suggest the following statute: whoever feels he has to satisfy his sexual needs goes to such houses, passes a medical examination, etc.[16]

"In all the questionnaires, naked sexual instinct reigns supreme," Gel'man summarized. "Blind sexual need flourishes and transports a youngster from one sexual encounter to another."[17] A number of sexologists confirmed Gel'man's findings. Thus N. Gushchin's study regretted to observe that the worst kind of pornography flourished in the universities. "No less than eight obscene homemade journals had to be confiscated from students." And V. Kliachkin noted that many students longed for sensuality, "no doubt suffering from deviations of the psychophysical sphere."[18]

Such fixation on bodily instincts, however, was defended by an important camp in the 1920s scientific establishment and, at least for a while, could even have been described as the cutting edge of theory.[19] When physiologists and medical doctors referred to the sort of opinions Khokhorin embraced as "materialist," they legitimized whatever he said as intellectually sound. Many Bolshevik dignitaries praised the "new, objective psychology" as a timely reaction to the "idealist" psychology of the prerevolutionary period. Armed with quantitative methods of investigation, physiology, with its "objective" knowledge of the operation of the human organism, came to replace psychology in the early 1920s.[20] Ivan Pavlov and Vladimir Bekhterev, the doyens of Soviet behaviorism, physiologists with a considerable reputation in the West, insisted that human behavior was a biological phenomenon to be studied not by psychologists but by natural scientists.[21] V. Borovskii, their follower and an expert in "animal psychology," claimed that "man thinks with his entire organism. Each time we talk about thinking and mental processes, what we actually have in mind are organic phenomena." Marxist psychology, Borovskii triumphantly stated, "is the only school of psychology capable of overcoming philosophical dualism."[22]

Even the term "psychology" itself fell out of favor as "idealist" once its etymology was traced to the Greek mystical notion of the soul *(psyche)*.[23] The proponents of naturalism argued that the "physiological method can meet the Socratic challenge of 'know thyself' better than any introspectionism," a practice believed to be tainted by such "antideterministic" concepts as "will" and "spirit." Instead of searching for "causes" of behavior, psychologists posit a "free will," Pavlov famously said—and went on to declare the subjective method "totally unscientific."[24] Pavlov suggested that even though individuals had a subjective feeling of freedom, it was only an illusion, which science had to unmask in order to demonstrate the determinate nature of all human phenomena. Psychology was a part of physics, a similarly inclined expert maintained, "because what we call a psychic process is a misnomer for a flow of physical energy."[25] The founder of American behaviorism, John Watson, who asserted that "thinking is nothing but a complex material process," was translated approvingly into Russian.[26]

Emmanuil Enchmen's Theory of New Biology was widely regarded as a legitimate scientific position, consistent with the early 1920s physiology.[27] Its author, trained in psychology in the prerevolutionary capital, and who later became known for his extremist futuristic outlook, tried to do away with the mind/body problem Descartes had bequeathed to Western philosophy. Enchmen elected to cut the Gordian knot. Following Pavlov, he dismissed dualism as a "philosophical delusion" and argued for an ontology based on matter alone. According to Enchmen, "thinking" was but a chain of reflexes. For these his theory had a better name: "analyzers" *(analizatory)*, that is, "a special kind of reactions, called by some [wrongheaded idealists] 'notions.'"[28] The "mind," which since Descartes had presented so many problems to philosophers, was, for all intents and purposes, thereby demolished as a concept.

Enchmen was sure that he had managed to efface the Cartesian duality between the spatial and the nonspatial by demonstrating that "consciousness is a material phenomenon like any other."[29] He vehemently denied subjective states any empirical reality. "True scientific method consists in establishing the interdependence between spatial phenomena only, without recourse to the so-called 'psychic phenomena,' which, some wrongly believe, occur simultaneously. Subjective states cannot be verified by experience. All that can be said about 'psychological states' is that they are acoustic reverberations," by which he meant that although the words that referred to psychological states existed, the entities to which these words were supposed to refer did not.[30]

The popular scientific literature of the time reiterated many of Enchmen's reductionist contentions. The very title of Amar's 1923 *The Human Machine* suggested that humans were automatons.[31] As part of its effort to disseminate materialism, the Proletarian Library published a similarly titled brochure—*Man-Machine*—a year later. Its author, M. Gremiatskii, declared, "not only am I not embarrassed to state that I function like a sophisticated machine, but I am proud that I can pay myself this compliment." Much like Enchmen, Gremiatskii erased all distinctions between mental and physical states. The brain, he argued, operated on the principle of the calculating machine. "Thought is nothing but a reflex. Consider a headless frog. It, too, can be made to act 'intelligently.' What happens when we spray some acid on its leg? The frog immediately raises its other leg and brushes the stimulated place, attempting to remove the bothersome liquid. The scientist calls it a 'reflex,' the layman 'thought.'"[32]

The uniqueness of the mind, what some regard as the locus of the spiritual, the animated, the subjective, was thereby denied. Man was seen as one with nature, its pinnacle perhaps, but a creature qualitatively similar to other animals.[33] The popular treatise *The Soul of Animals and Men*, published as part of the Workers' Bookshelf series, displayed the same reductive tendency. In two of the book's charts man was placed at the top of nature's chain of being. The first chart, representing a "zoological ladder," began with the simplest one-celled organism and ended with man; the second chart depicted the human brain as simply an enlargement of the brain of animals. In both cases the human mind was viewed only as an extension and improvement of the faculties also possessed by other creatures. The treatise maintained that the uniqueness of human mental functioning was a myth, connected to a religious notion of the soul: "We are told that the soul is not constructed in the same way as other parts of the human body.

It is invisible. Yet somehow that does not keep it from summoning humans to action." Denying the viability of spiritual notions, the treatise stated that "the 'soul' does not exist. Everyday actions of men are a chain of conditioned reflexes."[34] Other scholars added that the "soul," to the extent that they had to speak in such terms, was "a material thing."[35]

"Mind" *(intellekt)* was discarded in favor of the "brain" *(mozg)*. "Brain" represented the purely material; it was one bodily organ among many. One of the first to issue the call for Marxist psychology and its separation from idealist philosophy (a call that enabled him to inherit the Psychological Institute from his now-discredited mentor, Giorgii Chelpanov), Konstantin Kornilov presented Marxism as an "intrascientific" methodology that could turn the study of man into an experimental science.[36] Kornilov saw no difficulty in applying the law of energy conservation to the process of thinking: "What is called the 'mind' is nothing but an inhibited energy . . . The more intensive is the consumption of energy in the brain, the less energy remains for the use of our peripheral organs."[37]

Such crass materialist ideas found poetic expression in a number of early Bolshevik utopians. Vladimir Kirilov, the famous Proletkult poet, proudly declared in 1918: "Growing close to metal, we fuse our souls with machines." Aleksei Gastev, another prominent futurologist, maintained that true proletarian culture was about a "mechanized collectivism"—"a face devoid of expression, a soul without lyricism, and emotions measured not by laughter or screams but rather by manometer and taximeter." Gastev's proletarian vision included a period when "the will of machines and the will of human consciousness would be unbreakably connected . . . and machines would move from being managed to being managers."[38]

Supported by the central Marxist tenet "Consciousness is always determined by practice," some physiologists even dared to call for the destruction of the core Communist notion of consciousness itself. Many declared the ideational content of consciousness to be a mere "reflection" of underlying physiological processes.[39] The real psyche resided in the unconscious, said Bekhterev. "The importance of unconscious processes in the subjective life of man militates against the ascription of a serious role to conscious factors."[40] In the view of Borovskii, consciousness was a concept irrevocably "contaminated" by the use to which it had been put by "idealist psychology." He noted that although in recent decades "psychologists have substituted 'consciousness' for 'soul,' the qualities of the former remain unfortunately as imprecise and abstract as the attributes of the latter."[41]

Physiologists either recast all mentalist notions in materialist language or had them abolished. Highly ranked among physicians and physiologists in the 1920s, I. Sapir kept using the terms "soul" and "consciousness," but always put them in quotation marks.[42] Taking an even more extreme position, Mikhail Reisner denied the scientific credentials of mentalist notions altogether: "Had we upheld the position of the old psychology, we would have had to deal with such imponderables as 'subjective thoughts' or 'will' . . . But our modern 'psychology without a soul' excludes this scientifically unqualified material and treats man as a natural force." A reflex could pass through the centers of consciousness in the brain or bypass them and operate directly through the spinal cord, Reisner noted. "Thus the difference between the unconscious and the conscious turns out to be quantitative and not qualitative, depending on how many neural paths are affected by a given discharge."[43]

Reisner dared to take even the fathers of Marxism to task for using a "somewhat obfuscating" mentalist vocabulary. "The combination of two sets of terms in the terminology of Marx and Engels to denote man's psychic life is equivocal. On the one hand Marx and Engels use objective and material terms such as 'production of ideas,' 'ideological superstructure,' 'human brain,' and 'human heads.' On the other, they mention 'passions,' 'consciousness,' and 'will.'" But the first set of terms, Reisner pointed out, referred to an objective process, while the second referred to subjective states. "Marxists, who have passed through a serious school, must understand that terms have a meaning only if they describe objective facts. All talk of 'parallelism' between the 'physical' and the so-called 'psychic' is wrong. The psychic is nothing but a material process occurring in the brain, a physical phenomenon like any other."[44]

Such attempts to play down the importance of consciousness made some Soviet physiologists sympathetic to Freud. It was generally believed that "his psychic pandeterminism is the best antidote to the entire doctrine of free will, conceived as a faculty of the soul."[45] Physiologists praised psychoanalysis for maintaining that "nothing in the mind was accidental" and that every psychic event had a cause "even if our consciousness is not directly aware of it."[46] Thus interpreted, Freud's theory became both objectivist (because the search for the cause of a mental event had a clearly defined procedure) and materialist (because psychoanalysis postulated internal drives that had biological, and therefore material, underpinnings).

It is against this background that the endorsement of "Freudism" (*freidizm*) in the early 1920s should be understood.[47] Drawing an analogy between those places in the works of the founders of Marxism where they suggested that "men create their history unconsciously" (Engels) or that "relations of production form behind the backs of men, remaining for the most part outside the realm of consciousness" (Lenin) and the psychoanalytic notion of the unconscious (*bessoznatel'noe*), Freud's adherents in the Soviet Union legitimized Freud's theories.[48] Bernard Bykhovskii, a young Soviet scientist, maintained that the Freudian concept of conflict resolution in human life was methodologically consistent with the Marxist concept of class struggle: "The conflict between the psychological needs of men and the social demands placed upon them, censored, mediated, and transformed in the unconscious, moves irrevocably toward a resolution that is determined by heredity and by our environment."[49]

According to Aleksandr Luriia, a sociobiologist specializing in behavioral disturbances, the focus of "dualistic and subjectivist" inquiry had unfortunately been on the attempts to divide the realm of the mind from the realm of the body, and to provide static and isolated categories to define "sensation," "reason," and "will." Freudism had made very important steps toward the scientific understanding of human behavior by postulating the unity of psychic functions. The real contribution of psychoanalytic research resided in the light it cast on the motives impelling people to create ideological systems. Another virtue Luriia found in the Freudian focus on unconscious mental activity was that it allowed him to conduct his analysis "objectively," that is, in accord with the scientific rules of physiological inquiry. Unconscious activity, as Luriia defined it, was a "somatic process." The psychic energy governing it was analogous to physical energy: "Unconscious energy cannot disappear, but it can be transformed into other forms of energy and channeled in a different direction."[50]

Trotsky was happy to note that Freud's theory, no less than Pavlov's, was "inherently materialistic." The two theories differed in their method of inquiry, not in their philosophical presuppositions. "Your teaching about the conditioned reflexes," Trotsky wrote to Pavlov in 1922, "includes Freud's theory as a particular instance. The 'sublimation of sexual energy'. . . . replaces what you call the 'formation of conditioned reflexes.'" In this view, following an inductive method, Pavlov proceeded from physiology to psychology. Taking a more suppositional approach, Freud postulated in advance the physiological urge behind psychic processes. Both Freud and Pavlov, however—and hence their strong affinity in Trotsky's view—would have nothing to do with the idealist who claimed that the mind was a "bottomless well" that could not be subjected to rigorous scientific investigation. Both insisted that physiology formed the bottom of that well which we call the soul.[51]

Different as the theoretical vocabularies proposed by physiologists were, they converged in a depreciation of mentalism. Suspicious of any romanticization of consciousness as a self-transparent and omnipotent mystical entity, scholars construed it entirely in terms of reflex theory. Stripped of its position as the epistemological tool that organized reality, consciousness was reinterpreted as a property of well-organized matter, a token of the fact that a given neural system was sophisticated enough to account for its own functioning. The only remaining affinity between the sociological and the reflexological notions of consciousness was self-referentiality. Both "thought" (sociological vocabulary) and "mental labor" (physiological vocabulary) connoted a reflexive activity that generated self-knowledge. But whereas for the sociologists consciousness meant freedom, and functioned as the primal cause and therefore the source of all phenomena, for the physiologists it meant a refraction in the upper story of our being of a generally independent process.

Attempting to explain everything according to a rigorous and monistic system and further armed with the necessary "materialist," "determinist," and "scientific" credentials, physiology laid claim to the title of the "sole legitimate Marxist science of human behavior."[52] In the physiological scheme, the model of man was naturalistic. Psychic causality was described as operating on a purely physical level. Man might have known the forces operating within him, but he could do little by way of controlling them.[53]

Denouncing all psychology and mentalism as the worst possible tools of exploitation, Soviet scientists who supported the physiological view of man claimed to represent the interests of the proletariat in science. Subjective notions, besides being described as unscientific, were also blamed for constraining the self-expression of the working class and undergirding the domination of thought over work.[54] That ethical imperative of liberalism—that the spirit should control the body—was, for Reisner, a microcosm of the bourgeois plot to dominate the working class.

No wonder that psychology as a science of the soul has become the favorite hobby of an intelligentsia that purports to embody the supreme "consciousness" itself, with its "delicate and lofty feelings" and a "goal-oriented will" . . . Subjective psychology functioned as a weapon in the hands of the monopolistic intelligentsia, which transposes its view of the correct relations between the body and the chimerical "soul" onto class relations.

The inversion of the class hierarchy, such that the owner was on top and the producer at the bottom, had its corollary in the unnatural denigration of the material and the real in favor of the insubstantial and the chimerical. In Reisner's scenario, the soul, together with the rest of subjective psychology, had become nothing but shackles on the bodies of the workers, a "tool of class domination."[55]

The argument of Enchmen, whose scientific rationale was presented above, had a strong political component. In this scenario, too, the main enemy of the proletariat was not the bourgeoisie but the intelligentsia, which induced in the workers chains of predetermined responses that held them in check. Enchmen set out to transcribe the classic Marxist distinction between the physical and the mental aspects of proletarian subjugation into his own theoretical language. The ruling class, he posited, "produces the desired physiological reaction among the organisms it exploits through the deployment of two kinds of 'subjugation analyzers.'" These were "material excitations" injected by the army and the police, and "intellectual excitations" injected by the ruling class of the intelligentsia. The combination of both kinds of excitation produced the type of reflexological "hybridization" *(skreshchivanie)* that inhibited workers.[56] Enchmen believed he had sufficiently demonstrated that with each new historical epoch the intelligentsia only deepened and improved its mechanism of exploitation. Instead of co-opting it, the proletariat had to defeat the intelligentsia at its own game. The working class could be emancipated only if it countered the analyzers of the intelligentsia with analyzers of its own.

The second stage of a proletarian revolution, the assault on mental labor, was elaborated in great detail. Enchmen proposed the creation of a new institution—a Revolutionary Scientific Soviet of the Republic—dedicated to "facilitating joyful reflexes and reactions in the workers' organisms." These were to begin with the injection of fifteen analyzers into the workers that would start a chain of "cataclysmic revolutionary reflexes. All the analyzers implanted in the organisms during millenniums of exploitation will thereby be removed." As a result of this radical revolutionary action, "millions of rebellious proletarian organisms" would experience organic happiness.[57]

The destruction of everything intellectual was the ultimate goal of this particular vision of the proletarian Revolution. Enchmen discarded all mediation of thought in human activity as a matter of principle. For him, "emancipation" meant the emancipation of work from thought. The concept of equality was reformulated accordingly. In Enchmen's kingdom of the future, the equal distribution of the stock of the "positive organic excitation" was to be ensured through a system of "physiological passports." These passports were to indicate the quantity of intensity of the most important chains of reflexes in the individual organism, in order to secure a fair allocation of the "pleasure factor." Thus perfected, the "system of class rations" was to "lay the foundation for World Communism."[58]

Many physiologists tended to articulate the fundamental class divide along the mental/manual axis rather than along the owner/laborer axis. Venerating work, which they regarded as the defining characteristic of the proletariat, these theorists developed a marked hostility toward mental labor, which they regarded as the defining property of the intelligentsia. Contemporary students' denial of the so-called spirituality of emotions squared well with the physiological argument that human states of spiritual elevation were in fact illusions. And their vehement rejection of subjective ideals as chimeras spread by the bourgeoisie echoed the antimentalist position of the behaviorists.

Physiologism, the behaviorist reformulation of psychoanalysis, and Enchmenism provide the discursive backdrop against which Khokhorin's championing of uninhibited sexuality has to be read. Gumilevskii makes clear that Khokhorin's sexual libertinism was inspired by the fashionable reduction of the human being to his inner drives. His favorite word, "instinct," was defined as a "complex of unconditioned, innate reflexes" that responded to "predetermined excitations."[59] In effect, Khokhorin had considerable expert opinion on his side when he interpreted the triumph of the proletarian revolution as the emancipation of the body, the "instinctual" and the "natural," from the fetters of the psyche and the spiritual.[60] In this framework, the Revolution was a physiological event and sexual libertinism one of its most direct expressions. With the Revolution, the body broke free from the soul, the instincts shook off conscience. For this view, Khokhorin was indebted to Enchmen, who hoped that the contemporary social upheavals would free the sexual instinct, which is to say that they would liberate the noncerebral activity of human beings. The Revolution meant here a collective and equal bodily cataclysm. Put in the simplest terms, Communism, in Enchmen's scenario, was a state of workers' "perpetual orgasm" (orgasm [*stevizm*] being defined as "joyful reflexes and reactions").[61]

Sexual inhibition was in Khokhorin's eyes nothing but useless "bourgeois morals." Khokhorin construed sex as an instinct, a bodily need, to be respected and duly satisfied. Here, too, he was supported by the medical community. "In the process of phylogenetic evolution from lower animals to higher ones, humans included, the basis of the sexual drive retains the same innate reflexive mechanism," one sexologist pointed out. "Instinct determines behavior, selects and directs. It harnesses to itself all the resources of the brain, including the highest manifestations of the intellect."[62] In other words, human sexual behavior was a reflex responding to stimuli.[63] If mental entities did not exist, Khokhorin was correct in placing the instinct at the forefront of his existence. To buttress his position he could have referred to somebody like A. Stukovenkov, who identified "love" with sexual libido. "The thirst for closeness," this expert argued, "stems from the active sexual centers in the head."[64]

A number of physiologists who inspired Gumilevskii's Khokhorin drew parallels between the sexual lives of animals and men. "The dependence of students' sexual interest on the time of the year," so ran a typical statement by one of them, "is a token of the human link with the animal kingdom . . . An increase in the quantity of sexual emissions improves our organism's chance to nurture itself."[65] When an expert criticized Gumilevskii's novel as "untrue to life," he did so in the name of the same reductionist language put in Khokhorin's mouth. "But surely the intensity of desire the novelist attributes to Khokhorin violates the established laws of physiology. Is Gumilevskii unaware of Lavoisier's law of energy transformation? He conjures up an unlikely image of a student who studies, works, engages in Party and public activity but who still cannot use up his sexual drive."[66]

Gumilevskii was not alone in inscribing ideological health in the flesh. Hewing to late nineteenth-century Marxist naturalism, many experts attempted to deduce a person's moral qualities not from one's actions but from one's physique. According to these scholars cum hermeneuts, it was not the soul but the body that was testifying: meaning resided in the flesh, not in the word. However, this attempt to prefer the body over the mind and to make one's material substance—one's musculature, skeleton, circulatory system, and the gamut of other signs purportedly inscribed in the body—the witness of truth was destined to fail. The subject could not be made into an object stripped of subjective intentions and construed as a

heap of bones, tissues, and nerves without the notion of emancipation itself being seriously imperiled. The leap to freedom necessitated making
something out of nothing, and such voluntarism could not be deduced
from the principles of reductive science.

Sublimation

Khokhorin's encounters with fellow students were meant to persuade the
hero and the reader alike that sexual excess was unhealthy. Contrary to the
physiologists' expectation that sexual release would generate a feeling of
personal emancipation, it is the sexually obsessed scientist Burov, not the
celibate peasant student Bobrokov, who is deeply disturbed, unhappy with
himself, and seriously ill.

Immediately after his encounter with Babkova, who refuses to satisfy his
sexual needs, Khokhorin comes face to face with Bobrokov. Though both
protagonists fought in the civil war, the conflict's impact on their sexuality
has been very different. Whereas Khokhorin has lost all ability to control his sexual drive and he often buys love on the market, Bobrokov
has learned to sublimate his sexual energy. "Taking Bobrokov aside,
Khokhorin asks him, 'Tell me, how do you get your way with chicks?' . . .
'Me, brother, I barely understand these things,' Bobrokov replies." Bobrokov's physical constitution is excellent, while Khokhorin's physique shows
clear signs of degeneration. Bobrokov has to "shake Khokhorin's hand
gently, with exaggerated caution, as any strong person would shake the
hand of a weaker one" (pp. 38–39).

For the physiology-minded Khokhorin, sex with a prostitute is a convenient means of energy release. In his eyes, a prostitute is a semen receptacle
whose function ensures health; she definitely is not a source of illness.
Bobrokov, on the other hand, fully supported by the Soviet social hygiene
campaigns, associates the prostitute with venereal diseases. Soviet sexologists did not generally regard Khokhorin's behavior as unusual. One study
even claimed that "worker-students first experienced sex with a prostitute
more frequently than other students."[67] Khokhorin and his like had not yet
realized that pollution of the body and class pollution went hand in hand.
Later on he will understand what Bobrokov has known all along—that the
prostitute passes on her venereal disease and with it her alien consciousness.

A bit later Khokhorin asks Bobrokov with thinly concealed derision,

"Are you a virgin, or what?" His antagonist's virginity would have indicated to Khokhorin not only inadequate masculinity but also, in all likelihood, physical illness caused by the pressure Bobrokov's pent-up sexual energies would have exerted on his body. Bobrokov's answer revives the dialogue:

> "What? Me, brother, I am married . . . True, it has been two years since I last had sex . . . but I would rather go without it for two more years than be with a prostitute or do it only out of need."
> "Then how do you survive?"
> "I wait for a vacation . . . "
> "You are not a normal human being! . . . You cannot understand the state I am in! My mental stability and my working capacity hinge on it . . . "
> "Don't make a fool of yourself! You spend your life boozing and carousing and grow fussy! Do some gymnastics instead!"   (P. 40)

Khokhorin is totally controlled by his sexual drive; Bobrokov has attenuated his sexual desire and learned to control it.

For a long time sexologists were not in full agreement on the merits of sexual abstinence.[68] The debate, which kept resurfacing in the professional press, centered on the role of hormones in the human body.[69] The argument that was critical of abstinence may be summarized thus: abstinence induced tension in the prostate gland as a result of the influx of blood to that region. Reaching its peak, this tension was likely to impair the growth of seminiferous glands. The entire sexual apparatus could eventually reach a state of "torpor." Since the functioning of glands that stimulated life by their internal secretions was tightly linked to the operation of the nervous system, dysfunction in any one section of this chain affected the entire organism. "Hence the abnormalities in the life of mature adults who abstain from sex—hypochondria, irritability, dizziness, and even melancholy."[70] Many Khokhorins embraced this view. "Students," it was noted, "generally hold to the opinion that 'sexual abstinence makes us depressed and crazy,' and that celibacy is harmful to their health."[71]

Other experts, however, held that abstinence was a good thing.[72] In a scenario in which bodily energies answered to the zero-sum principle, sexual restraint actually saved the body a large reserve of neural and muscular energy, which could then be diverted toward a "higher" sort of activity. "Redirect secretion!" was the slogan directed toward youth from this corner.[73] "Abstinence is healthy!" Doctor Sigal maintained. "The virgin should not be embarrassed by the jeers of his 'know-it-all' comrades." While they irresponsibly wasted whatever energy nature gave them, "his organism will prove in the future well stocked with sexual energy."[74] The sexual activity of the male, pro-abstinence sexologists argued, involved an expenditure of protein, present in the discharged semen. The loss of sexual cells harmed men, primarily because the glands of internal secretion influenced all parts of the organism. Even a singular sexual encounter demanded from the organism a significant expenditure of nervous energy. Doctor Kaminskii, for example, calculated that "each sexual act reduces our weight-lifting capacity by a quarter of a kilogram."[75] The belief in a lethal connection between hypersexuality and exhaustion percolated outside scientific circles.[76] The Bolshevik moralist E. Lavrov lamented students' "squandering of sexual energy," Aron Sol'ts professed knowledge that "chaotic sexual relations weaken the organism," and Emel'ian Iaroslavskii was "not surprised to see youngsters who spend their energies on sex in hospitals and sanatoriums."[77]

An activity that had everything to do with circulation and nothing to do with production, unfettered sexual activity became in the hands of pro-abstinence sexologists a metonym for bourgeois lifestyle. According to what can be called the Bolshevik political economy of the sperm—an elaborate sexual theory that pronounced on the dosage, supply, and preservation of the bodily assets such that the human organism would be prevented from decaying—the excitation that stimulated the sexual drive had to be decisively inhibited. "The creation of a new, healthy generation of Communists will be impossible if it destroys its health by early sexual relations," argued one pro-abstinence sexologist. "Does a Komsomol member have to succumb to the power of the self-styled sexual science and let himself be sucked dry by sexual intercourse?" Bodies had to be trained and systematically prepared for abstinence in the name of the "principle of economy of nervous energy" and "energetic balance."[78]

Abstinence was declared the key to proletarian health around the time Gumilevskii embarked on writing his novel. It was a "prerequisite" to the very important mechanism of "sublimation" (zameshchenie), "the transformation of a lower form of energy into a higher one." Sexologists explained that there were two kinds of sexual glands: "reproductive glands" that produced external secretion in the form of semen and a "gland of internal secretion" that produced hormones.[79] It was further pointed out that "mental and physical retardation, idiotism, and feeble-mindedness often depend not on the working of the brain but on the condition of the glands of internal secretion."[80] Maintaining that the psychophysiology of sexual life had two means of sexual release—semen emission and sublimation— Professor I. Ariamov held semen to be the first substance produced by the sexual glands. But if the release of semen was obstructed, sexual glands would produce hormones instead. This process of conversion was the essence of sublimation.[81]

Sublimation was considered all-important because it ostensibly facilitated the production of hormones, which propelled "the development of cerebral processes." Equilibrium, one expert explained, was the key: "since in a living organism various organs and tissues share the same pool of energy, an increased functioning of one set of bodily organs necessarily weakens the functioning of others." As sexual energy was "very close in its nature to the highest forms of nervous-cerebral energy," the development of the human creative function was "directly dependent on the quantity of the unspent energy of the sexual glands."[82]

From this, the victorious pro-abstinence sexologists concluded that abstinence, which made sublimation possible, was particularly important during maturation, "when our sexual glands produce hormones that the body does not emit but keeps in the blood, hormones that facilitate the growth and development of the human brain." Experts warned that the premature expenditure of precious sexual products emphasized the "lower functions of the organism" and could even "retard the development of mental capacities" and render youngsters asocial. Promiscuity was blamed for "squandering the body's energies and preventing them from creating the tension within the organism necessary to maximize human productivity." Evaluating the issue "from the biological as well as from the social angles," Doctor Gradovskii supported "sexual abstinence prior to the period of full sexual maturation."[83] So did Zalkind, who explained that "there is no reason to assume that abstinence damages the health of the youth." Zalkind recommended that proletarians "abstain from sex before marriage and marry only when they are in their sexual prime (around the age of twenty to twenty-five), because proletarian premarital sexual activity is chaotic and sporadic and stimulates only the most superficial excitations."[84]

Sexologists accepted that sexual drives could be stimulated or inhibited according to social setting. Gel'man, for example, posited that "drives can become an object of conscious intervention and influence by sociopolitical instead of biological powers, and directed in the interest of the race or the state."[85] Zalkind concurred: "it is an indubitable Marxist truism that social existence determines our sexual consciousness. In changing his nature, man changes his psychophysiology."[86] Dramatic social upheavals rechanneled bodily energies.[87] Iaroslavskii maintained that the Revolution could have nothing to do with "a waste of a very precious life force . . . The easiest and most pleasant expenditure of sexual energy, the path of the least resistance," sexual satisfaction was unbecoming to a real Bolshevik.[88]

Doctor Kaminskii posited unequivocally that "Revolution led to sublimation."[89] A number of sexologists went on to prove that 1917 had reduced the "sexual excitability" of students. At Sverdlov University they found that the number of male students who argued that the Revolution had slackened their sexual drive was twice the number of students who claimed it had intensified it (in the case of female students the proportion was one to three). Kliachkin observed that "many students noticed deflation of their sexual activity during the Revolution because sexual energy was released in the form of social action." And Gel'man added that this happened because the great event, "consuming all the time and strength of students, reduced their sexual need."[90]

Following the Revolution, one student-worker learned to "redirect the energy that provokes sexual arousal into other pursuits." His peer was successful in "rechanneling his sexual energy into class hatred." Austere times taught Gumilevskii's Bobrokov to conserve his vital energy. This type of response to a crisis was regarded as typically proletarian: "When class struggle escalates, the proletariat finds it easier to sublimate its sexual energy . . . The needs of class imperiously call upon all the energies of the proletariat, and none are left over. Emotionally enriched, the proletariat diverts parasitic sexual energy into public life. The sexual loses its supposedly 'rightful place.'"[91]

But, much to the sexologists' chagrin, this was only half the story. As the plot of Gumilevskii's novel suggests, although 1917 could teach Bobrokovs to sublimate, it could also unleash the sexuality of Khokhorins. Those individuals who had experienced the Revolution and the civil war unprepared were often overwhelmed by their sexual drive. "When separated from normal life and put in an atmosphere of constant excitement," youngsters allegedly went sexually berserk. For example, many young soldiers "professed their right to have sex with women living in the quarters where they were billeted." One immature student confessed that during the civil war "I had sex with seven hundred women, some of them sixty years old," and another reported that "during the civil war I had sex with two women at once. Sometimes I even tried to have a third simultaneous partner." A number of students brought up the idea that an individual's stock of sexual force was finite to explain their heightened sexual excitability at the front. One of them thought, "What the hell, I am going to be killed anyhow. Why not use up the stock of my sexual energies?!"[92]

In short, the civil war, "an unimaginable bacchanalia," "a period of complete sexual license," had led to a "reign of animalist spontaneity and libertinism."[93] One expert hypothesized that "young people who are weakened by poor nutrition, tuberculosis, and anemia normally experience a precocious sexual maturation followed by pederasty and bestiality."[94] Another added that the tremendous military effort had drained the energies of student Communist youth. "During the war youth had to be constantly tense, all the time on the alert. But as the danger passed, nerves loosened . . . Today's youth easily succumbs to temptation and is prone to panic attacks; its self-restraint is dulled and atrophied." Many sexologists concluded that the protracted battle against the Whites, having thrown the energies of the human body into "disarray," had induced "sexual disorientation," not to say "mass psychosis."[95]

Even Party theoreticians who generally preferred to see the civil war as an ideal period of class purity conceded that it could have had an adverse impact on the young.[96] Bukharin maintained that he knew "good Komsomol lads" as yet unable to abandon those "fraternal values of War Communism" that condoned antisocial behavior.[97] In the view of Lunacharskii, the years 1918–1920 were a period of depravity "typical during a transitional period, a time when human beings have departed from their animal existence but have not yet arrived at a true humanity."[98] This set of attitudes was generally labeled "War Communism nihilism." For a time, it was a positive phenomenon that helped to break the "spell of the old moral code, held sacred by both our consciousness and the unconscious." But during the reconstruction of the mid-1920s this combative attitude was pronounced out of place; sexual nihilism had to recede into the past. The capacity for abstinence became a touchstone for determining whether the civil war had had a sublimating (Bobrokov's case) or a degenerating (Khokhorin's case) influence on a student.[99]

Sports could be of major help in easing the process of sublimating the sexual drive. Though sent to the university, Bobrokov has kept in touch with his proletarian self through sports, a surrogate labor of sorts. Gumi-levskii underscores the importance of sports in effecting the healthy synthesis between work and thought: "The link between the university and the factory was solidified by our sportsmen who struggled for the leadership of the soccer team, our constantly competing skiers, skaters, and our chess players . . . A tall, invariably good-humored student," Bobrokov is someone who "breathes heavily and cheerfully works his muscles, thinly covered by a shirt thrown over his shoulders" (p. 84). It was of men like him that Liadov said: "When I see a well-developed figure of an athlete I see the ideal. This is the harmoniously developed man of the future."[100]

The primary importance of sports lay in its substitution for the premature sexual activity that "overburdens the nervous system, destroys the organism and gives rise to decadent tendencies."[101] Sports could also counteract "bookish deviationism" and the sexual excitability that all too often accompanied it in students.[102] This is why Semashko urged students to "train their muscular systems to function selectively and accurately," and why Iaroslavskii likewise maintained that the young need "gymnastics, swimming and other physical exercises."[103] "My own experience demonstrates," one student confided to sexologist D. Lass, "that sports and light athletics are the best means to ensure sexual restraint . . . How true this is I learned when I sprained my tendon. My predicament prevented me from engaging in sports for two months. During all this time I felt wretched, as a result of a strong nervous fatigue induced by constant sexual excitement."[104]

The Party initially considered sports part of the "bourgeois cult of competition." Toward the mid-1920s, however, it decided to sanction sports, now rehabilitated as a "collectivist and sublimating activity." The April 1925 Central Committee instructions echoed scientific insights of the time. "Care for one's health is not, as many think, 'care for one's personality only.' It has to evolve into a movement for collective physical recovery." In this context, impressing the population with the importance of sports was the "first measure that ought to be taken."[105] Of course, sports could create "dedicated fighters for the revolutionary ideals" only if "linked with social construction. Not the athlete's selfish desire for individual victory should be the aim . . . but his desire to sublimate his energy and contribute it to his class."[106] "In view of the observed tendency of the student youth to degenerate physically," stated the Thirteenth Party Congress, "the Komsomol has to increase its activity in the sphere of physical culture."[107] The July 13, 1925, Party decree on "The Tasks of the Party in the Field of Physical Culture" elaborated: "there is nothing like sports to develop the will, the collective habits, persistence, composure, and other precious qualities."[108]

If Bobrokov did everything right, Khokhorin did everything wrong. Abstaining from sports but not from sex, Gumilevskii's hero exacerbated the dangers to his organism. Studies by contemporary physiologists repeatedly demonstrated that "an enormous percentage of students are mentally burnt out."[109] The students had failed to take into account that the brain core needed to rest after stimulation. "Everywhere one can see them studying without rest, spending nights without sleep." Unless they worked out regularly, exhausted students stood the risk of remaining mental invalids for the rest of their lives. Specialists on the "hygiene of mental labor" maintained that intensive thought produced more poisonous wastes in the brain than the idle body could remove, eventually leading to the destruction of brain cells.[110] "Has it ever happened to you that because of studying too hard you no longer understand what you are doing? The head and the hands come down, and you fall asleep." This phenomenon was called in the scientific literature "overstimulation of the brain. If it spreads all over the brain core, this condition cannot be relieved. The result is lunacy."[111]

There were good reasons why mental overwork and sexual excess went hand in hand. One sexologist explained it thus: whereas animal sexual excitation triggered purely instinctual motor activity, with humans the mechanism of sexual attraction was compounded by central cerebral mechanisms, whose function was the enhancement of intellectual activity. The brain geared itself toward the achievement of its sexual goals, and its work intensified in manifold ways. "Incidentally, this explains the well-known ingenuity of lovers."[112] Conversely, another sexologist related to the last point, "eunuchs are usually imbeciles."[113] If sex and brain activity stimulated each other, then overindulgence in one sphere would lead to overindulgence in the other sphere until both would exhaust themselves. Two types of sexual aberration were rampant in the case of mental laborers, Zalkind wrote: "(1) a reduction of sexual prowess as a consequence of the transfer of sexual chemistry into the work of the brain, or as a consequence of brain exhaustion; (2) an artificial upsurge of sexual activity triggered by strenuous cerebral concentration that "creates the wish to diversify cerebral processes through obsessive copulation and frequent change of partners. Burdened by strenuous mental concentration, such a mental laborer was driven to diversify and to rejuvenate the monotonous cerebral processes (attraction to frequent sexual changes, superfluous sexual acts etc.)."[114]

Bolshevik experts had to teach students how to deploy their stocks of energy without undermining their bodies. In the 1920s, physiologists offered suggestions to better regulate dormitory routine and to budget time effectively. "Scaling-down campaigns," in which student energy expenditure was rationalized, also enjoyed a certain vogue. The key question was how to maintain an equilibrium between the erotic and the cerebral sphere so that both would develop normally. What was crucial was achieving a healthy life "tone" *(tonus)*—a vague notion that meant something like a basic vitality that was supposed to enable the organism to coordinate its various functions and achieve healthy sublimation. "The vivacity of one's general 'tone,' one's emotional uplift," played a crucial role here. If a vibrant life tone was absent, Zalkind explained, sexual chemicals were not "sublimated" but "converted," that is, switched into "parasitic energy paths." This created an acute form of anxiety, depression, excitability, and other manifestations of general neural exhaustion.[115]

V. Kashkadamov, a sexologist, argued that "the physiological condition of an organism characterized by what we call 'health' can be defined as a balance between various organs, that is, by the congruence of various bodily functions."[116] All pleasurable activity beyond the basic act of intercourse was deprived of any "biological justification" and qualified as obsessive or perverse, and therefore bourgeois and decadent. Not that Soviet sexologists objected to sexuality as such. Lass, for example, argued that "the social-biological function of sexual instincts should not be destroyed."[117] The task then was to achieve a balance between mental activity and sex, not to sacrifice one for the other. "What is the purpose of the mental laborer's 'sexual economy'?" Zalkind asked himself.

The first was to preserve the chemicals needed for complex cerebral processes. The second was to guard the brain against frequent and stormy physiological upheavals. We must keep in mind that the mental laborer's brain core is a fragile, sensitive mechanism that reacts sharply to any physiological traumas and that the sexual act is always a major cardiac, and generally endocrine, shake-up of the organism . . . The third is not

to admit the core of the brain too often into the lower psychophysiological sphere. The sexual instinct, when it breaks out in sudden discharge, temporarily reduces the sensitivity and the complexity of the
higher cortical processes . . . And finally, the fourth is the need to limit
the variety of sexual objects. New sexual positions, creating new areas of
excitation, compete in the core of the brain with the creative activity
proper.[118]

Accepting that the combination of sexual activity and mental labor put
the student in double jeopardy, Zalkind objected to the simplistic inference
that mental labor must produce sexual infirmity. "True, the notorious
'professorial impotence,' stemming from the physiological emasculation
that follows from the principle of 'pure mind, no body,' is characteristic of
the Western intellectual's one-sidedness. But the mental labor of our Soviet
scholars," Zalkind assured his readership, "is invested with vibrant emotional supply. A cerebral task infused with the right emotional purpose sta-
bilizes their entire psychochemical sexual apparatus."[119]

Supposedly trapped in a vicious circle of direct energy expenditure, students like Khokhorin, bereft of the capacity to control and sublimate their
sexual drives, embodied the truth of experts' warnings. The "acute sexual
sensitivity" observed in the universities was regarded as a "symptom" of
"the exhaustion of nervous energy and . . . degeneration."[120] What better
proof could there be of the perniciousness of sexual excess than the number of real-life Khokhorins who, swayed by lust, became involved in sleazy
criminal affairs?[121] Although it is unlikely that they inspired Gumilevskii
directly, police cases such as the two examined below certainly contributed
to an atmosphere in which the plot of his novel would have felt familiar to
contemporary readers.

In the first case, the police established the following story. In 1919 two
students became acquainted.

Common interests united them: both were consumed by social life, participated in discussion circles, attended proletarian rallies . . . He was an
unskilled worker, very raw. She, Anastasiia E., twenty-four years of age,
was much better developed that he. While she wanted to turn him into
a cultured person, he, ferocious and indomitable, kept demanding her
body. In 1922 Anastasiia finally succumbed: "I hoped that intercourse
would calm my boyfriend down, that it would put an end to his nervous
fits," she recalled. "The beginning of our sexual relations was a turning
point in my life. While earlier I had been guided by reason, afterward my

emotions started to set the tone. My heart and my mind were now in discord."

When Anastasiia discovered that her lover, whom she had eventually married, was polygamous, she suffered a nervous fit, became convinced that, as she put it later, "'it' was the cause of all her troubles," and "at seven in the morning on October 10, 1923, severed her husband's penis half an inch from the pelvis."[122]

Both Khokhorin and Anastasiia were driven by their sexual instincts into crime. Both believed that sex was the road to health, only to learn that it was in fact the road to mental degradation and criminality. The Soviet legal system displayed the same compassion for Anastasiia that Gumilevskii does for his hero. On November 10, 1924, a Moscow provincial court found that Anastasiia's crime was committed while she was suffering from "a temporary psychological disorder. Affective impulses [*affektivnye impul'sy*] overshadowed her consciousness. She carried out her crime in a degenerated condition [*v sostoianii upadka*] . . . Behind the perpetrator's behavior was a drive to emancipate herself, to find her normal self, which had retreated in the face of the sexual attachment that turned her into a slave." Anastasiia got away with a light sentence.[123]

Three years later another criminal case corroborated the moral of the story: when instincts take over, man turns into an animal. Here, the juridical narrative also suggested that the noble savage was not a true proletarian, but a bestial libertine. Here are the details of the police report:

> During Lenin Levy [1924], K-ev's factory cell decided to send him to study law at an unnamed university. It was there that K-ev met his future wife and victim, R-na. Soon their relationship soured. On February 26, 1926, K-ev struck R-na, knocking out her left eye. He also stabbed her nose and cheek with his penknife. Another worker-student had gone berserk.

It was immediately clear to the police that two very different types had united in this marriage. "The citizen K-ev is endowed with a primitive, rudimentary personality. He is a brute with immediate and unsophisticated reactions to his environment . . . His self-infatuation, his adoration of his own body, are betrayed by every move he makes. The inflating of his chest and his periodic magnanimous smiles further corroborate his psychological infantilism." Finally, K-ev's restiveness, cynicism, and coarseness suggested a mechanism of "supercompensation. There is, for example, the perpetrator's fondness for blood and raw meat, suggesting an atavistic, primeval personality. A preponderance of the instinctual over all else is evident." At the end of the day K-ev was chastised and "put under surveillance," but not "isolated."[124]

The lightness of his punishment resulted from the juridical version of the solar-eclipse line of defense. Experts summoned to court had concluded that "a low impulse [*nizmennoe pobuzhdenie*] triggered K-ev's crime—the discharge of tensions that had built up over a long period. The impulse had traveled by the shortest path, circumventing the personality," creating a sort of a psychic "short circuit." K-ev had reverted to an instinctual state, and even as he was mutilating his wife he was beside himself, "unaware of what he was doing [*nevmeniiaemyi*]." It stood to reason that had he been healthy the worker-student would have assimilated his wife's superior consciousness and successfully transcended his bodily drives.[125]

The court went further in exculpating R-na's attacker: it implicated her in the crime. R-na was a "bourgeois young lady who never had to attend the school of physical labor and was quite spoiled by a careless existence. Depraved beyond measure, she had sought in her husband a man capable of satisfying her voracious sexual appetite." She had taken advantage of his naiveté to awaken a primeval lust he had nearly extinguished. The depravity of the victim (an intelligentsia female) was to be expected; the depravity of the perpetrator (a proletarian male) was the unfortunate result of degeneration. Clearly, there was a good deal of ambivalence in the court's assessment of the two parties: it contrasted a pure but brainless male with a perverse but resourceful female. The crude worker, the noble savage, had had to conquer his intelligentsia wife because he needed her consciousness; conversely, she had ostensibly entertained something like a rape fantasy because she envied his elemental proletarian energy.[126]

The erotic violence naturalized in police protocols and in Gumilevskii's novel simultaneously articulated and obfuscated the structure of the Communist eschatological narrative. A true worker (male) had to transcend (here "sublimate") his fundamental psychological traits, which had been absorbed through tedious, continuous, physical labor. Conversely, the bourgeois (female), desperate for sexual gratification, needed to attach a body of a worker to her mind. All this had a long philosophical pedigree. Ludwig Feuerbach, a seminal influence on Marx, had maintained that eschatological fulfillment would follow the unification of a nonabstract "suffering heart" with a "head" that possessed the universality of reason.[127] Or, in Marx's own formulation, proletarian emancipation required both an "idea" and a "material force that would embody it."[128]

The logic of the solar-eclipse line of defense clearly penetrated Communist legal theory insofar as the latter evaluated not discrete actions as such but the "personality of the culprit taken in all its complexity." In elaborating on the conditions that rendered a culprit not responsible for his actions, articles 24 and 25 of the penal code acknowledged that a culprit's mind could have been in a "twilight condition" *(sumerechnoe sostoianie)*. Even when the culprit's behavior was "goal oriented," it could still have been "unpremeditated."

When "breakdown of mental functioning" *(dushevnoe rasstroistvo)* was established as a legal concept in the 1920s, Soviet jurists believed that an individual did not necessarily lose the comprehension of what one was doing *(libertas judicii)*, but that it was possible to lose the capacity to make a choice between various courses of action *(libertas consilii)*. The distinction between "insanity"—a condition that assumed that "consciousness was muddled"—and "compulsion" corroborated the thesis that in the Communist view of the self, consciousness and will were two discrete components. To be guilty, a comrade had at one and the same time to be conscious of evil and to choose evil deliberately.[129]

Acknowledging the possibility that students might lose their minds and allow themselves to be driven by their baser instincts did not mean that the Communists approved of this condition. A man driven by his raw energies was not the New Man but a degenerate, a bourgeois persona. Hence Gumilevskii's denunciation of Khokhorin's tyrannical body. In principle, Khokhorin's health could be restored if his animalistic forces could be defeated and his Bolshevik consciousness—the consciousness that had once earned him Party admission—reestablished.

Gumilevskii's novel can be read as a literary treatment of the solar-eclipse line of defense. Elaborated by Soviet literature and legal theory, the physiological explanation of the solar eclipse endowed a defense strategy central to Party hermeneutics of the 1920s with scientific legitimacy. To blame the body and excuse the mind was more than a rhetorical maneuver. It was in essence a scientific argument. Eventually, when the solar eclipse disappeared from Soviet psychology, it also disappeared from the Communist hermeneutics of the soul. At that point, nothing could any longer mitigate guilt.

The Rehabilitation of the Mind

Was the human psyche an object or a subject of the Revolution? The third and final part of Gumilevskii's novel, which consists of Burov's sexual edification and Korolev's eulogy over Vera's open grave, addresses this key question head on. Gumilevskii proclaims the New Man to be master of his own body, not the other way around. He demotes Khokhorin, the self-styled candidate for New Manhood, from the leadership of the university's Party organization and elevates Korolev, a student who is well aware of the importance of consciousness as a bulwark against excessive sexuality.

The question of consciousness highlighted a basic difficulty with materialist reductionism. Materialist theory could not be consistently naturalistic and at the same time preach sexual restraint. Prescriptive, it had to invoke social conventions, not the state of nature. The whole point about sublimation was that it resisted nature and tamed it rather than going along with it. As a process unique to humans, one that diverted the natural flow of instinctual energy, sublimation could not be explained in naturalistic terms. Because it served a purpose, sublimation could not be an unintended product of routine organic functioning.[130] Sublimation brought intentionality into Soviet materialism through a back door. Discredited concepts such as "purpose" and "will" were needed to explain why Bobrokov succeeded where Khokhorin had failed.

Physiology came under attack by the Bolshevik scientific establishment because of its lack of interest in the social aspect of human existence and the concomitant premeditated planning of collective life. The psychologist M. Velikovskii complained that those scientists who "deal with questions of class organization through bizarre notions such as the 'reflex of purpose' or the 'reflex of freedom' leave it unclear as to what was the referent of the term 'reflex' here."[131] Equally unlikely was the match between "instincts" and intentionality. One contemporary sexologist did ask: "What is the 'purpose' of human instincts?"[132] And another even attempted to talk in almost Lamarckian terms of "acquired instincts," by which he meant instincts that had been socialized. Both formulations were groping toward a resolution of the contradiction between the teleology assumed within the notion of purpose, and the blind causality implied by the notion of the instinct. Since instinct was an innate, not an acquired, property, however, there was no choice but finally to admit that "there can be no social instincts, only social habits."[133]

Implying the existence of culture, a modification of the instinctual basis of humanity, "habits" exploded the physiological picture of man. If men were to be able to rearrange instincts purposefully, the psyche had to be defined as qualitatively, and not merely quantitatively, different from the instincts. Behaviorism reached a dead end on this point. Its analytic tools had proven sufficient to show that the notion of the psyche had to include a material dimension. But the radical ambition of reducing all psychological processes to the realm of the material collapsed when it became apparent that such reductionism did not leave space for intentionality.

The vicissitudes in the prestige of intentionality in the 1920s reflected the contemporary Marxist debate between the mechanists and the dialecticians. There were two broad methodological issues at stake. The first issue involved the meaning of the order of causality, that is, causality as an interaction of forces working themselves out toward resolution (the position of the mechanists), versus the causality of events organized and directed by man (the position of the dialecticians). The second issue addressed the nature of evolution in general. The mechanistic conception of development saw events as proceeding along a linear trajectory; the emphasis on the importance of inheritance and instinctual characteristics, prevalent in mechanistic circles, served to reinforce its determinism: the future was a direct projection of the past. In the broadest sense, the passivity of the organism in relation to its surroundings was a direct function of the attempt to explain human behavior in biological terms alone and of the exclusion of such proximal causes as man's thoughts. The dialectical point of view, on the other hand, saw evolution as a discontinuous chain of development, involving periods of crisis and revolution, which produced sudden, fundamental changes in the organization of the elements in the system. The subjective intentions of man were a factor here, and in many cases the prime cause of leaps from one stage to another.[134]

In taking on the question of the proper relation between necessity and freedom, Gumilevskii captured an important shift in the Soviet discourse. Industrialization had been on the agenda since the Fourteenth Party Congress (December 1925), and revolutionary transformations had to be accelerated. If the resumption of the proletarian Revolution was to be justified, scientists had to show that an autonomous, more active subject had come into existence to support it. The importance of consciousness had to be reasserted at the expense of sexuality—the locus of the instinct and of a cleavage between the individual and the collective. Man was being called on to become his own master, a subject of history and not its object.

The behaviorist-mechanistic picture of man was rejected along with the NEP as "overly fatalistic." Dialecticians articulated the need for a person who was able not only to adjust to reality but actually to revolutionize it.[135] One Bolshevik dialectician derided mechanism thus: "Some argue that the New Man will come on its own, created by the socialist economic order. Why bother, they ask. Time will pass, and the dirt will come off on its own. Pushing such arguments to their logical conclusion, one may say that capitalism will die off on its own and Communism will come without any human intervention." This was a cardinal sin: "In essence, such 'orthodox Marxists' deny Revolution . . . Unfortunately the old does not die on its own . . . The New Man has to be struggled for."[136] Developing this thought, another dialectician maintained that "if we want to dodge the fatalist deviation, we have to acknowledge that the laws of subjectivity participate in the objective laws of history."[137]

With the advent of Abram Deborin's dialectical school in the late 1920s and the concomitant discrediting of mechanism in the prestigious philosophy department of the Institute of Red Professors, objectivist physiology was denounced.[138] The Party accused mechanism (associated now with Bukharin's Right Opposition, which rejected intervention in economics) of trying to explain all phenomena in terms of the "twin concepts of equilibrium and adaptation," a framework that was said to produce a passive, mechanical view of man.[139] Speaking at the Socialist Academy, one expert went so far as to claim that mechanism supported the relations of exploitation. "Insofar as objectivist psychology . . . posits no intrinsic link between the thinking of workers and their labor process, thereby presenting a 'soulless' [obezdushennaia] and 'senseless' [obessmyslennaia] picture of workers' activity, it legitimizes workers' alienation."[140]

As early as the mid-1920s physiologism had come under heavy criticism. Indeed, the pejorative term "Enchmenism" was coined to ridicule the "vulgar materialism" of the Opposition.[141] Official Party theorists such as P. Sapozhnikov warned that "Pavlov's materialism and Bekhterev's reflexology are attempts to replace Marxism with something else." Debunking Enchmenism (and de facto rehabilitating Descartes), Bukharin posited the existence of two separate orders of phenomena: "those that have an extension and those that cannot be felt, seen, or measured."[142] To a large degree, Enchmen acquired notoriety as a pseudoscientist because of the suggested linkage between his theories and political heterodoxy. To be sure, by the time of the New Course Discussion (1923–24), which witnessed Trotsky's onslaught on "the bureaucratism of the apparatus," Enchmen was already dead. Yet Enchmenism was linked with the Opposition because Enchmen had criticized the "insufficiently radical" philosophy of the old Party guard. The supporters of the Central Committee claimed that Enchmenism was embraced by the petit-bourgeois student Communist cells. In one of the most vitriolic attacks, Enchmenites were condemned as "arch-individualists." It was alleged that in several universities in the capitals Enchmen followers, labeled "Echmeniata," had formed clubs of "Teenbists" (the acronym for supporters of the Theory of New Biology).[143]

The assumed link between Enchmenism and student Oppositionism discredited the proponents of physiologism.[144] An article in *Pravda* noted that the fashionable tendency to explain relations between the sexes as purely instinctual "has already been proposed by Enchmen, who completely denied the reality of the psychological process." The fruit of such an explanatory tendency—"the theoretical expulsion of the psychological state in the name of a physiological reflex and the practical expulsion of the psychical and the emotional from student life"—was blamed for the "Enchmenization of the everyday." Enchmenism was held to have inspired "simplificationism," "vulgarizationism," and "mechanistic materialism."[145] In representing his main hero as a lascivious degenerate, Gumilevskii expressed an official diagnosis that Trotskyism was a form of lapsed Marxism. Through the image of the depraved Khokhorin, he criticized not only student political beliefs but also the scientific notions that legitimized them. The view that sexual indulgence secured health and happiness—the crux of Khokhorin's entire physiologist worldview—was henceforth tainted by its association with the Opposition.

The demise of Enchmenism and mechanist physiology, and the affirmation of dialectics and "autogenetic movement," resulted in the establishment of psychology as a science independent of physiology. Beyond becoming the norm of conduct of the ideal Soviet citizen, purposive action now became the central preoccupation of Soviet science. Subjective factors were pronounced accessible to study and endowed with autonomous regularity. The concept of the reflex, the basis for the construction of human action as a passive response to the environment, came under heavy fire. The new conception of the psyche was directly tied to action, not reaction. In the dialectical view, the most important function of the psyche was to free man from the constraints of his immediate situation, and to permit him to direct his actions toward goals that lay beyond him. If sense was to be made of the notion of the Revolution as a purposeful change in the human condition, a preliminary awareness of the goal of action had to be presumed in the revolutionary agent.[146] Russian psychological subjectivism, which had never been entirely abandoned, even during the early 1920s, was given new life. As the NEP folded, the old theories gained increasing prominence and legitimacy.

Gumilevskii spells out the necessary adjustments in the Bolshevik theory of the psyche in the pivotal encounter between Khokhorin and Burov near the end of the novel. As the episode begins, Burov notices that he and Khokhorin have a "shockingly similar handwriting." The implication is that Burov, the sexually obsessed professor, is in many ways Khokhorin's alter ego. Khokhorin puts a cigarette into his mouth and, "intoxicated by it and the beer he has drunk" (i.e., overwhelmed by his bodily sensations), invites Burov to have a frank conversation. Yet this is not the same confident Khokhorin we have met at the beginning of the story. He has begun to question his belief system. Because Burov is a scientist, the conversation takes a very learned turn.

> "Tell me, Fedor Fedorovich," Khokhorin opens, "do you know what brings you down in our eyes, what undoes you as a scientist?"
> "It would have been strange had I not noticed what others do . . . "
> "But if you are conscious of it . . . ?!"
> "How naive you are! Voltaire was an atheist, did not believe in God or in the devil, and ridiculed religious prejudices. But he used to get really upset when he saw three candles and steered clear of cats that crossed the street. The upper consciousness is one thing, and the unconscious, where instincts reign, is something completely different. What takes place in the sphere of upper consciousness I can follow as well as anyone else, of course!"

Khokhorin is confused. "'Bifurcated personalities . . . otherness? This is rubbish. In your view, who then commands whom?" he asks Burov. "It's a struggle," the latter replies, "a constant struggle—consciousness and instincts do not always live together peacefully."

Halfheartedly, Khokhorin attempts a last defense of physiology. "I think the struggle with instincts is a mistake, since they are natural—an unnatural instinct is a contradiction in terms. One should simply obey one's instincts and satisfy them." But Burov, very up-to-date regarding current research, debunks his theory and argues that sexuality is only one component of the psyche and must be integrated into a coherent whole (pp. 74–81).

Reisner also sought a theory that would account for the essential unity of the mind, torn since Plato between three faculties—sensation, will, and reason. "Sensations are inseparable from reason," this developmental psychologist argued. "When the two combine, the will is born."[147] But as the deterioration of Burov's own mind clearly shows, this ideal scenario did not always materialize. A sick mind could be cleft into separate components. "It is quite possible that the neural complex of personality and the mechanism of the sexual drive operate separately. They can even enter into conflict." At such a time, either instinct or personality prevailed, depending on which was stronger.[148] According to this view, the specificity of the sexual instinct arose because the "instinct resides not in the conscious but in the unconscious sphere, and it is up to our consciousness to take it over and control it."[149] No longer an obedient servant of the instincts but acting as a strong check upon them, consciousness had clearly become an irreducible concept.[150]

The distinction between "symbol" and "sign" underlay the contrast psychologists drew between man, a creature that operates with symbols that convey the meaning of its action, and the bee, which uses signals that are mere extensions of its physiological organization. Whereas bees, being limited to the use of signals alone, can never intentionally alter their behavior, humans can do so through the use of symbols, conventional signs that can be changed. Arguing that human activity was based "not merely on signals but also on symbols," Reisner and other erstwhile behaviorists came close to admitting that the human condition was unique.[151] Indeed, the fact that Reisner resorted to symbols, his reflexological sympathies notwithstanding, was one other symptom of the failure of Soviet physiology to account for all human phenomena in terms of signs that automatically come with the instinctual apparatus. Symbols came to the fore with the importance given to intentional aspects of human behavior involved with the Five-Year Plan. Intention, the ability to invent something new, assumes language, dialogue, shared meaning—in short, human communality; a shared vocabulary of malleable symbols becomes crucial to all these constituents.

The writings of Soviet psychologists from the mid to late 1920s elaborated the new, less reductionist view of consciousness in great detail. Linking the notion of consciousness with the capacity of the central nervous system for "deliberate attention" *(proizvol'noe vnimanie),* Luriia, now a major expert on conflicts within the psychological apparatus, explained that we are recipients of a great number of internal and external stimulants. Had we always given all stimuli equal attention, he went on, our conduct would have looked like a set of chaotic motions carried out by disjointed organs. "We would not have been able to deal with . . . the demands of labor. Life in society and the imperative to focus on the socially significant stimulations demand that we respond not to the most intense stimuli but to the most significant ones."[152] According to Zalkind, consciousness—a superreflex that integrated reflexive chains and brought them under a central control—assumed the existence of an aim. "If the core of the brain is to be controlled, the content, stability, and fluctuation of the mind have to be mastered by what we may call a 'supper-reflex of purposefulness' [*tseleustremlennost'*]." To shorten this theoretical term, Zalkind drew on the concept of the "dominanta," a system that determined the goal of the body's activity.[153]

Prince Ukhtomskii, a prerevolutionary neurophysiologist who had accepted the Revolution and become a teacher at Petrograd University in 1919, defined the dominanta as "the dominant reflex, which sets itself in opposition to other reflectological chains, takes command of the entire reflectological apparatus, and inhibits bodily responses to stimuli."[154] Dominanta, a term that Ukhtomskii admitted he had borrowed from Richard Avenarius, a German physiologist once castigated by Lenin for "idealism," made human responses depend not only on external stimulation but also on the central nervous system (the brain).[155] "The dominanta controls the brain," Zalkind commented. "It attracts the majority of excitations, represses those that enter into a contradiction with it, and absorbs their energy. All processes which the dominanta does not steer pale, wilt or slow down. By contrast, all processes that do fall under its command accelerate, become more resilient and more persistent."[156]

To be sure, efforts continued to be made to interpret consciousness physiologically. In explaining how man learned to yoke his body to a higher purpose Zalkind insisted on the reinterpretation of consciousness as a "conditioned reflex." The brain core "becomes a complex of reflexes that may produce a 'psychic' impact on the body . . . A change in the environment impacts the refractory chain and through the operation of conditioned reflexes affects the bodily functions."[157] Continuing in this key, Kashkadamov contended that "we have to distinguish between the hereditary lower reflexes residing in the lower and middle layers of the brain and the very complicated reflexes residing in the core of the human brain." In this scheme, consciousness became a "compounded reflex that permits self-awareness."[158]

In describing consciousness as a "reflex," albeit a special one, Zalkind and Kashkadamov hoped to narrow the gap between consciousness and the instincts. Yet the distinction between "conditioned" and "unconditioned" reflexes that was now forced upon them could not but impose a qualitative difference between instinct and consciousness. Consciousness was henceforth a "superreflex," a unique reflex that somehow had a "purpose" and a "rationality." The attempt to reduce consciousness to something more basic failed. Summarizing these scientific endeavors, contemporary scientists admitted that their success was only partial and that "while the hypothesis regarding superreflexes is acceptable in itself, it still fails to explain . . . all the workings of the mind."[159]

If man was to be studied as an "active agent," the problem of that archmentalist notion, the "will," could not be avoided. The literary critic G. Iakubovskii praised the will as the organism's "executive committee."[160] A notion such as "will," argued Mikhail Basov, an important developmental psychologist, became indispensable when the scientist had to account for the conglomerate of conscious, purposeful actions fully compliant to the acting subject. Whereas instinctual acts are carried out in a predetermined and uniform manner, the mechanism of will makes us capable not only of responding to immediate stimulations but also of taking into account the past and, to an extent, of determining the future. In order to identify the distinctive aspects of willful acts Basov advanced the following three-tiered "structural analysis of behavior":

> (1) The elementary behavioral process: This consists of a simple chain of contiguous but unconnected acts. The purely external continuity of this process results from the sequentiality of its discrete acts. Utterly unconnected to willful action, it unfolds only because new external or internal stimulations constantly arrive and demand, regardless of the previous stimuli, an appropriate reaction. [See Figure 1.]

1. The elementary behavioral process (M. Basov, "Volia," in *Bol'shaia Sovetskaia entsiklopediia,* 13: 106)

(2) The associative-determined process: This more sophisticated process is that in which the continuity of behavior is not merely external but results from an organic link between the acts that, sharing a common meaning, influence one another. Taken as a whole, however, this type of process remains arbitrary. Having no aim . . . or plan, it does not involve our will. Since every discrete action is linked with the preceding one only by association, the noncontiguous acts may have nothing in common . . . Given this mode of organization, neither the subject nor the outside observer can predict what this process will amount to and how it will end. Thus a man can give himself away to the freefloating images that populate his memory, images that, linking up one to another, carry him into a remote past at one moment and return him to the present at the next. [See Figure 2.]

2. The associative-determined process (M. Basov, "Volia," in *Bol'shaia Sovetskaia entsiklopediia*, 13: 108)

(3) The apperceptive-determined process: This process subsumes all those processes that take place when a man sets himself a goal. It is to this category that "willful processes" [*volevye protsessy*] belong. Here discrete acts do not have to be sequential in order to be connected—every act is connected to the preceding and the following act not only locally but also through the intervention of a basic, central stimulation that fulfills the role of a "determining factor" . . . that introduces order into our behavior. [See Figure 3.]

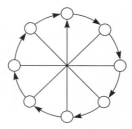

3. The apperceptive-determined process (M. Basov, "Volia," in *Bol'shaia Sovetskaia entsiklopediia*, 13: 110)

What was crucial here is that, in cases of willful behavior, according to Basov, contiguous acts linked up not sequentially, from first to last, but in the opposite order. Will, in other words, went hand in hand with teleology and so with intentionality and meaning.[161]

The ambivalent position of the will in a system of thought that otherwise tolerated only objective interpretation of its notions reflected a tension between strictly deterministic materialism, according to which human agency was historically determined, and the official aspiration to create a free revolutionary subject. Admitting that will usually went hand in hand with a "subjective sense of freedom of behavior," Semashko hastened to contain the implications of the resuscitation of human freedom, which brought up the specter of idealism in Bolshevik minds. "We all know that, objectively, not even the hypercritical personality can divert the wheels of history. But subjectively," he insisted, "a person remains 'free.' Historical reality is constructed from the combination of the so-called 'free acts of will.'"[162]

Unless young Communists cultivated a will, psychologists warned, "the instinct would pose a threat to their well-being."[163] The will had to be carefully nurtured, disciplined, and taught so that it would be able to "rise above instincts and take control of them."[164] "Restraint is an act of will. It leads to victory over oneself, over one's excitations and one's temptations." The struggle against oneself forges one's "character"—another mentalist notion with a long pedigree in Western ethics that could no longer be ignored.[165] The country, Lass pronounced, needed individuals with a strong "will" and a strong "character."[166] "Gymnastics of the will" was highly recommended so that will could be brought into accord with rationality. A strong will, specialists explained, linking one mentalist notion to another, "has to go in tandem with the intellect."[167]

Now that "will" had elbowed the "soma" (from the Greek word for body) out of the limelight, the notion of personality *(lichnost')* was also partially rehabilitated. For a long time "personality" had been condemned as an idealist notion through and through. Bogdanov had defined personality as a small particle of the "living tissue of the organism" and claimed that "its subjectivism only proves how limited a thing that is."[168] Whereas the anarchists, so the argument went, assigned precedence to personality, bestowing upon it qualities such as "uniqueness" or "creativity," a proper Marxist had to reject such individualistic virtues. Soviet experts prided themselves on the conviction that "personality," far from being an individual expression, was "socially conditioned and absorbed the values of the class to which the person belonged."[169]

Deployed to encourage collectivism and to show the link between individual destiny and class, this argument eventually backfired. By putting personality second to the objective material conditions that determined it, Marxists ended up with a notion of a subject that could not swim against the current. If a subject capable of creative action was to be constructed, "personality" had to regain autonomy from the environment. A locus of subjecthood, the agency able to affect material reality, not just obey it, was badly needed. A Leningrad youth newspaper bemoaned in 1926 what it called "the effacement of personality" and demanded a "focus on that which is personal within us."[170] "I hope that socialism, superseding its initial, collectivist phase, will reinstate the idea of personality and encourage it," Gel'man remarked. "We need a synthesis between the personal and the social."[171]

Applying himself to the task of saving the proletariat from a herd mentality, Reisner attempted to remove the theoretical ambivalence inherent in Marxist discourse by isolating the individualistic, antisocial sense of personality and relegating it to the domain of the strictly "individual" (*individual'noe*). As an alternative, Reisner proposed the notion of the "personal" (*lichnoe*), which was to be wholly socialized. "The 'individual' and the 'person' should not be confounded. An individual concentrates only on his base, animal needs, his habits, and herd drives all in defiance of 'will.' A person, on the other hand, is a socially organized unit that is immersed in the social and that carries out tasks on behalf of the collective." Furthermore, argued Reisner, users of the term "personality" had to distinguish between "personality as such" and "conscious personality." Here he made an ingenious reference to the highest Party authority. "In his writing and speeches, Lenin always came back to the issue of 'consciousness.' A thousand times over he stressed the need for a conscious mode of thinking, contrasting it with the unconscious spontaneity of the masses." In the proposed interpretation of Lenin, "spontaneity" (*stikhiinost'*) was loosely identified with the realm of the instinctual. "Consciousness," by contrast, was "a crucial proletarian weapon." From this, it followed that one of the greatest tasks of Communist politics was to transform toilers into "conscious personalities" capable of functioning as "independent actors in the socialist construction."[172]

How was personality to be scientifically defined? Most psychologists acknowledged that Kornilov's archreductionist definition—a "lump of protoplasm"—was too simplistic.[173] For the Marxists who adhered to psychophysical monism but who wanted to introduce some intentionality into their theory, "personality" denoted a "unitary complex that united physical and psychic attributes."[174] Ukhtomskii met the challenge through the concept of the "other" as an "independent essence . . . Only when he recognizes the person of the other," he argued, "does one deserve to be spoken of as a person himself."[175]

"Personality" received a comprehensive defense within the Marxist framework. "In our everyday speech," Doctor Vladimirskii wrote, "the personal and the social present themselves as mutually exclusive." An act performed for the sake of society was typically construed as a personal sacrifice. Frequently, the concept of the "large personality" was associated with "limitless egotism, a sharp disassociation from one's surroundings, upon which one feeds, parasitically." Vladimirskii saw it differently: "In my understanding, the fullest development of the personality actually coincides with the highest manifestation of sociability." According to this expert a complete, harmonious personality could not exist without a manifest social component. In fact, a growing indifference to society was the first sign of the disintegration of personality. "Antisocial behavior indicates an onset of mental illness." Vladimirskii assigned a positive meaning to personality, similar to that suggested by Reisner. Although he found it difficult to foresee how far personality could grow, it was still "obvious even to one who is not a philosopher" that personality could expand beyond the body, beyond physical individuality. Indeed, the possibility of such extension appeared to Vladimirskii to be the very essence of personality.[176] Vladimirskii posited four stages in the evolution of the personality. Type A was the "primitive personality." Its concerns did not extend beyond the body. Such a personality belonged to individuals interested in nothing but their physical well-being and the satisfaction of their instinctual needs. Type B was more complicated. "Consider the mother who stayed all night next to the bed of her sick child. She was not sacrificing herself, since it was her own personality that compelled her to behave in this manner." In type C, the personality was expanded further. Here Vladimirskii gave the example of national sentiment, which could prompt an individual to put his life in jeopardy in the name of his ethnic group. The pinnacle of this peculiar ladder was personality type D, referred to as the "ideally expanded personality." Its interests were coextensive with the interests of all humanity. The archetype of personality of this kind resided in the "wonderful legend of the human God who sacrifices himself to atone for the sins of humanity as a whole." The personality of the "free man"—a New Man, of course—"is the pinnacle of human development." In the ideal society there was to be no contradiction between personality and society. In the highest state of consciousness, "one who satisfies the personal benefits the social."[177] To attain that state of bliss, continued the psychologist A. Makarov, "we have to harmonize the human collective and the human 'I' without the former crushing the latter, so that the collective will be able to benefit from the inherent capabilities of its members." The New Man had to be "not a contemplating, egotistical, self-absorbed man . . . but an active person with an intense will."[178] In Semashko's formulation, "consciousness and personality had to unite in a physiopsychic 'I.'"[179]

In the process of demonstrating how the intentional and the subjective could be reintegrated into a Marxist theory of man, Soviet thinkers presented an elaborate critique of reflexology.[180] Professor Semen Sem'-kovskyi, a philosopher, faulted this approach for adopting the position of "Spinozism," according to which the psychological played no role in determining the physical. In this reading of the history of philosophy, it was Spinoza's use of the concept of "substance" that was problematic, since by "substance" Sem'kovskyi understood an entity that was not just material, but "material and psychological at one and the same time. In fact, Spinoza's substance has endless 'attributes,' of which we know only two— the material attribute and the psychic attribute." In his philosophy of mind "everything is bifurcated." The result, according to Sem'kovskyi, was not a "psychophysiological monism" but a "dualism," allowing what Spinoza regarded as two equal points of view on substance. Schematically, this position—one that Sem'kovskyi alleged had been adopted by the Menshevik Georgii Plekhanov—could be represented in the following way:

$$A \longrightarrow B \longrightarrow C$$
$$a \longrightarrow b \longrightarrow c$$

Capital letters stand for physical phenomena, lowercase letters for psychological phenomena. The chart indicates that the lowercase row—the psychological—is construed merely as a reflection of the upper. Thus Plekhanov's Menshevik view of the mind, a view that was characterized by

Sem'kovskyi as "reflexologism," was said to have postulated "psychophysical parallelism."[181]

Sem'kovskyi's primary interest was to show that in the reflexological theory of man the psyche was superfluous. Even if it was explicitly discussed, the psyche did not participate in determining material (i.e., real) processes and thus could be dispensed with. According to Sem'kovskyi, Engels became the father of the new science of the psyche. Unlike the reflexologists, Engels never divided the psychological and physical into two separate tiers. Rather, "Engels postulated a gradation of forms. 'Consciousness' was one form of energy; 'thought' another." Approving of this science of man, which was monist but not reductive, Sem'kovskyi represented Engels' position thus:

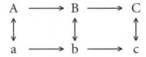

In Engels' theory of man, the psychological became a full participant in the determination of reality. To be sure, it was endowed with a material form and construed as "energy." But disguised or not, it reappeared as a factor qualitatively different from rudimentary physiological processes taking place in the human body. The ascent from matter to consciousness, Engels was said to have argued, was a qualitative (dialectical) leap, not an incremental improvement.[182]

The Imperative of Sexual Restraint

The revised theory of mind reviewed above is more or less the same as the one Gumilevskii sets forth through Burov—after all, Burov is a scientist. Clearly, he knows something Khokhorin does not, namely, that in order to produce a properly functioning organism the lower drives have to be carefully governed. Tediously and meticulously, Burov explains to Khokhorin that the body contains a multitude of instincts—reflexive chains with contradictory tendencies. In their original chaotic form, he says, instincts can lead only to destruction. It is therefore crucial that the individual form a unifying principle, a "psyche" that consolidates instincts and makes them a part of a purposeful chain of command. Burov's lecture to Khokhorin reads like a reformulation of Sem'kovskyi's position: both agreed that a sense of purpose, an integration of the organism to serve the larger society, was needed. As their conversation progresses, Burov denounces Khokhorin's pretense to scientism: "Superficial knowledge of biological sciences sometimes leads to conclusions such as yours . . . that everything is simple, satisfied by sexual intercourse and that is it! . . . The relative simplicity of the sexual exchange between simple organisms becomes much more complicated in humans. In the latter case, human emotion is enriched by various visual and spiritual balances, producing the specific aroma of a personality." Gumilevskii's scientist goes on, couching moralistic notions in heavy, hyperscientific language: "In the case of a coupling that is accidental, unjustified by the fullness of feeling . . . one is only partially satisfied. Separation of the various components of the sexual act is not only a vice and a disaster, but also a psychological malady! A tangled web of needs, feelings, and sensations . . . becomes disjointed and gives rise to tormenting internal chaos . . . My self-destructive obsession with Vera, as you noted yourself, reached a very high pitch. It led to acts that escaped the control of my higher consciousness" (pp. 76–77). Here Gumilevskii mentions a bunch of open bottles lying around—a token of Burov's intoxication and dissipation. Burov teaches the novel's hero an unequivocal lesson: lust has to be inhibited. Or, as an expert put it, "Tragedies happen because . . . sexuality, instead of being contained, is decided by us, that is, not by us, but by our sexual element."[183]

This last phrase is highly symptomatic of the equivocation with which radical psychology wrestled with the identity of the emancipated subject. Who was supposed to emancipate himself, and from whom? Should the subject's positive, material instincts emancipate themselves from the idealistic and bourgeois ego? Or should it be the other way around, with the subject's conscious ego emancipating itself from the blind instincts? In urging Khokhorin to employ his mind to discipline his body, Gumilevskii clearly tilts the scales in favor of the second position. His writing echoes experts who wished to "condition the youth to respect the mind," and to have the body "controlled by newly created restraining centers."[184]

Gumilevskii's own position is best expressed in Korolev's eulogy to Vera, the victim of Burov's sexual obsession. This eulogy praises "will," "personality," and "consciousness" and condemns unrestricted sex, individualism, and physiological reductionism: "Comrades," Korolev opens, "the meaning of the proletarian revolution is the awakening of human personality! . . .

Naked animal sensations that evoke our primordial beastliness can only lead humans back to the Stone Age. They are the root of evil . . . Hiding behind what they call the materialist understanding of history, Khokhorin and his like . . . reduce the richness of human personality to nothing but mechanism to satisfy natural needs. The tomb before us shows where this attitude leads . . . Sexual depravity undermines our physical and our psychic powers, poisons our will, and leads us into a blind alley. Sexual restraint, resistance to one's pure sexual instinct, a comradely attitude toward the woman one loves—this should be the highest Communist ideal of sexual relations" (pp. 201–205).

While Khokhorin erroneously couches his theory of sexual revolution in terms of the health of an individual organism, Korolev shifts the emphasis from the primacy of a proletarian individual to the primacy of the proletarian collective. In this he echoes those who recommended "sexual maturity," defined as a "coordination" between sexual life and public activity in the lives of Communist youngsters.[185] Alongside the training of the body, experts pronounced, "it is important to develop the child's character, the strength of his will, the consciousness of his responsibility."[186] If, for Khokhorin, the new society is an aggregate of sexually emancipated individuals with an equal right to orgasm, for Kovalev, who announces the new orthodoxy, it is a society in which individuals fit into a larger whole, which must always take precedence. An example of a sentiment that takes a step in the direction of the collective is "love," which Khokhorin steadfastly denies by mistakenly thinking it unscientific. "Do you know what love is?" Burov asks Gumilevskii's hero at one point toward the end of the novel. "Khokhorin shrugs his shoulders, 'I think I have a clear idea of that.' Burov leans toward him: 'Love is a great creative force. Many works of art and deeds of heroism have been achieved thanks to its force.' 'But you . . . ' Khokhorin tries to protest. 'You—in Vera's case?' Burov calmly raises his hand to interrupt him: 'It only means that my attitude toward this girl is not love!'" (pp. 74–78).

Khokhorin advocates sexual promiscuity because it ensures health and prevents the dyadic attachments that threaten exclusive loyalty to the Party. "Love always sins," many young Bolsheviks said, "in that, absorbing the thoughts and feelings of the 'two loving hearts,' it at the same time isolates, separates off the loving pair from the group."[187] Love was defined as "egotism for two," a bourgeois aberration whereby "one member of a collective is preferred to everybody else."[188] Student questionnaires had the following to say about love:

"I do not acknowledge love. It is simply a matter of habit, becoming accustomed to one person."

"I believe that love is a certain psychological condition. Every individual manifests it differently, depending on his development, but its basis lies in the desire for the continuation of the species."

"Discarding the bourgeois mystical shell, I believe love is the strongest bond between two individuals of the opposite sexes and should consist of sexual attraction."

Lass summarized these findings by noting that "our student youth often denies love's existence and poorly understands its psychological underpinnings."[189] Dismayed by student views, sexologists warned that such an approach to love "may bring more suffering than joy. When unrestrained, rash attraction is indiscriminately satisfied, the entire affair becomes squalid and ugly."[190] Sigal explained to the young that "no matter how sexually close a couple is, its cohabitation will turn into hell if it is not enlightened by a spiritual harmony."[191]

The notion of romantic love was brought back into favor. The new orthodoxy maintained that a "purely sexual act can never gratify a genuinely conscious person."[192] The updated "dialectical" view posited that "love is actually a very complicated group of conditional reflexes that permits us to derive pleasure from an object"; these reflexes were important because they were "permanent."[193] Now it was possible to speak about "gradations of love," from "bestial" to "noble," depending on the "weight of the spiritual element in the sentiment in question."[194]

Gumilevskii has Burov hint that Khokhorin's disdain for love is self-deluding. The novelist clearly agreed with the view that "while classes vary in their attitude toward love, it does not follow that the proletariat should prefer crude, animal satisfaction to warm, comradely ties." Soviet psychologists now blamed the "self-absorbed" intelligentsia for claiming that "a worker is a soulless, stern beast that is incapable of feelings."[195] They declared that the true emotional tie between two proletarians was not a blind, instinctual liaison along the lines of Khokhorin's or Burov's relationship with Vera, but a "conscious love," much like the steady relations that a Korolev would form.

Whether love was a "Platonic idea" or a "biological need" was now opened to reexamination.[196] Zalkind posited that in order for love to promote "happiness, the physical attraction and sexual desire must be coupled with spiritual closeness. No longer an everyday affair, love can only become more precious."[197] True love was considered possible only between a couple that shared the same level of development. A model proletarian student put it thus: "Moral considerations led me to pursue sexual partners whose consciousness was equal to mine."[198]

A strong psyche, "our savior from selfishness," could help students learn how to integrate themselves into society. "Those who obsequiously bow to the invincible power of sex are mistaken," wrote Gel'man. "Man is no animal; he is capable of controlling his drives. The will of the individual can influence the darkest among his instincts and inject them with meaning." The unrestrained sexuality of revolutionaries like Khokhorin reflected retrograde ideology that many Communists had yet to rid themselves of. "The old psychology still rests solidly in the depths of our only partially enlightened consciousness." Indifference toward future sexual organization and sexual morals, Gel'man admitted, "is a significant lacuna in the thought of the ideologues who prepared our Revolution." Gel'man declared that the old psychological makeup had to be reshaped. Rationalizing the expanded sphere of medical intervention was in his eyes a prerequisite for that. "The task of preparing the psychology of the New Man for the New World opens an enormous field for intervention in human sexual life." Special enlightenment work, "forging moral consciousness" was supposed to mediate the relationship between the sexes, "make them more genuine, more normal . . . Sexual mores of the future have to reconcile the interests of the individual with the interests of the race."[199]

That he used class and race interchangeably suggests that Gel'man's program of sexual hygiene was influenced by eugenics. Adapting the Marxist opposition between the "individual" and "class" to their own concepts, the Soviet proponents of this science linked what they called the "genus" and the "species" and repeatedly asserted that the individual could not be indifferent to his environment.[200] According to Zalkind, the working class, destined to become "a revolutionary savior of all humanity," was "faced with what was essentially a eugenic challenge—to improve the quality and the health of its posterity. Preobrazhenskii, the Party's wayward theoretician, applied eugenics to sexual engineering when he wrote that "matters of family and race assume a particular importance with the proletariat's ascent into power, since henceforth proletarian sexuality will determine the physical health of our race as well as its future." When he urged workers to be "conscious" in their selection of life partners, Doctor L. Vasetskii was clearly recasting themes from Korolev's eulogy into the terminology of eugenics. Vasetskii even considered breeding proletarians, although he finally had to concede that such a plan was somewhat "impractical."[201]

Many experts conceptualized the question of how the proletariat managed its sexual resources through the vocabulary of eugenics. Zalkind suggested that the working class should consider its sexuality a "biological weapon," a "vehicle of self-perpetuation," a "means of production" as important as any other. Echoing Korolev's call for every Communist to be responsible for the stock of sexual energy entrusted to him by his class, Zalkind wrote: "A worker's sexual attraction to a class-antagonistic object is no less depraved than sexual attraction to an orangutan or a crocodile. Invariably based on a purely sensual enticement, such a liaison will provoke frequent intercourse and . . . eventually exhaust his cerebral energy . . . We must set up regulators, blocks, and stimulators that, while preventing the squandering of class wealth, will also rechannel sexual energy into class-creative avenues." Zalkind declared a "strict proletarian sexual dictatorship" the order of the day. The first society in history to be "rationally organized," Soviet society was "ripe for a sexual revolution." What Zalkind had in mind was new restraints on sexuality mediated by consciousness. "In order to struggle with sexual abnormalities," Vasilevskii commented half sarcastically, half seriously, "Zalkind wants to construct a proletarian pump that will suck all sexual energy out."[202]

Proletarian sexual behavior was to be totally transformed. The New Man in this scheme was to be a being of "sophisticated" sexuality. Arousal would require the presence of numerous qualities in the object, and stimulation would occupy a longer time. The frequency of sexual acts would be reduced, but "their quality will be enhanced in compensation."[203] Reluctant to posit immutable human properties, Soviet scientists adopted the nearly Lamarckian assumption that human sexuality was open to improvement. The belief in human adaptability was related to two central tenets of the Marxist materialist doctrine: the principle of continual, universal change; and the principle that man could be conditioned.

Laymen looked forward to sexual engineering with high expectations. A number of letters to the editor published by Leningrad youth newspapers testified to the widespread hope that "sexual revolution" was imminent. One writer, who introduced himself as a "Communist sympathizer," offered the following plea: "Most respected comrades! We should take into account the great successes of science and technology as they stride inexorably forward to overcome the laws of nature. Now, when ninety-year-olds are rejuvenated [*omolazhivaiutsia*] . . . I expect that science will soon be able to relieve me of my attraction to the female sex." Another letter expressed similar hopes about the role that scientific knowledge would play in engineering sexual feelings. "Since the depravity of modern youth stems from clothing that stimulates the senses and deflects us from socially useful activity, and since I cannot look indifferently at a woman's décolletage, I suggest that we . . . cover the body completely."[204] Given such an intellectual environment, it was only natural for sexology to yoke itself to the task of creating the New Man.

In the late 1920s Soviet sexologists took a new look at Freud. Prominent Party leaders had suddenly recalled that whereas Lenin had reportedly called psychoanalysis a "fashionable whimsy," the disloyal Trotsky had supported it. Although the proponents of Freudianism managed to deflect the political onslaught for a few more years, the emphasis in its interpretation had to undergo a considerable change. Now that consciousness and will had been rehabilitated, dialectics had to replace behaviorist reductionism in any reading of Freud.[205] What had been affirmed in the early 1920s—the absolute importance of somatic processes, for example—was now denied; what had been denied—the unique role of the psyche as a bastion of rationality, for example—was now affirmed.

Bolshevik psychologists objected to Freud because of what they now perceived as his extreme sexual determinism. After all, Lenin had remarked (as became known only in 1925) that "I do not trust Freud or any others who are obsessed with sex as an Indian fakir is with his navel."[206] Freud's theory struck at a contemporary shibboleth: that the bodily experience controlled consciousness and not the other way around. Spearheading the revision of Freudism, Zalkind rejected the absolute primacy of the sexual instinct "as insisted upon by psychoanalysis." He postulated instead three general and equiprimordial forms of energy in man: biological, social and sexual. Zalkind believed that the explosion of sexual hyperactivity was due to contingent historical circumstances produced by capitalism; "about three-fourths of contemporary sexuality," he reckoned, "is a parasitic outgrowth of other instincts . . . The stock of energy originally at the disposal of other drives is absorbed by the carefree, simple, and happy sexuality." For Zalkind, the social drive was repressed by the hypertrophic sexual drive rather than the other way around; it was the libido, not the ego, that was the real transgressor.[207]

At its roots, the argument between Freud and Zalkind in the 1920s was metapsychological. Freud believed that sexual energy (libido) underlay all human phenomena. For him, the ubiquity of the sexual was a metaphysical truth, a perennial order of things. The sexual could be expressed, repressed, or sublimated but never obliterated. For Zalkind, the predominance of the sexual was historically true but not inevitable and eternal. Freud understood "creativity" as a sublimated manifestation of the sexual. For Zalkind, "creativity" was a natural expression of the social drive once the latter was released from the demands of the sexual drive and its original energy pool replenished. "From the sociological point of view," Zalkind wrote, "Freud's attempt to explain all creativity as sublimation, that is, as sexual renunciation, an appropriation of unused sexual energy by the creative process, is unfounded. The origin of human creativity is in the social drive, and not in the sexual drive in whose horrible clutches humanity resides only temporarily."[208]

Although the Bolshevik reading of Freud changed his emphasis, psychoanalysis remained for the time being a legitimate branch of the Marxist science of man. "Many argue that since the germ of Freudianism is the theory of the sexual drive," wrote Zalkind, "a critique of that aspect of the theory supposedly demolishes its very foundations." But psychoanalysis, Zalkind insisted, had its merits. He applauded the work of the "ego" in restraining and sublimating unruly sexuality. Turning the tables against the behaviorist reading of Freud, Zalkind praised Freud's "conscious ego" and denounced the "unconscious instinct." The agency that set out to restrain sexual drives, the "ego," was declared a notion parallel to those of "personality" and "will," whose standing had recently been elevated.[209]

Zalkind made the ego a drive (what he called the "social drive"), thus relegating it to the realm of irreducible psychological entities. He interpreted the Freudian pleasure principle as a bundle of "unconditioned reflexes"—the organism's innate drives—which expended their energy along the path of minimal resistance. The psychoanalytic "ego," by contrast, was a bundle of "conditioned reflexes." In Zalkind's view, the work of the "social drive" came down to the strengthening of some reflexes and the inhibition of others. If the ego weakened and the inhibiting reflexes slackened, repressed reflexes broke through. Until such a moment, they remained latent, as they should be, kept under control by socially oriented conditioned reflexes. According to this new version of psychoanalysis, the ego was not a foe but a friend. From a tool that repressed the natural inclinations of man, it was transformed into the protector of the social in man, the part of man that separated him from the beast.[210]

Did that mean that man was split into two irreducible agencies, the conscious ego and the unconscious instinct? And if so, was that not a violation of the monist view of man held by every good Marxist? Hoping to preserve his monist credentials, Zalkind tried to minimize the difference between the unconscious instinct and the conscious ego, arguing that the same energetic laws governed both. The only difference was that the energy of the conscious ego was expressed, while the energy of the unconscious instinct was repressed. Hard as he tried, however, Zalkind was unable to explain the work of the psyche in energetic terms alone. To be able to inhibit some instincts while allowing others expression, or, in energetic terms, to be able invest some instincts with energy but not others, the human organism had to possess some sort of criteria for discrimination. Since the criteria for distinguishing between the instincts had to be based on ideational representations of the aims that various instincts targeted, the qualitative specificity of the various instincts had to be taken into account. For example, instincts aiming at sexual gratification had to be denied but instincts aiming at class cooperation encouraged. As a sort of judge of instincts, an agency able not only to measure the energy of various instincts but also to represent to itself their aims, the ego had to be invested with a subjective rationality.

Degeneration in the Physiological Key

The revival of mentalism and the new interpretation of the role of the ego in psychoanalysis asserted themselves in *Dog Alley*, providing the narrator with a framework explaining the degeneration of mental laborers. Burov's failure to develop the strong ego needed to control sexual instincts was the beginning point for his lamentable predicament. That Burov could not contain his imagination indicated that he was obsessed. "Obsession," experts explained, "can take not only the form of anxiety but also obtrusive images that appear before our mind despite us, taking control of us," something that was happening to Burov all the time.[211]

Gumilevskii dwells at length on the etiology of Burov's disease. Answering Khokhorin's question "How then did you reach such a state, Fedor Fedorovich?" Burov delves into his past: "Only yesterday I received a letter from my sister reminding me of my childhood. She recalled that because of my gloomy disposition and passion for books kids ridiculed me as 'know-it-all' . . . It all started with everybody calling me 'professor' and trying to teach me the real joys of life . . . In the gymnasium it was considered a truism that a guy with pimples was in need of a woman . . . Our ideas about sex were 'original' . . . We were all jealous of one boy whose mother brought home a good-looking servant. He became a better pupil because the girl let him close to her only when his grades were good" (p. 78). In this short passage Gumilevskii heaps upon Burov most of the stereotypes associated with the petit-bourgeois body. "First sexual encounter was with servants" was regarded as typical petit-bourgeois vice.[212] Sexologists explained that "sex with domestics was encouraged by bourgeois parents who wanted to shield their offspring from prostitutes."[213]

On top of everything, Burov's morphology—he is impulsive, compulsive, and full of tics—bears clear marks of degeneration. The attention paid to Burov's body was in keeping with contemporary physical anthropology. "We have to discover the link between physique and psychology," experts argued. "Just as the length of man's fingers corresponds to the size of other organs in his body . . . so a correlation exists between the structure of his organs and tissues and his mental capacity."[214] In this context, "constitution" was an important analytical term, understood as "the way in which the organism responds to the outside world."[215] Several studies from the 1920s posited a strong connection between the "physical constitution" (three generic types were postulated), "character," and "susceptibility to mental decline."[216]

Professor N. Belov, a physical anthropologist, had individuals with Burov's pattern of behavior in mind when he maintained that individuals who developed prematurely sexually "often have short legs and a prolonged trunk, small facial features, and pronounced secondary sexual characteristics such as a beard and a hairy body. Despite being totally incapable of real passion, such impulsive types carry themselves like little womanizers, mice-size stallions . . . Avoiding physical labor, these sex maniacs develop a tendency to depravity [porochnost'], sexual hyperdevelopment, lasciviousness [pokhotlivost'], and voluptuousness [sladostrastie]."[217] Belov was not alone in attributing degeneration to a distinct morphology. A number of Soviet criminologists maintained that the deviant body exhibited primordial characteristics—various physical deformities—no longer visible in more fully developed humanity. Those forensic doctors who were thinking along similar lines systematically examined corpses of suicides for signs that self-destruction had been imminent. It was assumed that suicidal individuals could be discerned, for example, by alterations in the shape of the skull affecting the exchange of fluids in the brain. If

Lambroso's theories about the body's clues to moral deviance were by and large rejected by sociologists, they enjoyed some prominence among the more physiologically inclined scientists.[218]

When implying that Burov correctly diagnosed himself as a textbook "neurasthenic" *(nevrastenik)*, Gumilevskii was invoking another important psychomedical notion. The American physician George M. Beard had coined the term "neurasthenia" in 1869 to account for nervous problems, and his diagnostic invention was readily integrated into Marxist physiology.[219] Soviet doctors defined neurasthenia as an illness that spread over the entire nervous system and consisted in "nervous exhaustion" and "general weakness of the nervous apparatus." Its most obvious symptoms were "irritability" and "deterioration in concentration."[220] Burov is a classic neurasthenic because, though suicidal, he is not insane. His ability to lecture Khokhorin about his own malady is proof of his capacity for rational deliberation. Burov's morbid tendencies stem from his extreme sensitivity and impressionable nature and the weakened state of his nervous system. A product of the urban petit bourgeoisie, this alter ego of Khokhorin is ironically the type of person most easily victimized by the academic environment. His refined nervous system has too often been dangerously overstimulated. In using Burov's neurasthenia as a way to account for the incessant and exaggerated exaltation of the nervous system of a typical student,[221] Gumilevskii relied on Doctor L. Merel'zon, who noted that "we frequently encounter neurasthenia among university students . . . because the nervous system of the mental laborer is exposed to repetitive stimulations along the same nervous cords."[222]

Sexologists regarded the issue of the physical and the psychic constitution of students as of paramount importance, not only from the biological but also from the social-eugenics point of view. There was much interest in "tracing students' class genealogy."[223] Healthy proletarian genes, Lass believed, contributed to good health. A decadent, petit-bourgeois genetic stock, on the other hand, was responsible for youngsters' degeneration. "Affecting first the highest organ of the intellect, the brain, and the central nervous system, a pathological inheritance makes its impact on the sphere that is most sensitive and receptive to negative influences, namely sex."[224] Conceived by Gumilevskii as somebody born and raised among the wanton intelligentsia, Burov could have been predicted to have an unstable sexual constitution. "It is well known that children of promiscuous, lascivious, wanton parents," one expert maintained, "tend to indulge in sexual excess more than other children."[225]

Experts were confident that the earlier sexual activity began, "the more frequent it is, the faster the stock of sexual cells is depleted. Early evacuation of sexual fluids facilitates premature aging."[226] In this regard as well, Burov's milieu was supposedly the worst off. Extensive data were produced to prove that "by the age of thirteen premature sperm emissions are most frequent among the petit-bourgeois kids." Experts were not surprised that an "idle youngster who is alienated from physical labor tends to develop a precocious sexual interest." His underdeveloped will was too weak to stave off the influences of the surrounding atmosphere. Dirty talk, bad books, and dances aroused the youngster's dark drives. "Unable to control their nervous systems," intelligentsia youngsters were said to be organically unable to abstain from sex.[227]

Sexologists frowned upon "internal drive" *(vnutrennee pobuzhdenie)*—a motive for sexual intercourse frequently reported by students—which they saw as a purely instinctual, bestial sexual impulse to be contrasted with the healthy proletarian sexuality that was a natural response to outside excitation. "We have to bridle our internal drive!" one of them exclaimed.[228] In this connection, Bolshevik expert opinion clearly sided with nurture in the nature/nurture debate. "An inborn sexual call" was negatively contrasted with a sexual interest that "developed under the influence of literature and friends."[229] Thus one sexologist was sorry to register the preponderance among students of what he called "automatic semen emissions."[230] Lass's survey found that petit-bourgeois students indeed specified "need" as the most prevalent motive for their earliest sexual encounters. "Sexual need" *(seksual'naia potrebnost')*, this sexologist explained, "had grown organically in the luxury of a middle class environment." One report by a petit-bourgeois student was particularly symptomatic: "My first sexual experience occurred without any attraction to the object, out of a sheer need to satisfy an internal sexual drive. It was only natural that when I by chance witnessed my parents having sexual intercourse my precocious sexual interest woke up." Proletarians did not experience artificial sexual arousal with the same frequency. Workers, Lass reported, listed "need" less frequently as a primary sexual stimulator; among peasants "sexual need" was barely a factor at all.[231]

The extent of masturbation registered by scientific surveys conducted in Soviet universities throughout the 1920s repeatedly corroborated the Bolshevik moralists' perception of youngsters as physically and politically abnormal. Defined as a "deviation [*uklon*] of sexual desire," masturbation corresponded with Oppositionism, widely defined as a "political deviation."[232] Masturbation was deplorable.[233] "An immature organism suffers physically from this practice," Merel'zon commented. "The young resort to masturbation very frequently, thus bringing about a general emaciation [*iskhudanie*] of their bodies."[234] A frequent waste of "precious nervous matter," Doctor Faingol'd concurred, "exhausts the brain, weakens memory, and leads to spiritual depression."[235] But—and this was even more important in an academic context—the malady had a very important mental aspect as well: "A sense of guilt, the fear of retribution for the sin of masturbation, dominate the youngster, enhancing his sense of dissatisfaction . . . If we add to that doubtful satisfaction the cognition of the fact that the masturbator is dirty and iniquitous and that he is easily recognizable by his external appearance, we are in a position to understand the emotional suffering the young masturbators undergo."[236] When sexologists added that "constant excitation of the nervous system following excessive masturbation creates sexual neurasthenia," the circle of explanation was closed and the etiology of degeneration established.

It still remained to be explained why students were more promiscuous than other sectors of the population and why masturbation was so widespread among them. In grappling with this question a number of Bolshevik sexologists suggested that a strong sexual drive was the manifestation of an autoeffective physical constitution. "Masturbation activates fantasies and therefore puts heavy demands on the sexual center in the brain," posited Faingol'd. "If during the normal sexual act the brain barely participates, when masturbation takes place the brain plays a central role. Masturbation involves full participation of the faculties of imagination."[237] Self-perpetuating arousal was believed to be linked to self-reflection, a basic feature of mental labor. The resemblance between these two aberrations—the self-referential activity of thinking and self-induced sexual excitation—supposedly explained why universities, "the factories of thought," were hotbeds of the crime of Onan. Both thinking and masturbating were activities that recoiled, that acted back upon themselves. The ancient vice was now scientifically redefined as autoeffective behavior, "a sexual abnormality that entails excitation of one's body without recourse to another person."[238]

This connection was not lost on Soviet sexologists, who presented students as victims of enormous dosages of reflexivity.[239] Sexual excess, they argued, was induced by the disharmony between students' physical and mental faculties. Students admitted that frequent masturbation harmed their mental capacity. Masturbation made them "timid," "feeble," "hypochondriac," "depressed," "neurasthenic," "anemic," "impotent," "taciturn," "sleepy," "prone to fantasizing," "indecisive," "weak in character," "psychologically indifferent," "disillusioned," "consumed with guilt," "unable to maintain a train of thought," as well as "antisocial and devoid of any inclination to mix with others." One student questionnaire cited by the sexologist Grosser contained the following handwritten addition on its margins: "Following ten years of daily masturbation I turned myself into a monster that no longer needs terrestrial life with its joys and griefs. Now everything is alien and detestable to me, myself included. I am done and over with."[240]

The complaint that masturbation harmed the neural system was particularly rampant. One masturbating student felt "pains in his head and back"; a second experienced "discomfort in my spinal cord"; a third suffered from "an accelerated heartbeat and heavy breathing"; a fourth was "not only lacking physical strength even in the legs and arms . . . but also mentally enfeebled"; and a fifth admitted that "my once wide and muscular chest became narrow and flat following five years of masturbating every other day." "I feel weak," a sixth sinner complained. "My muscles are slack, although this might also be caused by the fact that for the last four years I have not engaged in manual labor. It is enough for me to turn sharply once on one leg to have my head spin. Besides all this, my face has until recently been very drawn, for which I also blame masturbation." Masturbating students stood the risk of "contracting a degenerate nervous constitution, a high level of sexual excitability, and a low irritability threshold."[241] Psychologists found that masturbation was the reason behind "student melancholy" and that it induced "hypochondria and suicidal impulses." Generally, autoerotic processes that did not require contact with another were said to cause a "pathological increase in egocentrism and to cultivate loners locked in themselves and oblivious to social life."[242]

In characterizing Burov, Gumilevskii omits none of these symptoms. From a masturbating child, Burov turns into a sexually obsessed adult. He develops a gloomy outlook, cannot find happiness with a woman, and ends up shooting himself. During his encounter with Khokhorin, Burov reminisces about the day he told his father he practiced masturbation. "My father listened to me, put his hands in the pockets, and walked away, saying, 'Well, so you will become an imbecile!'" (p. 78). Like the sexologists of his day, Burov's father must have believed that profuse sexual spending destroyed brain tissues. Experts would have urged him to see the origins of his son's masturbation thus: "Under the influence of servants and friends, the sexual instinct is aroused prematurely, before the restraining apparatus is fully developed. The insatiable sexual drive triggers the most basic and readily accessible form of autoeroticism—masturbation." The earlier the sexual instinct appeared, the graver was the danger that masturbation would become a habit: "The inhibiting centers of consciousness—poorly developed at a young age—are required if masturbation is to be prevented."[243] To curb masturbation that had run out of control, sterilization was sometimes recommended.[244]

All this being said, masturbation did not lead ineluctably to degeneration. Other negative influences had to be at work as well. Experts noted that students themselves were not always certain whether masturbation was "just another manifestation of sexual activity" or actually led to excessive "cerebral emissions, which severely weaken the spinal cord." At least one sexologist was sure that a student with a "robust constitution could endure masturbation without damage to the organism."[245] Generally, there was a consensus that so long as students periodically returned to manual labor, masturbation was harmless. One student reportedly testified: "Since I do much heavy labor, I masturbate quite often without any physical fatigue. Perhaps the devil is not as terrible as they make him out to be." A civil war veteran reported that "while in the infantry I masturbated countless times but remained healthy because . . . I worked so hard that mushrooms grew on my shoulders." The testimony of this student was used as another piece of evidence demonstrating that the influence of masturbation on one's health depended on the individual's specific "psychophysical organization." It was the combination of masturbation with unmitigated cerebral activity that was regarded as absolutely and unquestionably harmful. "If only artificial stimulation could be avoided, masturbation would be so much less detrimental," claimed the sexologist A. Stratonitskii.[246]

Soviet sexologists deduced from a careful study of questionnaires that masturbation was "virtually rampant" among students of nonproletarian background. "Idleness" was said to be the "mother of all vices, masturbation included."[247] Conceived by Gumilevskii as someone who came from a comfortable background, Burov was evidence for this generalization. Precocious sexual development and excessive masturbation prevented creation of inhibiting centers in Burov's psyche. Since his early interest in mental labor developed at the expense of manual activity, Burov failed to bring his psyche into harmony.

Having abandoned physical activity, Khokhorin is only one step behind Burov. The etiology of Khokhorin's degeneration, however, is somewhat different. The reader is never allowed to forget that Gumilevskii's hero comes from a working-class family. This means that his childhood must have been healthy and that his constitution was prepared to meet the challenges of mental labor. Unfortunately, the civil war intervened, interrupting his normal course of development. Moving to the university after the end of the war, Khokhorin fell into the trap of Burov's degeneration syndrome and became Burov's shadow.

Gumilevskii's emphasis on mental labor in the etiology of degeneration distinguishes him from Malashkin and his fixation on students' social environment. Gumilevskii implies that even proletarian psychophysiology is not immune to the adverse influence of academic labor. Most of the evidence on sexual degeneration amassed by Soviet sexologists on whom Gumilevskii relied pertained to students from lower classes. A. Platovskii, who studied the Iakutsk workers' faculty, emphasized that the student pathologies he found had to be attributed to "primarily workers and peasants." And Gel'man contended that his 1922 study of Moscow students was very important precisely because he had examined "proletarian and peasant students (whereas similar prerevolutionary studies focused on petit-bourgeois students)."[248]

Whatever their class background, students faced the dangers of hyperreflexivity in the explanatory scheme adopted by Gumilevskii. At the university, the proletarian Khokhorin and the petit-bourgeois Burov become nearly indistinguishable. "Don't be afraid, who hasn't been in Dog alley!" Burov says to Khokhorin. "The secret is to get out of there as soon as you can!" Drawing on his last reserves of strength, Khokhorin tries to pull himself up, "thinking of his superiority before this ill person. But then, recalling the entire evening, as if stricken by lightning, he is seized with fear. Khokhorin starts thinking of himself and others, like Burov, who got entangled in the web of a huge, white, heavy sexual spider that fed not on blood but on the best in a person—his brain" (p. 77).

At the end, however, Khokhorin is saved. In this respect, Gumilevskii's and Malashkin's agendas fuse quite neatly. It is very important for both novelists to impress upon Bolshevik readers that the proletarian kernel— whether it be physical constitution or social inclination—can never be irretrievably lost. In Gumilevskii's prescription, if he is to redeem himself, Khokhorin must return to manual labor, sublimate his sexual energy, and achieve the transformation from animalistic individualism to proletarian collective consciousness. So that they might be worthy of the future class-less society, the Bolshevik leaders instructed Khokhorins "to learn how to make instincts transparent and clear, bringing the areas below the threshold of consciousness under the direction of the will and thus making oneself a higher biological type, or, if you like, a Superman."[249]

Dramatic prescriptions of this kind signaled a momentous shift in the Bolshevik discourse. By the end of the 1920s, more or less voluntarist notions, "will," "consciousness," and "personality" chief among them, gained in importance. Thenceforth, student lapses into Trotskyism would not be dismissed as a temporary weakness, a physical failure. The return of voluntarist notions to Soviet Marxism pulled the rug from under the Oppositionists' solar-eclipse line of defense. From the perspective of the Party hermeneutics, compassion would be unlikely: it was increasingly difficult to claim that the body temporarily perverted the consciousness of the student Party member. The followers of Trotsky were now described as endowed with a counterrevolutionary state of mind.

5

Looking into the
Oppositionist Soul

Alongside the students who had attained enlightenment and were bathed in the purifying light of Communism were those fallen souls who had allegedly betrayed the Party—the Oppositionists. Two "outbreaks of Oppositionism" among the intra-Party struggles of the 1920s, the Discussion with Trotsky (1923) and the Discussion with the United Opposition (1927), will suffice to trace how the Opposition was diagnosed and how this diagnosis evolved over time.[1]

The Discussion with Trotsky broke out during the winter of 1923. Lenin lay dying, the struggle over succession was visible around the corner, and a host of hardships—cuts in wages and a wave of industrial strikes—brought tensions to a head. The disagreements between the "triumvirate" (Kamenev, Zinoviev, and Stalin) and Trotsky's Opposition had to do with economic policy and the Party's internal regime. The Discussion lasted until the opening of the Thirteenth Party Conference (January 16, 1924); contentious issues were ferreted out. At the conference itself the Opposition was condemned, its crime construed as a factional attempt to provide a power base for the petite bourgeoisie within the Party. Stalin's challenges received little support in 1924: according to the January Central Committee plenum, 98.7 percent of the Party had voted for the theses advanced by the Central Committee majority.[2]

More important here, however, is the great success Trotsky enjoyed in the university Party cells. Given that every tenth Communist in the country was a student, this was sufficient cause for alarm.[3] This popularity stemmed from the stress on "Party youth" in Trotsky's rhetoric. In a series of articles initiated in the fall of 1923 and collectively titled "The New Course" Trotsky argued that the main problem with Party life was not the "chimera of factionalism" but the "unchecked growth of bureaucratic practices . . . The older Bolshevik cadres are barring the younger generation's path to advancement." Trotsky maintained that students best represented the general state of the Party because they were its most heterogeneous echelon. Drawn from different classes, they made the university cell a microcosm of the Party, the most "sensitive" and "representative" Communist milieu.[4]

When Trotsky lamented the "suppression of the youth," Communist students responded enthusiastically.[5] Moscow Oppositionists hoped that this rank-and-file support would sweep them to victory in the capital.[6] When the votes had been counted the Opposition had indeed prevailed at Moscow's universities: forty academic cells had voted for the Opposition, compared with thirty-two for the official Party line. But this was a pyhrric victory: the factory cells, the administrative cells, and even the military cells, formerly believed to be a bastion of support for Trotsky, had overwhelmingly supported the Central Committee majority.[7]

In Petrograd, then Zinoviev's fief, the Opposition fared even worse. Trotsky's "factionalism" had already been condemned outright by the Nineteenth Petrograd Party Conference on December 1.[8] In the city on the Neva, as in Moscow, university Party cells were the exception: while most students endorsed the official resolution, "On Party Building," what criticism was leveled at Stalin and the Central Committee came from academic quarters. Trotskyist propagandists sent from Moscow had enjoyed moderate success in their efforts to raise the temperature of debate.

At Leningrad State University the Discussion was fierce. Almost the entire membership of the cell came to the university auditorium to discuss the political issues on the agenda. Evenly split (three members supported Trotsky and three Zinoviev), the buro failed to send an unequivocal signal. The main reporters protested "Trotsky's attempt to unleash the youth against the leaders." The pro–Central Committee resolution offered a warning: "We must beware of democratic phraseology; it is dangerous to set up Communist youth against the Party veterans." Gorbachev, a supporter of Trotsky, offered a vigorous response: "Instead of keeping up with the changing moods of the mass of the Party, the Party apparatus labels Trotsky 'petit bourgeois.' What good does it do to sweep problems under the carpet?" The Oppositionist resolution maintained that "the Central Committee's accusations against Comrade Trotsky are utterly groundless." The Opposition was defeated by a vote of 48 to 101.[9] In the Leningrad University workers' faculty, however, the situation was reversed, and the Opposition carried the day, 94 to 46.[10] According to the subsequent apology offered by the loyalist buro, the "accidental" Oppositionist majority was born of an abnormal union between lapsed students and alien elements. Despite the buro's claim that "our cell is not really thoroughly Oppositionist: with a few insignificant exceptions we all endorsed the resolutions of the Thirteenth Party Conference," a secret report maintained that some local Communists continued their Oppositionist activity at the workers' faculty well into 1924.[11]

The Leningrad Party organization and the official press focused on students as a special type of Communists whose unique problems hindered the development of their consciousness. Although only a minority of university students expressed objectionable opinions, the Party apparatus blamed the university milieu as a whole for the spread of Oppositionist attitudes. Local loyalist sources reported that of the 300 "active Oppositionists" in Petrograd, 165 were registered in higher educational institutions, compared with only 54 in factories and mills.[12] "The tertiary institutions turned out to be the weakest link in our Party organization," insisted a front-page article in *Petrogradskaia pravda*. "Many students took advantage of the Discussion to vent some spleen. One gets the distinct impression that our university Party cells are full of individuals with swollen egos. They do not seem to appreciate the Party's goals at all, and complain that they are, if you please, 'cramped' and 'stifled' and that their initiative is being blocked."[13] Statisticians in the employ of the Petrograd Party apparatus marshaled a battery of data to prove that it was students and other nonproletarian types who were swallowing Trotsky's bait; a staggering 73 percent of the Leningrad Oppositionists were classified as intelligentsia, compared with a meager 6 percent of workers from the bench.[14]

There was an obvious problem with this argument: at Leningrad State University it was not the main faculty, dominated by the intelligentsia, but the workers' faculty, dominated by the lower classes, that supported Trotsky. To explain how a petit-bourgeois doctrine could sway what was supposed to be a loyally proletarian organization, it was said that the workers' faculty in question was not truly proletarian. To substantiate the claim, the local buro drew up a list of fresh attributes for each Party member. After examining newly amassed biographical information, an internal committee found far more petit-bourgeois elements than had been apparent earlier: whereas according to the old count there had been 237 proletarians in the cell, according to the new calculation their number stood at only 167. By contrast, the number of employees increased dramatically, from 10 to 61. "Others," a dubious category from the point of view of class purists, was now constituted into existence (two students were relegated to this category).[15]

Another strategy involved the now-familiar notion of degeneration. "Why is it that we have almost no Oppositionists in our factory collectives but many Oppositionists in our university collectives?" a summary report by the Petrograd provincial committee wondered. "It is not 'because students are better developed,' as Oppositionists would argue, but because workers who enter the universities find themselves hemmed in by bourgeois decadence."[16] New medical imagery developed by Soviet moralists had penetrated the very heart of the Party discourse. Students who supported the Trotskyist Opposition in 1923–24 were diagnosed as "unhealthy comrades" who, having submerged themselves in the academic environment, had lost their clear view of the Party line.

Degeneration was for all purposes a satisfactory diagnosis, since it explained how even Communists of proletarian descent could oppose the Party line. As long as this diagnosis held, the spiritual predicament of Oppositionist students was believed to be dangerous, but by no means hopeless. Party leaders surmised that the academic environment had turned Communist students into "unprincipled opportunists." The official press carried discussions of the etiology of student deviation. "Recently a quite noticeable trend has emerged," Zinoviev stated on the pages of a prominent youth journal. "The enveloping influence of the petite bourgeoisie has been seeping into our Party through the student milieu, rendering apparent the latent threat of the student Party members. An old Bolshevik worker confided to me that 'once upon a time we used to say that street kids make mischief [*rebiata buziat*]. Now we have to say that 'college kids make mischief [*rebiata vuziat*].'"[17]

Unimpressed, Sverdlov University students disputed the labels Zinoviev was attaching to them: "These days we cannot show our faces in workers' quarters. 'Aaaa!' we hear. 'Sverdlovets, a member of the intelligentsia!' Whence comes this allegedly petit-bourgeois tag? We live in dormitories, among Communists. The devil knows what we are to make of ourselves! . . . To be sure, not too many of us are real workers—if one has been in the army or the Party since the age of seventeen it is not easy to become a worker. But it is no easier to become a member of the intelligentsia! And yet, we are now being 'extolled' with this epithet. "[18]

But the Party leadership remained unmoved. "Petite bourgeoisie," Stalin stated, could be a "mood"; it need not necessarily be an objective class position.[19] Clearly, it was time to recall Lenin's "Better fewer but better."[20] Accordingly, the Thirteenth Party Conference decided on a "limited Party verification."[21] The 1924 cleansing operation was to involve only administrative and educational Party cells, a total of 230,000 Communists. As Iaroslavskii put it, "these cells must be purged of their decadent elements, those carriers of petit-bourgeois influence."[22] The decision to exclude productivist Party cells underscored the official assumption that factory Communists were immune from degeneration and that comrades who engaged in mental labor were especially susceptible to the influences of the NEP.[23]

In what was now renamed Leningrad, verification was announced in March 1924, much earlier than in other areas. Official announcements made no mention of Oppositionism. "The Party Conference alerted us this January to our contamination by socially alien, demoralizing elements," proclaimed the guiding statement by the provincial committee. "We must implement its decisions and purge the ballast. This is necessary for the recovery of our Party."[24] Day-to-day supervision of the process was carried out by a special Party committee. Accountable only to the Central Control Commission, this body had to draw up lists of nonproductive cells to be examined as well as lists of highly distinguished Bolsheviks worthy of sitting on the three-man verification tribunals, often called "troikas" (partproverktroiki). The troikas were overwhelmingly working class in their composition and their members of long Party standing; many were distinguished veterans whose Party seniority dated back to 1904–05. Clearly, these were trustworthy hermeneuts of the soul, well equipped "to separate the wheat from the chaff."[25]

The troikas treated each Party cell as one indivisible collective. Once a cell had been classified as "nonproductive"—and all university cells naturally fell under that category—its entire membership, irrespective of class origins, was carefully scrutinized. The actual interrogation of students was carried out on the premises of the cell's buro—proof of the troika's supreme power to pass sentence. Quickly dispensing with general issues such as the profile of the cell and its level of discipline, the troika invited individual comrades to present themselves for "comradely discussion" (tovarishchskaia beseda). At this stage, the key issues were the comrade's occupations, revolutionary involvement, and public service. Once it had completed its task, the troika sent personal files, Party cards, and protocols to the committee and reported its findings at a general meeting of the cell.[26]

Perhaps the most meticulous verification was the one that took place at Leningrad State University, the second-largest academic institution in the country. As Zinoviev's entire apparatus looked on, the investigation proceeded strictly by the book. First Nekmodov, the representative of the Vasilevsk Island district committee, lectured students on the expediency of the verification. The main faculty promised "to assist the work of the troika in every possible way."[27] Anxious to dissociate itself from heterodox elements, the loyalist buro of the workers' faculty issued even more enthusiastic public statements: "Even before the center decided on a verification," it boasted, "we had already requested permission to cast out the degenerated, anti-Party element."[28]

If we can judge by the failure of the district committee's pro-purge resolution to gain massive support among workers' faculty students, the unanimity suggested by this declaration was imposed on the cell by its new buro. A group of defiant students proposed a reorganization of the ballot, this time counting the votes of Party candidates as well, hoping that the official decision endorsing a purge would be overturned. But this motion was voted down. A week later Nekmodov was bemoaning students' lingering resistance: "Frightened by the sight of us, many comrades are reluctant to help the troika. On several occasions they have hid their wedding rings, standing before the commission's table hat in hand or wearing kerchiefs. All this is done in hope of confusing us [i.e., to present themselves as typical proletarians]. But we know very well what to ask and of whom."[29]

Individual student interrogations took place on April 5–11. According to the troika's official summary, verification reduced the main faculty cell's membership from 331 to 270; 44 students (8 percent) were purged from the Party; many others were sent back to the factories; 105 were censored. In the workers' faculty cell the rate of attrition was of course significantly higher: 28 of its 105 members were expelled, 10 placed on probation.[30]

Extant verification protocols permit a tentative assessment of the criteria employed by the troika. Although the data on all the cases in the Leningrad University main faculty have survived, the information is dry and formulaic. The paperwork left behind by the 1924 troikas contains only very stereotyped descriptions of those examined and the verdicts; there are no minutes of the actual interrogations. Only in rare cases do we know how students presented their biographies, so the data are broken down below statistically, supplemented whenever qualitative material illustrates a quantitatively established trend. Ultimately the method yields a link between the verdicts and those key variables distinguished in the Communist autobiography: class, former party affiliations, enlistment with the various armies, and Party record.

From the moment the Soviet leadership established the official premise that those who supported the Opposition were social aliens, a spotlight was thrown onto the issue of class. When the Leningrad leadership described the students, it claimed that the overwhelming majority were "individuals from a nonproletarian background," by and large employees and intelligentsia who naturally embraced the Opposition. Speaking before the Leningrad State University students, Nikitin, a Party functionary, made the connection between class and political orientation quite explicit: "15–20 percent of our cell consists of students who came from a nonproletarian background, all Opposition supporters."[31] When the verification at Leningrad State University had run its course, the local buro noted with evident satisfaction: "The social composition of our cell has markedly improved: the percentage of workers has increased, while that of intelligentsia has dropped."[32] Table 1 vividly conveys the impact of class on the troika's verdicts.

Although workers and peasants were rarely purged (14 and 18 percent respectively), over half of the intelligentsia (56 percent) and a high per-

Table 1 Incidence of purge among Leningrad State University Communists by social origins, 1924

Social Origins	Number (%) of students	Number (%) of purged students
Workers	35 (20%)	5 (14%)
Peasants	44 (25%)	8 (18%)
Intelligentsia	25 (14%)	14 (56%)
Employees	14 (8%)	5 (36%)
Artisans	46 (27%)	11 (24%)
Merchants	1 (1%)	0 (0%)
Nobles	5 (3%)	3 (60%)
Clergy	3 (2%)	1 (33%)
Total	173 (100%)	47 (27%)

Source: Calculated from material in TsGA IPD, f. 984, op. 1, d. 58, ll. 1–37.

centage of employees (35 percent) were expelled. Since class and political stance could not be disentangled in the official discourse, these statistical regularities can be interpreted in more than one way: we can say that the troikas were looking for "intelligentsia," but we can also argue that when Trotsky's supporters were identified, they were labeled "intelligentsia" in the purge rolls.

In several instances the verification commission presented individuals as "class aliens" who would otherwise seem to have been likely candidates for the proletariat. Thus Rebrova, the daughter of a blacksmith, was marked as a member of the intelligentsia, most likely as a result of her support of Trotsky. How else can we explain the purge of this deputy chief of Olenetsk province's People's Education Department? Although Rebrova was prominent in the local Zhenotdel (Women's Department), she was purged for "passivity" and "political illiteracy." Clearly, this was a shorthand for her failure to cooperate with the loyalist Party organs. Or take the case of Kantor, a member of a supply detachment during the civil war as well as a "partisan under Narva and Kronstadt" who had worked long enough as a blacksmith to be counted among the proletarians; but the behavior of this student during the Discussion apparently made such classification impossible, and he was purged.

The frequency with which student deviancy was explained in terms of "insubordination to Party discipline" or a "background in petit-bourgeois parties" helps measure the incidence of purging among comrades with tainted organizational backgrounds, summarized in Table 2.

Because of the cloud of duplicity that hung above them, the vast majority of second-time Party members were purged. Having failed to remain in touch with the Bolshevik organization during Denikin's conquest of Vladikavkaz, a bricklayer's daughter named Gagorina had received an in-

Table 2 Incidence of purge among Communists with a tainted Party record

	Number (%) of students	Number (%) of students purged
Former members of Non-Bolshevik parties	24 (13%)	8 (67%)
Readmitted Bolsheviks	10 (5%)	8 (80%)
Unblemished Bolsheviks	152 (82%)	33 (22%)
Total	186 (100%)	49 (26%)

Source: Calculated from material in TsGA IPD, f. 984, op. 1, d. 58, ll. 1–37.

delible stain. His unauthorized departure from the Vitebsk Party organization in 1920 led, in a similar case, to the purge of Gal'brakh.

Former members of "petit-bourgeois" parties were also censored more
often than students who had pure Bolshevik records. It was official doctrine that Communists with checkered political records were naturally
drawn to heterodoxy.[33] The reasons cited by the troika in passing judgment
add detail to the picture: although former Mensheviks and Socialist-Revolutionaries (SRs) were frequently listed among the "ideologically alien,"
none of them was accused of "passivity." Students who had gone politically
astray before joining the Bolshevik ranks could not be regarded as having
drifted on the winds of political fashion during the Discussion; these were
the active enemies of Soviet power.

Although former SRs were censored more frequently than former Mensheviks (their party had taken up arms against the Bolshevik regime),
some former SRs who told convincing stories of their conversions managed to survive the verification process. A peasant's son and an SR from
July 1917 to January 1918, Gorodskoi was retained because he had joined
the Bolsheviks after a "kulak uprising proved to him that SRs sided with
the village rich." An "SR sympathizer in 1917," Maegova also made it
through the verification because by 1918 she had discarded her illusions of
bucolic socialism and become a Bolshevik. A daughter of a clerk and a
nurse, Avarykina, by contrast, had more experience as an SR: exiled from
Petersburg for membership in a quasi-SR organization in 1914, she had
formally joined the SR party during the Revolution. It was the Left SR anti-
Bolshevik coup that had inspired her defection. Good enough: instructed
"to deepen her knowledge of Bolshevik tactics" and "eradicate the SR petit-
bourgeois ideology," she was allowed to retain her Party membership.

The timing of one's political conversion mattered, and the verification
commission tended to retain former Bundists, Mensheviks, and SRs who
had joined the Bolsheviks in the midst of the civil war: of those who had
made the mistake of being members of a "petit-bourgeois party," one of
five who had joined the Bolsheviks during the peak of the civil war was
censored, compared with one of two among those who had made the
switch after it became apparent the Bolsheviks were prevailing.

A combination of former Socialist-Revolutionary affiliation, petit-bourgeois social origins, and late arrival to the Party rendered a student's prospects of surviving the verification process dim indeed. Gar, for example,
joined the Bolsheviks only in 1920. The daughter of a *zemstvo* employee

and an SR until August 1918, she was charged with "philistine deviation" and "political vacillations" and was promptly purged. Although Benfeste, a civil war veteran and a political instructor in the Red Army, was herself apolitical, "her husband remained a Left SR as late as 1919," long after the party had been outlawed by the Bolshevik government. "Having failed to denounce her husband" (who was under GPU arrest at the time of her interrogation), she, too, was expelled as an "alien."

Whereas a history of disciplinary problems reduced a student's chances of preserving his Party card, extraordinary service to the Party naturally had the opposite effect. The son of a shop assistant who had been in the Bund around 1905 and had gone even further in the wrong direction by joining the "Jewish Socio-Democratic Party of Poalei Tsion," Margolin escaped censure because he "had joined the Bolsheviks during the advance of Iudenich's forces against revolutionary Petrograd." Tomson, another student whose background was solidly bourgeois (his father was a landowner who leased out land, and he himself had enjoyed private tutoring as a boy), survived verification thanks to his zealous service in the Red Army in 1919.

Given that his father had been a deputy governor of Tver' under the old regime, the retention of Mikhailov in the Party was nothing short of spectacular. Having received the proper upbringing for a future navy cadet, the young Mikhailov rebelled against his background and left home to enlist as a stoker in the navy; in 1917 he joined the SRs. Apparently it was in his capacity as a Red Army officer that Mikhailov, already baptized as a Bolshevik, "took Iudenich on." Serving as the organizer of Marxist circles in Zinoviev University during the Discussion, this truly extraordinary Communist was never hindered by his family origins. (Whereas Mikhailov was praised for "helping to put down the Kronstadt rebellion," Polonskii, also a child of the nobility who had joined the Party in 1920, was purged when two denunciations were received establishing that his brother had been among the Kronstadt rebels.)

Because the Thirteenth Party Conference had declared that "the Party does not consider the Oppositionists a lost cause," there is no discussion of Trotskyists in the verification protocols.[34] The Party leaders insisted that the verification was not an "act of revenge" against Communists who had "accidentally slipped into petit-bourgeois practices through misunderstandings."[35] In a statement typical of the time, authorities at Moscow's Institute of Communication Engineers claimed they had removed "not so much Oppositionists but only individuals who degenerated as a result of NEP influence."[36] In his report to Leningrad State University, Aleksandrov likewise noted that "despite claims that the verification is connected with the Discussion, it was in fact sparked by the need to relieve ourselves of socially alien elements."[37]

Despite the official reluctance to target Oppositionism directly, some casual remarks in the verification interviews at the Leningrad State University show that heterodoxy was not treated lightly. The charges against Rokotov, for example, suggest that his real sin may have been his political stance: "Having made an unauthorized address before non-Party students," he was purged for "ideological deviation." The mysterious characterization of both Grodnetskii, who had lectured at a Party school, and Glazkov, who had worked in the Cheka during the civil war, as "ideologically alien" and "politically unprepared" suggests that the troika was dissatisfied with their conduct during the Discussion. Nor is it easy to explain why Berezina, an administrator of political courses on Vasilevsk Island, was instructed to "improve her grasp of Bolshevik tactics in the struggle against petit-bourgeois parties," unless she had fallen into the trap of the Opposition.

Communists of Jewish extraction were commonly suspected of heterodox orientation. Indeed, at least two female Jewish students purged from the Leningrad University Party organization without any real explanation must have suffered on account of their Trotskyist sympathies. Among them was Rubinshtein, a revolutionary since 1904 who had shouldered a variety of pubic assignments, now accused of "petit-bourgeois inclinations"—a known euphemism for Jewishness. Minskaia had, together with her entire Bund cell, joined the Party in February 1919 and had spent two months in a Latvian jail as a Bolshevik prisoner; but this history did not prevent her purge as "petit bourgeois" and "ignorant of Party ethics."

In the mid-1920s the Opposition was treated as a political manifestation of the NEP and the concomitant sociocultural degeneration affecting weak echelons in the Party. No one claimed that the supporters of Trotsky were deliberate saboteurs of Bolshevik unity, let alone dangerous enemies. A sustained proletarian influence, combined with effective moral-ideological edification (the metaphors consistently invoked images of medical treatment), could surely return them to the fold. Even the purged—hardly the majority of those who adhered to Trotsky's program in one way or another—were not regarded as incorrigible. The Party hermeneuts believed that after a short stint in the factory they were likely to regain their political senses and apply for readmission. The official press dubbed Oppositionists as "deviators" *(uklonisty)* not "counterrevolutionaries" *(kontrrevoliutsionnery)*. "Straight-liners" and "deviators" had an identical destination: Communism. Having temporarily lost clear sight of the Party goals, the Trotskyists had simply chosen an ill-advised, lengthy, and hazardous route to that destination.

The Left Opposition on the Bench

Internal divisions continued to plague the Party throughout the 1920s. The New Opposition challenged the Central Committee majority during the Fourteenth Party Congress (December 1925). Zinoviev's collaborative report criticized most planks of official policy, embarrassing Stalin severely. But since only the Leningrad Party organization followed the Opposition, it was easily defeated early in 1926. The most powerful challenge to Stalin's leadership, the "United Opposition," grew out of the wedding of a pair of former rivals. A fusion of Trotskyism and the Leningrad Left called for the restoration of Party democracy and the defense of the working class against Stalin's tyrannical regime.[38]

The year 1927 witnessed a marked escalation of the intra-Party struggle. Heavy rhetorical blows were exchanged, the Opposition blaming the Central Committee for relying on the apparatus instead of the Party rank and file and thus "betraying the working class," and the loyalists claiming that the Opposition had attempted to set up a second party, thereby putting itself outside the camp. When things came to the fore that fall, the Central Control Commission decided on an all-out crackdown on the Opposition. On November 11, 1927, it issued a directive urging provincial organizations "to prevent illegal meetings and to purge without hesitation all Communists who oppose Party policy at non-Party meetings."[39] When the Fifteenth Party Congress convened on December 2, 1927, the leaders of the Opposition found themselves excluded from the proceedings. The Congress declared the Opposition "an anti-Leninist second party . . . which capitulated to the bourgeoisie." Adherence to the Opposition was "incompatible with membership in the ranks of the Bolshevik party," so the congress set up a commission to recommend a series of measures to be taken. The principal recommendation the commission offered was simple: "Oppositionists must recant or they will find themselves outside the Party."[40]

For all intents and purposes, the Opposition was rendered illegal. For the first time, purge was an acceptable punishment of political heterodoxy (following the Fourteenth Party Congress, Oppositionists had been banned from ideological posts but allowed to occupy administrative positions). Verification commissions were set up across the country to examine comrades with suspect profiles. As a result of their work, 2,270 Communists across the Soviet Union were expelled for "factionalism" between December 1927 and June 1, 1928. Another 3,098 Communists declared their "departure" from the Opposition during the same period.[41]

Communists who appeared on the official "list of Oppositionists" were strongly advised to submit a "recantation" *(zaiavlenie ob otkhode)*.[42] Addressed either to the buro of the cell or to the provincial Party committee, recantation letters classically proceeded as follows: "I, so-and-so, 'disassociate myself' [*otmezhevyvaius'*] from the Opposition and endorse the position of the majority." Or, a bit less tersely: "After a detailed review of the literature—both the materials produced on the subject at the Party Congress and the speeches made by leaders of the Central Committee—I, so-and-so, admit that my position was erroneous." Verification commissions carefully inspected the recantations, comparing their contents with evidence collected by the circuit control commission. Afterward Oppositionists were interrogated in person, first by the buros of the local Party organizations, and next, if necessary, by the entire Party cell.[43]

As students recanted, they typically did their best to show that they had purged themselves of all counterrevolutionary thoughts. Reapplying the poetics of the traditional Communist autobiography, a proper Oppositionist recantation traced the spiritual history of the writer's consciousness. But unlike the autobiography, with its single account of conversion, a typical recantation spoke of no fewer than three quasi-conversions. Since all the narrators were Party members, the first of the three conversions was always in the background. Succumbing to the temptation of the Opposition was the second conversion. The crux of the narrative was the attempt to explain and somehow justify this lapse; generally this meant depicting the act of defiance as fleeting. The third conversion was of course the one that allowed the repentant to claim that he had returned to Party orthodoxy.

District committees across the country prepared periodic reports in which they classified the recantations they had received; during December 1927 and January 1928, the period when most recantations came in, such reports were prepared every three days. The Party kept track of the exact dates when recantations were submitted, the class position of their authors, their Party standing, and, most important, the extent of their deviation (e.g., "vacillator," "sympathizer," "activist").[44]

It was not unusual for students to submit a number of increasingly contrite recantations. A Communist University student named Karmannikov stated in his first recantation: "Recent events have forced me to reevaluate my views. I have concluded that the Opposition line is politically unsound and tactically disastrous" (December 19, 1927). This plea was denied because "it did not contain specific self-accusations." The authorities saw the letter not as a confession but as an attempt to smooth things over. In Karmannikov's second recantation (January 23, 1928) he admitted to having signed the Trotskyist program:

> Whether the sum of my Oppositionist activity is great or small is not for me to judge . . . Following the Fifteenth Party Congress, however, my views changed radically. I need hardly point out that, having decisively and wholly distanced myself from Trotskyist ideology, there can be no question of my involvement in further divisive activities. In addition to the remorse I feel for what I have done I also long to make amends to the Party for my guilt.[45]

That "sincerity" *(iskrennost')* was the ultimate touchstone for these recantations highlights the role of the verification as a court of conscience patterned after the inquisition and not as legal court geared to establish objective crimes. Only the absolutely sincere were believed to be truly remorseful; "recantations suspected as phony" were forwarded to the control commission for closer investigation; recantations found to contain "ambiguity" *(dvumysel)* were dismissed.[46]

The detailed proceedings left behind by the verification commission at Tomsk Technological Institute provide a glimpse at the Communist hermeneutic of the soul in the aftermath of the Discussion with the United Opposition (1927). The language employed by the verification commission hammered out a rich psychological vocabulary to show how various classes succumbed to sin. The Discussion at the institute had been protracted and bitter, pitting the deputy rector of the university, Kutuzov, and a group of students who followed him against the loyalist secretary of the

Party organization, Klikunov. Turning in October–November into an all-out war, the Discussion came to an end only when the resolution of the Fifteenth Party Congress reached Tomsk. Kutuzov was purged from the Party and expelled from the institute, and his adherents had now to face charges that they had participated in an illegal, nearly counterrevolutionary organization, the "Tomsk Center."[47] The verification commission was reluctant to declare too many Oppositionists lost souls. Klikunov preferred to describe his sinning comrades as uprooted workers: "victimized by separation from their native milieu, our students miss the factory."[48] The rest of the buro obligingly seconded his view: "Any Communist surrounded by books is in danger of becoming an Oppositionist, no matter how strong he is."[49] Only three students were actually purged from the Party by the institute's verification commission. The remaining few dozens emerged from the verification process with the innocuous label "disgruntled individuals." They had confessed their sins and were prescribed a refresher course in "the Bolshevik struggles against deviation" and sent home, pardoned.

Whereas a proletarian upbringing was assumed to serve as a strong antidote to heterodoxy, doubts and deviations were held to be natural to the intelligentsia. Influential as class was in assessing the character and sincerity of the defendants, however, conclusive proof of thought crimes overrode a good class background. Just as members of all classes could attain the light, so could members of all classes succumb to the temptations of evil; this was a basic assumption of the verification commission. If convicted of wrongheaded thinking, both workers and nonworkers were purged from the Party. In fact, workers often had it tougher; whereas they were expected to be perfect, the Party demanded less from members with less respectable class backgrounds.

That the verification commission treated nonproletarians severely meant that Grinevich, a student "with no experience of physical labor," was in serious trouble when he stood before the buro. Klikunov presented Grinevich as a typical member of the intelligentsia. "Grinevich's recent conduct has sorely disappointed us. He is completely oblivious to the seriousness of the situation and spends all his time pontificating." Other interrogators pointed out that Grinevich himself "admits that 'there is nothing straight about him.'" While he accepted some of the charges brought against him, Grinevich rejected others: "Because I lived in the same house with arch-Oppositionists, I was naturally exposed to 'Lenin's Testament' and the countertheses"—two crucial tools in the hand of Trotsky, who had tried to show that it was the Opposition, not the Central Committee majority, that was truly Leninist.

> Since it seemed to me that the Central Committee was keeping the Party in the dark at a crucial moment, I referred to Party leaders as schismatics [raskol'niki]. If we view the Discussion as a febrile struggle, a struggle that took place not only within the Party but also outside of it, then my support for Kutuzov was a grave crime. But I had no organizational ties to the Opposition. I give you my word, the word of one who has been a Bolshevik since 1917, that I am speaking the truth.

Grinevich also characterized the Discussion as a great ordeal that had ultimately contributed to his intellectual growth: "For me the Discussion was a laboratory of political thought. I now support the seven-hour work day [a Central Committee gesture to the working class coinciding with the tenth anniversary of the October Revolution] and have no doubts about the Komintern's foreign policy."

For better or worse, the implications of Grinevich's class identity dominated the hearing of the case. The healers of his soul formed a sort of a medical conference, discussing the patient's chances of recovery:

> *Obrazov:* Grinevich is a nice guy, but he has his shortcomings. The main one is that he attacks without any idea of what he is doing. Then he suddenly comes to his senses and mends his ways. He is indirect and tumultuous.
>
> *Fel'belbaum:* I've heard Grinevich's speeches for several years. He's always going off on tangents, swerving and zigzagging. His problem is that his mind is way too philosophical, too academic. His theoretical equipment is shaky, he tends to emphasize secondary problems, and he's always getting into hot water.
>
> *Klikunov:* If you look at how Grinevich acted during the recent events, it's clear that he feels accountable only to himself. Thanks to his frivolous concerns, he helped infect the Party with a "talking fever."

As they cited their complaints about Grinevich, the commission summarized a virtual encyclopedia of intelligentsia character limitations drawn up over the years. The defendant had indulged in vain rhetorical flourishes; he had enjoyed giving bookish and long-winded speeches during the Discussion, which for him had been nothing but "an opportunity to chat." Grinevich had been absorbed into the disputatious student existence to the point of "lacking proletarian straightforwardness." Besides sincerity, the more direct sense of "straightforwardness" *(priamolineinost')* was meant here—the capacity to follow the line charted by the Party to show the way to full proletarian victory. A self-indulgent individualist and free spirit, the defendant, so the accusation went, liked to draw fancy lines of his own—not exactly straight ones.

"You are right," admitted Grinevich; "I am sometimes circuitous." He was quite happy to let the buro infer his weaknesses from his class background rather than from the intrinsic qualities of his soul. Grinevich received a warning and was allowed to retain his Party membership.[50]

The verification commission was disposed to be merciful to "errant proletarians."[51] It had been instructed by the Central Control Commission "to be careful about purging workers." When Iarygin was asked, "What brought down a worker like you?" he replied, "When I returned to my native province for practical work, I encountered small abnormalities in how our transport and agriculture work. Those set me on the wrong path. I had insufficient theoretical preparation [to understand the real sources of the trouble in our everyday life]." Because he was a worker and still displayed "immaturity" *(nedorazvitost')*, Iarygin's punishment was light.[52]

Garan'ko was "a worker with seventeen years of labor experience." Although he had endorsed Kutuzov in every vote, this student showed himself so adept in manipulating working-class stereotypes that his judges let him off with the lightest of sentences. Witness the following exchange:

Q: How could a worker like you take a stand without having figured out the issues?

A: Though it has four feet, even a horse sometimes stumbles [*Kon' o chetyrekh nogakh i tot spotykaetsia*].

Through homely proverbs and a sort of proletarian patois, Garan'ko turned himself into the living embodiment of the quaint laborer and received a worker's discount.[53]

Panov's interrogators were puzzled that this worker-student had not only endorsed all the Oppositionist theses, but had at one point even entertained the idea of becoming an Oppositionist delegate to the circuit Party conference. Panov explained his vacillations thus: "I figured that if there was smoke there had to be fire, and I was confused by the form the

Discussion had taken." He had never been organizationally close to Kutuzov, but he "used to talk to him." But all this lay in a distant past. In the present, Panov was sparing himself no efforts to persuade his interrogators that his recantation corresponded with a spiritual awakening: "I no longer harbor any Oppositionist views. If I follow the Party line today it must be because I am convinced it is correct. Why else would I?" His strident and direct tone, the crudeness of his formulations, and the prescribed mixture of naiveté and doctrinal orthodoxy were crucial touches in the portrait of an authentic, slightly crusty member of the working class.[54]

Among those who were haled before the institute's verification commission, a number of student-workers could not deny their highly visible Oppositionist activities; the best they could do was to present their heterodoxy as temporary and unrepresentative of an otherwise firm commitment to the Party. In these circumstances, the solar-eclipse defense came in handy. In the hands of Kochkurov, for example, it became a trump card, saving him from certain expulsion. Kochkurov's "general level" was said to be low: "he clearly is unprepared to combine academic studies with theoretical development . . . He gave little thought about where Kutuzovshchina might lead the Party." Clearly, this was a case of degeneration; Volkov, all in all a benefactor of Kochkurov, piped up. "My general impression," he noted, "is that Kochkurov had been thoroughly brainwashed." As Obrazov put it, "Something came over Kochkurov [*ego chto-to zakhlestnulo*]. Yes, I recall him telling me, 'I can't understand what's happening to me.'" Kochkurov had been beside himself, had "lost his mind" (*poterial golovu*) for the duration of the Discussion. But all was well that ended well. In the spring of 1928, the sun was again shining down on Kochkurov. "The lad is sincere," remarked his confident interrogators. "He has learned his lesson, and in the future he'll think twice." The cell would bear responsibility for "ventilating" (*provetrivat'*) Kochkurov's consciousness, monitoring his behavior to make sure that he had returned to normal.[55]

Where Kochkurov succeeded Lugavier dismally failed. His years spent as an unskilled laborer and blacksmith constituted an impressive labor record, and Lugavier's misconduct originally appeared no graver than Kochkurov's: he was accused of fraternizing with Oppositionist leaders and reading illegal tracts. But unlike Kochkurov, Lugavier was only a Party candidate, somebody who had yet to prove he was loyal and worthy. It emerged from the interrogation that Lugavier had read some Trotskyist documents. "I wanted to form my own opinion," he explained. "Yes, if I had been allowed to vote, I would probably have voted in favor of the Opposition."

Having been described as "childish" and "hysterical," Lugavier set about making these characteristics the basis for his solar-eclipse argument: "I lost my way and developed a bias [*predvziatoe mnenie*]. My political shortsightedness has to be blamed." Although this apology sounded terribly familiar, the defense was stillborn. Rather than a lapsed Communist, concluded the interrogators, Lugavier was not a Communist at all. "As a Party candidate, Lugavier proved unrestrained and unstable . . . He failed his rite of passage and must be purged as politically unstable." There could be talk of solar eclipse only when a proper consciousness had antedated degeneration.[56]

Once Stalin severed his alliance with Bukharin and the right and intensified the industrialization and collectivization drives, cracking down on the kulaks in the villages and the speculators in the cities, even the most obstinate Left Oppositionists began streaming back into the Party. In 1929 and 1930 former Oppositionists who submitted letters of recantation were returned to positions of authority. Kamenev and Zinoviev confessed their sins at every opportunity, pledging their loyalty to the Party and its Stalinist leadership. Their supporters joined the Party and were given important posts in the government apparatus. Only the diehard Trotskyists who would not renounce their exiled leader remained ostracized.

The students of Leningrad Communist University also returned meekly to the fold. "After 1927," the official history of the university stated, "no group opposed the Leninist Central Committee." Once the Party made the transition to a "wide-scale socialist offensive, our Party organization proved so mature and ideologically committed that it met any attempt to pervert the meaning of Leninism with fierce resistance." The main enemy was outside the Party: the kulak in the village, the petit-bourgeois in the city.[57] The attitude toward Oppositionists was correspondingly conciliatory. This is why "political heterodoxy" was mentioned in only a handful of personal evaluations composed during the May 1929 purge at Communist University. Party organizers mentioned Kozlov's "ideological vacillations" and Kudamanov's "mingling with Trotskyists," but once they had produced "honest recantations" these students were warmly accepted. Many "errant comrades" were even commended for the "forthrightness of their soul-searching statements."[58]

Mikhailov was one of the very few former Oppositionists at Communist University who faced the real prospect of being purged.[59] "This crafty student," the buro noted, "never set down his recantation in writing, so it is not clear whether he has fully repented." According to some sources Mikhailov had persevered in making heterodox speeches. The interrogation opened with the reading of a deposition by Morozov, a Party secretary no longer present in Leningrad, who was considered the best authority on Mikhailov's soul. "Mikhailov renounced his Oppositionist views orally," Morozov had stated.

Despite the positive tone of this authoritative reference, the buro was reluctant to vouch for Mikhailov: "Although he has ceased his factionalist work we cannot be sure that he will always cleave to the Party line." If his detractors were to be believed, "Mikhailov still clings to the Zinovievist definition of Leninism . . . He has become aloof, self-enclosed." A number of students claimed that Mikhailov's refusal to propagate the Party line was a symptom of his persistence in heterodoxy. But Mikhailov vehemently rejected all charges of this sort: "To say that I refused practical work is not true . . . Had I known that my work as a propagandist would be reproved here, I would have brought documents from the factory stating that I am not a Trotskyist." Mikhailov's rhapsodies about the marvelous job he had done as a staunch loyalist were buttressed by statements from others in the cell: "During the struggle with the Trotskyists in 1923–24 he always actively defended the Party line"; "In the Caucasus Mikhailov treated the non-Party mass well; the entire local population lent him its support."

As usual, the issue boiled down to the defendant's consciousness, and in this case the focus was on his theoretical knowledge. While a number of speakers claimed that "Mikhailov boasts to everybody about how clever he is" and that "Mikhailov used to say that Trotsky's formulations were more precise than Lenin's," the overwhelming majority of students in his cell could not divine "where the notion that Mikhailov is highly literate can possibly have come from. As things stand many theoretical issues mystify him. Yes, Mikhailov brags that he knows Lenin by heart, but in fact he often fails to grasp Lenin's exact meaning and quotes incorrectly." According to his benefactors, there was nothing reprehensible about Mikhailov's voicing his doubts. "After all, he never insists on his mistakes, always says, 'Help me understand what is what.'"

Mikhailov's concluding plea built on this justification: "Comrades, remember that it was only in the Army that I learned to read and write . . . One of you said that my formulations regarding Leninism are 'insufficiently firm.' Now that I have read further I have realized that I made some cardinal mistakes. I supported the Oppositionist positions only objectively and not subjectively . . . Following the Discussion with the United Opposition you decided to retain me in the Party, and I have used the last two years to correct myself." Since everybody agreed that "his recent behavior is free of vacillations," the purge committee eventually decided "to retain Mikhailov and closely monitor his conduct."

Here was the Party at its most clement: at the close of the 1920s, Oppositionism was an opinion that had to be corrected, one belief in a baggage of beliefs, in short an ideological confusion or a character weakness that could be overcome. The 1929 Communist University purge commission was lenient because it construed heterodoxy as a wrongheaded opinion, not an incorrigible heresy. The Opposition served mainly as a kind of benchmark, a standard measurement of disquieting error, and right-thinking Party members might use it to sharpen their theoretical tools; it was not regarded as a hopeless condition. The personal evaluation of the following "former Trotskyist" is a case in point: "During the Discussion Comrade Chirkunov stated openly that he shares Oppositionist views. After the Discussion he rejected those views, just as openly. Irreproachable and honest, this comrade always presents his doubts sincerely."[60]

But even in the full flush of the season of tolerance that lasted from 1929 to 1934, there were warnings of trouble ahead. The sensitive seismograph of Communist poetics registered a certain intensification of manichean rumblings. Autobiographies from these relatively quiet years indicate that refinements in anti-Oppositionist consciousness directly affected narratives of personal growth. Consider the 1933 autobiography of Anastarenko, a student at the Leningrad Institute of Red Professors. As an anonymous member of the Putilov factory Party cell he had reacted "instinctively" to the Fourteenth Party Congress by mechanically embracing the right side; two years later, when he had become much more aware of the dangers of heterodoxy, he was already "personally unmasking Oppositionists in my shop."[61]

When students wrote of boldly opposing Oppositionists within their own cells, the heroic Stalinist self began making an appearance. Nikitin, another student at the Institute of Red Professors, recalled the work he had done in the 1920s for a local soviet, "then still in the hands of the Rightist opportunists." Undeterred, he had "steadfastly defended the Party line against all odds."[62] Describing his glorious struggles with the various manifestations of Oppositionism in excruciating detail, Kosol'pov, a third student from the same institute, distinguished between the various degrees of conviction with which he had been persecuting political heterodoxy:

> During the Tenth Party Congress the Workers' Opposition made lots of noise in our Party cell at the Naval Academy; at the time I was undecided. The Kronstadt mutiny sharpened my suspicions that the Opposition was doing harm. Three years later, when the country was undergoing a wave of Trotskyism, our institute was unaffected and the Discussion uneventful. Still, it would be presumptuous to say that I was politically super-developed at the time. What kept me from joining the Oppositionism were (1) Lenin's authority and (2) . . . my dislike [of complicated ideological debates]. Finally, when Zinovievism appeared, I knew quite a bit about politics, and began taking on our homebred Oppositionists.[63]

Although it is difficult to talk about a systematic campaign to suppress Oppositionism in the early 1930s, there was little allowance for the expression of political heterodoxy. With every week the cult of Stalin gathered momentum, and it could not be long before the Opposition came under fire. This is not to say that the indiscriminate persecution of Opposition that followed Kirov's assassination was not a dramatic change in policy, but this reversal had roots in the official political discourse.

The New Man: From Metaphor to Metamorphosis

During the 1930s the Soviet notion of man underwent a number of important changes. Schematically speaking, two concepts of the Soviet subject emerged: the developing subject of the early part of the decade, and the already-perfected, omnipotent, and omniconscious subject of the second half of the decade. Postulated into existence in 1936, the latter subject, the New Man, was the yardstick by which individuals were judged during the period of mass repressions. We turn here to the genealogy and contours of such a subject as conceived by Soviet sociologists and psychologists.

During the early 1930s, Bolshevik partisanship was the order of the day. Psychologists commented that the link between science and politics became particularly palpable. "All the fundamental questions, political as well as theoretical, are presently set edgewise."[64] Social psychology "assisted proletarian class struggle" by assigning workers for a particular type of labor on the basis of their "psychophysiological characteristics," and by teaching them "how to acquire the necessary work habits."[65] What was in the process of being created during the first two Five-Year Plans was, first and foremost, the New Man himself.[66] "The creation of a new type of human being has become our first priority," wrote contemporary developmental psychologists.[67] Soviet citizens of the future were to be characterized by creativity in socialist construction, purposefulness, discipline in labor, ideological resolve, habits of self-organization, and domination of class stimulations even in private life. A shock worker—the ultimate hero of the First Five-Year Plan—was someone who "reworked his habits, skills, and personality" and learned how to embrace his labor activity lovingly.[68]

Communists appropriated the Marxist concept of "labor" for the process of self-realization and advocated an authentic existence of the human subject as a creature that expressed itself though a world-modifying activity. "Labor," in the Communist discourse, should be understood not in its narrow sense as a description of human economic practice, but as the aggregate of those mental and physical capabilities which a human being exercised whenever he produced—that in which every single activity was founded and to which all activities returned. During the era of the first Five-Year Plan (1927–1931), psychologists emphasized "labor's constructive role, the tight connection between the physiology of labor and the psychology of the laborer."[69] Through the labor process, a Soviet worker was supposed to do much more than simply realize his natural psychological "traits" (*priznaki*) or his "inherited dispositions" (*zadatki*). Soviet men and women were expected to reforge themselves by themselves, becoming, in the process of labor, brand-new creatures with unprecedented "socialist psychology."[70]

Genuine Marxist psychology had to reject the reduction of psychic processes to "reaction," a term that implies a theory of balance.[71] According to early 1930s science, plasticity of human nature, its susceptibility to radical reworking, was the key trait distinguishing proletarian psychology from the bourgeois one. "When a scholar takes the dynamic positions and affirms the 'malleability' of man," one Soviet expert explained, "he is one of us. If, by contrast, he construes biology as destiny [*rok*], he is one of them."[72] Another expert added: "the contention that the Soviet proletarian can change itself while changing his environment—this is the quintessence of Marxism."[73]

Excessive affirmation of the plasticity of the human psyche—Lamarckism—was believed to have its own dangers, however. "Lamarck turned man into a passive creature that reacts to stimulations but is incapable of creativity." On the one hand, effecting a change in human features so that they approached the features of the New Man called for a belief in a flexible subject. On the other hand, purposeful work of the self necessitated an already-formed self, one that could set goals and take resolute steps toward achieving them. Dialectics was the solution. Holding the stick at both ends, Zalkind maintained that "circumstances shape the subject; and vice versa, the subject shapes his circumstances."[74] Applying themselves to a refutation of "bourgeois psychology" that either separated the psyche from the physiological processes turning the psyche into a "self-enclosed monad" or, inversely, "present[ed] the psyche as an automaton doomed to react passively to external stimuli," Soviet psychologists braced themselves for a struggle on two fronts: against "mechanism" (which assumed the man was totally malleable) and "idealism" (which ran to the opposite extreme, ignoring the historical conditions that shaped man).

What the Party demanded from the Soviet scholarly community was an "integral psychology" that would recognize that social man represented a complex, dynamic system of relations. Psychologists were asked to dedicate themselves to the study of "conscious personality" and the manner in which it "interacts with reality."[75] The most pressing task on the theoretical front was to develop a theory of "man's self-activation."[76] "Psychotechnics" was designed to deal with the "concrete and manysided ways" in which creative personality could be engineered.[77] Reconceptualized as an "active" *(deistvuiushchaia)* and not "contemplating" *(sozertsatel'naia)* entity, personality was conceived as the agency that guided men, that planned their economic activity.[78]

However strong the emphasis on self-generation, the transformation of man's consciousness was not understood as a voluntary process that unfolded outside any systematic laws of behavior. The internal constitution of the psyche, the expert Rudnik was certain, was not beyond the grasp of science: "We have to admit that man inherits a physiological structure of the organism, including the brain."[79] Zalkind agreed that "we have no need for the mystical, vitalist position of those who venerate powers that are supposedly hidden in our organism. There is nothing that is not determined."[80] Autonomous and self-activating, personality was still presented in this scheme more as an object of study than as its subject, "for otherwise it will be impossible . . . to work out its development prognosis . . . and imbue it with class content."[81]

Insofar as the growth of man's psyche was subjected to a law, man remained a part of nature. This is particularly evident in Kolbanovskii's methodological ruminations: "Marx enables us to fully understand psychological phenomena. His scientific method explains the biological regularities in the development of the human mind." Although Kolbanovskii pronounced man qualitatively superior to animals, his conflation between psychology and biology thrust man back into the natural world: "We do not exclude but assume the evolution from lower organisms to higher ones, the evolution from monkey to man. The qualitatively new features of the psyche on different rungs along this ladder are the subject of our study."[82]

This theoretical background explains the quick rise to prominence of pedology (pedologiia). Although a "pedological Five-Year Plan" had been announced as early in 1929 and pedology was linked to the "science of youth" (iunoshestvovedenie), it was only around 1931, when the Central Committee instructed psychologists "to collect and generalize the findings of educators who work directly in production," that pedology reached its zenith.[83] Zalkind defined pedology as a "discipline dealing with the complex unity of the science of man."[84] Aiming at a "systemic study of the contents of personality," this science of the "regularities, stages, and types of the sociobiological formation of the individual" attempted to map an important aspect of a psychological, but nevertheless objective, component of reality—the stages of human growth, from childhood to adulthood.[85] The Party hoped that pedology—the scientific basis for training the New Man—would make a crucial contribution to the success of Stalin's Revolution. The jewel in the crown of Marxist sciences of the psyche in the early 1930s, pedology was said to stand "not alongside physiology and psychology but above them."[86] Only a Marxist dialectical synthesis, as pedology was defined by Zalkind, "united the separate psychoneurological disciplines . . . exposing man in all his complexity."[87] Experts in the field declared that pedology was indispensable for a successful transformation of men. "Connected with the contemporary imperative to teach the toiling population new ways of thinking and prepare it for classless society," they proudly maintained, "pedology could develop only in the Soviet Union."[88]

In this scheme, pedagogy was no more than "applied pedology."[89] Without proper pedological preparation it was impossible to direct pedagogical process scientifically.[90] Whereas the task of pedagogy was to teach, wrote Blonskii, the task of pedology was to investigate how the child absorbed what he was being taught.[91] According to the main Soviet pedological journal, "pedagogy will not be equal to its task unless pedologists tell it exactly what is the structure, the bulk, and the degree of plasticity of the mind it works on."[92] Indeed, for a while pedology managed to displace pedagogy with its "retrograde" educational principles, thereby discrediting much of the 1920s educational system. Claiming that inculcation of knowledge could take place only on the construction site, through the laboring process, Zalkind insisted that "the realities of class struggle teach youth much more than any program of studies."[93] Because the influence of the environment on the evolution of the human mind was immense, another pedologist explained, "we should not drum information into the head of the child but create external conditions that will stimulate his development."[94] Crucial to our purposes in all this pedological theorizing is that the New Man was still conceived as something in the making. Hence the contemporary emphasis on development (in social terms) and growth (in individual terms).

Retaining its status as an independent category, "youth"—a metonym for what distinguished growing Soviet society from full-blown Communism—was conceived as something very different from adulthood. Books and journals carried articles discussing "the peculiarities of youth's thinking" and "the unique features of youth's social behavior."[95] Pedologists were eager to discover "the regularities of childhood development," "how social content refracts itself at different ages," and "whether youngsters from different classes mature differently."[96] That environment played a role in the lives of children was evident from the fact that "the pace and character of maturation . . . were not identical in twins subjected to different circumstances."[97] To know what regulated childhood development was to find the key to the evolution of society in general. For example, children's creativity, one pedologist argued, "is a condensed recapitulation of the general sociohistorical process of the development of language."[98]

Pedological research into stages of children's growth was, of course, conducted in the service of developmentalism, not of geneticism.[99] During the early 1930s Soviet authorities considered any hint at genetic determinism as a direct attack on the very idea of revolution.[100] I.Q. tests were said to determine not "inherited dispositions" but "the existent level of development of a given mental function." A child's phenotype, experts reiterated, should not be seen as a direct product of his genotype.[101] "Individuality," the pedologist Vnukov argued, "can be understood not in the general but only through a historical prism, related to the entire history of its develop-ment."[102]

That the New Man was still a work in progress was widely acknowl-edged. Somewhat paradoxically, youth was seen as synonymous with back-wardness, insofar as both concepts denoted something unfinished.[103] Lebedinskii, a prominent pedologist at the time, observed that "certain forms of remembering are absent both in children and in primitive peo-ple."[104] Psychological weakness was also embraced as a legitimate aspect of Soviet reality; there was time to overcome it. One psychological journal noted that "stresses induced by the Five-Year Plan enhance nervous infec-tions," and another study demonstrated that "difficulties with adaptability to new social environment may be the cause of psychoneurosis."[105] It was still possible to argue that it was generally good that Soviet man and women experienced acute neurosis, since "neurosis liberates the reflectoro-logical fund needed for creativity."[106] In fact, experts insisted at the time that illness should be understood in social terms. "Rejecting biologism in the interpretation of disease," Soviet medicine examined infirmity not so much from the perspective of the "breakdown of the functions of the organism" as from the perspective of "breakdowns in the laboring pro-cess."[107]

Openly acknowledging an assortment of ailments that beset young men and women, scientific journals discussed such unpleasant issues as "neural infection," "epilepsy and schizophrenia," "manic-depressive psychosis," "acute psychological traumas," "breakdown of the thinking process," and "syphilis of the brain."[108] In a continuation of the 1920s tradition, students were tested by psychoneurologists who looked for "intellectual fatigue," "lowering of psychological capabilities under the influence of exhaustion," and "malfunctioning in the emotional-willful sphere."[109] The construction of the New Man appeared primarily as a psychosocial challenge.[110] Vowing to make their own contribution to the construction of Communism, neu-ropathological and psychological associations took it as their task to help the Soviet Commissariat of Health in the reconstruction of neuropsycho-logical work "for the benefit of the toiling masses."[111]

Since it was obvious that the New Man could not be realized by an act of will alone, pedology was asked to establish the stumbling blocks to his con-struction. Framing the realm of the possible, pedology put the link be-tween class, working conditions, and psyche at the top of the scientific agenda.[112] What intervention in the environment would bring the optimal results in human psyche was the question experts asked themselves. "The environment carves from the pliable and unformed child-material future personalities," claimed Basov.[113] Now if a child "can be sculptured," wrote Molozhavyi, expanding on this idea, "we should seek to understand the conditions that leave the greatest imprint on the child's life."[114]

Despite appearances, however, such emphasis on external determinants was hardly a return to the passive view of man in homeostasis with nature, which had prevailed in the early 1920s. In this era of heightened activism the crucial element in the man-environment equation lay elsewhere. Now the driving notion was that if man was to be revolutionized, reality had to be actively changed. Pedologists maintained that the predictability with which man was influenced by his surroundings could be exploited for revolutionary and not reactionary purposes: "Each interaction between man and environment," claimed Molozhavyi, "finds its resolution in . . . dissolution of previous balance, systemic change, rebuilding, and creation of a new type of connections."[115] Armed with this knowledge, Soviet science could build "a new infrastructure in the child's organism"; it deemed itself well positioned "to restructure the entire activity of the child by . . . changing his surroundings."[116]

Exclusive emphasis on the environment as the medium through which psychic identity could be manipulated brought Freud's final demise in the Soviet Union that much closer.[117] The Psychological Discussion that took place in 1931 in connection with the Central Committee's decree "On the Journal *Under the Banner of Marxism*," celebrated the end of Freudism, now harshly castigated as "idealism in the realm of psychology."[118] Soviet psychologists emphasized that man was a social being, a "product of his milieu." The role of the inner drives of man was discounted. "What Freud is completely incapable of understanding is the social conditioning of behavior," an authoritative article in the Soviet encyclopedia declared. "Consciousness plays only a secondary role in his theory of human psyche, and the impact of reality is reduced to nearly zero. Fond of talking about biological factors, especially sex," so went the charge, "Freud does not think much of the role of socioeconomic determinations and class struggle. It is not social existence but the unconscious that determines consciousness, he erroneously argues."[119]

Publicly renouncing his former views, Zalkind now referred to Freudism as a "reactological perversion."[120] It was time to focus on the "conscious aspects of personality" and to depreciate "the weight of the unconscious and the subconscious affects," he admitted in 1931.[121] And in more detail in the pages of the main pedological journal: "At present I have no doubt that the Freudian system . . . contains a number of dangerous elements, methodologically and politically . . . such as the belief in the rule of the elemental past over the conscious present." Furthermore, advances in socialist construction rendered Freud's perceived conservatism pernicious. "It is clear that belief in deep biological (sexual) roots of the psyche is counterrevolutionary and that it discredits the constructive, battle-ready orientation of the working class. The victory of proletarian consciousness over old instincts, the development in the proletarian mind of a counterbalance to unconscious elements, all this reveals what garbage Freudism actually is."[122] From Zalkind's perspective it appeared that Freud's crucial mistake was his attempt to heal the psyche by trying to access it directly, instead of using the environment as a tool toward that end.[123]

In the early 1930s, Soviet psychologists conceived of man as a social being emerging via a complex social process, an upshot of the dialectical and somewhat chaotic transformation Soviet Union was undergoing. Still not entirely pure and self-aware, the Party had to allow life itself—class straggle and all it entailed—to mold the future generation.

In June 1936 Stalin's constitution was proclaimed. The concomitant declaration that the foundation of Communism had been laid called for a revision in the official notion of the self. The Soviet scientific establishment did not have to wait long before receiving a signal that the New Man was a reality, too: the Central Committee decree of July 4, 1936, "On Pedological Perversions in Our Education System," criticized the only recently celebrated science as pessimist and defeatist. "Pedology," the Central Committee now argued, "could reach the position it did only as a result of uncritical transportation into Soviet psychology of bourgeois theoretical principles, namely that the exploiting classes and 'superior races' presumably have talents that entitle them to rule over the damned toiling classes and the 'lower races.'"[124]

In a widely publicized address entitled "On the Theory and Practice of Contemporary Pedology," Bubnov made the case that pedology was an "anti-Marxist theory . . . an eclectic hodgepodge in which Menshevik apologetics of spontaneity, Struve's objectivism and populism, and an assortment of Socialist-Revolutionary creeds mixed with reactionary psychological theories."[125] Soviet psychologists were presented in the official language as having been seduced by the bourgeoisie. Failing to raise their

voices in opposition to the "most detrimental, supercilious pedological experiments," they had "perverted" *(izvratili)* and "emasculated"
(vykholostili) the innocent Soviet youth.[126] What was perhaps most ominous in these condemnations was that the language they employed was
identical with the language used to describe the attractiveness of Trotsky
and Zinoviev to the rotten segments of the population.

Pedology was lambasted for a fatalistic belief in an "irreversible conditioning of children's development." "Deeply reactionary," the laws of pedology were said to "glaringly contradict Marxism as well as the entire
Soviet practice of socialist construction." What pedologists did, so the accusation went, "equals denial of the very prospect for a successful reeducation of man." As a result of the "biosocial" and "sociobiological" principles
of their theory, "our children were doubly shackled: by the fatalistic chains
of heredity and by the environment they supposedly could not modify."[127]
The updated Stalinist historians of science heaped scorn on the "biological
roots" of the "pseudoscience" *(lzhenauka)* of pedology and its "vulgar use
of mechanism."[128] Blonskii was denounced for "treating human being as a
puppet," and Vygotskii's brand of pedology was charged with "metaphysical foundations."[129] The pedologist Lebedinskii could hardly dismiss lightly
the accusation that by thinking along the theoretical lines laid out by the
now totally discredited eugenics, he had been attempting to prove the existence of such a thing as "hereditary gifts in humans."[130]

According to the new Stalinist orthodoxy, theories of mental determination went hand in hand with impermissible social pessimism. Post-1936
Soviet psychological theory connected "pedological distortions" in educational policy with the heretical view that Soviet children could not accelerate their development and become adults in an instant. A new generation
of experts blamed pedologists for "presenting social environment as a dic-
tator and the child as a soulless object, a piece of marble from which the
environment mechanically sculptures future personality."[131] According to
Fomichev, "the counterrevolutionary charge of pedology" was expressed
best in what pedology had insisted on presenting as its "supposedly inexo-
rable law"—that children were influenced by adverse biological and social
factors "and that the marks these influences leave are for some reason in-
delible."[132] No one was willing to forgive Kolbanovskii for having asserted
the existence of "objective biological boundaries . . . that delimit the effec-
tiveness of educational undertakings."[133] Thus, so the iron-handed rebuttal
of pedology went, "pedologists reduce behavior to the sum total of its determinations. No place is left for human initiative and creativity."[134]

In all this we witness echoes of the criticism of the mechanistic view of man as a passive creature, a theory now ominously rechristened as the "Rightists' opportunist theory of involuntary social process." Although the parallel is indeed striking, there had also been important changes in the articulation of the main line of criticism. During the early years of Bolshevik psychology, psychic determinism was attacked because, by taking external obstacles as given, it depicted Soviet men and women as almost helpless. Unlike Bukharin, who blamed society, pedologists of the early 1930s blamed men who experienced difficulties in adapting to the fast-changing society. In the interim, however, the political context in which Soviet science operated had changed considerably. Once the Five-Year Plans had turned society into something nearly perfect, pedology was criticized for its outdated and overzealous emphasis on changing the psyche. Positing that citizens had to go on working on themselves, pedologists were suspected of implicitly suggesting that the Great Transformation was not yet fully accomplished, and that the New Man embodied in the Stalinist constitution was premature.

When viewed against the axiom that the current social environment was perfect, the deficiencies that contemporary pedologists continued detecting in Soviet youth could indeed lead to only one, very embarrassing conclusion: that native children were mentally retarded.[135] This was precisely what Boris Anan'ev claimed: pedology broke the development of a child into "time stretches" with supposedly natural and constant qualities. "When during a pedological 'inquiry' it turns out that a child of such-and-such an age cannot solve a problem that supposedly matches his age group, such a child is immediately declared underdeveloped."[136]

An array of organizational measures against pedology followed. Acting first, the Commissariat of Enlightenment banned I.Q. questionnaires from schools and ordered the removal of pedological material from children's personal files.[137] The Party apparatus followed suit, terminating in December 1936 all work in "psychotechnical laboratories." The Leningrad Dzherzhinskii Party committee explained this step: "Pedological tests, questionnaires, and contraptions are by and large counterrevolutionary in that they depict Soviet toilers as imbeciles or degenerated drunkards."[138] Official press demanded that the impermissible victimization of the children of the working class be immediately stopped. "Propagating physical and spiritual hopelessness in the toiling classes," pedology, one article after another now claimed, had "infested Soviet schools with a humiliating and soulless attitude toward the children of toilers."[139] In July 1936 a confession was extracted from Comrade Kniazeva, the head of the Leningrad Pedological Institute, that over the years her institute alone had dispatched 13,000 children to "health-improving schools" *(ozdorovitel'nye shkoly),* where the situation with regard to educational work "is known to border on criminal irresponsibility."[140]

The Central Committee was troubled by the apparent parallels between pedological disbelief in children's ability to skip stages of psychological development and the Opposition's denial of the Soviet Union's ability to skip stages of historical development. "The pedological notion of growth," Anan'ev's trend-setting article argued, "is based on a vulgar, evolutionary theory of development. Pedologists would not move beyond the notion of growth." Development, according to Anan'ev, was not "something preordained [*predopredelennyi*]—a realization of what was there in the embryo from the very beginning," but a set of qualitative leaps.[141] Emphasis on revolution in the psyche was not new, of course, but now this transformation was conceptualized as an event, not a process, and, most importantly, an event that lay in the past. Soviet psychology was desperate for voluntarist concepts. "Active reeducation of man" was stressed as a key component of "the transition of human society from capitalism to Communism."[142] According to the standards of 1937, one of the main faults of the pedological movement was that it had advocated that "a 'child' is not a 'small adult' but a unique creature with its own, specific properties. Essentializing age groups as standardized, frozen, and inert emphasized predetermined factors in human condition, factors that do not depend on education."[143]

Pedologists, in other words, were guilty of entertaining the possibility that childhood, and, by extension, backwardness and illness, could last. Luriia, who made his career in the early 1930s as an expert on human defects specializing in disorders in the brain, found himself in a sensitive position. His study of the psychology of the native Uzbeks and the distinction he posited between their "situational thinking" (typical of children and primitives) and "rational thinking" (typical of the civilized adults) were discredited. Vygotskii's work on defects in children and the mental disorder of schizophrenics was also declared unorthodox.[144] Indeed, the notion of "backwardness" disappeared from Stalinist anthropology. In the late 1930s the small peoples of the Russian north, for example, were not simply encouraged to be like everybody else but were assumed to be like everybody else.[145]

Finally declared to be a reality, the New Man was advanced and, no less important, healthy.[146] Scholars who denied proletarian prowess in the slightest degree were denounced. Zalkind was ridiculed: "Years after the Revolution he still believes that the working class was only 'trying' to become the master of production."[147] Any mention of "inferiorities" *(nepolnotsennosti)* was punished.[148] Among others, pedology was condemned for its "closeness to defectology [*defektologiia*]," and what was described as the unholy alliance of medical and educational establishments came under heavy fire.[149] Periodicals dealing with psychological illness or sociological backwardness were closed down in mid-1936. Other publications, celebrating health and consciousness and sponsored by the resurgent pedagogical institutions, were launched instead.[150]

Now that nervous illness was out, all psychoanalytic research was terminated.[151] It had been six years since Zalkind had recanted "my unfortunate defense of a mechanistic-reflexological Freudism."[152] Psychoanalysis had continued a truncated, shadowy existence after the attack of 1931, recognized at best as "an important scientific theory that explains the behavior of the nervously disturbed." By 1936, however, Freud was accused of "extrapolating his entire scheme of human development from ill patients," a terrible crime in an intellectual environment that did not admit illness as such.[153] Luriia, an early advocate of psychoanalysis, now maintained that it was "an erroneous theory that sees nothing but biology behind the complex, historically conditioned human consciousness." The effects of this position were not only antiscientific but also politically reactionary: "society itself is understood by psychoanalytic theory not as an entity that creates new forms of psychological life but as a negative force that inhibits man's basic drives."[154]

Noting archly that "the first word in pedology's pseudoscientific mumbo jumbo always belonged to Professor Zalkind," Bubnov made the veteran Soviet psychologist out to be the villain of the science drama of 1936; Zalkind was to die later that year.[155] Paradoxically, from the point of view of the students of the nature/nurture debates, Zalkind was vilified both for overemphasizing the effect of environment and for overemphasizing the effect of heredity. The trouble with pedology, then, was not this or that scientific stance but its deterministic overtones as such. What Zalkind had neglected to acknowledge, according to his detractors, was unfettered creativity—Stalinists' claim that laws of nature could be "overturned" by people.[156] A. Zaluzhnyi dedicated an entire pamphlet to discrediting the pedological teaching of his former teacher: "What Zalkind advocates is the bourgeois creed according to which human behavior responds only to external stimulation . . . Personality appears here as some sort of a biological entity . . . Zalkind believes that only the peaceful transformation of the human environment can prepare us for collectivism . . . and that revolutionary intervention into the course of what he calls 'natural social development' will only obstruct progress." The importance of psychic voluntarism—the crucial importance of man as the source of freedom—emerged quite forcefully in these criticisms. Zalkind drew such intense fire in part because the notion of "autogeneration" *(samodvizhenie)* was seen as totally absent from his writings.[157]

Naturalistic metaphors were swept from the stage of human psychology: "beast and child," late 1930s psychologists firmly affirmed, "are qualitatively incomparable."[158] The human mind was no longer seen as a simple extension of the animal mind. "The unique features of the human psyche should not be denied," the scientific press argued. "Today's mechanists have not yet given up their hopes of finishing off the psyche. They make it out to be a phantom and believe that its qualitative uniqueness arises out of the chance combination of material particles. This leads to an attempt to reduce the subjective to the objective, the ideal to the material."[159] Despite their naturalist training, Luriia and Leontiev essentially concurred with the criticism: "In differentiating itself from organic matter . . . the human psyche undergoes a series of qualitative changes. The main leap in this process is the transformation of the instinctual activity of animals into conscious activity." It was this that made a man a man.[160]

The New Man possessed a unique sense of individuality thanks to the unprecedented liberation of human faculties taking place in the Soviet Union.[161] "In the process of learning," wrote Professor Odintsev, "Soviet man strengthened his thinking capacity and his conscious Will."[162] Another expert, F. Georgiev, warned that the antiquated, "physiological reading of the will violates the socialist notion of the will, depriving it of all meaning."[163] "Only in our schools . . . where the interests of personality and society no longer conflict," the resurgent Soviet pedagogues maintained, was the true "individualization" of teaching possible.[164] Having almost disappeared during the egalitarian era of the early 1930s, "personality" could no longer be identified with consciousness or self-consciousness (concepts that could be interpreted as reflective and thus still somewhat passive), at least not without a residue. Instead it had become the "quintessence of human existence," not at all abstract or self-absorbed but a "concrete and active medium," the sum total of man's "actual relations with nature and with other individuals."[165]

This is not to say that mind was pronounced superior to matter; such a position would have brought Soviet Marxism dangerously close to its arch-rival, idealism. Rather, mind and body were collapsed into one. "Psycho-physiological unity" became the new dogma: "the psychic," it was said, "never exists outside and beyond the physical."[166] The unity of the psychological and physiological, a new orthodoxy stated, "is the precondition for human activity . . . Psychic phenomena not only accompany complex life processes; they are their precondition."[167] Once any meaningful distinction between mind and body had been invalidated, the idea of one acting upon the other had to be ruled out. Everything that happened to the body had to be somehow immediately registered in the mind, and vice versa. A bodily event without a corresponding mental experience diminished the omni-conscious New Man. Conversely, everything the mind could envisage had to become at once material reality; now fused with the mind, the body could not hinder the realization of the ideas envisaged by the omnipotent New Man. During the late 1930s research into the somatic underpinnings of the psyche was not interrupted. It was, rather, the idea of bodily illness hindering the psyche that would no longer be tolerated.

Emotions—the main product of somatic processes—were not ignored. Rather, psychologists postulated that the Soviet citizen's emotional life had fully engaged with the Communist project. Instead of diminishing the mind, emotions became, as it were, conscious. Only shortly before this period Kornilov had felt free to distinguish between "lower, individualistic emotions," linked with the "self-preservation of a separate species (e.g., hunger, fear, anger, joy)," and "higher emotions," which had "social significance (e.g., sympathy, morality)."[168] This hierarchy of emotions was now vehemently rejected. "According to Kornilov's anti-Marxist theory of emotions," so the condemnation read, "the mighty anger of the toilers against the enemies of the Soviet people, for example, is not a 'higher emotion.' Neither, if we heed this wrongheaded theorist, is the joy of the Soviet people at having destroyed the exploiting classes and built socialism a 'higher emotion'!"[169]

Now that pedology had been annihilated, it followed naturally that pedagogy would enjoy a rehabilitation. Indeed, on June 23, 1936, the Central

Committee passed a resolution titled "On Work in the Field of Higher Education," heralding its return. "The notion that schools will simply 'wither away'" was, according to the resolution, "anti-Leninist." Attending to the Communist education of the masses was pronounced "the main task of pedagogical psychology."[170] It was time to "reinstate fully pedagogy and pedagogues," Bubnov stated.[171] Pedagogy would teach students to be "politically firm and unbendable . . . and would instill in them a high degree of Marxist-Leninist consciousness . . . and inculcate hatred of class enemies." In the late 1930s, the pedagogical task had changed: not to create the New Man—he had already been born—but to serially reproduce him. "Cultural experts," the Central Committee resolution stated, "must train specialists versed in all the achievements of humanity."[172] Soviet students were taught by the best pedagogues to display "initiative" *(samodeiatel'nost')* in denouncing each other's crimes.[173]

High expectations generated enormous anxiety: now that society had been declared perfect, only the individual could be blamed for negative actions. Since it stood poised on the threshold of the Communist paradise, the new self was healthy and mature. Those who thought otherwise—pedologists or any other retrograde psychologists—were, quite simply, criminals. And so, in a crucial shift in the articulation of the Bolshevik moral enterprise, Party institutions deprived the psychological establishment of the right to diagnose the soul. Heretofore the object of scientific investigation had been the relation between environment and self or between the body and self. The key question now, however, was not genealogical but ontological. The question was no longer "How?" but "What?"—not "How do we produce a new self?" but "What is the inner self of this or that individual all about?"

It would be simplistic to say that in 1936 or 1937 science lost out to messianic spiritualism. These domains of theory and practice were intertwined in a myriad of ways, and any attempt to rigorously separate them would produce only a one-dimensional picture. The Soviet theoretical establishment, inside as well as outside the Party, announced that Soviet society had been perfected. This provoked hermeneutical tribunals, in the Party, in the NKVD, and in the Soviet legal system, to use the blueprint of the New Man as a measure of men. The implications were ominous: psychological clinics were replaced by courts, diagnosis by judgment. The road to the Great Purge opened.

The Hunt for the Opposition Gathers Momentum

In the mid-1930s, the demonization of the Oppositionists significantly intensified. The knot around them started tightening after December 1, 1934, the day Kirov was assassinated in Smol'nyi by a disgruntled Communist, a certain Nikolaev. The Politburo claimed that the "most treacherous Zinovievist faction" stood behind the assassination. Oppositionists, supposedly linked with the "Leningrad and Moscow Terrorist Centers," could no longer be simply purged but had to be arrested. Trotskyists, who had been anathematized since the late 1920s, and Zinovievists, who had been forgiven at that time because their leader had duly recanted, were amalgamated into one group.[174]

Countless articles assailing Zinoviev filled the pages of the Leningrad press. Zinovievists, described as "poisonous snakes," "human scum," "the vilest, most ignoble, and deceitful enemies of the working class," could finally compete with the Trotskyists in the arena of official demonization.[175] The city was reportedly "wild with rage." If there was little hard evidence against Zinovievists, this was beside the point. As one NKVD employee explained, "every member of Leningrad's proletariat wanted those who were directly or indirectly linked with the Opposition to be sent into exile, including those in their midst who worked well and had nothing to do with Kirov's death."[176]

Named as the masterminds behind Nikolaev's deed, Kamenev and Zinoviev were arrested and tried. In retrospect, their sentences were remarkably light. On January 16, 1935, Kamenev was sentenced to ten years of imprisonment and Zinoviev to five. Soon after the sentence was pronounced, the Central Committee dispatched to all Party organizations a secret letter titled "The Lessons of Kirov's Wicked Assassination." The preamble announced that "Zinoviev's group is the first group in the history of our Party to turn two-faced behavior into a requirement. The Opposition's willingness to bash its own platform openly and systematically . . . just to win our trust is unique. Zinovievists mask their wicked deeds with solemn vows of fidelity."[177]

The letter did not erase the image of the Oppositionist's perverted body but rather fused it with a deeply wicked mind. According to the Central Committee, counterrevolutionaries manipulated sexual temptations: "corrupting monsters—Nikolaev, Kotolynov, and other Zinovievists—turned

them into a tool for the satisfaction of counterrevolutionary passions
[*vozhdeleniia*]." The Soviet jurists aimed at settling a question very much
in the air: Were these men mad? Although Nikolaev's condition at the time
of his arrest "raises doubts . . . regarding his sanity," a juridical-psychiat-
ric examination, mandated by article 79 of the penal code, was not conducted.[178] When the Leningrad NKVD established that Nikolaev was "not a
weak neurasthenic but a composed and fearless fanatic," it was clear that
Communist hermeneutics would no longer assail the Opposition in medical language; the time had come for demonization.[179] Among the "opera-
tive conclusions" listed in the secret letter from the Central Committee was
a change in how Oppositionists would be punished: no longer would they
be "simply purged"; henceforth they were to be "arrested and isolated."[180]

Leningrad Communists contended that Kirov's assassination had completely altered the political atmosphere inside the Party. Endless meetings
and rallies tried to sort out the "recent counterrevolutionary operation,"
proclaimed to be "much more self-critical these days."[181] Heartened by the
bellicose stance of the leaders who vowed to enhance vigilance and exact
brutal revenge on the enemy, comrades on the lower rungs of the Party
ladder joined in the fray. The flow of denunciations and counterdenun-
ciations reached unprecedented proportions, and a good number of seasoned Communists who had spent years teaching Marxism and Leninism
in Leningrad factories and academic institutions suddenly found themselves threatened with expulsion from the Party and worse. An NKVD cir-
cular dated March 31, 1935, urged the Party grassroots organizations to
track down any Oppositionist who had ever set foot in their midst so that
they could be tried.[182] So quickly did the Great Purge gather momentum in
the early months of 1935 that expulsions were universally and unanimously endorsed. It had supposedly taken the death of Kirov for the people to begin reviewing old convictions with an eye toward harsher sentencing. The Party Control Commission pronounced old recantations null and
void. If they wished to call their souls their own, former Oppositionists
were expected to confess their old sins all over again and much more con-
tritely.[183]

In the wake of Kirov's assassination the profile of the very worst suspects
comprised two traits: Party members who had joined "petit-bourgeois"
political parties first and had indulged in Oppositionism second. This
sort of continuity was a sure sign of ideological waywardness. A series of
early 1930s trials of "petit-bourgeois parties" had preceded the onslaught

against former Oppositionists. In 1930 the GPU had arrested Aleksandr Chaianov and Nikolai Kondrat'ev, two of the country's most renowned agricultural researchers, and accused them of leading the "Party of the Toiling Peasantry." The "National Menshevik Union," accused of widespread industrial wrecking during the trial of the "Industrial Party," was linked with this SR-inspired group. During the trial of the "National Buro of the Central Committee of RSDRP" Krylenko had insisted that there were intimate connections between the "Mensheviks on the bench" and similar "kulak-SR counterrevolutionary organizations." The long and short of this crusade was that by the mid-1930s little remained of the once all-important distinction between "socialist" and "counterrevolutionary" parties.[184]

A striking example is that of the Bundists. Considered legitimate precursors to Bolshevism in the 1920s, they came to be identified with Jewish nationalism by the mid-1930s. Former Bundists who had succumbed to the temptation of Oppositionism were rounded up almost to a man. To justify the arrest of Professor Krivitskii, known for his "conciliatory attitude toward a Trotskyist," an NKVD protocol stressed that "Krivitskii was a member of the Bund between 1917 and 1918." Another Bundist, Professor Katsenbogen, was also arrested; his additional sins included supporting Trotsky in the 1920s and then, recently, having the impertinence to state that "Stalin's speech at the Seventeenth Party Congress did not exactly invent the wheel [otrkyl ameriku]."[185]

The arrest and exile of Kofman rocked Leningrad's scholarly community. The transformation of this highly respected scholar from Jewish socialism to Bolshevism had seemed a great success story, but in January 1935 his erstwhile Menshevism and Zinovievism returned to haunt him. Kofman's metamorphosis from Old Bolshevik into suspicious fellow traveler illustrates many aspects of the redefinition of political identities after Kirov's assassination. The dramatic deterioration in the public image of this professor of political economy, who had for many years been a significant presence at the Communist University, demonstrates how the renewed attack on Zinovievism catalyzed a reinterpretation of other, related sins. Those elements of an individual's past that everyone had been willing to overlook suddenly became intolerable.[186]

"Kofman has never been censured," read a personal evaluation of this Party member. "Students are satisfied with his lectures." To be sure, other, less attractive details were known as well: "In 1925–26 Kofman booed

Party policy"; "In 1932 he edited a textbook in political economy that included articles by a former Oppositionist." But considering that there was no evidence that "Kofman had persevered in his heterodoxy," the Party committee felt comfortable in entrusting a study circle devoted to Party enlightenment to the leadership of this highly experienced scholar—an honor that underscored Kofman's political loyalty.

Then, in January 1935, an outpouring of denunciations provoked grave doubts about Kofman's character. "Kofman wanted to affirm his break with Zinoviev in no uncertain terms," one letter stated; and yet, "even when plenty of compromising material against him was amassed, he hesitated to submit his recantation." Another, shriller text described the distinguished professor as "an active factionalist who exerted a strong anti-soviet influence on his students." An annotation in pencil stated: "Kofman had the nerve to object when Molotov came to Leningrad to draw students away from Oppositionism." Aspersions fell like hail over the next days. Kofman complained that "it is very hard for an honest Party member like myself to live and work in the sort of atmosphere of distrust that now surrounds me." Feeling "compelled to confess," he dispatched a long letter to the university committee: "My conversion to Zinoviev's point of view in late 1925 was triggered by a number of subjective causes," he opened. "I believed that the Opposition was struggling against Trotsky—this was what its leaders were stating."

Although Kofman admitted to having believed that "I have the right to express myself," he swore that he had never been a factionalist. "Honest comrades, I said to myself, could not be undermining the Party." When Zinoviev aligned with Trotsky, "my eyes were opened. In October 1926 I severed all ties to the Opposition." Later, when the United Opposition appeared, Kofman realized that he bore an obligation to work for its defeat, specifically in the realm of theory. "In the Vyborg district I conducted a Party seminar in which I set forth a critique of the economic program of the Opposition." His slip had taken place in the distant past, and Kofman—an Old Bolshevik whose mistakes had to be seen against the background of long revolutionary activity—was now absolutely loyal. "It is with great aversion and acrimony that I think of the ignoble Zinovievist terrorist gang, sworn enemies to the Party and to me. I cherish an untainted memory of our leader, Comrade Kirov, whom they treacherously assassinated." A reformed Kofman hung on Stalin's "every word"; he promised to "make sure that no one ever again moves me an inch from the proletarian line."

Remarkably, the protocols for such investigations in 1935 did not impose silence on the topic of battles within the Party of the mid-1920s. As Kofman's garrulous narrative suggests, the Central Committee encouraged the discussion of Oppositionism and played an active role in intensifying, reorienting, and modifying it. Kofman's 1935 autobiography written in response to Kirov's assassination should be seen as part of a deployment of a set of elaborate practices for refashioning the past. These practices were not supposed to reconstruct the past accurately, nor were they meant to distort it. They were meant as a creative effort to establish, by the light of fresh revelations, the deeper truth about the treason of such leaders as Trotsky and Zinoviev. Kofman had to understand the need to come face to face with his past once again and the importance of narrating his story in accordance with an updated, Stalinist historiography.

Kofman's recantation weaves the new history into autobiography, the macro into the micro, simultaneously reinterpreting the general course of the mid-1920s Discussions and his own role in the events. While he had to relive his traumatic past, Kofman's task was not to overindividualize what had happened by presenting it as a strictly personal memoir, but to insert himself even more firmly into the Party's collective memory. Together with the Party, Kofman would traverse a long path of development: at first a trifle insecure in his political convictions, he was gradually to become an incontrovertible Stalinist. This was how Kofman narrated those crucial events, nearly ten years old by 1935. "During the purges of 1929 and 1933 he made a clean breast of what had happened," and the purge commissions told him that since the Party had already established his naiveté and confusion, the issue was dead.

Having circumscribed his guilt, Kofman turned to preempt his detractors by explaining the origins of his misstep:

My Oppositionism can be interpreted as a belch of my bourgeois past. Comrades, surely you know that after years of underground revolutionary work, I, who had been a Social Democrat and, after the schism, a Bolshevik, sank in 1908 into the bourgeois "swamp." My philistinism [obyvatel'shchina] showed that I was then an intelligentsia fellow traveler and not a true Bolshevik. Surely you also know that in the spring of 1917

I committed a grave misdemeanor: by accepting a job with the Society of Factory and Mill Owners I yoked myself into service for the bourgeois spirit. At some time during the second half of 1918, however, I fully comprehended the greatness of the Revolution and its intimate link with the endeavor to which I had dedicated my youth. With all my soul I submitted to the proletariat.

Kofman told the story of the making of a New Man. He concluded his supplication with a passage nearly purple in its excesses: "From my new perspective the baleful pages of my past appeared to me so alien, so irreconcilable with my present, with my new life, that I could scarcely believe that I had ever done the things I did."

But times had changed, and the Party authorities would have none of it. They pulled no punches: "Kofman's speech at the Party meeting of December 25 and December 28, 1934, and his letter to the Party committee are exceptional evidence of a double-faced self . . . Only one conclusion is possible: this champion of Zinoviev has no place in our Party." When Kuz'minov, the Party secretary, sat down in January 1935 to compose a fresh evaluation of Kofman, what came out of his pen read, to all intents and purposes, like a denunciation. The autobiography of the accused was contested point by point, and important lacunas in his story were diligently singled out. It was evident to Kuz'minov that "his class origins predisposed Kofman to harbor an active bourgeois spirit." It turned out that the future professor was the "son of a rich Odessa merchant. He was born in 1879 and attended a series of prestigious universities in Odessa, Berlin, and Heidelberg between 1902 and 1904. According to Kuz'minov, Kofman had completely distanced himself from the revolutionary movement after 1905. "He had become a barrister in St. Petersburg and served until the Revolution as the head of the Department of Law at the Military-Industrial University. In 1918 he undermined workers' control of the factories." Although Kofman claimed to have been a Bolshevik during the 1905 revolution, Kuz'minov maintained that "during that period he worked primarily for Menshevik organizations and collaborated with people like [Vladimir] Voitinskii, who now lives in exile." Furthermore, "when Kofman applied to the Party he concealed his social origins, and during purges he never mentioned his mother's emigration to France."

In a summary of Kofman's new physiognomy the university journal spoke of a "political chameleon dressed up in the toga of Party-mindedness," a servile type "hastily adjusting to Soviet power," a Menshevik accepted into the Party on the strength of recommendations from Zinovievists and Trotskyists. "An insolent Zinovievist yesterday, today he composes declarations of repentance [*pokaianie*]. Feigning modesty and remorsefully bowing his head, Kofman keeps crawling back into the Party."[187] Every aspect of Kofman's record was excoriated. Kofman was obliged to admit that some of his autobiographical silences were indeed "criminal," but he clung to extenuating circumstances. "Bear in mind," he pleaded, "that I was motivated by the fear that the Party would not believe that I had broken with my past. Yes, I once served the bourgeoisie, but this is something that upsets and disgusts me enormously . . . But I was never an active Oppositionist, and I did not endorse the views of the Opposition in their entirety."

Eventually Kofman was reduced to groveling. "Every fiber of my being is connected to our university, but if it has been decided that every former must be sacked, so be it . . . But I absolutely cannot imagine my existence outside the Party." A few days later he had become reconciled to the inevitable: "Though I know you will purge me—such are the times—I intend to dedicate my life to unmasking the enemies of the working class." The hint of defiance that had crept into Kofman's testimony did not leave his auditors indifferent: "What do you mean, 'such are the times'?" "A time of tension," Kofman sheepishly mumbled, "when everyone is extremely hostile toward former Oppositionists, and rightly so." Kofman claimed that his purge was preordained. His hermeneuts, by contrast, appreciated the importance of stressing that Kofman was being examined as a concrete individual and condemned as such as well. Labeled "a bourgeois who after ten years in the Party has not been reeducated one tiny bit," Kofman was purged and driven from the hall with boos and catcalls.[188]

On January 26, 1935, the Central Committee resolved that 663 former Leningrad Oppositionists were to be exiled and sent to Siberia and the Arctic area.[189] Of those arraigned, most were students and professors who had allegedly joined the "entourage of the Leningrad Center." Kofman was arrested as part of an "operation for the liquidation of the Zinovievist-Trotskyist Counterrevolutionary Underground." The Leningrad NKVD carried out the operation in February 1935, exceeding by a few hundred the target figure set by the Party heads.[190]

One of those taken into custody was Gorlovskii, a colleague of Kofman's and the head of the Leningrad Institute of Philology and Linguistics. On February 5, 1935, the Special Council of the NKVD resolved to purge this

Party instructor and send him to Iakutsk. Gorlovskii's political career had been especially checkered: a Bundist for a number of years and a Bolshevik from 1919, he had been an ardent supporter of Trotsky in 1923. Although when he was given a chance Gorlovskii recanted profusely, his Party organization alleged that "he remained attached to former Oppositionists."[191]

A few months later Nikolai Ezhov, then the chairman of the Central Control Commission, and Andrei Zhdanov, the chairman of the Leningrad Party Committee, received an appeal from Gorlovskii:

> The main charge against me is that during my directorship I hired a number of Zinovievists, thus polluting the institute that was under may care. I have to say that the instructors I accepted had all been passed along to me by the Party's culture and propaganda department . . . Be that as it may, I admit my mistake, which unfortunately I perceived only after Kirov's assassination. However, I never had ties to enemies of the Party, certainly not ideologically and never consciously attempted to help them . . . I beseech you to reexamine my case carefully and sensibly [chutko] and to see whether I can be rehabilitated. I have never been a two-faced person.

By referring to a "juridical mistake" Gorlovskii let fall a clue that things were changing. No longer an intra-Party affair, Oppositionism had became a state crime, a form of counterrevolutionism. Still, it is immediately striking that the supplicant identified the loss of his Communist honor as his greatest concern. He talked not about the hardships of a life in exile but about the "stigma" (kleimo) borne by the traitor, a stigma he "could not go on carrying." Gorlovskii denied ever having been a real Oppositionist. "True, in December 1923 I committed a grave political mistake by giving a Trotskyist speech at a Party meeting. But within a few days, once I had become aware of my mistake, I openly renounced my speech." Old verdicts were hardly binding, as he well knew, but Gorlovskii nevertheless added that "I was never censored for Trotskyism." As a historian he had never accepted the "Trotskyist 'theory of permanent revolution' or his conception of the Russian historical process." As a propagandist, he had been instrumental in "unmasking Trotskyist libels against the Bolsheviks in connection with Trotsky's 'Lessons of October.'" As to Zinoviev, "I fought against Zinovievists in the Military-Technical Academy and in Herzen Pedagogical Institute."

Gorlovskii's language was infused with the manichean lexicon and imagery of 1935. His appeal became an indirect denunciation of a number of Leningrad scholars as he swore to having always been an enemy of all Zinovievists. In his self-presentation, Gorlovskii was a most vigilant anti-Oppositionist, so deeply concerned about the ideological purity of the students in his institute that he had routinely attended the classes of suspect professors to make sure that they were not deviating from the Party line and had checked up on them again by reading students' lecture notes. The supplicant did return to Leningrad, but not as he had hoped. In the spring of 1936 an alleged Trotskyist-Zinovievist terrorist organization based in Leningrad academic institutions was "unmasked." Gorlovskii was interrogated by the Leningrad NKVD as one of the conspirators, tried by the Special Council of the Military Collegium, and executed.[192]

After Kirov's assassination it became much more difficult for former Oppositionists to convince their interrogators that they had broken completely with their pasts.[193] Still, not every Party member who had endorsed a heterodox position at some point in the past was pronounced a lost soul. That stigma was automatically attached only to those who had supposedly deceived the Party and craftily concealed their political lapses. If, on the other hand, one recognized Zinovievism as a counterrevolutionary creed and denounced one's former collaborators, the road to self-transformation was open.[194] Those who vowed that they would "invest all their energy in the struggle for which Kirov had sacrificed his life" might well receive a somewhat sympathetic hearing.[195]

However important the tectonic shift in Communist discourse, the Great Purge did not assume its final contours before the summer of 1936. As late as March the third plenum of the Central Control Commission was preaching a more permissive response to those who violated Party norms: "Even as they struggle ceaselessly against alien groups . . . our organizations must be warm and comradely as they edify and persuade, must show sensitivity and attentiveness to each comrade."[196] Many traits later associated with the Great Purge had not yet appeared. Class language was still intact and, with it, the belief in reeducation through labor. No less importantly, the idea of fusing hermeneutical tribunals within the Party and organs of state justice—that deadly combination that came to stand at the heart of Ezhov's reign—was rejected. "We have to distinguish," the Central Control Commission stated, "the censures meted out to individuals for violating Party statute, Party discipline, or Party ethics from the censures meted out for breaking the law."[197]

Even more significantly, the Central Control Commission still clung to the distinction between the innocent offense and the willful crime: "When a comrade whose purge is being considered shows that his misdemeanors are the result not of a conscious violation of statute but of an insufficient absorption of the basic principles of Bolshevik organization and discipline, and that Party organs have not yet provided him with full political training, he should not be purged . . . Party committees must treat comrades sensitively if they honestly and fully admit their mistakes and if they vow . . . to reform themselves."[198]

The Advent of Messianic Times

The year 1936 marked the crucial transition from the Party's reacting, even if belatedly, to assertive formulations of heterodox political belief, to actively seeking out heretics on the assumption that they must have been there to be found. Any failure on the part of the NKVD to uncover the whereabouts of the enemy only confirmed that Oppositionists were able not only to cover their tracks but also to infiltrate official organizations.[199] Following the condemnation of Trotsky, Kamenev, and Zinoviev as deliberate traitors, the predicament of former Oppositionists became worse still. Stalin's notorious "Sochi telegram" of September 25—clearly a watershed in the history of the Great Purge—pushed for a particularly comprehensive reevaluation of Opposition activities.[200] On September 29 a Politburo directive, "Concerning Measures Regarding Counterrevolutionary Trotskyist-Zinovievist Elements," demanded the elimination of all surviving Oppositionists.[201]

As Stalin's constitution was promulgated in July and preparations for the first Moscow Show Trial began, people became aware that they had entered a new stage in history. The most zealous were already sniffing the eschatological horizon. An invigorated Party declared that the Communist personality would soon be given its head and encouraged to find its own way to enlightenment. Mark Mitin, one of the state's leading philosophers, declared that "the victory of socialism represents the end of prehistory. The actual history of humanity has begun."[202] In a well-orchestrated campaign, the official press all around the country trumpeted: "The dreams of the toilers of the entire world became reality," "We are the happiest men and women on earth," "Thank you, Comrade Stalin," and so on.[203]

Full-blown Communism was, however, still around the corner. Party propagandists argued that "the transition from capitalism to socialism is over, but the transition to Communism still continues" and that "some vestiges of capitalism have not vanished from people's consciousness."[204] Socialism had triumphed, but, as the official line reiterated, this "does not mean that all enemies have been defeated."[205] Omnipresent and dangerous, the enemy within remained a source of anxiety. To understand the historical significance of the new constitution, Communists had "to appreciate the crucial junctures in Lenin's and Stalin's battles against deviations."[206] "If for so much as a moment that vile scum Trotsky and Zinoviev had triumphed within our Party," stated the *Leningradskaia pravda*, "we would never have lived to see the new constitution."[207]

In 1936 it was once again the biblical apocalypse that provided the framework adopted by the Party to interpret the current situation. The historical process was conceived as a struggle of essential virtue against a virulent, but ultimately transitory, vice. If before counterrevolutionism had retained some internal gradations and shades of meaning, now its various manifestations—Whites, Fascists, or Oppositionists—were definitely all hewn from the same timber. "The different enemy camps," in one pithy formulation, "cannot be told apart."[208]

The Party now claimed that it had at last realized how foolishly lenient it had been, sparing outright counterrevolutionaries who had infiltrated Party ranks. Correspondingly, the curve of arrests among former Oppositionists grew steeper and steeper: from 1,871 in 1934 it climbed to 5,068 in 1935 and then leaped to 23,373 in 1936 and 56,503 in 1937.[209] Research into Communists' pasts was pursued with astounding meticulousness and care. Materials on purges and transcripts of antiquated Party meetings were backchecked for any heterodox speeches. Special teams pored over the cells' archives, making lists of the heterodox, compiling new lists on the basis of unprocessed material from years before, and cross-listing and indexing all personal information on Oppositionists that they could lay their hands on. Such interest in political biography reflected the conviction that evil was innate and that any now proven to be tainted must have betrayed hints of their true nature at different points in their past.

Evil was immutable and timeless. It had always been there, though only now was it fully unmasked. As the new orthodoxy put it, "Trotsky was an enemy of the workers' movement from the earliest times [*izvechnyi*]."[210] Asked in August 1936 whether Trotsky had become a counterrevolutionary before or after being deported, Il'in, the secretary of the Party organization at Communist University, dismissed this question as "nonsensical."[211] Four days later Communist University's Zhukov made the mistake of referring to the Oppositionists as "our former comrades" and was immediately corrected: "They were never 'our comrades'; it was our blindness that made us believe such nonsense."[212]

As it adapted to the new ontology of evil that summer, the hermeneutics of the self was undergoing important changes. Few retained their earlier confidence that class origins were a reliable clue to the soul. On the contrary, it was a fundamental assumption of the new hermeneutics that class and loyalty to the cause did not necessarily go hand in hand: workers could reject Communism just as the bourgeois could unexpectedly embrace it. Stalin's constitution proclaimed guilt to be individual, not social. This was explained by the propagandist Rybenov to students at the Leningrad Institute of Red Professors in 1936: "Recall what used to happen to an immaculate [*neporochnyi*] Party member with wrong class origins. He himself would certainly get purged, and if he had a son—even if the kid was in the Komsomol—he would get purged, too. I have no better term for this than persecution, harassment of people . . . Now the Party has resolved that everyone, regardless of social origins, is equal."[213]

For a while it seemed as though ideological heterodoxy would replace class as a criterion for identifying the enemy. Oppositionist recantations no longer convinced, and the formerly heterodox were arraigned once again, this time not by Party courts but by the NKVD, with all that this entailed; any contributions the suspects might have recently made to socialist construction were irrelevant. Ultimately, however, even so promising a criterion as a heterodox past proved to have limited utility. Authorities at the Leningrad Institute of Red Professors noted that "although formers were barred from Communist universities from as early as 1932, the enemy found other cracks and succeeded in infiltrating our camp. In trying to identify the enemy it is not sufficient to ask whether they have participated in Oppositionism."[214]

Appearing in article 131 of Stalin's constitution, "enemies of the people" referred to a new type of villain, a villain linked to the epoch of victorious socialism. The term had been in desuetude since the end of the civil war; in the 1920s the Supreme Executive Committee of the soviets had spoken of "enemies of the toilers" (*vragi trudiashchikhsia*), not "enemies of the people" (*vragi naroda*).[215] Talk about "enemies of the people" amplified the manichean undercurrents present in Communist discourse. During the

Great Purge, the enemy was no longer the bourgeois class as such ("that class has been essentially liquidated") but a loose assemblage of vaguely defined evil creatures, obsessed with the desire to reverse history and restore capitalism.[216]

"Enemies of the people" was so broad a term that it burst all attempts at definition. Old hermeneutical categories had been undermined, and a radical rethinking of the enemy's identity was clearly on the way. The crucial innovation of 1936 was the essentialization of heterodoxy to such a degree that past crimes and current crimes were collapsed into one and the same thing: yesterday's Oppositionists metamorphosed into the active counterrevolutionaries of today; conversely, the counterrevolutionaries of 1936 assumed the stereotyped traits of Oppositionists, who had schemed against the Party all along.[217]

Such a worldview provided a congenial climate for evaluating an individual's ethical makeup in explicit and sharply delineated terms. Loyal Communists would at last move beyond "superficial signs" and begin to probe the "true essence" of their associates.[218] But "essence" *(sushchestvo)* should not be confused here with "personal qualities" *(lichnye kachestva)*: the former term had a moral-eschatological meaning, the latter a more restricted, psychological one, and the distinction was generally honored. The Communist's soul should not be confused with the individual's psychology: it was closer to the Socratic impersonal or, rather, suprapersonal daemon. Schneider, a Leningrad Communist, was taken to task precisely because his condemnation of the Oppositionist leaders missed this key distinction. "The makeup [*natura*] of Zinoviev and Kamenev is such that they cannot bring themselves to agree with our policy," he had stated during a Party meeting in 1936. "Their personal qualities lead them to swerve constantly from the Party line." For assuming that human weaknesses could be improved, Schneider had his knuckles rapped: "Instead of making manifest the counterrevolutionary essence of the anti-Leninist leaders, Schneider maintains that their mistakes stem from habit."[219] When "personal qualities" were reviewed, something external and fairly random was meant; the Party hermeneuts averred that "character" or "nature" was something contingent and circumstantial; every individual had his idiosyncrasies, his own inclinations. The "essence," by contrast, was the deepest and most fundamental feature of the soul; there were only two kind of human essences—good and evil.

According to the new hermeneutics, it was no longer sufficient to assess individuals solely on the basis of their questionnaires and autobiographies. What one had become, what one had been at the core of one's being, was more important than one's past behavior. The following instructions, issued by Leningrad Party heads, captured these subtle alterations in hermeneutical technique: "Look not only into how someone studies and works but also into how he spends his leisure hours, into his routine. What does he say at home? What does his little son say he is saying? What does his wife say he is saying?"[220] Objectification was proscribed. The university press chastised Party organizations for "presenting the mass as abstract human object [*chelovekopredmet*]."[221]

The pros and cons of various hermeneutical methods were widely discussed. A letter by a certain Vybonov, intercepted by the Leningrad Party apparatus in 1936, showed that these issues could even become subjects of private correspondence:

> Just returned from the Party meeting: in our organization everything is all right, no one has been purged, no cards withdrawn. *I am lucky that I was in the group checked by Klenov. I like his method. Klenov conducted the interrogation superficially, taking only the biographical angle. Eglit, by contrast, checked much more carefully, from all perspectives; he's the one who exposed so many aliens. If it had turned out to be Eglit who examined me, I was going to tell him plenty about myself; not only about my origins, they are clean, but also about my degenerate moods;* but to Klenov I said nothing.[222]

Klenov, the easygoing hermeneut, focused on Vybonov's past, thereby neglecting what was now all-important, the current state of comrades' souls. The fact that the Party official who examined the letter marked the lines that testified to his oversight suggests he was to be duly punished.

While biography lost ground as a hermeneutical technique the study of physiognomy left its mark on many reports. Strange facial expressions, lip-biting, brow-mopping, and stammering were the sure signs of counterrevolutionary students. "I do not know this person," admitted many an interrogator. "But I can tell by his eyes he is an enemy of the people."[223] One of Stalin's closest collaborators, Lazar Kaganovich, said apropos the show trial of Kamenev and Zinoviev, "By looking into their eyes you can sense an enemy; there is no light in such individuals, no soul in their work."[224] "Livshits," Kaganovich once asked his deputy, "why do you have such a somber mien? Should I conclude that you still harbor vestiges of Trotskyism?"[225] Skillful hermeneuts were supposed to know that the meaning of signs must sometimes be inverted. "According to bourgeois ethics, eyes are the mirror of the soul," Belov told Voroshilov, the head of the Red Army. "But the eyes of those accused at the show trial never revealed their bottomless wickedness." Other signs, however, did bear direct witness to the truth. "The posture of the accused was extremely abnormal," they had a grim and hammered look, and the "seal of death was written all over their faces."[226]

At the threshold of a new era the soul was becoming transparent, and the distinction between the surface and what lay beneath—the core problem in Communist hermeneutics in the past—was greatly diminished. This explains why the art of physiognomy, with its emphasis on surfaces—face, body language, dress—did not collide with the "unmasking" technique that emphasized the soul's interior. Advances in Stalinist hermeneutics meant that its practitioners could move freely between essence and appearance; one's "Party face" *(partiinoe litso)* and "deepest core" *(glubokaia sushchnost')* were interchangeable.

As Party officials busied themselves with the "exchange of Party documents" for much of 1936, the Communist hermeneutics of the soul expanded to suit the redoubled search for the enemy within.[227] A close inspection of the reports on the exchange of documents yields an accurate map of the important shifts in the enemy's profile. In May the exchange had hardly begun: the exchange board described the purged as the children of kulaks and speculators.[228] But by the time the final results of the exchange were presented in October, little remained of the language of class. "In the process of the exchange," the Party organization now reported, "we expelled enemies of the people," among them "Whites," "alien elements," and "Trotskyist-Zinovievists."[229]

The discourse moved another step closer to wholesale demonization of the Oppositionists. Not only were more Oppositionists assailed than in the 1935 purges, but also there was an important shift in terminology. Now they were designated not as "formers" but as "Trotskyist-Zinovievist active counterrevolutionaries," not something relegated to the past but something very much alive.[230] Two additional linguistic innovations merit attention. First, a record number of nine students were pronounced "spies," indicating a growing obsession with the violation of Communist borders, geographic and ideological; second, "alien elements" *(chuzhdyi element)*, those class aliens who were potentially enemies, became "enemy elements" *(vrazdebnyi element),* that is, actual enemies. After all, Stalin had declared in his constitution that class war in the Soviet Union was over, and this change in terminology explains the ease with which the exchange board admitted that the majority of those purged were "workers" in terms of their social standing: class could no longer be relied on in identifying the enemy.[231]

The charges Toffer faced before his Party card was eventually reclaimed by Communist University go a long way to show how Party discourse transformed Oppositionism into a vague description applied to all untoward political behavior.[232] Members of this Estonian Communist's cell denounced him as a "haughty worker" who looked down on the peasantry, a telltale sign of Trotskyism. "Toffer engages in needless disputation and swears at the drop of a hat. Calling us 'toadies who shiver as we fondle our Party cards,' he tells us to 'boil for another five years in the proletariat cauldron, then teach me something.'"

Toffer pinned his hopes to his proletarian autobiography.

> Believe me, I was always loyal to the Party and will remain so. What are the chances that one who was raised by the Komsomol, who has supped at the Party's table, would turn out a rascal? In 1919 I was already at the front, and somehow I managed to survive. My father's name is hanging on a blackboard in Narva [among the Bolshevik heroes who paid for the victory of the Revolution with their lives].

But the new generation of inquisitors had little patience for autobiography. "Do not bother to go four generations back just to exculpate yourself. You speak about your proletarian origins and give us the 'I-am-a-son-of-the-toiling-people' line. No one doubts your origins, but that is not why you are being interrogated."

Seeing that this was getting him nowhere, Toffer opted to reassess his proletarian skills and to seek refuge in his growth potential. "Maybe my behavior is due to my inadequate cultural development," he said. "I do not understand how a student should behave." But recourse to backwardness as an excuse was also an old game; it did not square with the assumptions underlying Stalin's constitutions that the New Man had already been perfected. This stratagem was brushed aside with the comment that "instead of admitting his mistakes Toffer philosophizes."

Things looked bleak indeed, but Toffer had not given up. In fact he tried a number of fairly sophisticated identity maneuvers. He spoke of his working-class coarseness: "Nothing penetrates my head these days. My diplomas are the ten fingers on my hands. When so many accusations are being leveled at me . . . I grow numb, smack my fist on the table and yell at everybody. Yes, I have a big ego, a loose tongue." This was not much of an apology, and once again Toffer was not allowed to finish his sentence: "Instead of simply repenting, you say you are hotheaded." Proletarian straightforwardness was useless against suspicions that a thought-crime had been committed.

As the Soviet subject became transparent, the solar-eclipse line of defense lost much of its support. But Toffer tried it anyway: "Comrades, I am not saying I am demented. Perhaps my tongue slipped, but I did not consciously say anything wrong. When I described our pricing policy as 'crafty' [*khitraiia*], what I really meant was 'clever' [*umelaia*]. You cannot read too much into that; I speak bad Russian." His tone belligerent, he announced, "I cannot accept that I am a conscious Trotskyist. You are mechanically applying the term 'Trotskyist' to me."

Toffer insisted that he himself had the best access to his soul. "Am I an enemy today? Who knows better than I that nothing can be worse for a Communist than to be expelled from his Party?" But Prem, the secretary of the local Party organization, had his own ideas about how the mind of the accused was to be explored, and he rejected this autohermeneutics: "Do not preempt us, Toffer. Comrades here know you quite well, and they will decide who you are." One of the purgers, Comrade Shal'gin, brought some clarity to the challenge the exchange board faced: "It is our task to figure out whether Toffer's belief that the peasantry is reactionary is a systematic view or an expression of his political illiteracy. The two scenarios are mutually exclusive." Duev, another interrogator, was inclined to show some clemency: "Toffer has no substantial critique of the Party; he took his words back, didn't he?" But even this gesture had to be hedged: "Of course, if everything attributed to Toffer is true, then he is indeed a Trotskyist." The condemnation by another student, Lovtsikov, was more persuasive: "Toffer starts out by saying that he knows everything and that we must learn from him and ends up claiming that he lacks consciousness."

Toffer insisted that none of this meant that he "harbored Trotskyist thoughts . . . I can correct myself. For me, being expelled is like being led to the scaffold." He burst into tears. But even this extravagant display backfired. The physiognomists were pitiless: "Toffer's whimpers and sniveling are not the behavior of a Communist but of a Trotskyist. Where is his self-command? Toffer, you are basically suggesting that if you don't like the Party's decision you are going to stick your neck in the noose. Is that proof of Communist character?"

His defense strategies struck down one by one, Toffer was unanimously purged. Duev, the questioner who had expressed some sympathy for the accused, was reprimanded, although he had spoken so cautiously that he must have been very anxious of the outcome. "I admit that I erred by underestimating Toffer's Trotskyism," he said. Then Duev challenged his tormentors: "But I am the scapegoat for our entire cell; I would rather remain a non-Party Bolshevik than be censured for supporting Trotskyists." It remained for Prem to note that "what Duev just said has only exacerbated his guilt."

A Transparent Soul

Modifications in the autobiographical genre, always an excellent barometer for what was going on with the Communist self, point unmistakably toward the essentialization of moral features. In the 1920s, the autobiography had been a complex genre that dwelt on the phenomenological evolution of the individual's worldview and on his arduous work of self-correction and self-discovery, highlighting his dramatic conversion to Communism. Now the autobiography was an extremely monotonous literary form that presented an unchanging, unalterable picture of the autobiographer's soul. Whereas in the past autobiographers had drawn on a range of model selves, now there were two basic types: the good soul and the wicked soul. Inevitably new reading practices also arose. Rather than measure the author's proximity to the light, the inquisitors practiced a form of rudimentary indexing to determine only whether the accused was with "us" or with "them."

The wonderful stories of self-transformation had been replaced by compendiums of the actions most illustrative of a moral ontology. To be sure, a certain interest in the life persisted: before the 1936 exchange of Party documents, for example, students were told to prepare fresh autobiographies, their most "candid" to date. "Comrades must recount their life stories at our meetings," said Dertin, a student at the Leningrad Institute of Red Professors. "How can I be ignorant of the biographies of those in my own cell?"[233] But the focus of the autobiographies had nothing to do with following the soul through its metamorphosis; all the Stalinist inquisitors wanted was to find previous illustrations of the individual's moral kernel.

Those who wrote their autobiographies in the mid and late 1930s did not speak of becoming Communists; they simply insisted that they had never been anything else.

The mature Stalinist autobiographer had ceased to function as an individual and had completely internalized the perspective of the collective. Hence the widespread practice of including excerpts from personal evaluations in the story. The autobiography had come to resemble a completed questionnaire: they were not "composed" *(sochinit')* but "filled out" *(zapolnit')*.[234]

The following questions established the framework for Communist autobiographies in the mid-1930s:

(1) What is my date of birth and my social origins? (2) What is the social standing of my parents? What is their relation to Soviet power? (3) Who are my brothers and sisters and how do they relate to Soviet power? (a) Have any of my family members been disenfranchised? (b) Does anybody from my family live abroad?

Later, and especially from 1936 onward, those first four clauses, dwelling on class background, were either dropped or deemphasized. The questions continued thus:

(4) When and where did I begin working? (5) Was I a wage laborer? (6) What Party work or social work do I do? (7) What is the record of my education from childhood to the present?

Communists were now invited to discuss their present before turning to their past. One's contribution to Soviet economic construction was usually examined prior to one's political development. The issue of education, which appeared sixth in the scheme, was the first that demanded some sort of chronological presentation.

Items arranged around the theme "the Party and I" came next:

(8) Who accepted me to the Party and when? (9) Was I in the Opposition? (10) For what have I been censured by the Party? Give a detailed account of the charges [*sostav prestupleniia*]. Have the censures been removed? (11) Was I ever elected to any public post?

Insofar as one's Party record had to be discussed before one got to the circumstances of one's admission, there was no possibility of a conversion narrative.

Let us examine the autobiography of Il'in, the Party secretary at Communist University from October 1936 and a model young Stalinist:[235]

> Born in 1900, I attended a public high school close to my parents' house. In 1920 I was conscripted. Demobilized in 1921, I returned to the bench at my old factory in Moscow . . . In 1930 the Moscow Party Committee sent me to study in Leningrad . . . In 1934 Narkomzem sent me to study at the Planning Institute's political department . . . In mid-1936 I was transferred and became an instructor at the university.

Extremely monotonous, the text is structured after a chronicle—something steadfastly avoided earlier. Since spiritual transformation did not figure in the story, the narrator's use of the passive voice was more or less consistent; Il'in remained what he had always been, a loyal proletarian dedicated to Party duties. The Central Committee had moved him from place to place like a pawn, and he loved it, just as he embraced the opportunity to strip himself of all agency.

Given its utter lack of narrative, it is hardly surprising that Il'in's autobiography subordinated chronology to a thematic presentation. After inventorying his contributions to socialist construction up to the present, Il'in traveled backward in time to discuss his family background: "My father, a tanner, and my mother, a clothmaker, worked in the same factory. My older brother is a driver, the younger is a pilot. My older sister is a weaver." Indefatigably committed to this dry style, Il'in gave similar details about the careers of his other sisters. Next the autobiographer turned to his own Party record and reviewed yet again the years, and some of the material, he had already discussed:

> I entered the Party in November 1920; in December of that year the Krasnaia-Presnia district committee sent me to work as a political commissar at the preenlistment compound park. In June I was mobilized and sent . . . to the southwestern front . . . In 1927–1930 I worked in an executive committee; in 1931 I was sent to study; while formally I was a student in reality I was employed in grain procurement . . . I worked as a cultural propagandist in the district committee until November 1935, at which time I became deputy chairman of the Donetsk district committee.

At no point in the presentation of his Party record did Il'in offer any sort of phenomenological observation about himself. There was no talk of personal commitment to the victory of the movement, no excitement about the classless society looming ahead; not so much as a hint of these rattled the format of a digest. Il'in's autobiography was no more than a compendium of good deeds spread around the calendar.

Toward the end of his text Il'in added something about his disciplinary record. Again, the text's organizing principle was not storytelling but list-making:

> Having joined the Party in 1920 I left it in 1921 because I had missed verification. I joined for the second time in 1925, and my Party standing officially begins on that date . . .
> Never in Opposition.
> No Party censures.
> Have no relatives who were alien elements or joined the Opposition.

This is a text that could well have turned up in a juridical setting; it is informative and careful, not enlightening and sensational.[236] In Il'in's autobiography there is no personal development—how could there be in one perpetually conscious?—even as the Soviet Union was undergoing great upheavals.[237]

What is significant in the autobiography from the time of the Great Purge is not that its protagonist is docile and deprived of initiative (such a generalization would exclude all the Stakhanovite shock workers, famous arctic explorers, and other recordbreakers) but that the autobiographer's personality remains entrenched and does not evolve through the course of his life.

If Il'in was always passive, his peer Rabinovich was always active. It is difficult to find a sentence in Rabinovich's 1936 autobiography written in the passive tense. A young Jewish man of twenty, this instructor at the Leningrad Institute of Red Professors moved from Smolensk to Petersburg to engage in underground activity at a very early age. Rabinovich never mentions his conversion to the revolutionary cause; Social Democracy was second nature to him. What is more, he seems to have been a Bolshevik even before Bolshevism was born. The narrator was linked to Lenin's newspaper from his first days in the capital and surrounded himself with diehard Leninists. "I joined the party committee devoted to *Iskra* and collaborated with Babushkin (executed), Dolivo-Dobrovol'skii (committed suicide), and Rozenberg-Esen (lives in Moscow)." As if these ties with the founders of Bolshevism were not impressive enough, Rabinovich attests that he also "worked with the professional revolutionaries who played a leading role in the preparation of the Second Party Congress," where Bolshevism split off from Menshevism and a new type of party was born.

Soon Rabinovich was arrested and exiled to Siberia. But a vigorous figure such as he would not succumb to tsarist dictates: "I escaped and arrived in Geneva where I met Ilich as well as Orlovskii (Vorovskii) and Voinov (Lunacharskii)." As a hero among heroes, he was "in the same organization with Deborin (Ioffe) and Zinoviev (Radomyl'skii)." The narrator insists on giving the real name behind the pseudonym, not in order to boast of his intimacy with key Bolsheviks or in an effort to unmask revolutionary self-fashioning. Rather, the tacit suggestion here is that conversion is no longer significant, and name and pseudonym are equally valid. All true Bolsheviks, Rabinovich implies, were revolutionaries from birth, and since their original names embodied something of that truth, he never found it necessary to adopt a pseudonym.

Rabinovich retains an active voice throughout the text. During the Revolution the narrator, now a doctor of philosophy, found his natural place in the proletarian movement. He was immediately recognized for the leader he was. "Following the raid of the Whites on my apartment, railway workers brought me to Baku together with a number of my students . . . My revolutionary activity brought me close to the 26 executed Baku commissars. In 1918 I worked in the information department of the local executive committee alongside Beriia, the author of the History of the South Caucasian Party Organization," a book famous in the late 1930s for the major role it assigned to Stalin in the history of the Bolshevik movement.

Escaping with the Reds "following the de facto establishment of the Menshevik and SR dictatorship" in the area, Rabinovich was arrested and spent two months in jail. A bit later he was taken hostage by the British stationed in Persia. "But at the end of April 1919, the British high command, under the pressure of local workers, delivered the detainee from the Enzemiisk jail in Baku." Having established for himself nearly divine status, the autobiographer speaks here in the third person. The Bolshevik leadership recognized the greatness of Rabinovich. "Mikoian, the representative of the Baku Party organization, came to the steamboat to greet me. The Baku press carried the following news item (April 25, 1919): 'Rabinovich was arrested by the Azerbaijan police and, without being properly charged, was expelled from the republic. He is now free.'" In using newspaper clippings in his autobiographical text, Rabinovich integrates himself into Bolshevik history without leaving any trace of his private self.

Much like Il'in, he has never had an independent existence outside the Bolshevik movement.

Leaving Azerbaijan for Menshevik Georgia, the indefatigable Rabinovich took an intimate part in the publication of a semilegal newspaper, *Wave*, which appeared in Tiflis. "I signed my articles 'Friend of the Toilers.' My work brought me close to various Georgian Bolsheviks—Kas'ian, the brothers Okudzhava, Mariia Orakhelashvili, Saverdova, and others." This list of local luminaries with whom the autobiographer was on an equal footing indicates, once again, Rabinovich's level of perfection; he has nothing to learn even from the greatest minds. The remainder of the autobiography consists of a list of prominent positions the protagonist occupied, indicating that the Party fully valued his merits.[238]

The fact that Il'in was a cog in the Party machine and Rabinovich was its operator did not, paradoxically, alter the basic configuration of the self in the late 1930s. This self was a utopian self, outside of time and space, a self fused in its entirety with the Bolshevik movement. Since the protagonist and the Party were inseparable, cause and effect were interchangeable. The autobiographer might speak as an extension of the Party, in which case he would assume the passive voice, or as the Party's driving force, thus preferring the active voice.

The flattening of subjectivity so visible in Il'in's and Rabinovich's self-portrait resulted directly from the messianic assumption, prevailing during the Great Purge, that the gap between the signifier and the signified had been completely erased. One was what one appeared, without residue or supplement. This simplified picture of the self was just one manifestation of the assumption, critical to Stalinist language, that "ought" and "is" were at long last identical. "A unity of essence and appearance," Party propagandists maintained, "is one of the unique features of our times."[239]

The Party had no patience for what it deemed an artificial separation between speech acts and actual happenings. "Bear in mind the latest events in our Party," Stalin urged the faithful. Then he explained that by "events" he meant "our latest slogans."[240] This erasure of the gap between word and act becomes particularly significant as we consider Vyshisnkii's instruction to his prosecutors to discard any distinction between "terrorist statements and terrorist acts."[241]

The total collapse of the distinction between signifier and signified persuaded Stalinist zealots that to name was to summon into existence. As a result of this leap of faith, Petrov, an official speaker at the Institute of Red

Professors, was reprimanded for "superfluous citations from enemies of the people."[242] Writers were instructed to avoid "unnecessarily dividing a hyphenated word at the end of a line." The hyphenated word "counterrevolutionary" was a prime example: should the unwary reader miss the negative prefix left dangling at the end of the line, great and potentially treasonous confusion might well arise.[243] Iogikhes, a teacher of German grammar at the Institute of Red Professors, was censured for using the sentence "I am not a fascist" to teach German declinations; the Party committee suspected a cipher. Was it not likely that Iogikhes was inviting students to treat such a declaration as nothing but a string of abstract words, any one of which might be manipulated or inverted? Was not "I am a fascist" as semantically valid as "I am not a fascist"? An investigation protocol noted that "it is very difficult nowadays to tell whether Iogikhes' would-be 'mistake' is a belch from the old school or a conscious dissemination of fascist chauvinism. We must study her more closely, not only in class but also outside it."[244]

Accidents had no place in the world of the Great Purge; everything done was fully intended. A tailor was arrested because when he stuck a needle into a newspaper he pierced the eye of Kaganovich. A sailor who wrapped a belt around a huge bust of Stalin to make it easier to carry it to his club allowed the belt to slide down and catch the general secretary by the neck; he, too, was arrested.[245] The pages of *Bol'shevik* explained that what might appear to be a misprint was actually intentional sabotage: "Most often, the so-called misprints assume the following form: one or two letters of a word are transposed, or one letter is omitted, giving the sentence a new and counterrevolutionary meaning. Thus instead of 'to reveal' [*vskryt'*] one finds 'to conceal' [*skrtyt'*]; instead of 'ominous warning' [*groznoe*] one finds 'ruinous warning' [*griaznoe*, literally 'squalid']." There was, according to Vinokurov, incontrovertible evidence that the enemy had inserted, with consummate artistry and skill, portraits of enemies of the people into seemingly innocuous photographs; these could be recognized when the reader turned the page upside down. "Those who refuse to see the hand of the enemy in this and prefer to blame misprints on the inexperience of the proofreader or the typesetter are terribly mistaken."[246]

All actions were intentional. Any student whose record showed bad behavior now had to explain his political blunders not as a lapse into unconscious, atavistic modes of thinking, but as a result of literally automatic behavior. The solar-eclipse defense strategy had to be taken to its logical extreme. It was not that consciousness was eclipsed; rather, the body, now taken in its literal sense, labored to undermine it. When asked why he had not unmasked Serebriakov, that enemy of the people, a student at the Leningrad Institute of Red Professors named Pal'tsev defended himself by saying, "I withdrew into myself as my hearing dimmed." There had been nothing wrong with Pal'tsev's consciousness, but, lacking input, it had offered no judgment. The classic version of the solar-eclipse defense, one he did not dare to marshal now, would have led Pal'tsev to blame the primitive recesses of his psyche.[247]

Nervous diseases, anxiety attacks, fainting, the sort of psychological breakdowns that would normally have postponed the work of a hermeneutical court, if not hastening it to clemency, were totally disregarded. On one occasion Voitlovskaia, a Leningrad history student arrested in 1936, passed out during her investigation. "I could smell camphor and heard the doctor say that 'the accused has acute anemia of the brain, we must take her to the hospital,'" she recalls. But Voitlovskaia's interrogator simply threw her back into her prison cell.[248] In her complaint to the NKVD dated April 23, 1936, the wife of an arrested Oppositionist leader, Mrachkovskii, complained that her husband had received similar treatment. "My husband's condition is grave: doctors have diagnosed a disease affecting the nerves and nervous centers. How can his interrogation be going ahead as usual?"[249]

An attempt to have recourse to something like a degeneration is evident in Eva Findlender's Supreme Court appeal from 1938. Frau Findlender protested the NKVD's decision to deport her Communist husband back to Nazi Germany. "My husband is mentally ill," she explained. "His condition was not detected by the Cheliabinsk interrogator because it does not manifest itself externally. Not breaking out in a form of a rash or a delirium, it nonetheless suppresses my husband's desire to go on living. Thus affected, he is not capable of taking the opportunity to write to me, his wife or, more important, to appeal the verdict himself." Psychological weakness being irrelevant according to the regnant view of the subject, this appeal went unanswered.[250]

Bereft of layers of meaning, the subject of the Great Purge was flat and transparent. If the Communists were omnipotent, they were also extremely vulnerable. Their potential culpability had grown immensely since the last time their souls had been weighed. All the defense strategies open to them in previous years had been swept away, leaving them accountable for the smallest offenses. Whenever an infraction had to be interpreted, the worst was made of it. Ezhov's judges snuffed out the distinction between "misde-meanors" *(prostupki)* and "crimes" *(prestupleniia)*. And criminality, now that everything was conscious and intentional, meant resistance to Communism and almost certain death.

It is tempting to present the Great Purge as a contest in which different factions of the Party became intoxicated by the struggle for power and thus ultimately destroyed themselves in the process. This contest consisted of a number of rounds beginning shortly after 1917 and intensifying after Lenin's illness and death. In 1923–24 supporters of Zinoviev and Kamenev accused Trotskyists of deviation, only to succumb a few years later to similar charges. After Kirov's assassination late in 1934, the leaders of the universities, now regarded as the purest among the pure, smeared their older colleagues as unrepentant Oppositionists. When the next round began in the spring of 1936, so the story continues, they had to swallow the same bitter pill, ultimately being purged from the Party and exiled. Often transcending generational and occupational alignments, alliances in the university Party organizations proved to be highly unstable. Students could denounce the same instructor in unison and ten minutes later sink their teeth into each other. Friendships were frequently betrayed, and arbitrary denunciations meant that some members of the same faction survived the purge while other members were destroyed. The carousel kept spinning in 1937 and 1938, the intervals between rotations becoming shorter and shorter as the Great Purge picked up momentum. Eventually, almost all the heads of the university Party cells and many of the students were executed.

Historians who explain the dynamic of the Great Purge as a struggle between actors who cared about nothing but the maximization of their access to spoils—be they bureaucratic agencies, high-ranking officials, or rank-and-file Party members—present the Communist self-fashioning as window dressing, a decoy used to conceal utilitarian, self-interested goals, whether career advancement or simple survival. However, the distinction between the imperfect reality of factionalist struggles and the prescriptive unanimity of the future was frequently berated by the Stalinist contemporaries themselves. The point is not that Communists failed to live up to the ideals of "unanimity" *(edinstvo)* and "purity" *(chistota)* that were constantly on their lips, but rather that these ideals functioned as justifications for widespread persecution of difference. Once the Communist discourse is understood as a multilayered and contested web of meanings woven by succeeding activists, an effective account can be given of the internal contradictions of theory and practice and the degree of abandon that characterized the Great Purge without divesting the process of its ideological overtones. It was precisely because so many Party members did not merely adapt to the evolution of state policy in an attempt to advance their own interests but instead sought to preserve the purity of the society in which they lived, that they participated in the hermeneutics of the soul and thereby propelled the purges to ever-greater heights.

The problem with the commonplace observation that the Great Purge brought out the best and the worst in people is that it tends to judge the actors by the standards of the normative subject, that is, a historical subject as the moralizing philosopher conceives of him. Such an approach presents the Stalinist true believers as ethically bankrupt, while anti-Communist resisters are accorded the laurels of heroes who preserved their personal integrity in trying times.[251] Despite their opposite judgments of historical figures, both assertions—the one that condemns the enemies of Stalinism for obstructing emancipation and the one that praises them as conscientious objectors—remain trapped within manichean ethics. The fact that many victims of the Great Purge denounced others shortly before their own arrest calls into question the distinction between victims and perpetrators.

Each generation of scholars of the Great Purge returns to the same set of basic questions: Were the confessions of the accused sincere? Why did Communists confess crimes they could never have committed? Sidestepping these questions, this book attempts to understand to which discourse the notion of "sincerity" belonged and what assumptions made it all-important in the eyes of so many contemporaries. Unless we remind ourselves that "sincerity" was a Communist obsession and not only our own, we risk getting hopelessly trapped within the terms of the phenomena we are analyzing.

Communist autobiographical confessions cannot be regarded as accurate descriptions of a consistent life. Such a view is predicated on the assumption that one's moral essence remains the same through time and circumstance. By contrast, this study shows the Communist self to have been structured around a discontinuity, not a locus of a preexisting moral identity but something constantly in the making. Only by treating the historical actor not as a stable ethical persona but as an agent and product of an ever-changing official discourse can we reconstruct the actual dynamic the led to the Great Purge. Changes in how people perceived themselves, which usually take centuries to unfold, occurred in Bolshevik Russia every few years, an acceleration that resulted from the breakneck speed of this historical experience. Once the Revolution severed all cultural moorings, the Bolsheviks could alter the most fundamental truisms regarding the human condition. Redefinition of the self was expected to keep up with developments in economics: just as the Bolsheviks aspired to effect in less than a decade the socioeconomic transformation that had taken Great Britain centuries to accomplish, so they were seeking to reforge human identity in record time.

The Great Purge can be seen as a result of growing expectations that men and women would be ever more self-conscious, ever purer, and of the consequent harshening of the hermeneutics of the soul. Legal norms and administrative considerations took a back seat when the contest between scientifically armed moral selves occupied center stage. Each time Moscow signaled that it had found another way to define the New Man, local leaders were condemned as failed hermeneuts, unable or unwilling to unmask the enemy. Leaders were always the first to be wiped out, not because Stalin was settling personal accounts with local bosses, nor because the masses punished their undeserving vanguard in a fit of righteous rage, but because, setting the moral standards and declaring themselves to be the best readers of human souls, they were held personally responsible for breakdowns in vigilance. When the stakes in Communist diagnostics rose following the announcement of the creation of true socialist society in the summer of 1936 and every hermeneutical failure was declared intentional, there was no way around accusing prominent comrades who erred of aligning with the counterrevolution. It was the inherent inability of the hermeneutical discourse to hand down indisputable verdicts that made Stalinist power extremely volatile: to fail purging an enemy, or to purge the wrong individual, meant to risk your own life. A supreme token of Communist authority, the mandate to diagnose souls could easily turn into a boomerang.

What made Stalinist politics unique, then, were not the mundane interests that motivated its actors but the prevalence of the soul-judging framework that could present anyone as an enemy in disguise. The Great Purge crisscrossed the country with such ferocity and speed not because little collusions and intrigues activated each other but because of the Communist belief in the existence of one great counterrevolutionary conspiracy. As Vyshinskii put it, "concrete crimes committed by this or that individual are only particular cases of one, general plan of criminal activity, a plan shared by all the criminals united by the same counterrevolutionary goal."[252] The drive to find links between the guilty across regions, ages, and walks of life had to do with the fundamental Communist belief that evil was universal and that it must be unmasked and eliminated on a universal scale. In the final account, the Stalinist discourse postulated only two archfactions: the good and the evil.

Epilogue:
Communism and Death

In the Bolshevik tradition, death linked the individual in a final embrace with the brotherhood of the elect. Death could be a sublime, highly positive experience of self-sacrifice, or a negative experience, in which one's expulsion from the society of men was rendered eternal. The unidirectional structure of the official autobiography takes us nearer to the meaning of death in Communism. If in order to realize one's true self one had to become a Party member, failure to do so meant cutting the story short. A life lost to the Party was a life aborted, an unfinished life, and it could be narrated as such. But nothing short of a conversion to Communism fully satisfied the demands of the genre. This seemingly innocuous feature of Communist poetics inspired a morbid conclusion: the individual who was absolutely unable to see the light of Communism—human dross at best, a menace to universal salvation at worst—had to disappear. This resolution began as a mere possibility and ended as terrible reality: whereas at first Communist misfits were given a second and a third chance to reform, properly to complete their life's journey and become good Communists, from 1936 onward they were shot.

During the lull of the 1920s many of those who were spared nonetheless despaired of reaching the light and chose to condemn themselves to death. Suicide was the final step taken by the individual who realized his worthlessness in a system that defined the self solely in relation to the collective. Communist autobiographers accompanied their applications to the Party with the threat that refusal would leave them no choice but suicide; outside the Party their lives were meaningless. For example, Andronov concluded his autobiography with a thinly disguised ultimatum: "The thought that I

stand outside the Party pains me. It is very important for my future development that I not remain a 'loner.' I realize that I do not yet stand shoulder
to shoulder with the proletariat, and this knowledge depresses me and
brings me down. It is pointless to go on living this way!"[1] When he said
that his life outside the Party was meaningless, Andronov meant that the
narrative of his life outside the Party had become unintelligible to him,
that an existence that failed to move toward a climax lacked all motive.

Self-inflicted death could be an ignoble escape from the struggles of life
or an act of martyrdom. If Andronov's thoughts of suicide were due to a
total loss of meaning, Adolf Ioffe's successful suicide was a self-affirming
act. Ioffe killed himself in 1927 to reestablish the system of life's values that
he had believed in as an Oppositionist. His brave act fostered enormous interest in the Party because he had challenged its assessment of itself. In the
suicide note he left behind Ioffe claimed that there was no point to life now
that Trotsky, whom he regarded as the fulcrum of proletarian consciousness, had been elbowed out of Party leadership. Clutching a pistol in one
hand, he scribbled his note with the other:

> Thirty years ago, I adopted the belief that human life has no meaning ex-
> cept in the service of something infinite. Since humanity alone is infinite,
> while everything else is limited, any endeavor to prolong a meaningless
> existence must be condemned . . . All my life I have believed that the po-
> litical man is duty-bound to abandon life if he becomes aware that he can
> no longer be useful to the cause he wants to serve.

Ioffe wanted to live only so long as he could continue serving the movement. When he became convinced that in delegitimating the Trotskyist
camp the Party was rejecting his services, he made that ultimate gesture of
protest against loss of purpose in the public world. "I hope," his note concluded, "that the coincidence of the two events, the great [the ongoing
struggle within the Central Committee] and the little [his own suicide],
will awaken the Party. The thought should make me happy, since then my
death will not have been in vain."[2]

The eschatological substrate of the Communist notion of the self goes a
long way to explain why the evaluation of Ioffe's dramatic gesture hinged
on whether his suicide was construed as a conscious act or not. If, in shooting himself, Ioffe had acted consciously, Party leadership had to be in the
wrong. Leaping into the hermeneutical breach, an underground Oppositionist leaflet asserted that "Ioffe's suicide was that of a true revolutionary

who values class interests over personal interests." Among those sympathetic to Ioffe, Victor Serge saw in his suicide "the best possible expression of the revolutionary's communion with mankind."[3]

Others saw it differently, and their hypothesis, that Ioffe had lost his sense of purpose, meant that both he and his mentor, Trotsky, had been renegades and had richly deserved death. Emel'ian Iaroslavskii, a loyalist, took this position, declaring that "Ioffe's suicide was induced by psychosis," an act of despair carried out by a man weakened in body and soul. He called Ioffe "a psychotic with a history of mental problems" and insisted that he could not have been a truly conscious Party member. Iaroslavskii maintained that only "the weak-willed and the weak-nerved, those who lose faith in the strength of the Party, commit suicide these days," and he saw an obvious connection between a rash of Communist suicides and a time of "vacillations in the Party, a certain loss of ideological compass." Whatever the state of Ioffe's mental health may have been, neither side found anything unreasonable or even strange in politically motivated suicide.[4]

In keeping with the prevailing therapeutic discourse, the Party opted to grapple with the "epidemic of suicides" of the 1920s. It was only during the Great Purge that suicides were transformed from a disease into the expression of a wicked will. Consider the case of Mikhail Tomskii; this Right Oppositionist who committed suicide on August 22, 1938, was described as an "enemy of the people" and held fully responsible for his desperate step.

In a suicide note addressed to Stalin, Tomskii wrote: "I am approaching you not only as the head of the Party but also as an old comrade in arms. This is my last request: do not believe a single word of what Zinoviev has said against me. I never joined him in any bloc and I have never conspired against the Party."[5]

Far from feeling pity or regret at the death of a former leader, the Party swiftly pronounced this text utterly deceitful and self-serving. Whereas Ioffe's suicide was medicalized, Tomskii's was criminalized. "Tomskii's suicide is a premeditated act, a part of a conspiracy," Viacheslav Molotov argued in 1938. "Tomskii accepted his friends' suggestion that such an act would help inflict a final blow against the Central Committee."[6] Klement Voroshilov was equally brutal: "Tomskii found a simple solution to his personal problem. But he certainly did not make the defense of his collaborators any easier; now that he has killed himself 50 percent of their verdict is set, if not 75 percent."[7]

A surge in suicides accompanied the Great Purge. According to official statistics, 728 Red Army soldiers attempted suicide in 1937 and 832 in 1938.[8] Two members of the Central Committee—Ian Gamarnik and Panas Liubchenko—took their own lives. Nikolai Skrypnik, Vissarion Lominadze, F. Fur'er, and Agasii Khadzhian were among the other prominent Party leaders who killed themselves in the 1930s. Largely responsible for setting the Stakhanovist movement into motion, Furer committed suicide late in 1936. He tried to turn his farewell note into a blow against the Great Purge, declaring, "I cannot accept the arrest and execution of innocent people."[9] Stalin, speaking at the November 1936 Central Committee plenum, sardonically shrugged off the criticism. "What a letter Furer left us! Makes me want to bawl."[10]

As the number of those who seemed to be exploiting suicide to wipe their records clean rose, Stalin's chancellery reacted, pronouncing "anti-Party acts" of this kind decisive proofs of guilt. "All these people kill themselves in order to cover their tracks . . . to deceive us for the last time and to put us in a ridiculous position," claimed Stalin. "One kills oneself because of the fear of being unmasked, because one does not want to watch idly as one is disgraced . . . Suicide is one of the most extreme ways and one of the simplest ways to spit in the Party's face for the last time before leaving this world."[11] (Stalin's private opinion must not have been very different. When his son attempted suicide in the spring of 1928, Stalin wrote to his second wife, Alilueva, "Tell Iasha that he acted like a hooligan and a blackmailer and that I want nothing to do with him in the future.")[12]

Stalin appears to have been successful in imposing his interpretation of suicide, as the case of Uziukov makes clear. Commenting on the self-exculpatory note left behind by the latter, a prominent member of the Sverdlov Party committee who killed himself in early 1937, Vladimirov, the director of a machine-building factory in the Urals, sounded like an echo of Stalin: "These days we cannot believe suicide notes—even these may well turn out to be false . . . In committing suicide an individual is trying to threaten the Party, to tell it that by mistreating those who commit political crimes, the Party cripples people and forces them to put revolvers to their own heads." Whatever one's lot, Vladimorov concluded, "a suicide has to be regarded as an anti-Party gesture."[13]

During the Great Purge an attempted suicide might have precipitated an arrest. Even the suicides of rank-and-file Party members were routinely investigated by the special political department of the NKVD, and the results of the investigations were collated in special Central Committee files.[14] Official communiqués explained that those killing themselves had done so because of "having become entangled in criminal affairs." When Gamarnik, the head of the Red Army's political department, killed himself in 1937, the Soviet press announced that "having become involved with anti-Soviet elements, this former Central Committee member committed suicide on May 31."[15] At around the same time Pshenitsyn, a high-ranking provincial Party secretary, was summoned to Moscow, apparently to be arrested. On the morning of his departure he shot himself. His colleague Stoliar commented: "Pshenitsyn's suicide suggests that he was suffering from a guilty conscience; he must have somehow wronged the Party." One of Stalin's lieutenants, Andreev, agreed: "Certainly a man whose conscience is clean, whose past and present are devoid of criminal behavior, has no reason to spill his own blood." Speaking of Kolotilin, the secretary of the Don Party committee who committed suicide early in 1937, a member of Stalin's team had similar things to say: "By shooting himself Kolotilin fully proved his guilt . . . He who kills himself has no idea what to do with himself, and he is looking for a unique way to avoid interrogation."[16]

A number of suicide notes drafted by the Party's rank and file considered the notion that self-annihilation was an ultimate act of subversion. Deprived of the drama and invective they had carried in the 1920s, suicide notes from the period of the Great Purge tended to be apologetic. An ailing Party member shot himself in a Leningrad hospital in the winter of 1937. His suicide note strongly asserted his innocence of any counterrevolutionary intent: "I simply can no longer take the pain. To look for political meaning in my act would be pointless. I was always loyal to the Party and remain so. The great Stalin must adopt a tough and decisive approach to demolishing all of what remains of enemy parties and classes. There must be no retreat. I regret that my strength has abandoned me at this moment."[17]

When a Communist named Yevsey Zaretskii threw himself from the window of his Leningrad apartment on December 20, 1935, he blamed himself, not society. This was not, he wrote, a critical statement directed at the Party; his suicide note reaffirmed fundamental Communist values. Zaretskii wrote of the "crimes" he now bitterly regretted having concealed from the Party, among them a forged registration on the Party rolls at the district committee and his mendacious claim to have been a veteran Komsomol worker. The note concluded with a touch of pathos: "I stumbled, but I lived an otherwise honest and irreproachable life, as is fitting for a Communist-Stalinist. It is ironic, of course, to end one's life with suicide. In our country, suicide is a rare phenomenon . . . I had no political disagreements with the Party . . . but I was so distrusted that I could no longer imagine going on with my life and work."[18]

It was one thing to die gloriously for the Revolution, quite another to be condemned to death by the proletarian state. Even when they were sent to the gallows by their own Party, Communists wanted to believe that they were dying for the right cause. Kamenev's last note to the NKVD opened with "Comrades, dear ones."[19] Even Ezhov, the former head of the NKVD, exclaimed when he saw his executioners: "I have always been a conscientious Leninist! . . . Tell Stalin that I will die with his name on my lips."[20]

The last words of convicted revolutionary leaders contained fascinating ruminations on the meaning of death. "I have seen death staring me in the face more than once," Ivan Smirnov said, recalling his civil war experiences, "but I felt no fear of death then because I was fighting for my class and for my Party." But he added ruefully that "towards the end of my life I made a terrible mistake: I participated in a Trotskyist struggle against the Party." He knew he would be sentenced to death, but Smirnov seemed unconcerned about the end of his physical existence; it was the meaninglessness of his imminent death that shook him: "Now the sword of proletarian justice is raised above my head. It is terrible to die by the hand of my own state." To die while fighting a hated foe frightened him not at all, but to die as a traitor—"How disgraceful!"[21]

Another convicted Party leader, Iakov Drobnis, also contrasted dying for the proletariat with dying because one had opposed it. "Is there," he wondered, "the slightest possibility that I can be allowed to die without disgrace? Could you permit me, after the great suffering I have endured in the name of [the proletariat] all my life, to rejoin the ranks of the class to which I was born?"[22] The tension in Drobnis' speech was not between life and death—no Communist wasted his time with dreams of eternal life— but between meaningless death and meaningful death.

Once he had been arrested in connection with Kirov's assassination, Zinoviev became consumed by the fear that he tarnished his good Bolshevik name at the close of his political career. "I never dreamed that I would end up accused of terrorism against Party leaders," he wrote. "I find myself now in the company of degenerates and fascists and I am, before history, terribly frightened. For what remains of my conscious existence and until my last breath I will remain dedicated in my soul to the international proletariat." On July 10, 1935, Zinoviev explained to the NKVD that it was not death but life without a purpose that he feared most: "Comrades! Dear ones! What troubles me is not the deprivation of my freedom, my illness or anything like that. I know that I am dead. Morally I have been killed. I will survive a bit longer only if I am sent to a concentration camp and given the right to work." His final comment seems strange to those who might rate consignment to a labor camp as marginally preferable to execution; for Zinoviev and all right-thinking Communists it was the exact opposite: a chance to reform oneself through labor.[23]

Zinoviev's thoughts foreshadowed Bukharin's more famous ruminations on beautiful death:

> I ask myself, "If you must die, what are you dying for?" With startling vividness a black void immediately rises before my eyes. "There is nothing to die for, if one wants to die unrepentant. If, on the contrary, one repents, everything fine and good that shines in the Soviet Union acquires in one's mind a new dimension." In the end it was this thought that completely disarmed me. I went down on my knees before the Party.

In one of his last letters to Stalin Bukharin was telling the secretary general how he had been preparing himself for death: "My hunger for life is gone. My soul is ready to make its exit. I harbor no animosity toward the Party, toward all of you, toward our common life work. I am filled with enormous, limitless love."[24]

Bukharin said that he agreed with Vyshinskii's verdict that his crimes merited "being executed ten times over," but still he sued for mercy. The rhetoric of his final plea to the judge, a reluctantly expressed wish that his body might be permitted to continue existing, was extraordinary. The accused styled himself as somebody whose hopelessly corrupted soul meant that only his brain could still be offered to the Revolution:

> The old Bukharin is dead; he no longer walks the earth . . . What endure in me are my knowledge and my capabilities—the machine called my mind. The activity of this machine used to be criminal, but its mechanism is now wound the other way . . . The sole justification for this request for forgiveness is my possible use to the Revolution. Give the new Bukharin, a second Bukharin, a chance to grow. Call the new Bukharin Petrov if you like; but know that this new man will be the exact antithesis

of the man who is already dead. The new Bukharin is already born; allow him to work . . . If permitted to continue my physical existence . . . I will do my best to show you that your gesture of proletarian generosity was justified.[25]

The basis of Bukharin's argument was utility. In his plea Bukharin spoke as the inheritor of a body, not as a repentant comrade whose present self had important connections to his past self. A highly personal document, Bukharin's supplication letter can hardly be classified as an autobiography. Although we have seen autobiographies that describe, even stress, acute discontinuities in their authors' lives, a fundamental continuity of the narrating self was presumed. But when he proposed that he be called "Petrov," Bukharin gave up on his very self.

Apropos Bukharin's plea that his physical existence be prolonged, it is interesting to note that NKVD agents intercepted rumors in the late 1930s that suggested the convicted leaders of the Opposition had not been executed and were living on some distant island under new names. Heavily guarded, they supposedly continued to fulfill Central Committee assignments. "Do you see how great Stalin is? He got just what he wanted: when Zinoviev and Kamenev confessed they blackened their own names. Then Stalin absolved them so that he could use their knowledge for the Party's benefit."[26]

The notes Bukharin kept while in prison suggest that the soul had become a subject of much importance during the Great Purge. When he wrote, after Hegel, "world history is the world's court of judgment," Bukharin did not mean, as some have contended, that matters of individual conscience were insignificant; he meant that he who judged the conscience was not transcendent (God) but immanent (Party). Bukharin's "Letter to the Future Generation of Party Leaders," written in 1938, expressed the wish that a new generation of Communists would restore his Party membership. Why should he have cared about posthumous reinstatement? Why should the Party have obliged, no matter how belatedly? (Bukharin was solemnly reinstated on July 21, 1988.)[27]

Indeed, a Party member continued his existence through the suprapersonal medium of history. According to Marxism-Leninism, the mortality of individual Communists was not a serious issue. "Man's individual life and the life of the species are not different," Marx explained, "although, necessarily, the mode of individual existence is more particular than the life of the species." That which was particular was mortal, but the essential was eternal. It was on this ground that Marx based his contention that true Communists would experience their essential connection to the species so strongly that they would cease to treat the death of the individual as a tragedy.[28] Thus the early Bolshevik poet Aleksei Gastev identified himself with the life of his Party to such an extent that his life would be infinitely prolonged:

> I do not live for years
> I live for hundreds of years, for thousands of years
> I have been alive since the creation of the world
> And I shall live for millions of years to come
> And there is no limit to my career.[29]

The manichean language of disjuncture, of the absolute moral opposition between revolutionaries and counterrevolutionaries, was coupled with a discourse of harmony, just as eschatologically motivated—this was the spiritual unity of those who followed the Party, dead or alive. Trotsky was proud that his followers "learned not to despair when they found out that historical laws did not match individual inclinations . . . Not everybody will get to the safe shore; many will drown along the way. But to participate in this movement with open eyes and an intense will—this alone provides a sentient being with its highest moral satisfaction!"[30]

The wretchedness of death meant nothing when held up alongside the bliss of Party membership, the only thing that saved man from time. This viewpoint accounted for Bukharin's devout prayers for posthumous reinstatement. If Communist martyrology is to be believed, the last request of some Red Army soldiers was that they be counted among the brotherhood of the elect. If they were obliged to leave the safety of their trenches for a desperate attack on the enemy lines, they reportedly were wont to exclaim: "If I am killed, I wish to be counted a Communist! [*Esli ub'iut, shchitaite menia kommunistom!*][31]"

Communists had access to salvation precisely because they could overcome death. The dead lived within the Party's collective memory. In the spring of 1917 newspapers described the "fallen fighters" of the revolutionary movement as "people's saints."[32] Shortly before his execution Bukharin wrote to his wife, urging her to "remember that the great deed called the Soviet Union lives; only this is really important. Our personal fates are transient and pitiful [*perekhodiashchie i mizerabel'nye*]."[33] When a Party member paid for the cause with his life, he died only to be transfigured. His body might have perished, but his spirit lived on. The "resurrection" of the revolutionary hero through the movement might be symbolized by a comrade picking up a fallen banner (a constant theme in Soviet art and the cinema) or by the transformation of his tomb into a wedding chapel (regularly done in the Soviet Union). The habitual distribution of red handkerchiefs to children initiated into the Young Pioneers had a similar symbolic value. The children were told that what they had tied around their neck was a "sacred talisman that represents the blood of revolutionary martyrs."[34] A Komsomol membership card that had been pierced by the enemy's bullet was prominently exhibited in the Leningrad War Museum, and it served a similar role.[35] For the Communists, history was endowed with such overwhelming importance that everything about an individual, his physical self included, was important only if it was assigned a symbolic function. Since history was somehow more real than mundane reality, even the climactic moment of death was a mere shadow of the ritual of Party admission, that moment when the individual ceased to belong to himself and became a member of a larger-than-life collective.[36]

Communist conversion made of death a curious paradox. Converts could see that the only way to realize the meaning of their lives was by living, but in a radically new way, transindividually and transhistorically, and thus to die. In a sense, entrance into the Party was suicide, the death of an autonomous, self-sufficient individual. Biological death left a stinking corpse; social death signaled a loss of meaning. Party enrollment, on the other hand, was a clean and tidy death—it was the consummation of a Party member, his ultimate fusion with the soul of the movement. A Communist lived between salvation and damnation. Life outside the Party was not a life worth living.

Notes

The following abbreviations are used in the notes.

BSE   Bol'shaia Sovetskaia entsiklopediia [Great Soviet Encyclopedia], 65
         vols. (Moscow, 1926–1947)
PANO   Partiinyi arkhiv Novosibirskoi oblasti
PATO   Partiinyi arkhiv Tomskoi oblasti
PSS   V. Lenin, *Polnoe sobranie sochinenii*, 5th ed. (Moscow, 1963–1977)
TsGA IPD Tsentral'nyi gosudarstvennyi arkhiv istoriko politicheskikh
         dokumentov

Introduction

1. *Detskaia defektivnost', prestupnost', i besprizornost'* (Moscow, 1920), p. 11.
2. A. Solzhenitsyn, *The Gulag Archipelago, 1918–1956,* trans. Thomas P. Whitney (New York: Harper and Row, 1973–1978), vol. 1, pp. 173–174.
3. On the recent uncovering of Stalin's mass graves and the debate this process instigated in post-Soviet society, see K. Smith, *Remembering Stalin's Victims: Popular Memory and the End of the USSR* (Ithaca: Cornell University Press, 1996), pp. 163–165; and I. Paperno, "Exhuming the Bodies of Soviet Terror," *Representations,* no. 75 (2001).
4. Hans-Henning Schroeder claims that the human losses during 1936–1938 were "far fewer than those of forced collectivization, which are generally reckoned at 5–6 million"; "Upward Social Mobility and Mass Repression: The Communist Party and Soviet Society in the Thirties," in *Stalinism: Its Nature and Aftermath. Essays in Honor of Moshe Lewin,* ed. N. Lampert and G. Rittersporn (New York: Sharpe, 1992), p. 175. See also V. Kyritsyn, "1937 god v istorii Sovetskogo gosudarstva," *Sovetskoe gosudarstvo i pravo,* no. 2 (1988), 113–114.

5. R. Tucker, *Stalin in Power: The Revolution from Above, 1928–1941* (New York: Norton, 1992), p. 309.

6. B. Nicolaevsky, *Power and the Soviet Elite* (New York: Praeger, 1965), p. 79.

7. M. Malia, *The Soviet Tragedy: A History of Socialism in Russia, 1917–1991* (New York: Free Press, 1994), p. 248.

8. "O sud'be chlenov i kandidatov v chleny TsK VKP(b), izbrannogo XVII s"ezdom partii," *Izvestiia TsK KPSS*, no. 12 (1989), 82–113; *Istoricheskii arkhiv*, no. 2 (1994), 40.

9. V. Kravchenko, *I Chose Freedom* (New York: Hillman Periodicals, 1946), p. 212.

10. R. Thurston, "Fear and Belief in the USSR's Great Terror: Response to Arrest, 1935–1939," *Slavic Review* 45 (1986), 219. A very substantial number of the executed had at some point been members of the Communist Party; A. Getty, G. Rittersporn, and V. Zemkov, "Victims of the Soviet Penal System in the Prewar Years," *American Historical Review* 98 (1993), 1023. Olga Adamova-Sliozberg, who spent many years in Stalin's prisons, recalled that in 1949 only about 10 percent of her cellmates were Party members, whereas in 1936 the share was 90 percent; O. Sliozberg, *Put'* (Moscow: Vozvrashchenie, 1993), p. 175.

11. Quoted in A. Walicki, *Marxism and the Leap to the Kingdom of Freedom: The Rise and Fall of the Communist Utopia* (Stanford: Stanford University Press, 1995), p. 463.

12. D. Zatonskii, "Pochemu oni ogovarivali sebia i drugikh," *Nedelia*, no. 28 (1988).

13. A. Iakovlev, ed., *Reabilitatsiia: Politicheskie protsessy 30kh–50kh godov* (Moscow: Izdatel'stvo politicheskoi literatury, 1991), p. 184; "Prosti menia, Koba: Neizvestnoe pis'mo N. Bukharina," *Istochnik*, no. 0 [*sic*] (1993), 23–25.

14. Steven Kotkin, *Magnetic Mountain: Stalinism as a Civilization* (Berkeley: University of California Press, 1995), pp. 198–237.

15. K. Papaioannou, *Marx et les marxistes* (Paris: Flammarion, 1972); Malia, *The Soviet Tragedy*.

16. Leszhek Kolakowski, *Main Currents of Marxism*, vol. 3 (Oxford: Clarendon Press, 1978), p. 86.

1. Good and Evil in Communism

1. "Hermeneutics of the soul" is used here after Michel Foucault's "About the Beginning of the Hermeneutics of the Self," *Political Theory* 21, no. 2 (1993), 198–227. In the Communist discourse the inner self could be variously referred to as "consciousness" *(soznanie),* "inside" *(vnuterennost'),* "soul"

(dusha), or, if the self was deficient, "little soul" *(dushonka)*. The term "her-meneutics of the soul" is mine, although "exposure of the face" *(vyiavlenie litsa)*, occasionally used by Party courts of conscience, comes close. See, for example, Tsentral'nyi gosudarstvennyi arkhiv istoriko politicheskikh doku-mentov (hereafter TsGA IPD), f. 408, op. 1, d. 1175, l. 91.

2. On the Bolshevik "cultural revolution," that is, the attempt to revolutionize the way people perceived things, see René Fueloep Miller, *The Mind and Face of Bolshevism: An Examination of Cultural Life in Soviet Russia* (New York: Knopf, 1927); Richard Stites, *Revolutionary Dreams: Utopian Vision and Ex-perimental Life in the Russian Revolution* (New York: Oxford University Press, 1989); L. Mally, *Culture of the Future: The Proletkult Movement in Revolution-ary Russia* (Berkeley: University of California Press, 1990).

3. For the evolving definitions of the "new man" *(novyi chelovek)* in the 1920s and 1930s, see A. Gol'tsman, *Reorganizatsiia cheloveka* (Moscow, 1924); P. Kerzhentsev, "Chelovek novoi epokhi," *Revoliutsiia i kul'tura*, no. 3–4 (1927); M. Ianovskii, *Za novogo cheloveka* (Leningrad, 1928).

4. Maxim Gorky, *Untimely Thoughts* (1917) (New Haven: Yale University Press, 1968), p. 7.

5. Nadezhda Krupskaia, "Idealy sotsialisticheskogo vospitaniia," in *Pedagog-icheskie sochineniia*, ed. N. Goncharova, I. Kairova, and N. Konstantinova, 11 vols. (Moscow, 1958–1963), 2: 83.

6. Quoted in I. Druzhnikov, *Donoshchik 001* (Moscow, 1995), p. 139.

7. Czeslaw Milosz, *The Captive Mind* (New York, 1955), pp. 193, 199.

8. Hannah Arendt, *On Revolution* (New York, 1963), p. 100.

9. Arthur Koestler, *Darkness at Noon* (New York: Macmillan, 1948), pp. 73–75. Oleg Kharkhordin maintains that throughout Russian history a search for the soul has been a search for features of the self revealed through observable deeds rather than through the hermeneutic of desires; *The Collective and the Individual in Russia* (Berkeley: University of California Press, 1999).

10. John Hazard, "Soviet Law: The Bridge Years, 1917–1920," in *Russian Law: His-torical and Political Perspectives*, ed. W. Butler (Leyden: A. W. Sijthoff, 1977), p. 241; Robert Tucker, *The Soviet Political Mind* (New York: Norton, 1972), p. 69. The Bolshevik practice of preventive executions directed at those merely "willing" to engage in counterrevolutionary actions is discussed in P. Holquist, "Conduct Merciless Mass Terror: Decossackization on the Don, 1919," *Cahiers du monde russe* 38 (1997).

11. V. Viktorov, *Bez grifa "sekretno"* (Moscow, 1990), pp. 95–96, 97–98.

12. K. Rigel, *Konfessionsrituale im Marxismus-Leninismus* (Graz, 1985).

13. Robert Conquest, *The Great Terror: Stalin's Purge of the Thirties* (London, 1968), pp. 209–210; R. Sharlet, "Stalinism and Soviet Legal Culture," in *Stalin-ism: Essays in Historical Interpretation*, ed. Robert Tucker (New York, 1977),

pp. 163–168. For the role of confession in Stalinism, see B. Unfried, "Rituale von Konfession und Selbskritik: Bilder vom stalinistischen Kader," *Jahrbuch für historische Kommunismusforschung* 2 (1994), 148–164.

14. *Voprosy istorii*, no. 6–7 (1992), 3.

15. Tucker, *The Soviet Political Mind*, p. 85.

16. Arch Getty, "The Politics of Repression Revised," in *Stalinist Terror: New Perspectives*, ed. A. Getty and R. Manning (Cambridge: Cambridge University Press, 1993), p. 42.

17. Leonard Wessell, *Prometheus Bound: The Mythic Structure of Karl Marx's Scientific Thinking* (Baton Rouge: Louisiana State University Press, 1984), pp. 103–104.

18. Hannah Arendt, *Between Past and Future: Six Exercises in Political Thought* (New York: Meridian, 1954), p. 102.

19. On Marxism's blurring of the distinction between ethics and aesthetics, see B. Groys, *The Total Art of Stalinism: Avant-Garde, Aesthetic Dictatorship, and Beyond*, trans. C. Rougle (Princeton: Princeton University Press, 1992); L. Boia, *La mythologie scientifique du communisme* (Caen, 1993).

20. Alan Besançon, *The Rise of the Gulag: Intellectual Origins of Leninism* (New York, 1981), p. 282.

21. Karl Marx and Friedrich Engels, *Collected Works*, vol. 4 (Moscow: Progress, 1976), p. 37.

22. G. Kostomarov, ed., *Listovki Moskovskoi organizatsii bol'shevikov, 1914–1925gg* (Moscow: Gos. izd-vo polit. lit-ry, 1954), pp. 189–190.

23. N. Bukharin, *Etiudy* (Moscow, 1932), pp. 13, 16.

24. See G. Carleton, "Genre in Socialist Realism," *Slavic Review* 53 (1994), 1002.

25. J. Marcus, "The World Impact of the West," in *Myth and Mythmaking*, ed. H. Murray (New York: Braziller, 1968).

26. M. Abrams, "Apocalypse: Theme and Variations," in *The Apocalypse in English Renaissance Thought and Literature*, ed. C. Patrides and J. Wittreich (Ithaca, 1984), p. 346.

27. *Kentavr*, July–August 1992, 103.

28. V. Naumov, A. Kraiushkin, and N. Teptsov, eds., *Nepravednyi sud: Poslednii stalinskii rasstrel. Stenogramma sudebnogo protsessa nad chlenami Evreiskogo antifashistkogo komiteta* (Moscow, 1994), p. 7; Iu. Stetsovskii, *Istoriia sovetskikh repressii*, 2 vols. (Moscow: Glasnost', 1997), 1: 458, 490–491.

29. The will was defined in the first edition of the *Large Soviet Encyclopedia* as "a faculty placed under the full command of the subject"; M. Basov, "Volia," in *BSE*, 13: 106.

30. *The Case of the Anti-Soviet "Bloc of Rights and Trotskyites" Heard before the Military Collegium of the Supreme Court of the U.S.S.R., Moscow, March 2–3,*

1938 (Moscow: People's Commissariat of Justice and the U.S.S.R., 1938), p. 776.

31. Iurii Lotman and Boris Uspenskii, "Binary Models in the Dynamics of Russian Culture," in *Semiotics of Russian Cultural History*, ed. A. Nakhimovsky and A. Stone-Nakhimovsky (Ithaca: Cornell University Press, 1985), p. 32.

32. The importance of Marxism for the evolution of the Soviet political system is forcefully argued by Leszek Kolakowski, "Marxist Roots of Stalinism," in Tucker, *Stalinism*, pp. 184–187.

33. Jacob Talmon, *The Origins of Totalitarian Democracy* (London: Sphere, 1955), pp. 5–6, 249.

34. Iosif Stalin, *Sochineniia*, 13 vols. (Moscow, 1946–1955), 13: 93.

35. *Istoriia grazhdanskoi voiny v SSSR*, vol. 1 (Moscow, 1935: Gos. izd-vo polit. lit-ry), pp. 24–25.

36. Michel Foucault, "Governmentality," in *The Foucault Effect: Studies in Governmentality*, ed. G. Burchell et al. (Chicago: University of Chicago Press, 1991) p. 97.

37. For the Bolshevik interest in what people thought, see N. Werth and G. Moulle, eds., *Les rapports secrets sovietiques: La société russe dans les documents confidentiels, 1921–1991* (Paris, 1995); and Varlen Izmozik, "Voices from the Twenties: Private Correspondence Intercepted by the OGPU," *Russian Review* 55 (April 1996).

38. Jochen Hellbeck, "Self-Realization in the Soviet System: Two Soviet Diaries of the 1930s," in *Stalinismus vor dem Zweiten Weltkrieg*, ed. M. Hildermeier (Munich, 1998).

39. Peter Holquist, "'Information Is the Alpha and Omega of Our Work': Bolshevik Surveillance in Its Pan-European Context," *Journal of Modern History* 69 (1997).

40. Michael Walzer, *The Revolution of the Saints: A Study in the Origins of Radical Politics* (Cambridge, Mass.: Harvard University Press, 1965), pp. 222, 224.

41. Katerina Clark, *The Soviet Novel: History as Ritual* (Chicago: Chicago University Press, 1981), pp. 42, 47.

42. The hyphenating of "auto-biography," "auto-biographer," and the like, in books printed about 1840–1850, suggests the relative newness of these compounds. "Autobiography" appeared in English dictionaries soon after 1820 and in French, German, and Italian dictionaries somewhat later; A. West, *Roman Autobiography* (New York: De Vinne, 1901), pp. 23–26.

43. Toby Clyman, "Autobiography," in *Handbook of Russian Literature*, ed. V. Terras (New Haven: Yale University Press, 1985), p. 28. On Soviet autobiography's debt to the Russian nineteenth-century literary tradition, see S. Mashinskii, "O memuarno-avtobiograficheskom zhanre," *Voprosy literatury* 6 (1960).

44. Charles Taylor, *Sources of the Self: The Making of Modern Identity* (Cambridge, Mass.: Harvard University Press, 1989), pp. 288–289.

45. James Bernauer, "Michel Foucault's Ecstatic Thinking," in James Bernauer and David Rasmussen, The Final Foucault (Cambridge, Mass.: MIT Press, 1988), pp. 53, 63; Vladislav Todorov, *Red Square, Black Square: Organon for Revolutionary Imagination* (Albany: State University of New York Press, 1995), pp. 29–42; Katerina Clark, "Utopian Anthropology as a Context for Stalinist Literature," in Tucker, *Stalinism*, pp. 180–198.

46. Jean-Jacques Rousseau, *Emile*, trans. B. Foxley (London, 1911), p. 358.

47. "Vladimir Ilich Lenin," in Vladimir Maiakovskii, *Sochineniia v dvukh tomakh* (Moscow, 1988), p. 233.

48. J. Hellbeck, "Fashioning the Stalinist Soul: The Diary of Stepan Podlubnyi (1831–1838)," *Jarhbucher für Geschichte Osteuropas*, no. 3 (1996).

49. Elaine Pagels, *The Origins of Satan* (New York, 1995), p. 167; Wayne P. Meeks, *The Origins of Christian Morality* (New Haven: Yale University Press, 1993), p. 124.

50. A certain Antipov, for example, was arrested in 1936 because he "falsely identified himself in his autobiography as non-Party although he once was a former Communist purged for Oppositionism"; TsGA IPD, f. 408, op. 1, d. 52, l. 43.

51. *Listovki peterburgskikh bol'shevikov, 1902–1917*, vol. 1 (Leningrad: Gos. izd-vo polit. lit-ry, 1939), p. 244.

52. Aleksandr Kosarev, *O perestroike raboty komsomola: Doklad na IX plenume TSK VLKSM IX sozyva* (Moscow: Molodaia gvardiia, 1935), pp. 23–24.

53. "Prosti menia Koba: Neizvestnoe pis'mo N. Bukharina," *Istochnik*, no. 0 [*sic*] (1993), p. 24.

54. L. Lebedinskii, "Khudozhestvennaia ucheba i proletariat," *Oktiabr'*, no. 3 (1927), 161–162.

55. Stalin, *Sochineniia*, 13: 68.

56. "Nevol'niki v rukakh germanskogo reikhsvera: Rech' I. V. Stalina v narkomate oborony," *Istochnik*, no. 3 (1994).

57. Evening session, August 22, 1936, in *The Case of the Trotskyite-Zinovievite Terrorist Centre: Report of Court Proceedings Heard before the Military Collegium of the Supreme Court of the USSR, Moscow, August, 19–24, 1936* (Moscow: People's Commissariat of Justice of the U.S.S.R., 1936), p. 166.

58. A. Iakovlev, ed., *Reabilitatsiia: Politicheskie protsessy 30kh–50kh godov* (Moscow: Izdatel'stvo politicheskoi literatury, 1991), pp. 192–193.

59. A. Ball, *Russia's Last Capitalists: The Nepmen, 1921–1929* (Berkeley: University of California Press, 1987), pp. 10–11.

60. Lenin, *PSS*, 1: 27.

61. N. Popov, "O sotsial'nom sostave RKP(b) i o Leninskom prizyve," *Krasnaia nov'*, no. 3 (1924), 310–311.

62. Ibid., p. 311.

63. *Pravda*, October 27, 1921.

64. T. Rigby, *Communist Party Membership in the U.S.S.R., 1917–1967* (Princeton: Princeton University Press, 1968), p. 103.

65. A. Selishchev, *Iazyk revoliutsionnoi epokhi: Iz nabliudenii nad russkim iazykom poslednikh let (1917–1926)* (Moscow: Rabotnik prosveshcheniia, 1928), pp. 99–100.

66. *Pravda*, December 18, 1921.

67. *Pravda*, October 15, 1921.

68. P. Sakulin, *Sotsiologicheskii metod v literaturovedenii* (Moscow: "Mir," 1925), p. 117.

69. L. Engelstein, *Castration and the Heavenly Kingdom: A Russian Folktale* (Ithaca: Cornell University Press, 1999), p. 231.

70. L. Trotskii, *Sochineniia*, vol. 21 (Moscow, 1927), p. 460; idem, *Literatura i revoliutsiia* (Moscow: Gos. isd., 1924), p. 197. On the Russian category of the "everyday" *(byt)* and its relation to sexuality, see L. Engelstein, *The Keys to Happiness: Sex and the Search for Modernity in Fin-de-Siècle Russia* (Ithaca: Cornell University Press, 1992); and Svetlana Boym, *Common Places: Mythologies of Everyday Life in Russia* (Cambridge, Mass.: Harvard University Press, 1994).

71. In capitalizing the Opposition, I want to alert the reader to the fact that this was how the regime perceived opponents and suggest that this perception is an important historical fact in itself. I am writing not about the empirical reality behind the opposition but about the real effects of the construct called "The Opposition."

72. For standard histories of intra-Party struggles in the 1920s, see L. Schapiro, *The Communist Party of the Soviet Union*, 2d ed. (New York, 1959); I. Deutscher, *The Prophet Unarmed: Trotsky, 1921–1929* (Oxford: Oxford University Press, 1959); R. Daniels, *The Conscience of the Revolution: Communist Opposition in Soviet Russia* (Cambridge, Mass.: Harvard University Press, 1960); Robert Service, *The Bolshevik Party in Revolution, 1917–1923: A Study of Organizational Change* (London, 1979).

73. *Desiatyi s"ezd RKP(b). Mart–Aprel' 1920 goda: Protokoly* (Moscow: Gospolitizdat, 1960), pp. 77, 350; *Dvenadtsatyi s"ezd RKP(b) 17–25 Aprelia 1923 goda: Stenograficheskii otchet* (Moscow: Politizdat, 1968), p. 343.

74. Lenin, *PSS*, 25: 79.

75. G. Zinov'ev, "Skol'ko 'marksizmov' syshchestvuet na svete?" *Bol'shevik*, no. 16 (1928), 28.

76. *KPSS v rezoliutsiakh i resheniiakh,* vol. 2 (Moscow: politizdat, 1983), p. 300; Stetsovskii, *Istoriia sovetskikh repressii,* 2: 160.

77. Lenin, *PSS,* 41: 394, 541.

78. For the official image of the enemy see H. Guenther, "Der Feind in der totalitaeren Kultur," in *Kultur im Stalinismus: Sowjetische Kultur und Kunst der 1930er bis 50er Jahre,* ed. B. Gorzka (Bremen, 1994), pp. 89–100; J. Cassiday, *The Enemy on Trial: Early Soviet Courts on Stage and Screen* (De Kalb, Ill., 2000); A. Fateev, *Obraz vraga v sovetskoi propagande, 1945–1954* (Moscow, 1999).

79. Naum Jasny, *Soviet Industrialization, 1928–1952* (Chicago, 1961), p. 142.

80. Although Stalin's constitution entered into force only in 1937, the commission to draft a new constitution was set up in February 1935; *Pravda,* March 1, 1935.

81. *Voprosy istorii,* no. 2 (1994), 19–21; I. Stalin, *O nedostatkakh partiinoi raboty i merakh likvidatsi trotskistskikh i inykh dvurushnikov* (Moscow: OGIZ, gos. iz-vo politicheskoi literatury, 1937), p. 5.

82. *Voprosy istorii,* no. 4–5 (1992), 25–26, 33.

83. For a detailed study of the purges in the 1920s based on materials similar to the ones examined here, see M. David-Fox, *Revolution of the Mind: Higher Learning among the Bolsheviks, 1918–1929* (Ithaca: Cornell University Press, 1997), pp. 125–127, 147–151, 153–160.

84. J. Hellbeck, "Writing the Self in the Time of Terror: Alexander Afinogenov's Diary of 1937," in *Self and Story in Russian History,* ed. L. Engelstein and S. Sandler (Ithaca: Cornell University Press, 2000).

85. V. Rogovin, *Partiia rasstreliannykh* (Moscow: Novosti, 1997), p. 29.

86. A. Gorbatov, *Years of My Life: The Memoirs of a General in the Soviet Army* (London: Constable, 1964), p. 103.

87. Quoted in A. Avdeenko, *Nakazanie bez prestupleniia* (Moscow: Sovetskaia Rossiia, 1991), pp. 171–172.

88. L. Trotsky, "Obezglavlivanie Krasnoi Armii," *Biulleten' oppozitsii,* no. 56–57 (1937) 6.

89. This is the main thrust of the revisionist historiography. See A. Getty, *Origins of the Great Purges: The Soviet Communist Party Reconsidered, 1933–1938* (Cambridge: Cambridge University Press, 1985); and G. Rittersporn, *Stalinist Simplifications and Soviet Complications: Social Tensions and Political Conflicts in the USSR: 1933–1953* (Chur, Switzerland, 1991).

90. *Bol'shevik,* no. 9 (1937), 8.

91. B. Starkov, ed., *Na koleni ne vstanu* (Leningrad: Izd-vo polit. lit-ry, 1992), p. 33.

92. Tucker, *The Soviet Political Mind,* p. 60.

93. *Sotsialisticheskii vestnik,* no. 3 (1937), 3.

94. Stalin, *O nedostatkakh,* pp. 14–17, 26–27, 32–33.

95. *Izvestiia,* February 5, 1937; *Voprosy istorii,* no. 4–5 (1992), 16–18.

96. *Pravda,* January 22, 1937.

97. *Partiinoe stroitel'stvo,* no. 2 (1937).

98. V. Zenzinov, *Vstrecha s Rossiei: Kak i chem zhivut v Sovetskom Soiuze. Pis'ma v Krasnuiu Armiiu: 1939–1940* (New York: Rausen, 1944), p. 571.

99. *Sotsialisticheskii Donbass,* June 27, 1937, quoted in Hiroaki Kuromiya, *Freedom and Terror in the Donbas: A Ukrainian-Russian Borderland, 1870s–1990s* (Cambridge: Cambridge University Press, 1998), p. 219.

100. Avdeenko, *Nakazanie bez prestupleniia,* pp. 182–183.

101. *Voprosy istorii,* no. 2 (1994), 21–22.

102. *Ogonek* 28 (1989), 31.

103. Iakovlev, *Reabilitatsiia,* p. 153.

104. N. Bukahrin and E. Preobrazhensky, *The ABC of Communism,* ed. E. Carr (Harmondsworth: Penguin, 1969), p. 276; *Ugolovnyi kodeks R.S.F.S.R.* (Moscow, 1927), p. 9. On the Bolshevik application of noncustodial "compulsory work" to the "toiling classes" with the goal of spiritual rehabilitation, see Peter Solomon, "Soviet Penal Policy, 1917–1934: A Reinterpretation," *Slavic Review* 39 (1980), 196–203.

105. Peter Solomon, *Soviet Criminal Justice under Stalin* (Cambridge: Cambridge University Press, 1996), p. 33.

106. D. Dallin and B. Nicolaevsky, *Forced Labor in Soviet Russia* (London: Hollis and Carter, 1948), p. 251.

107. Ibid., p. 233.

108. *Pravda,* September 3, 1933 (Gorky); Carleton, "Genre in Socialist Realism," p. 995 (Iagoda).

109. Dallin and Nicolaevsky, *Forced Labor in Soviet Russia,* p. 233.

110. A. Vyshinski, *Ot tiurem k vospitatel'nym uchrezhdeniiam* (Moscow: Gosudarstvennoe izdatel'stvo Sovetskoe zakonodatel'stvo, 1934), p. 276.

111. Dallin and Nicolaevsky, *Forced Labor in Soviet Russia,* p. 255.

112. V. Glotov, "Bilet do Leningrada. Bol'shevik Zinaida Nemtsova kak ona est'," *Ogonek* 27 (1988), 5.

113. Solomon, *Soviet Criminal Justice,* pp. 118–119.

114. H. Berman, *Justice in the USSR: An Interpretation of the Soviet Law* (Cambridge, Mass.: Harvard University Press, 1963), p. 56.

115. S. Rubinshtein, *Osnovy obshchei psikhologii* (Moscow, 1946 [1st ed., 1935]), p. 475.

116. Dallin and Nicolaevsky, *Forced Labor in Soviet Russia,* p. 202.

117. "Iz dnevnika akademika V. I. Vernadskogo," *Sovershenno sekretno,* no. 8 (1990), 11–12.

118. *Voprosy istorii,* no. 1 (1994), 22–24.

119. N. Gel'perin, "Direktivy narkoma," *Za industrializatsiiu,* February 21, 1937.

120. Solomon, *Soviet Criminal Justice,* pp. 241–242.

121. D. Volkogonov, *Stalin: Triumf i tragediia,* vol. 1 (Moscow, 1991), p. 522.

122. *Svod zakonov SSSR,* no. 19 (1935), 155.

123. V. Rogovin, *1937* (Moscow: Novosti, 1996), p. 356.

124. *Voprosy istorii,* no. 10 (1994), 16–20.

125. Iakovlev, *Reabilitatsiia,* p. 246; Starkov, "Narkom Ezhov," in Getty and Manning, *Stalinist Terror,* p. 42.

126. *Case of Anti-Soviet "Bloc,"* pp. 626–629, 656–657.

127. Stetsovskii, *Istoriia sovetskikh repressii,* 1: 443.

128. *Izvestiia TsK KPSS,* no. 6 (1990), 112–113, 107, 111.

129. M. B., "Trotskisty na Vorkute," *Sotsialisticheskii vestnik,* no. 10–11 (1961); *Izvestiia TsK KPSS,* no. 10 (1989), 75–78; Dallin and Nicolaevsky, *Forced Labor in Soviet Russia,* p. 260.

130. The Jacobin term "enemies of the people" was used by Lenin as early as 1917 in reference to the leadership of the Kadets. In 1918 a decree by the Supreme Soviet applied the term to peasants who refused to give up grain. During the NEP the term went out of circulation, to be revived during the Great Purge; J. Rossi, *Spravochnik po Gulagu v dvukh chastiakh,* vol. 1 (Moscow: Prosvet, 1991), pp. 63–64.

131. R. Markus, *Saeculum: History and Society in the Theology of St. Augustine* (Cambridge: Cambridge University Press, 1970), pp. 124, 167–168.

132. N. Belov, *Lichnost' i vneshnost'* (Petrograd, n.d.), pp. 47–48.

133. Talmon, *The Origins of Totalitarian Democracy,* p. 4.

2. A Voyage toward the Light

1. J. Harris, "Autobiography: Theory and Praxis," in *Autobiographical Statements in Twentieth-Century Russian Literature* (Princeton: Princeton University Press, 1990), pp. 16–17.

2. G. C. Spivak, "Subaltern Studies: Deconstructing Historiography," in *Selected Subaltern Studies,* ed. R. Guha and G. Spivak (Oxford: Oxford University Press, 1988), pp. 3–32.

3. This methodology is outlined in C. Bynum, *Holy Feast and Holy Fast* (Berkeley: University of California Press, 1987), p. 8.

4. See, for example, L. Lezhaeva and G. Rusakov, eds., *Pamiatnik bortsam proletarskoi revoliutsii, pogibshim v 1917–1921 godam,* 3 vols. (Moscow, 1922–1925); G. and M., *Geroi i mucheniki proletarskoi revoliutsii,* vyp. 1 (Moscow, 1924).

5. A. Fil'shinskii, "Priemnye ispytaniia v Sverdlovskom universitete," in *Zapiski*

kommunisticheskogo universiteta imeni Sverdlova, vol. 2 (Moscow, 1924), p. 300.

6. L. Mink, "Narrative Form as a Cognitive Instrument," in *The Writing of History: Literary Form and Historical Understanding*, ed. R. Canary and H. Kozicki (Madison: University of Wisconsin Press, 1978), pp. 143–144.

7. TsGA IPD, f. 984, op. 1, d. 188, ll. 18–23, 29.

8. Hayden White, *The Content of the Form: Narrative Discourse and Historical Representation* (Baltimore: Johns Hopkins University Press, 1987), pp. 47–48.

9. Incidentally, the Communist poetics strictly forbade stylistic ornamentation; the Party applicant was summoned to be "simple like the truth" *(prost kak pravda)*. Katerina Clark, *The Soviet Novel: History as Ritual* (Chicago: University of Chicago Press, 1981), p. 52.

10. Charles Taylor, *Sources of the Self: The Making of Modern Identity* (Cambridge, Mass.: Harvard University Press, 1989), pp. 91–92.

11. Josephus, *Antiquities of the Jews* 1.14, trans. Thackeray (Cambridge, Mass.: Harvard University Press, Loeb Classical Library).

12. W. Spengemann, *The Forms of Autobiography: Episodes in the History of a Literary Genre* (New Haven: Yale University Press, 1980), pp. 25, 31–32; E. Vance, "Augustine's Confessions and the Grammar of Selfhood," *Genre*, no. 6 (1973), 24.

13. *Dvenadtsatyi s"ezd RKP(b) 17–25 Aprelia 1923 goda. Stenograficheskii otchet* (Moscow: Politizdat, 1968), p. 704.

14. TsGA IPD, f. 3, op. 1, d. 841, ll. 1–12.

15. Harris, "Autobiography," p. 32.

16. "Confession," in *Chambers Twentieth Century Dictionary*, ed. C. Schwarz et al. (Edinburgh, 1983).

17. George Gusdorf, "Conditions and Limits of Autobiography," in *Autobiography: Essays Theoretical and Critical*, ed. J. Olney (Princeton: Princeton University Press, 1980), pp. 41, 44.

18. L. Trotskii, *Moia zhizn': Opyt avtobiographii* (1929; reprint, Moscow, 1991), p. 24.

19. Lenin, *PSS*, 52: 224.

20. *Belomorsko-baltiiskii kanal imeni Stalina* (Moscow, 1934), p. 42.

21. Michel Foucault, *Technologies of the Self* (Amherst: University of Massachusetts Press, 1988), pp. 39–49.

22. Ignazio Silone, among others, explicitly compared the act of joining the Communist movement to a "conversion"; R. Crossman, ed., *The God That Failed* (London: Hamilton, 1950), p. 163.

23. William James, *Varieties of Religious Experience: A Study in Human Nature* (Harmondsworth: Penguin, 1983), p. 189; A. Nock, *Conversion: The Old and*

the New in Religion from Alexander the Great to Augustine from Hippo (London: Oxford University Press, 1933), p. 7.

24. TsGA IPD, f. 197, op. 1, d. 723, ll. 93ob.–94, 108. For related characterizations of the acquisition of revolutionary consciousness by Russian workers as something like a conversion, see R. Zelnik, "To the Unaccustomed Eye: Religion and Irreligion in the Experience of St. Petersburg Workers in the 1870s," *Russian History* 16 (1989), 316–318; D. Pretty, "The Saints of the Revolution: Political Activists in 1890s Ivanovo-Voznesensk and the Path of Most Resistance," *Slavic Review* 54 (1995), 300.

25. Foucault, *Technologies,* pp. 46–49.

26. Jean Starobinski, "The Style of Autobiography," in Olney, *Autobiography,* pp. 78–79.

27. René Girard, *Deceit, Desire, and the Novel* (Baltimore: John Hopkins Press, 1965), p. 294.

28. Arnold Van Gennep, *The Rites of Passage* (London: Routledge and Kegan Paul, 1960).

29. The distinction between the two types of conversion appears in James, *Varieties of Religious Experience,* p. 189; for a useful elaboration of this theme, see A. Hawkins, *Archetypes of Conversion* (Lewisburg, Pa.: Bucknell University Press, 1985).

30. Igor Golomstock, *Totalitarian Art in the Soviet Union, Fascist Italy, and the People's Republic of China* (London: Collins Harvill, 1990), p. 44.

31. R. Bultmann, *History and Eschatology* (Edinburgh: University Press, 1957), pp. 103–109.

32. R. Mathewson, *The Positive Hero in Russian Literature* (Stanford: Stanford University Press, 1975), p. 5.

33. TsGA IPD, f. 197, op. 1, d. 71, ll. 55–56.

34. Clark, *The Soviet Novel,* pp. 73–74.

35. TsGA IPD, f. 197, op. 1, d. 71, ll. 69–71.

36. "Politicheskie partii posle oktiabria," *Molodaia gvardiia,* no. 1–2 (1922), 103–104.

37. S. Fitzpatrick, "Lives under Fire: Autobiographical Narratives and Their Challenges in Stalin's Russia," in *De Russie et d'ailleurs: Feux croisés sur l'histoire. Pour Marc Ferro,* ed. Martine Godet (Paris, 1995), p. 225.

38. L. Kolakowski, *Main Currents of Marxism: Its Origins, Growth, and Dissolution,* vol. 1 (New York: Oxford University Press, 1987), p. 127.

39. S. Tretiakov, "Standart," *Oktiabr' mysli,* no. 2 (1924), 33.

40. "Dnevnik Prishvina: 1930 god," *Oktiabr',* no. 7 (1989), 164.

41. PATO, f. 320, op. 1, d. 7, ll. 26–27.

42. TsGA IPD, f. 197, op. 1. d. 734, ll. 30–31.

43. TsGA IPD, f. 984, op. 1, d. 148, l. 148.

44. V. Strel'nikova, "Son professora Mal'kova," *Krasnoe studenchestvo,* no. 1 (1927–28), 10.

45. "Instructions of the Petrograd Party Provincial Committee to all Primary Party Organizations," March 29, 1923, TsGA IPD, f. 138, op. 1, d. 1g, l. 1.

46. *Spravochnik partrabotnika,* vyp. 3 (Moscow, 1923), 81.

47. *Desiatyi s"ezd RKP(b) Mart 1921 goda: Stenograficheskii otchet* (Moscow: Gospolitizdat, 1963), p. 281.

48. *Dvenadtsatyi,* p. 160.

49. *Instruktsiia organizatsiiam RKP(b) o edinom bilete* (Moscow, 1920); TsGA IPD, f. 138, op. 1, d. 1g, l. 21; *Spravochnik partiinogo rabotnika,* vyp. 3 (Moscow, 1925), pp. 128–130.

50. A. Angarov, "Klassovaia priroda sovetskogo gosudarstva," *Molodaia gvardiia,* no. 10 (1926), 142–143.

51. Aleksander Bogdanov, *Voprosy sotsializma: Raboty raznykh let* (Moscow: Izdvo polit. lit-ry, 1990), p. 367.

52. TsGA IPD, f. 1085, op. 1, d. 26, l. 74.

53. Smolenskii arkhiv, WKP 326, l. 167.

54. How to define a peasant was a long-debated question among Soviet statisticians. See TsGA IPD, f. 3, op. 1, d. 841, ll. 1–12; PATO, f. 320, op. 1, d. 6, pp. 1–63; d. 114, ll. 24–25, 65.

55. TsGA IPD, f. 138, op. 1, d. 34, ll. 66–68.

56. TsGA IPD, f. 984, op. 1, d. 126, ll. 35–39.

57. Lenin, *PSS,* 39: 425.

58. Bertrand Russell, *The Practice and Theory of Bolshevism* (London: Allen and Unwin, 1920), p. 27.

59. PATO, f. 320, op. 1, d. 7, l. 17.

60. PATO, f. 115, op. 2, d. 7, l. 42.

61. *Dvenadtsatyi,* p. 664.

62. *Pravda,* April 17, 1923; *Dvenadtsatyi,* p. 849.

63. *Dvenadtsatyi,* p. 69.

64. *Odinnadtsatyi s"ezd RKP(b). Mart-aprel' 1922 goda: stenograficheskii otchet* (Moscow: Gospolitizdat, 1961), p. 255.

65. *Desiatyi s"ezd RKP(b),* pp. 254, 239.

66. N. Popov, "O sotsial'nom sostave RKP(b) i o Leninskom prizyve," *Krasnaia nov',* no. 3 (1924), 310–311.

67. Smolenskii arkhiv, WKP 326, l. 42.

68. Ibid., ll. 48–52.

69. *Odinnadtsatyi s"ezd RKP(b),* p. 374.

70. *Izvestiia TsK RKP(b),* November 11, 1920.

71. Z. Gitelman, *Jewish Nationality and Soviet Politics: The Jewish Sections of the CSPU, 1917–1930* (Princeton: Princeton University Press, 1972), pp. 444–445.

72. *Pravda,* April 1, 1921; *Spravochnik partrabotnika,* vyp. 2 (Moscow, 1922), pp. 109–110.

73. G. Haupt and J. J. Marie, eds., *Makers of the Russian Revolution: Biographies of Bolshevik Leaders* (London, 1974), p. 192.

74. Ibid., pp. 226, 227.

75. TsGA IPD, f. 984, op. 1, d. 126, l. 58.

76. PATO, f. 320, op. 1, d. 17, l. 12.

77. *Dvenadtsatyi,* p. 664.

78. TsGA IPD, f. 1085, op. 1, d. 26, l. 240; PATO, f. 1, op. 1, d. 97.

79. PATO, f. 1, op. 1, d. 97, l. 17.

80. TsGA IPD, f. 138, op. 1, d. 1g, l. 44.

81. PANO, f. 2, op. 1, d. 71, l. 233.

82. PANO, f. 2, op. 1, d. 261, ll. 117–120.

83. The words "temporary eclipse" *(vremennoe zatmenie)* were first used by the Bolsheviks in trying to make sense of the defection of Roman Malinovskii (later unmasked as a provocateur of the tsarist police) from the Duma and his sudden arrival abroad. While Malinovskii's unauthorized step was criticized, there were those who argued that it probably had no political underpinnings and was caused by "enhanced nervousness" *(obostrennaia nervoznost')* and "mental fatigue" *(dushevnaia ustalost');* Trudovaia pravda, May 31, 1914.

84. In 1926 one percent of expulsions from the Leningrad Komsomol had to do with "observance of religious rites"; N. Lebina, *Povsednevnaia zhizn' sovetskogo goroda, normy i anomalii: 1920–1930 gody* (St. Petersburg: "Letnii sad," 1999), p. 138.

85. TsGA IPD, f. 984, op. 1, d. 39, l. 66.

86. Smolenskii arkhiv, WKP 326, ll. 7–8.

87. *Pravda,* October 28, 1921.

88. Marrou, "The Fallen Angel," p. 76.

3. The Bolshevik Discourse on the Psyche

1. Space does not permit me to examine the biographies of the experts mentioned in the following pages or to discuss in any detail their relations to the political apparatus. Most of the experts cited were born in the 1880s and were more or less of the same age as the Bolshevik leaders. Although some of them enjoyed a national reputation, many others were only mildly distinguished in their day. A sociologist with an excellent prerevolutionary training, Mikhail Reisner, was one of the authors of the first Soviet constitution and also a founding member of the Communist Academy and the Russian Psychoanalytical Society. Sergei Rubinshtein, a leading theorist of psychology in the

1930s, was a young but already mature scholar with a Ph.D. when the Bolshevik Revolution broke out. He did not find it too difficult to translate his early interest in Hegel's idealism into hardcore Marxist materialism. See K. Levitin, *One Is Not Born a Personality: Profiles of Soviet Education Psychologies* (Moscow, 1982), pp. 126–127. Party voices will also intrude, far too important to go unheard. For the most part, Nikolai Bukharin, Emel'ian Iaroslavskii, Aron Sol'ts, and their like spoke as psychological or sociological authorities, a role that marked the particular convergence of knowledge and the Bolshevik art of government. Nikolai Semashko, a Bolshevik commissar, can be regarded as a classic example of a politician who could buttress his moralizing with the medical diploma in his possession. His professional background provided him and Party spokesmen like him with an indispensable scientific cachet. For biographical detail on Soviet psychologists see V. Bekhterev, *Avtobiografiia* (Moscow, 1928); A. Luriia, "Professor L. S. Vygotskii, 1886–1934," *Sovetskaia nevropatologiia, psikhiatriia i psikhogigiena,* no. 1 (1935), 165–169; P. Blonskii, *Moi vospominaniia* (Moscow, 1971); A. Kozulin, *Psychology in Utopia: Toward a Social History of Soviet Psychology* (Cambridge, Mass.: MIT Press, 1984); D. Joravsky, *Russian Psychology: A Critical History* (Oxford: Basil Blackwell, 1989), pp. 222–224, 248, 250–251; Kiril Rossianov, "Beyond Species: Ilya Ivanov and His Experiments on Cross-Breeding Humans with Anthropoid Apes," *Science in Context* 15 (2002).

2. R. Walter, "What Became of the Degenerate? A Brief History of the Concept," *Journal of the History of Medicine and the Allied Sciences* 11 (1956). On the various uses of degeneration see P. Baldwin, "Liberalism, Naturalism, and Degeneration: The Case of Max Nordau," *Central European History* 13 (1980), 99–120; R. Soloway, "Counting the Degenerates: The Statistics of Race Deterioration in Edwardian England," *Journal of Contemporary History* 17 (1982), 136–164; R. Nye, "Degeneration and the Medical Model of Cultural Crisis in the French *Belle Epoque,*" in *Political Symbolism in Modern Europe,* ed. S. Drescher, D. Sabean, and A. Sharlin (New Brunswick, N.J.: Rutgers University Press, 1982).

3. Charles Darwin, *The Descent of Man,* 2d ed. (New York: A. L. Burt, n.d.), pp. 160–161.

4. Karl Marx, *A Contribution to the Critique of Political Economy* (Chicago, 1904), pp. 21–24; Karl Marx and Friedrich Engels, *On Britain* (Moscow, 1953), p. 375; both quoted in L. Feuer, "Marx and Engels as Sociobiologists," *Survey,* no. 23–24 (1977–78), 115, 121, 128. See also R. Colp, "The Contacts between Karl Marx and Charles Darwin," *Journal of the History of Ideas* 35 (April–June 1974).

5. S. Gilman, "Political Theory and Degeneration: From Left to Right, from Up

to Down," in *Degeneration: The Dark Side of Progress,* ed. J. Chamberlin and S. Gilman (New York: Columbia University Press, 1985), p. 168.

6. Karl Marx and Friedrich Engels, *Selected Correspondence* (Moscow, 1965), p. 172.

7. Friedrich Engels, *The Origins of the Family, Private Property, and the State* (New York, 1942), p. 21.

8. E. Ferri, *Socialism and Modern Science: Darwin—Spencer—Marx* (Chicago: Charles H. Kern, 1909), p. 89.

9. On the reception of Darwin in 1920s Russia, see S. Iu. Semkovskii, *Chto takoe Marksizm (Darvin i Marks)* (Khar'kov, 1922); G. Broido, "Darvinizm i Marksizm," *Pechat' i revoliutsiia,* no. 3 (1923); G. Daian, "Darvinizm i Marksizm," *Sputnik kommunista,* no. 21 (1923); G. Gurev, *Darvinizm i Marksizm* (Gomel, 1924); M. Bublikov, *Bor'ba za sushchestvovanie i obshchestvennost': Darvinizm i Marksizm* (Moscow, 1926); Iu. Shaksel', *Biologicheskie teorii i obshchestvennaia zhizn'* (Leningrad, 1926); F. Duchinskii, "Darvinizm, Lamarkizm i neodarvinizm," *Pod znamenem Marksizma,* no. 7–8 (1926).

10. *Deviataia konferentsiia RKP(b)* (Moscow, 1972), pp. 188, 181.

11. G. Searle, *Eugenics and Politics in Britain, 1900–1914* (Leyden: Nordhoff, 1976); W. Schneider, "Towards the Improvement of the Human Race: The History of Eugenics in France," *Journal of Modern History* 54 (1982), 268–291.

12. N. Kol'tsov, "Uluchsheniie chelovecheskoi porody," *Russkii evgenicheskii zhurnal,* 1922, 26–27. See also idem, *Prichiny sovremennogo iskhudaniia* (Petersburg, 1922).

13. Iu. Filipchenko, "Anketa po nasledstvennosti sredi uchenykh Peterburga," *Nauka i ee rabotniki,* no. 1 (1922), 51; no. 2 (1922), 35–36.

14. On the attempt of Soviet scientists to pose the question of the relation between heredity and placticity in a Marxist way in the 1920s, see A. Serebrovskii, "Proiskhozhdenie vidov v svete posledarvinskogo izucheniia izmenchivosti i nasledstvennosti," in *Proiskhozhdenie zhivotnykh i rastenii* (Moscow, 1924); T. Morgan and Iu. Filipchenko, *Nasledstvenny li priobretennye priznaki?* (Leningrad, 1925); F. Dobrzhanskii, "K voprosu o nasledovanii priobretennykh priznakov," in *Preformizm i epigenesis* (Vologda, 1926); P. Serebrovskii, "Nasleduiutsia li priobretennye priznaki?" *Zapiski NOM,* no. 7 (1927).

15. A. Lunacharskii, *Meshchanstvo i individualizm* (Moscow: Gos. izd. 1923), p. 123.

16. On the precursors of the Bolshevik psychological discourse, see L. Engelstein, *The Keys to Happiness: Sex and the Search for Modernity in Fin-de-Siècle Russia* (Ithaca: Cornell University Press, 1992).

17. *Komsomol'skaia pravda,* March 1, 1927. Also interesting is the prerevolutionary V. Posse, *Vyrozhdenie i vozrozhdenie* (St. Petersburg: izd. "Zhizn' dlia vsekh," 1913).

18. Gilman, "Political Theory and Degeneration," p. 172.

19. P. Bessal'ko, "O poezii krest'ianskoi i proletarskoi," *Griadushchee,* no. 7 (1918), 24.

20. B. Pike, *The Image of the City in Modern Literature* (Princeton: Princeton University Press, 1981), quoted in S. Gilman, "Sexology and Psychoanalysis," in Chamberlin and Gilman, *Degeneration,* p. 88. For the Bolshevik context see Katerina Clark, "The City versus the Countryside in Soviet Peasant Literature of the Twenties: A Duel of Utopias," in *Bolshevik Culture,* ed. A. Gleason, P. Kenez, and R. Stites (Bloomington: University of Indiana Press, 1985).

21. Engelstein, *The Keys to Happiness,* pp. 287–288.

22. Engels, *The Origins of the Family,* p. 5.

23. P. Kerzhenstev, "Chelovek novoi epokhi," *Revoliutsiia i kul'tura,* no. 3–4 (1927), 18–19.

24. A. Zalkind, "Tseleustremlennost'," *Krasnaia nov',* no. 6 (1927), 187, 189.

25. The editions I cite are Sergei Malashkin, *Luna s pravoi storony* (Moscow: Molodaia gvardiia, 1927); and Lev Gumilevskii, *Sobachii pereulok,* 2d ed. (Riga: Gramatu draugs, 1928). At the time his novel was published, Malashkin, born in 1888 to a peasant family, was regarded as one of the best realist proletarian authors and had a "long-standing reputation of being a revolutionary, Communist, and proletarian writer." Gumilevskii, born in 1890, was a more obscure figure. Although Gumilevskii never joined the Party, the 1928–29 publication of a four-volume edition of his works indicates that he was well regarded by the official literary establishment. See I. Novich, "Kholostoi vystrel," *Na literaturnom postu,* no. 1 (1927), 4, 9.

26. I. Kiselev, "Pro cheremukhu shcho roztsvetae i pro liudinu shcho zagnivaet," *Student revoliutsii,* no. 2–3 (1927), 92; T. Ganzhulevich, "Literatura pro molod'," *Student revoliutsii,* no. 4 (1927), 49; T. Kostrov, "Zametki ob kommunisticheskom vospitanii molodezhi," *Revoliutsiia i kul'tura,* no. 7 (1928), 30.

27. T. Kostrov, "Revoliutsiia i meshchanstvo," *Revoliutsiia i kul'tura,* no. 3–4 (1927), 30.

28. I. Bobryshev, "Pereulki i tupiki," *Komsomol'skaia pravda,* March 2, 1927.

29. *Kakova zhe nasha molodezh'?* (Moscow, 1927), pp. 36, 49. See also S. Rodov, "Rabkory i proletarskaia literatura," *Oktiabr',* no. 2 (1924), 187; G. Lelevich, "Proletarskaia literatura i bytovaia revoliutsiia," *Oktiabr',* no. 1 (1925), 143.

30. Quoted in E. Naiman, *Sex in Public: The Incarnation of Early Soviet Ideology* (Princeton: Princeton University Press, 1997), p. 100.

31. L. Gumilevskii, "Sud'ba i zhizn'," *Volga,* no. 8 (1988), 105.

32. V. Polonskii, "O povesti S. Malashkina 'Luna s Pravoi Storony,'" in *Kakova zhe nasha molodezh'?* pp. 44–45.

33. Novich, "Kholostoi vystrel," pp. 50–53. See also D. Bukhartsev, "O pessimisticheskoi lune i pessimizme voobshche," *Molodoi bol'shevik,* no. 9–10

(1927), 16–17; G. Iakubovskii, "Psichologicheskii neorealizm Sergeia Malashkina," *Zvezda*, no. 1 (1927), 151; G. Bergman, "Za zdorovuiu zhizn'," in *Komsomol'skii byt* (Moscow: Molodaia gvardiia, 1926), p. 251.

34. "Disput v akademii kom. vospitaniia im. Krupskoi," *Molodaia gvardiia*, no. 12 (1926), 171.

35. N. German, "Iz zhizni rabfaka VTU," *Znamia rabfakovtsa*, no. 1 (1923), 36.

36. On the trial of literary heroes see *Iunost' boevaia: Vospominaniia starykh komsomol'tsev* (Moscow: Molodaia gvardiia, 1958), p. 248. The novels by Malashkin and Gumilevskii were discussed endlessly in student forums. See A. Gorelov, "Luna s pravoi storony," *Smena*, January 9, 1927; S. Rozental', "Pechat' i nasha smena," *Narodnyi uchitel'*, no. 12 (1927), 95.

37. In 1927 a literary evening took place in the Leningrad State University under the banner "Proletarian Literature—Collective Orator, Propagator, and Organizer of Proletarian Masses in the Soviet Union"; TsGA IPD, f. 984, op. 1, d. 242, l. 22.

38. E. Troshchenko, "Vuzovskaia molodezh'," in *Kakova zhe nasha molodezh'?* p. 169.

39. A. Ryndich, *Partiino-sovetskie shkoly* (Moscow, 1925), p. 62.

40. A. Zalkind, *Polovoi vopros v usloviiakh sovetskoi obshchestvennosti* (Leningrad, 1926), pp. 91–92.

41. *Izvestiia TsK VKP(b)*, no. 34 (1925), 5. For discussion see V. Tiazhel'nikova, "Samoubiistva Kommunistov v 1920-e gody," *Otechestvennaia istoriia*, no. 6 (1998). For contemporary treatment of suicide in the Soviet Union, see Ia. Leibovich, *1000 sovremennykh samoubiistv: Sotsiologicheskii ocherk* (Moscow, 1923); N. Brukhanskii, *Samoubiitsy: Sotsial'no politicheskoe obsledovanie 355 sluchaev okonchennykh i neokonchennykh samoubiistv s 1 dekabria 1923 g. po 31 maia 1924 g. v gorode Moskve* (Leningrad: Priboi, 1927); G. Bergman, "Esenin—znamia upadochnykh nastroenii," in A. Zharov, ed., *Protiv upadochnichestva: Protiv "eseninshchiny"* (Moscow: "Pravda" "Bednota," 1926), pp. 6–7.

42. TsGA IPD, f. K-601, op. 1a, d. 735, ll. 1–15.

43. David Khanin, "Bol'shevistskoe vospitanie molodezhi i oppozitsiia," *Molodaia gvardiia*, no. 9 (1926), 100.

44. A. Stratonitskii, *Voprosy byta v Komsomole* (Leningrad: Priboi, 1925), p. 37.

45. S. Smidovich, "O Davidsonovshchine," in *Komsomol'skii byt*, p. 142.

46. A. Sol'ts, "Kommunisticheskaia etika," ibid., pp. 65–66.

47. I. Bobryshev, *Melkoburzhuaznye vliianiia sredi molodezhi* (Moscow, 1928), p. 94.

48. T. Ganzhulevich, "Literatura pro molod'," *Student revoliutsii*, no. 4 (1927), 50.

49. Malashkin, *Luna s pravoi storony*, pp. 58–59. Hereafter page numbers are cited in the text.

50. P. Ionov, "Bez cheremukhi," *Pravda*, November 12, 1926.

51. Zalkind, *Polovoi vopros*, p. 42.

52. Bergman, "Za zdorovuiu zhizn," p. 251. See also "Protiv raspushchennosti," *Komsomol'skaia pravda*, November 6, 1927.

53. A. Sol'ts, "Ne nyt' a stroit," in *Komsomol'skii byt*, pp. 108–110.

54. A. Lunacharskii, "Studenchestvo i novaia ekonomicheskaia politika," *Proletarskoe studenchestvo*, no. 1 (1922), 6.

55. I. Stukov, "Trevozhnoe iavlenie," *Pravda*, Novemer 22, 1921.

56. S. Gusev, "Kakoiu dolzhna byt' nasha molodezh," in *Komsomol'skii byt*, p. 147; D. Manuil'skii, "Mysli vskol'z' o revoliutsii i chadiashchem byte," *Kommunist*, October 12, 1923.

57. "Disput," pp. 169, 172.

58. *Pravda*, December 11, 1923.

59. *Pravda*, January 1, 1924. On the problematization of the concept of "youth" (*molodniak*) following the New Course Discussion, see also A. Zalkind, "Kul'turnyi rost sovetskogo molodniaka," *Molodoi bol'shevik*, no. 19–20 (1927), 75–84; M. Kolosov, D. Kochetkov, and G. Shubin, *Molodniak* (Moscow, 1927); A. Slepkov, *Oppozitsionnye techeniia vnutri VKP(b)* (Moscow: Moskovskii rabochii, 1926), p. 25.

60. A. Gorlov, "Bogdanovsko-messianskie otkroveniia k molodezhi," in *Komsomol'skii byt*, p. 226.

61. K. Kirkizh, *Komsomol i Trotskizm* (Moscow, 1925), p. 39. On Bersteinianism and revisionism in their German context see Carl Schorske, *German Social Democracy, 1905–1917: The Development of the Great Schism* (Cambridge, Mass.: Harvard University Press, 1955).

62. Lunacharskii spoke at the Second National Conference of Proletarian Students in January 1927; quoted in N. Safraz'ian, *Bor'ba SSSR za stroitel'stvo sovetskoi vysshei shkoly, 1921–1927* (Moscow, 1977), p. 107.

63. Novich, "Kholostoi vystrel," p. 50.

64. *Upadochnoe nastroenie sredi molodezhi: Eseninshchina* (Moscow: Komakademiia, 1927), pp. 143–144, 30.

65. "Disput," p. 172.

66. Kirkizh, *Komsomol i Trotskizm*, p. 43.

67. Shamberg, "K novomu uchebnomu godu," *Krasnoe studenchestvo*, no. 7 (1926).

68. Gorlov, "Bogdanovsko-messianskie otkroveniia k molodezhi," p. 226.

69. *Pravda*, January 19, 1924.

70. The attitudes of students were a subject of numerous studies in Soviet universities in the 1920s. Some of these undertakings have been perused by Sheila Fitzpatrick. Fitzpatrick analyzed the quantitative results obtained through contemporary questionnaires and deduced from them the norms of students

sexual behavior in the 1920s. I, by contrast, concern myself with the nature of the questions, rather than with the statistical breakdowns of the answers to these questions. Imposing terms borrowed from the Party ethical discourse and the contemporary scientific community questionnaires were devices defining the parameters within which students could voice their personal concerns. Thus my focus is on a questionnaire as a language-creating device and not a scientific tool of inquiry.

See Fitzpatrick, "Sex and Revolution: An Examination of Literary and Statistical Data on the Mores of Soviet Students in the 1920s," *Journal of Modern History* 50 (1978).

71. Stukov, "Trevozhnoe iavlenie."
72. For the "academist deviation" among students see also A. Shliakhman, "Studencheskie organizatsii v epokhu diktatury proletariata," *Proletarskoe studenchestvo*, no. 1 (1922), 10.
73. "Dushevnoe nastroenie uchashcheisia molodezhi," *Krasnyi student*, no. 4 (1923), 13–14.
74. "Dukhovnyi lik studenchestva," *Student-proletarii*, no. 6–7 (1924), 69. For a similar sexual questionnaire addressing Saratov students, see S. Bykov, *Studencheskaia mysl'*, no. 3–4 (1923), 16.
75. "Disput," p. 171.
76. A. Khozail, "O bezpartiinosti v vysshei shkole," *Krasnyi student*, no. 1 (1924), 30.
77. N. Zagorskii, *Klassovaia bor'ba v sibirskikh vuzakh* (Novosibirsk, 1929), p. 71.
78. Mukhin, "Beglye vospominaniia. K 10-letiiu Sverdlovii," in *X Let. 1918–1928: Kommunisticheskii universitet imeni Ia. M. Sverdlova* (Moscow, 1928), p. 320; Arkad'ev, "Vospominaniia profkursnika," ibid., p. 317.
79. M. Liadov, "O zadachakh i perspektivakh kommunisticheskogo universiteta im. Ia. M. Sverdlova. (Doklad na studencheskom sobranii v Marte 1924 Goda)," ibid., p. 269.
80. Troshchenko, "Vuzovskaia molodezh'," pp. 160–161. For how workers supposedly became alienated members of the intelligentsia, see A. Volzhskii, "Otorvalsia," *Oktiabr'*, no. 3 (1924), 157–159.
81. *Pravda*, February 2, 1924.
82. *Naslednikam revoliutsii: Dokumenty partii o komsomole i molodezhi* (Moscow, 1969), pp. 77–78.
83. For a contemporary commentary on this scene, see Iakubovskii, "Psikhologicheskii neorealizm Sergeia Malashkina," p. 155. The connection between the poetry of Blok and students' notion of free love was discussed in Z. Gurevich, "Polove zhitiia studenchestva," *Student revoliutsii*, no. 1 (1927), 40.
84. *Komsomol'skaia pravda*, September 19, 1926.
85. G. Pokrovskii, *Esenin—eseninshchina—religiia* (Moscow, 1929), p. 57.
86. *Upadochnoe nastroenie sredi molodezhi*, p. 143.

87. "Disput," p. 171.

88. V. Maiakovskii, *Polnoe sobranie sochinenii*, vol. 12 (Moscow, 1959), pp. 97, 105.

89. N. Bukharin, "Zlye zametki," *Voprosu literatury*, no. 8 (1988), p. 227.

90. V. Dynnik, *Liricheskii roman Esenina* (Moscow, 1926), p. 2.

91. A. Kruchenykh, *Khuligan Esenin* (Moscow: Izd. avtora, 1926), p. 15; A. Reviakin, "Esenin i eseninshchina," *Na literaturnom postu*, no. 1 (1927), 14. Public disputes about the degeneration of the youth and Eseninshchina were conducted on December 20, 1926, in the Meerkhol'd theater, and on February 13 and March 5, 1927, with Lunacharskii, Maiakovskii, Polonskii, and Radek in attendance. See *Upadochnoe nastroenie sredi molodezhi*, pp. 31–38, 76–82; A. Gorelov and V. Rozov, "Bol'ny li Eseninym?" *Smena*, July 14, 1926; On Esenin as a spokesman for the kulak mentality see A. Evdokimov, *V bor'be za molodezh'* (Leningrad, 1929), pp. 70–73. On Esenin as an archetype of a peasant intelligentsia see A. Iamskii, "Upadochnichestvo i khuliganstvo v studencheskoi poezii," *Krasnoe studenchestvo*, no. 4 (1927), 57–58; A. Lunacharskii, *O byte* (Moscow, 1927), pp. 55–56.

92. A. Makarov, "Rabfakovets," *Put' prosveshcheniia*, no. 6 (1923), 168–169.

93. *Odinnadtsatyi s"ezd RKP(b). Mart-aprel' 1922 goda: stenograficheskii otchet (Moscow: Gospolitizdat, 1961)*, p. 449.

94. Makarov, "Rabfakovets," pp. 168–169.

95. Ibid., p. 171.

96. A. Makarov, "K psikhologii proletarskogo studenchestva," *Put' prosveshcheniia*, no. 5 (1923), 145–146.

97. Makarov, "Rabfakovets," pp. 159, 165.

98. D. Lass, *Sovremennoe studenchestvo (byt, polovaia zhizn')* (Moscow, 1928), p. 23.

99. V. Antonov-Saratovskii, "Eshche o nashem studenchestve," *Pravda*, January 22, 1922.

100. Makarov, "K psikhologii proletarskogo studenchestva," pp. 146–147.

101. Makarov, "Rabfakovets," p. 165. See also K. Ivanov, "Pis'mo na zavod," *Krasnoe studenchestvo*, no. 6 (1927–28), 62–63; M. Laptev, "Partiia, vuzy, proletarskoe studenchestvo i ucheba," *Student-rabochii*, no. 10 (1924), 7–8.

102. Makarov, "Rabfakovets," p. 171.

103. Makarov, "K psikhologii proletarskogo studenchestva," pp. 149, 155, 151.

104. M. Postnikov, "Polovoi vopros v srede sovremennoi uchashcheisia molodezhi," *Omskii rabfakovets*, no. 2 (1928), 39.

105. Troshchenko, "Vuzovskaia molodezh'," pp. 160–161.

106. Makarov, "Rabfakovets," p. 158. See also *Upadochnoe nastroenie sredi molodezhi*, pp. 22–23.

107. Makarov, "K psikhologii proletarskogo studenchestva," pp. 142–143; The "limited social horizon" of peasant students is discussed in Gorn,

"Obshchestvenno-politicheskaia deiatel'nost' Permskikh rabfakovtsev za tri goda," *Permskii rabfakovets,* no. 1 (1922), 14–15.

108. Antonov-Saratovskii, "Eshche o nashem studenchestve."
109. Makarov, "K psikhologii proletarskogo studenchestva," pp. 144–145.
110. Makarov, "Rabfakovets," p. 165.
111. Troshchenko, "Vuzovskaia molodezh'," pp. 171–173.
112. Bobryshev, "Pereulki i tupiki," pp. 94–98.
113. A. Zalkind, "Raboche-krest'ianskaia molodezh i vysshaia shkola," *Proletarskoe studenchestvo,* no. 1 (1922), 43.
114. Makarov, "Rabfakovets," p. 159.
115. Polonskii, "O povesti S. Malashkina," p. 45.
116. I. Figlin, "K bor'be s uklonami," *Krasnyi student,* no. 1 (1924), 21.
117. Makarov, "Rabfakovets," pp. 174, 173.
118. M. Reisner, "Sotsial'naia organizatsiia lichnosti," *Krasnaia nov',* no. 3 (1927), 144–145. On the concept of "anarchistic individualist" see A. Kurella, "Litso kul'turnogo konservatizma," *Revoliutsiia i kul'tura,* no. 14 (1928), 27; "Intelligentsiia v proshlom, nastoiashchem i budushchem: Lektsiia A. Lunacharskogo," *Biulletini literatury i zhizni,* no. 2 (1924), 128.
119. G. Iakubovskii, "Psichologicheskii neorealizm Sergeia Malashkina," p. 153.
120. Polonskii, "O povesti S. Malashkina," pp. 45–46.
121. *Upadochnoe nastroenie sredi molodezhi,* p. 114.
122. Ibid., p. 173.
123. Makarov, "Rabfakovets," p. 173; A. Lunacharskii, "O sotsialino-psikhologicheskikh gruppakh molodezhi," *Krasnoe studenchestvo,* no. 4–5 (1927–28), 31.
124. Antonov-Saratovskii, "Ishche o nashem studenchestve."
125. Makarov, "Rabfakovets," p. 165.
126. T. Kostrov, "O kul'ture, meshchanstve, i vospitanii molodezhi," in *Komsomol'skii byt,* p. 121. For the worries expressed by the Bolshevik moralists regarding the percolation of bourgeois mores into Communist marriages see E. Kviring, "Zheny i byt," *Kommunist,* July 17, 1923; "Kommunisticheskoe studenchestvo. Bytovye ocherki," *Proletarskoe studenchestvo,* no. 2 (1922), 50–51.
127. N. Semashko, *Novyi byt i polovoi vopros* (Moscow: Gos. Izd., 1926), p. 3; Lunacharskii, *O byte,* p. 8. For a similar definition see A. Zalkind, "Etika, byt i molodezh'," in *Komsomol'skii byt,* p. 77.
128. K. Koshevich, "Po povodu verkhnikh etazhei byta," *Revoliutsiia i kul'tura,* no. 14 (1928), 22; L. Sosnovskii, *O kul'ture i meshchanstve* (Leningrad, 1927), p. 76; TsGA IPD, f. K-141, op. 1, d. 1a, l. 7; PANO, f. 1, op. 2, d. 487, l. 23.
129. N. Bukharin, "O starinnykh traditsiiakh i sovremennom kul'turnom stroitel'stve," *Revoliutsiia i kul'tura,* no. 1 (1927), 17.
130. N. Bukharin, "Za uporiadochenie byta molodezhi," in *Komsomol'skii byt,*

p. 99. For an additional discussion see D. Sabchenko, "Kliuch k novomu bytu," *Krasnoe studenchestvo*, no. 5 (1927), 40; M. P'ianykh, "V bor'be za novyi byt," ibid., no. 4 (1927), 44–45.

131. K. Koshevich, "Po povodu verkhnikh etazhei byta," *Revoliutsiia i kul'tura*, no. 14 (1928), 22.

132. Ryndich, *Partiino-sovetskie shkoly*, p. 132.

133. E. Preobrazhenskii, *O morali i klassovykh normakh* (Moscow, 1921), p. 17; Lenin, *PSS*, 41: 309; N. Bukharin, *Teoriia istoricheskogo materializma* (Moscow: Gos. izd, 1923), p. 239.

134. N. Bukharin, "Vospitanie smeny," in *Komsomol'skii byt*, pp. 24–25.

135. A very prominent sexological authority, Aron Borisovich Zalkind was a paradigmatic case of a moralist who floated between domains of knowledge and power. A Jew born in 1883, Zalkind was highly regarded by the Party elite throughout the 1920s. He was even invited to deliver a very prestigious series of lectures in the Red Hall of the Moscow Party Committee. Still, while Zalkind's name will have to be mentioned many times, the analysis below consistently underemphasizes scholars' identity and intellectual itinerary. The unity of the Communist moralistic discourse was based not on the biographical commonality of its participants but on the space in which various notions emerged and were continuously transformed. The rules of formation of scientific concepts unfolded according to a peculiar uniform anonymity, as if they were speaking through the individual who undertook to participate in the new discursive field. Joravsky, *Russian Psychology*, pp. 222, 224, 248, 250–251.

136. Zalkind, "Etika, byt i molodezh'," p. 71. The moralist Ral'tsevich also posed the question of the relation of ten commandments to the Bolshevik ethics; V. Ral'tsevich, "Za klassovoe ponimanie morali," *Revoliutsiia i kul'tura*, no. 23–24 (1928), 13.

137. Iosif Stalin, *Sochineniia*, 13 vols. (Moscow, 1946–1955), 6 : 248.

138. *Revoliutsiia i kul'tura*, no. 1 (1927), 22.

139. T. Kostrov, "Revoliutsiia i meshchanstvo," p. 33; *Upadochnoe nastroenie sredi molodezhi*, p. 24; Bobryshev, *Melkoburzhuaznye vliianiia sredi molodezhi*, pp. 49–51.

140. Bergman, "Za zdorovuiu zhizn'," p. 250. See also M. Shchekin, *Kak zhit' po novomu: Sem'ia, liubov', brak, prostitutsiia* (Kostroma, 1923); T. Kostrov, "Zametki ob kommunisticheskom vospitanii molodezhi," p. 19.

141. A. Lunacharskii, "Kakoiu dolzhna byt' nasha molodezh'," in *Komsomol'skii byt*, pp. 150–151.

142. This argument is made in the various articles collected in A. Slepkov, ed., *Byt i molodezh'* (Moscow: "Bednota," 1926).

143. Kostrov, "O kul'ture, meshchanstve, i vospitanii molodezhi," p. 121.

144. E. Iaroslavskii, "Ob asketizme, vozderzhanii, i polovoi raspushchennosti," in *Kakova zhe nasha molodezh'?* p. 65.

145. V. Dunham, *In Stalin's Time* (Cambridge, 1976), pp. 20–21.

146. Kostrov, "Revoliutsiia i meshchanstvo," pp. 23–24; Iaroslavskii, "Ob asketizme," p. 65.

147. M. Liadov, *Voprosy byta. (Doklad na sobranii iacheiki Sverdlovskogo kommunisticheskogo universiteta)* (Moscow, 1925), pp. 6–7.

148. M. Reisner, "Meshchanstvo," *Krasnaia nov'*, no. 1 (1927), 150.

149. Koshevich believed that "when discordant tendencies in the everyday are locked in struggle a conscious intervention might be useful in order to prevent a slide into the bourgeois slump"; K. Koshevich, "Po povodu verkhnikh etazhei byta," *Revoliutsiia i kul'tura*, no. 14 (1928), 22.

150. Liadov, *Voprosy byta*, pp. 5–7.

151. V. Kuz'min, "Pis'mo o novom byte," in *Komsomol'skii byt*, p. 321; *Iunost' boevaia. Vospominaniia starykh komsomol'tsev* (Moscow, 1958), p. 175.

152. R. Stites, *Revolutionary Dreams: Utopian Vision and Experimental Life in the Russian Revolution* (New York: Oxford University Press, 1989), p. 118.

153. *Naslednikam revoliutsii*, p. 116; *Spravochnik partiinogo rabotnika*, vyp. 5 (Moscow, 1925), pp. 403–405; G. Zinoviev, "Chto takoe Komsomol i chem on dolzhen stat'," in *Partiia i vospitanie smeny* (Leningrad: Gos. izd, 1925), pp. 19–20, 46–49. On the Komsomol decadence theme see N. Chaplin, *Komsomol v polose sotsialisticheskogo razvitiia* (Kharkov, 1927); *Komsomol na perelome* (Moscow, 1927); and *Kuda idet Komsomol?* (Moscow 1927). On the Komsomol and the Opposition see David Khanin, "Igra s ognem. O politicheskikh rezul'tatakh raboty Komsomol'skoi oppozitsii," in *Protiv komsomol'skoi oppozitsii* (Leningrad, 1926), pp. 44–45; N. Chaplin, *Ob oppozitsionnoi klevete na komsomol* (Moscow, 1927).

154. Troshchenko, "Vuzovskaia molodezh'," pp. 164–165.

155. "K proverke vuzovskikh iacheek," *Oktiabr' mysli*, no. 3–4 (1924), 86–89.

156. Bukharin, "O starinnykh traditsiiakh," p. 22; I. Tsvalin, "Chto est' raspushchennost'," in *Komsomol'skii byt*, p. 334; Lunacharskii, *Upadochnoe nastroenie sredi molodezhi*, p. 116.

157. *VI s"ezd RLKSM. Stenograficheskii otchet. 12–18 Iulia 1924*, (Moscow, 1924), pp. 131–132.

158. "Disput," p. 169; Polonskii, "O povesti S. Malashkina," p. 42; Bobryshev, *Melkoburzhuaznye vliianiia sredi molodezhi*, p. 86.

159. Polonskii, "O povesti S. Malashkina," p. 92.

160. Iu. Grossman-Roshchin, "Tezisy ob upadochnichestve v literature," *Na literaturnom postu*, no. 1 (1927).

161. Reisner, "Meshchanstvo," pp. 149–150, 151–152.

162. "Disput," pp. 171–172.

163. Reisner, "Meshchanstvo", p. 153.

164. Korabel'nikov, "Strasti-mordasti," in *Kakova zhe nasha molodezh'?* pp. 96, 112.

165. P. Lepeshinskii, "V vol'no-diskussionnom klube," *Molodaia gvardiia,* no. 1 (1923), 99–100.

166. Korabel'nikov, "Strasti-mordasti," p. 112.

167. L. Vasilevskii, "Polovoe vospitanie i polovoe prosveshchenie," *Leningradskii meditsinskii zhurnal,* no. 2 (1926); N. Semashko, "Novyi byt i polovoi vopros," *Sud idet,* no. 7 (1926).

168. I. Kisel'ev, "Pro cheremukhu shcho roztsvetae i pro liudinu shcho zagnivae", *Student revoliutsii,* no. 2–3 (1927), 91.

169. A. Sol'ts, "Kommunisticheskaia etika," p. 63.

170. N. Semashko, *Iskusstvo odevat'sia* (Moscow, 1927); A. Sol'ts, *O partiinoi etike* (Moscow, 1925), p. 22. For a critique of "fancy dress behind which a philistine soul is hiding," see A. Kurella, "Litso kul'turnogo konservatizma," *Revoliutsiia i kul'tura,* no. 14 (1928), 28.

171. Although Kollontai opened the discussion on "free love" during the civil war, as can be seen in her *Novaia moral' i rabochii klass* (Moscow, 1919), the locus classicus of her outlook is A. Kollontai, *Svobodnaia liubov'* (Petrograd, 1924). For criticisms see, e.g., I. Lin, "Eros iz Rogozhsko-Simonovskogo raiona: Mysli v slukh o stat'e tov. Kollontai 'Dorogu krylatomu erosu'," *Molodaia gvardiia,* no. 4–5 (1923), 152–155; P. Vinogradskaia, "Voprosy morali, pola, byta i tov. Kollontai," *Krasnaia nov',* no. 6 (1923), 179–214.

172. Zalkind, *Polovoi vopros,* p. 53. Lavrov called to notice the "determination of love by class struggle"; E. Lavrov, "Polovoi vopros i molodezh'," *Molodaia gvardiia,* no. 3 (1926), 142; For the meaning of "free love" see Smirnov, "Mysli o sushchnosti staroi i novoi liubvi," *Student-proletarii,* no. 3 (1924). Also of interest is the questionnaire on "love" in F. Tatarskaia and D. Lass, "Voprosy liubvi," *Krasnoe studenchestvo,* no. 1 (1927–28), 37.

173. Iaroslavskii, "Ob asketizme," pp. 58, 65.

174. K. Tsetkin (Zetkin), *O Lenine. Vospominaniia i vstrechi* (Moscow, 1925); *Lenin o morali* (Moscow, 1926). See also Lass, *Sovremennoe studenchestvo,* p. 8; *Komsomol'skii byt,* pp. 16–20; Postnikov, "Polovoi vopros v srede," pp. 40, 46; N. Semashko, "Polovoe vospitanie i zdorov'e," *Komsomol'skaia pravda,* August 15, 1925.

175. Liadov, *Voprosy byta,* pp. 30–31.

176. Ryndich, *Partiino-sovetskie shkoly,* p. 133; Kostrov, "O kul'ture, meshchanstve, i vospitanii molodezhi," p. 121.

177. Kostrov, "Revoliutsiia i meshchanstvo," pp. 23–24.

178. Ionov, "Bez cheremukhi."

179. N. Bozhinskaia, *Prestuplenie Ivana Kuznetsova (Svobodnaia liubov')* (Moscow, 1927), p. 60.

180. S. Gusev, "Sud pionerov nad Romanovym," *Molodaia gvardiia,* no. 7 (1927), 141.

181. The argument here is drawn from, Naiman, *Sex in Public,* p. 115.

182. For an overview of these issues see S. Gilman, "Jews and Mental Illness: Medical Metaphors, Anti-Semitism, and the Jewish Response," *Journal of the History of the Behavioral Sciences,* no. 20 (1984).

183. For an implication of a link between Jewish youth and Trotskyism see, for example, *Izvestiia TsK VLKSM,* no. 13 (1928), 17.

184. TsGA IPD, f. K-598, op. 1, d. 70, ll. 2, 39–40.

185. G. Stocking, *Bones, Bodies, Behavior: Essays on Biological Antropology* (Madison: University of Wisconsin Press, 1988); D. Horn, *Social Bodies: Science, Reproduction, and Italian Modernity* (Princeton: Princeton University Press, 1994), p. 29.

186. On Lombroso's physiognomism see D. Pick, *Faces of Degeneration: A European Disorder, c. 1848–c. 1918* (Cambridge: Cambridge University Press, 1989), pp. 109–152.

187. P. Mirel'zon, *Gigiena nervno-bol'nogo* (Krasnodar, 1927), p. 9.

188. Gilman, "Jews and Mental Illness," pp. 150–159.

189. K. Sotonin, *Temperamenty* (Kazan, 1921), pp. 12, 36–37.

190. E. Carlson, "Medicine and Degeneration: Theory and Praxis," in Chamberlin and Gilman, *Degeneration,* pp. 127–128.

191. Sotonin, *Temperamenty,* pp. 79–81.

192. Lass, *Sovremennoe studenchestvo,* p. 80; A. Zalkind, *Polovoi vopros,* pp. 44–45; E. Demidovich also maintained that "sexual promiscuity leads to *atrophia testiculorum*"; "Polovaia zhizn' i zdorov'e studenchestva," *Krasnoe studenchestvo,* no. 8 (1927–28), 42.

193. Postnikov, "Polovoi vopros v srede," p. 46.

194. A. Zalkind, "Polovoi vopros s kommunisticheskoi tochki zreniia," in *Polovoi vopros,* ed. S. Kalmanson (Moscow, 1924), p. 13.

195. Ionov, "Bez cheremukhi"; D. Lebed', "Predislove," in *O morale i partiinoi etike* (Kharkov, 1925), p. 3; Liadov, *Voprosy byta,* p. 21.

196. Zalkind, "Polovoi vopros," p. 6.

197. L. P., "Bol'noe," *Krasnyi student,* no. 2 (1924).

198. Zalkind, *Polovoi vopros,* pp. 15–16, 64.

199. Lass, *Sovremennoe studenchestvo,* pp. 103–105, 134.

200. Engelstein, *The Keys to Happiness,* p. 238; Lass, *Sovremennoe studenchestvo,* pp. 17–118; Liadov, *Voprosy byta,* pp. 14–15; S. Grigoreev, "Vtoraia stikhiia. Eshche raz o polovoi zhizni studenchestva," *Krasnyi student,* no. 3 (1924), 38–39.

201. Lass, *Sovremennoe studenchestvo,* p. 110. Could Tania's femininity have anything to do with her sexual behavior? Or, to put the same question in more

general terms, what did Bolshevik sexology make of the differences between the sexes? Some experts claimed that "the mind of a working-class female resembles the mind of the man of her own class more than the mind of the woman of another class"; "Zhenshchina i novyi byt," *Izvestiia*, February 20, 1925. Nemilov, by contrast, maintained that the primacy of hormones in determining behavior "prevents us from speaking about the 'human being' as such . . . We know only man and women"; A. Nemilov, *Biologicheskaia tragediia zhenshchiny* (Leningrad, 1925), p. 39. Kollontai was also talking about the "physical and spiritual particularities of women," their "distinctive characteristics and qualities." A. Kollontai, *Polozhenie zhenshchiny v evoliutsii khoziaistva* (Moscow, 1922), p. 205.

202. A. Zalkind, "O iazvakh v RKP," *Pravda*, September 27–29, 1923.

203. G. Iakubovskii, "Psichologicheskii neorealizm Sergeia Malashkina," *Zvezda*, no. 1 (1927), 153.

204. I. Gel'man, *Polovaia zhizn' sovremennoi molodezhi: Opyt sotsial'no-biologicheskogo obsledovaniia* (Moscow, 1923), p. 111.

205. Polonskii, "O povesti S. Malashkina," p. 88.

206. "O povesti S. Malashkina," *Na literaturnom postu*, no. 1 (1927), 46–47, 50. For a similar criticism see Bobryshev, "Pereulki i tupiki."

207. Zalkind, *Polovoi vopros*, p. 12.

208. Katerina Clark, *The Soviet Novel: History as Ritual* (Chicago: University of Chicago Press, 1985), pp. 105, 111.

209. T. Gandzhulevich, "Novyi student v khudozhestvennoi literature," *Student revoliutsii*, no. 4 (1926), 12.

4. From a Weak Body to an Omnipotent Mind

1. PANO, f. 6, op. 1, d. 12, ll. 2–4.

2. I. Bobryshev, "Pereulki i tupiki," *Komsomol'skaia pravda*, March 2, 1927. See also the parody in P. Bul'ver, "Luna bez cheremukhi ili liubov' iz sobach'ego pereulka," *Smena*, no. 9 (1927), 10.

3. V. Kopp, "O neslykhannykh otkrytiiakh tovarishcha Enchmena," *Molodaia gvardiia*, no. 3 (1923), 89–90; A. Kalashnikov, "Sotsial'nyi i biologicheskii faktory v sovetskoi sisteme vospitaniia," *Narodnyi uchitel'*, no. 2 (1926), 23.

4. P. Kruglikov, *Sovremennaia psikhologiia i ee sblizhenie s naukami o kul'ture i obshchestve* (Kazan, 1922), pp. 9–11. See also L. Voitlovskii, *Ocherki kollektivnoi psikhologii* (Moscow, 1925), p. 7.

5. T. Hanzhulevych, "Literatura pro molod'," *Student revoliutsii*, no. 4 (1927), 51.

6. V. Bekhterev, *Obshchie osnovy refleksologii cheloveka*, 3d ed. (Leningrad, 1926), p. 13. For the rise of the physiological conception of the mind, see R. Young, *Mind, Brain, and Adaptation in the Nineteenth Century: Cerebral Localization*

and Its Biological Context from Gall to Ferrier (Oxford: Oxford University Press, 1970).

7. L. Minor found at least three meanings of "consciousness" in use: consciousness as an incarnation of the World Spirit in the body, consciousness as a function of the brain—a manifestation of psychic energy, and consciousness as a flickering self-awareness of the soul; "Pitanie truzhenikov uma," *Russkaia klinika*, no. 1 (1924), 26.

8. Experts admitted that they found it difficult to define mental labor, "because all forms of labor have both a physical and a psychic dimension"; I. Stychinskii, "Umstvennyi trud i utomlenie," *Studencheskaia mysl'*, no. 6–7 (1923), 22–25.

9. Bobryshev, "Pereulki i tupiki."

10. L. Faingol'd, *Polovoe bessilie: Ego prichiny, preduprezhdenie, i lechenie* (Odessa, 1927), p. 10.

11. A. Bogdanov, "Trud i potrebnosti rabotnika," *Molodaia gvardiia*, no. 3 (1923), 105–106.

12. "Sud pionnerov nad P. Romanovym," *Molodaia gvardiia*, no. 7 (1927), 141.

13. Lev Gumilevskii, *Sobachii periulok*, 2d ed. (Riga: Gramatu draugs, 1928), pp. 10–11, 22–23. Hereafter page numbers are cited in the text.

14. I. Kysel'ov, "Pro Leva Gumilevskogo i pro liubov deshevshu, nizh kvitok u kino," *Student revoliutsii*, no. 4 (1927), 53.

15. K. Chukovskii, *Dnevnik, 1901–1929* (Moscow: Sovetskii pisatel', 1991), p. 96.

16. I. Gel'man, *Polovaia zhizn' sovremennoi molodezhi: Opyt sotsial'no-biologicheskogo obsledovaniia* (Moscow, 1923), pp. 94, 96, 115–116; TsGIA IPD, f. 984, op. 1, ll. 244, 21.

17. Gel'man, *Polovaia zhizn' sovremennoi molodezhi*, p. 65; P. Lepeshinskii, "V vol'no-diskussionnom klube," *Molodaia gvardiia*, no. 1 (1923), 96–97; 102–103; L. Vasilevskii, "Polovoi byt uchashchikhsia," *Komsomol'skaia pravda*, March 19, 1927.

18. N. Gushchin, *Rezul'taty polovogo obsledovanie molodezhi g. Iakutska* (Iakutsk: Narkomproszdrav IaASSR, 1925), p. 5; V. Kliachkin, "Polovaia anketa sredi Omskogo studenchestva," *Sotsial'naia gigiena*, no. 6 (1925), 129.

19. See, for example, V. Borovskii, "K voprosu ob instinkte v nauke o povedenii," in *Psikhologiia i marksizm* (Moscow: Gos. isd., 1925); M. Lemberg, *Chto nuzhno znat' o polovom voprose* (Leningrad: Priboi, 1925).

20. E. Arkin, "Fiziologiia i mirovozzrenie," *Narodnyi uchitel'*, no. 2 (1926), 60–61.

21. A reductive theory of the mind was not specific to Bolshevism, of course. For a contemporary discussion of the influence of Watson's behaviorism in the Soviet Union, see *Ob"ektivnaia psikhologiia v Rossii i Amerike* (Moscow, 1925); V. Borovskii, "O bikheviorizme i materializme," *Pod znamenem marksizma*, no. 7–8 (1928).

22. "Sud pionnerov nad P. Romanovym," 141.

23. Iu. Frolov, *Mozg i trud* (Leningrad, 1925), p. 6; V. Bekhterev, "Sub"ektivnyi ili ob"ektivnyi metod v izuchenii lichnosti?" *Molodaia gvardiia*, no. 5 (1924).

24. Pavlov quoted in G. Volkov, *Ugolovnoe pravo i refleksologiia* (Kharkov, 1928), pp. 18–19.

25. K. Kornilov, *Uchenie o reaktsiiakh cheloveka s psikhologicheskoi tochki zreniia: Reaktologiia* (Moscow: Gos. Izd., 1922), p. 8.

26. D[zhon] Votson (John D. Watson), *Psikhologiia kak nauka o povedenii* (Moscow, 1926), p. 296.

27. Among the basic works that translated reflexology, physiology, and objectivist psychology into Marxist categories, the most prominent were N. Podkopaev, *Metodika izucheniia uslovnykh refleksov* (Moscow, 1924); Iu. Frankfurt, *Refleksologiia i marksizm* (Moscow: Gos. Izd., 1924).

28. E. Enchmen, *Vosemnadtsat' tezisov o "teorii novoi biologii" (proekt organizatsii Revolitusionno-Nauchnogo Soveta Respubliki i vvedeniia sistemy fiziologicheskogo pasporta)* (Piatigorsk: In. K. O. Severo-Kavkazkogo Revoliutsionnogo Komiteta, 1920), p. 5. His contemporaries argued that Enchmen was influenced by the famous psychologist N. Vvedenskii (1852–1922), who foreshadowed much of the Pavlovian paradigm. Such influence is plausible, since it is known that Enchmen worked in St. Petersburg, where Vvedenskii served as the president of a local philosophical society. However, whereas Enchmen was a vehement antimentalist, Vvedentskii's view is better characterized as skeptical. According to Vvedenskii "consciousness," existent or not, was not conducive to science: "Material processes are unaffected by psychic events. They follow their own logic as if the psychic does not exist . . . As no objective criteria prove to me that my interlocutor is a spiritual being, any such claim will have to remain unproved"; A. Vvedenskii, *Psikhologiia bez vsiakoi metafiziki* (St. Petersburg: Stasulevich, 1917), pp. 80–81; G. Chlepanov, *Psikhologiia ili refleksologiia* (Moscow, 1926), p. 15. See the discussion of these issues in E. Budilova, *Bor'ba materializma i idealizma v russkoi psikhologicheskoi nauke: Vtoraia polovina XIX—nachalo XX veka* (Moscow: Iz. Akademia Nauk SSSR, 1960).

29. E. Enchmen, *Teoriia novoi biologii i marksizm* (Petrograd: Rabochii fakul'tet peterburgskogo gos. Universiteta, 1923), pp. 1–2; K. Grasis, "O Tvoreniiakh odnogo zapozdalogo maga," *Krasnyi student*, no. 7–8 (1923), 44; L. Cheskis, "Neproizvoditel'nyi trud," in *Ocherednoe izvrashchenie marksizma: O teorii Enchmena* (Moscow, "Novaia Moskva," 1924), p. 16; K. Kornilov, "Psikhologiia i teoriia novoi biologii," *Pod znamenem marksizma*, no. 4–5 (1923).

30. E. Enchmen, *Vosemnadtsat'*, p. 27; idem, *Teoriia*, pp. 14–17. For a related attempt to critique "psychophysiological parallelism," see Bekhterev, *Obshchie osnovy refleksologii*, pp. 70–73.

31. Amar, *Chelovecheskaia mashina* (Moscow, 1923).

32. M. Grematskii, *Chelovek machina* (Moscow, 1925), pp. 122, 16, 117–119, 127.

33. Ibid., p. 124. One year earlier a treatise discussing human beings from the "biological point of view" argued that "man is constructed like a factory with many departments and rooms"; N. Shvarts, "Biologicheskii ocherk," in *Polovoi vopros,* ed. S. Kalmanson (Moscow: Molodaia gvardiia, 1924), p. 18. Cf. V. Savich, *Osnovy povedeniia cheloveka: Analiz povedeniia cheloveka s tochki zreniia fiziologii tsentral'noi nervnoi sistemy i vnutrennei sekretsii* (Leningrad, 1924), p. 121; S. Vasil'ev, "K kharakteristike mekhanicheskogo materializma," in *Dialektika prirody* (Vologda, 1927), p. 46.

34. E. Lubotskoi and M. Lubotskaia, *Dusha zhivotnykh i cheloveka* (Moscow, 1926), pp. 10, 126, 3–5, 102. See also the locus classicus in Paul Lafargue, translated into Russian as P. Lafarg, *Proiskhozhdenie i razvitie poniatiia o dushe* (Moscow, 1924).

35. Kopp, "O neslykhanykh otkrytiiakh tovarishcha Enchmena," p. 89. Also relevant on the "soul" in Marxism are A. Nimilov, "Uznaem li my kogda-nibud' chto takoe 'dusha'?" *Chelovek i priroda,* no. 4 (1924); Ts. Perel'muter, *Nauka i religiia o zhizni chelovecheskogo tela* (n.p., Bezbozhnik, 1927).

36. For accounts of these positions see A. Petrovskii, *Istoriia sovetskoi psikhologii* (Moscow, 1967), p. 59; and A. Smirnov, *Razvitie i sovrmennoe sostoianie psikhologicheskoi nauki v SSSR* (Moscow, 1975), p. 139.

37. Kornilov, *Uchenie o reaktsiiakh cheloveka,* pp. 128, 152.

38. V. Kirilov, "My," *Griadushchee,* no. 2 (1918), 4; A. Gastev, "O tendentsiiakh proletarskoi kul'tury," *Proletarskaia kul'tura,* no. 9–10 (1919), 42; idem, *Industrial'nyi mir* (Kharkov, 1919), pp. 50–70.

39. Votson (Watson), *Psikhologiia kak nauka o povedenii,* p. vi.

40. V. Bechterev, *General Principles of Human Reflexology: An Introduction to the Objective Study of Personality,* trans. Emma Murphy and William Murphy (London: Jarrolds, 1933), p. 41. For a contemporary appraisal of the relation of Bekhterev and Pavlov to Marxism see V. Nevskii, "Politicheskii goroskop uchenogo-akademika," *Pod znamenem marksizma,* no. 3 (1923); M. Velikovskii, "Pobeda materializma (O rabotakh akademika Pavlova)," *Sputnik kommunizma,* no. 23 (1923); Iu. Frankfurt, "Uchenie Bekhtereva i marksizm," *Pod znamenem marksizma,* no. 6 (1928); V. Protopopov, *Bekhterev kak refleksolog* (Kharkov, 1928).

41. V. Borovskii, "Chto takoe psikhologiia," *Krasnaia nov',* no. 4 (1927), 157.

42. I. Sapir, "Protiv idealizma v biologii—tak nazyvaemaia psikhicheskaia deiatel'nost' i materializm," *Sputnik kommunista,* no. 24 (1923), 311.

43. M. Reisner, *Problemy sotsial'noi psikhologii* (Rostov-on-Don, 1925), pp. 9–10, 21.

44. Ibid., p. 21.

45. A. Zalkind, *Ocherki kul'tury revoliutsionnogo vremeni* (Moscow: Rabotnik prosveshcheniia, 1924), p. 59.

46. A. Variash, "Freidizm i ego kritika s tochki zreniia marksizma," *Dialektika v prirode*, no. 1 (1925). For an influential critique of Variash see G. Bammel', "Filosofskii metod Lenina i nekotorye cherty sovremennogo revizionizma," *Voinstvuiushchii materializm*, no. 2 (1925).

47. Acceptance of Freud by the Soviet Marxists was not unanimous even in the early years. It was pointed out that Freud's psychological method is based on introspection (hence the charge of subjectivism) and that mental events in his theory are, in the last resort, independent entities irreducible to physiology (hence the charge of idealism). See V. Iurinets, "Freidizm i marksizm," *Pod znamenem marksizma*, no. 8–9 (1924); V. Gakkebuch, "K kritike sovremennogo primeneniia psikhoanaliticheskogo metoda lecheniia," *Sovremennaia psikhonevrologiia* 8 (1925); I. Sapir, "Freidizm i marksizm," ibid., no. 11 (1926); I. Perepel', *Freidizm i ego akademicheskaia oppozitsiiia* (Leningrad: Izd. avtora, 1926). For a discussion of the encounter between Freud and the Bolsheviks, see J. Marti, "La psychanalyse en Russie et en Union Sovietique de 1909 à 1930," *Critique* 32, no. 346 (March 1976); H. Lobner and V. Levitin, "A Short Account of Freudism: Notes on the History of Psychoanalysis in the USSR," *Sigmund Freud House Bulletin* 2, no. 1 (1978); C. Toegel, "Lenin und die Rezeptsion der Psychoanalyse in der Sowjetunion der Zwanzigerjahre," ibid., 13 (1989); A Belkin and A. Litvinov, "K istorii psikhoanaliza v sovetskoi Rossii," *Rossiiskii psikhologicheskii vestnik*, no. 2 (1992); M. Miller, *Freud and the Bolsheviks: Psychoanalysis in Imperial Russia and the Soviet Union* (New Haven: Yale University Press, 1998), pp. 53–92.

48. K. Veidemiuller and A. Shcheglov, "Freidizm," in *BSE*, 59: 188. That Freudism was legitimate only as a branch of knowledge studying the ill (neurotics) in the late 1920s and early 1930s is evident from D. Ozeretskovskii, "K kritike psikhoanaliza: O novykh putiakh v lechenii nevrotikov," *Sovremennaia psikhonevrologiia* 8 (1929), 311–319; B. Birman, "Psikhoterapiia, kak sotsiorefleksoterapiia nevropaticheskoi lichnosti," in *Psikhonevrologicheskie nauki v SSSR*, ed. A. Zalkind (Moscow: Gosmedizdat, 1930), pp. 321–322; and V. Vnukov, "Psikhoanaliz," *Meditsinskaia entsiklopediia* 27 (1933), 733.

49. B. Bykhovskii, "O metodologicheskikh osnovaniiakh psikhoanaliticheskogo ucheniia Freida," *Pod znamenem marksizma*, no. 11–12 (1923), 158–177.

50. A. Luriia, "Psikhoanaliz kak sistema monicheskoi psikhologii," in *Psikhologiia i Marksizm* (Leningrad: Gos. izd., 1925).

51. L. Trotskii, *Sochineniia*, vol. 21 (Moscow: Gosizdat, 1927), pp. 260, 430–431.

52. Marxists with strong scientific inclinations espoused similar positions. Bogdanov, for instance, wrote that "production" is a "socially organized system of reflexes" and that "historical materialism" is "social reflexology"; A.

Bogdanov, "Uchenie o refleksakh i zagadki pervobytnogo myshleniia," *Vestnik kommunisticheskoi akademii,* no. 10 (1925), 67. Also of interest in this context is N. Gredeskul, "Uslovnye refleksy i revoliutsiia," *Zvezda,* no. 3 (1924).

53. R. Bauer, *The New Man in Soviet Psychology* (Cambridge, Mass.: Harvard University Press, 1952), pp. 67–92.

54. V. Struminskii, "Marksizm v sovremennoi psikhologii," *Pod znamenem marksizma,* no. 3 (1926), 214–216.

55. Reisner, *Problemy sotsial'noi psikhologii,* pp. 3–5.

56. Enchmen, *Vosemnadtsat',* pp. 35, 39, 43–46.

57. Ibid., p. 39.

58. Ibid., p. 35.

59. A. Luriia, "Printsipial'nye voprosy sovremennoi psikhologii," *Pod znamenem marksizma,* no. 4–5 (1926), 134–135; Frolov, *Mozg i trud,* p. 105.

60. M. Reisner, "Intelligentsiia, kak predmet izucheniia v plane nauchnoi raboty," *Pechat' i revoliutsiia,* no. 1 (1922), 104.

61. Enchmen, *Vosemnadtsat',* p. 35.

62. S. Val'gard, *O psikhologii polovoi zhizni* (Moscow, 1926), p. 20.

63. D. Lass, *Sovremennoe studenchestvo (byt, polovaia zhizn'),* (Moscow, 1928), p. 57. See M. Zavadovskii, "Problemy pola v biologicheskoi postanovke," in *Polovoi vopros v svete nauchnogo znaniia: Sbornik statei* (Moscow: Gos. izd., 1926); G. Sakharov, "Fiziologicheskie predposylki i obshchii vzgliad na patologiiu polovoi zhizni," ibid.

64. A. Stukovenkov, "Gigiena polovoi zhizni," in Kalmanson, *Polovoi vopros,* pp. 13–137.

65. Lass, *Sovremennoe studenchestvo,* p. 127.

66. Kisel'ev, "Pro Leva Gumilevskogo," p. 53.

67. N. Semashko, *Novyi byt i polovoi vopros* (Moscow: Gos. izd., 1926), p. 25; Kliachkin, "Polovaia anketa sredi Omskogo studenchestva," p. 130. Prostitution was usually associated with the urban environment; see Gel'man, *Polovaia zhizn' sovremennoi molodezhi,* p. 121; A. Platovskii, *Polovaia zhizn' sovremennogo studenchestva* (Rostov-on-Don: "Burevestnik," 1926), p. 27; K. Kampfeir, *Prostitutsiia kak obshchestvenno-klassovoe iavlenie i obshchestvennaia bor'ba s neiu* (Moscow, 1925).

68. Ia. Golomb, *Polovoe vozderzhanie (za i protiv)* (Odessa: Svetoch, 1927). See also P. A. Vasilevskie and L. M. Vasilevskie, "Polovaia zhizn' cheloveka," in Kalmanson, *Polovoi vopros,* pp. 64–65.

69. *Vnutrennie dvigateli chelovecheskogo tela (gormony)* (Moscow: Gos. izd., 1923).

70. Lass, *Sovremennoe studenchestvo,* p. 195.

71. "Iz otzyvov chitatelei 'Pravdy' na stat'iu tov. Smidovich 'O liubvi,'" in *Komsomol'skii byt* (Moscow, 1926), p. 277; V. Gradovskii, "Polovoi vopros," ibid., p. 283.

72. A strong pro-abstinence stance was expressed by Vladimir Bekhterev in his *Znachenie polovogo vlecheniia v zhiznedeiatel'nosti organizma* (Moscow: Narkomzdrav R.S.F.S.R., 1928), pp. 17–18.

73. Kliachkin, "Polovaia anketa sredi Omskogo studenchestva," p. 137.

74. B. Sigal, *Polovoi vopros* (Moscow: Molodaia gvardiia, 1925), p. 49.

75. Ia. Kaminskii, *Polovaia zhizn' i fizicheskaia kul'tura* (Tver, 1927), p. 30.

76. V. Slepkov, "Ne edinoi politikoi zhiv komsomolets," in *Komsomol'skii byt,* p. 216; B. Landkof, "Do pytannia pro zanepadnytstvo," *Student revoliutsii,* no. 5 (1927), 75–76.

77. E. Lavrov, "Polovoi vopros i molodezh," *Molodaia gvardiia,* no. 3 (1926), 140; A. Sol'ts, "O partiinoi etike: Doklad na sobranii iacheiki TsKK i NK RKI," in *Sbornik materialov o partiinoi etike* (Chita, 1925), pp. 21–22; E. Iaroslavskii, "Ob asketizme, vozderzhanii, i polovoi raspushchennosti," in *Kakova zhe nasha molodezh'?* (Moscow, 1927), p. 49.

78. P. Merel'zon, *Gigiena nervno-bol'nogo* (Krasnodar, 1927), p. 4.

79. Kaminskii, *Polovaia zhizn' i fizicheskaia kul'tura,* p. 18.

80. Vasilevskii, "Polovaia zhizn' cheloveka," p. 35; N. Perna, *Stroiteli zhivogo tela: Ocherki fiziologii vnutrennei sekretsii* (n.p., 1924); Sigal, *Polovoi vopros,* p. 17.

81. I. Ariamov, "Biologicheskie osnovy polovoi zhizni," *Vestnik prosveshcheniia,* no. 9 (1925); idem, "Znachenie sokhraneniia polovoi energii dlia molodezhi," *Komsomol'skaia pravda,* February 7, 1926. On "rejuvenation" of the human body see N. Kol'tsov, *Omolozhenie* (Moscow: Gos. Izd., 1923); "Noveishie opyty omolazhivaniia liudei," *Chelovek i priroda,* no. 4–5 (1925).

82. A. Zalkind, *Polovoi vopros v usloviiakh sovetskoi obshchestvennosti* (Leningrad, 1926), p. 49. See also Golomb, *Polovoe vozderzhaniie,* pp. 7–8; Kaminskii, *Polovaia zhizn' i fizicheskaia kul'tura,* pp. 12–13.

83. Gradovskii, "Polovoi vopros," pp. 285, 284.

84. Zalkind, *Polovoi vopros,* pp. 48–49.

85. Gel'man, *Polovaia zhizn' sovremennoi molodezhi,* p. 7.

86. Zalkind, *Ocherki kul'tury revoliutsionnogo vremeni,* p. 102; idem, *Polovoi vopros,* p. 16; Reisner, *Problemy sotsial'noi psikhologii,* pp. 17–18, 135.

87. Platovskii, *Polovaia zhizn' sovremennogo studenchestva,* p. 7; Gushchin, *Rezul'taty,* p. 24.

88. Iaroslavskii, "Ob asketizme," pp. 61–62.

89. Kaminskii, *Polovaia zhizn' i fizicheskaia kul'tura,* p. 20.

90. Kliachkin, "Polovaia anketa sredi Omskogo studenchestva," p. 131; Gel'man, *Polovaia zhizn' sovremennoi molodezhi,* pp. 77–78.

91. Gel'man, *Polovaia zhizn' sovremennoi molodezhi,* pp. 74–76, 81.

92. Zalkind, *Polovoi vopros,* pp. 4, 64, 34; S. Grigoreev, "Vtoraia stikhiia. Eshche raz o polovoi zhizni studenchestva," *Krasnyi student,* no. 3 (1924), 39; Z. Hurevych, "Polove zhyttiia studentstva," *Student revoliutsii,* no. 1 (1927), 43.

93. Gel'man, *Polovaia zhizn' sovremennoi molodezhi,* p. 64; Kliachkin, "Polovaia

anketa sredi Omskogo studenchestva," p. 129; M. Ravich, "Bor'ba s prostitutsiei," *Kommunistka*, no. 1–2 (1920).

94. Lass, *Sovremennoe studenchestvo*, p. 8.

95. Kliachkin, "Polovaia anketa sredi Omskogo studenchestva," pp. 137–138; M. Liadov, *Voprosy byta. (Doklad na sobranii iacheiki Sverdlovskogo kommunisticheskogo universiteta)* (Moscow, 1925), pp. 32–33; Zalkind, *Polovoi vopros,* pp. 18, 30, 44; G. Lapidus, "Voprosy psikhologii kak elementy sotsial'noi gigieny," *Studencherskaia mysl',* no. 5 (1923), 17.

96. A. Zalkind, *Polovoi fetishizm: K peresmotru polovogo voprosa* (Moscow: Vserossiskii Proletkul't, 1925), pp. 36–37.

97. N. Bukharin, "Ratsionalizatsiia i uporiadochenie byta molodezhi," in *Komsomol'skii byt*, p. 103.

98. A. Lunacharskii, "Moral' i svoboda," *Krasnaia nov',* no. 7 (1923), 135; "O sotsialino-psikhologicheskikh gruppakh molodezhi," *Krasnoe studenchestvo,* no. 4–5 (1927–28), 31.

99. V. Kuz'min, "O 'molodoi starosti,' asketizme i kazenshchine," in *Komsomol'skii byt*, p. 214; Lavrov, "Polovoi vopros i molodezh'," p. 137.

100. Liadov, *Voprosy byta*, pp. 32, 39.

101. S. Smidovich, "O byte," *Komsomol'skii byt,* p. 165. See also L. Gerkan, "Zdorov'e studentov i fizkul'tura," *Krasnoe studenchestvo,* no. 10 (1927–28), 32–33.

102. A. Ryndich, *Partiino-sovetskie shkoly* (Moscow, 1925), p. 127; R. Tsypkin, "Fizicheskoe vospitanie v vysshikh uchebnykh zavedeniiakh," *Krasnyi student,* no. 9–10 (1923), 36; "Fizicheskaia kul'tura," *Molodaia gvardiia,* no. 3 (1923), 226–229; M. Borova, "Voprosy fizkul'tury," *Sputnik agitatora,* no. 10 (1927); M. Burova, "Fizkul'tura na novom etape," *Kommunisticheskaia revoliutsiia,* no. 13–14 (1927); M. Reikhrud, *Fizicheskoe vospitanie iunykh pionerov* (Moscow, 1927).

103. Semashko, *Novyi byt i polovoi vopros,* pp. 14–15; Iaroslavskii invoked the Latin proverb "a healthy spirit in a healthy body," which later became a set Bolshevik phrase; "Ob asketizme," p. 59.

104. Lass, *Sovremennoe studenchestvo*, p. 135.

105. Ibid., pp. 401–402.

106. Zalkind, *Polovoi vopros*, p. 102.

107. *Trinadtsatyi s"ezd RKP(b), mai 1924 goda: Stenograficheskii otchet* (Moscow: Gospolizdat, 1963), p. 675.

108. *Spravochnik partiinogo rabotnika,* vyp. 5 (Moscow, 1925), pp. 293–294.

109. D. Lass, "O prepodavanii seksual'noi gigieny," *Krasnoe studenchestvo,* no. 15 (1927–28), 48.

110. V. Levitskii, "Umstvennyi trud i utomliaemost'," *Nauka i tekhnika* 2–3 (1922), 11; V. Efimov, *Utomlenie i bor'ba s nim* (Moscow, 1924), p. 7; V. Kashkadamov, "Gigiena umstvennogo truda," *Narodnyi uchitel',* no. 5–6 (1927), 143.

111. Lubotskoi and Lubotskoi, *Dusha zhivotnykh i cheloveka,* pp. 107–108, 145–146; On students' "fatigue of the brain" see V. Efimov, *Utomlenie i bor'ba s nim* (Moscow, 1924), pp. 15, 49, 52; A. Stratonitskii, *Voprosy byta v komsomole* (Leningrad: Priboi, 1926), p. 77.

112. Val'gard, *O psikhologii polovoi zhizni,* p. 28.

113. G. Gordon, *Gigiena umstvennogo truda* (Moscow, 1925), pp. 14–15, 27.

114. A. Zalkind, "Mozg i byt," *Revoliutsiia i kul'tura,* no. 20 (1928), pp. 48–49.

115. Ibid.

116. Kashkadamov, "Gigiena umstvennogo truda," p. 140.

117. Lass, *Sovremennoe studenchestvo,* pp. 128–129.

118. Zalkind, "Mozg i byt," p. 51.

119. Ibid., pp. 49–50.

120. Lass, *Sovremennoe studenchestvo,* p. 126.

121. For materials relating psychological illness to criminality see N. Lavrent'ev, "Dushevnye bolezni i polovye prestupleniia," *Zhurnal nevropatologii i psikhologii* 1 (1928), 59–74.

122. N. Brukhanskii, *Materialy po seksual'noi psikhopatologii* (Moscow: M. and C. Sabashkovy, 1927), p. 9.

123. Ibid., pp. 10–16.

124. Ibid., pp. 25–26.

125. Ibid., pp. 26–27.

126. Igal Halfin, *From Darkness to Light: Class, Consciousness, and Salvation in Revolutionary Russia* (Pittsburgh: Pittsburgh University Press, 2000), pp. 121–148.

127. Ludwig Feuerbach, "Provisional Theses for the Reformation of Philosophy," in *The Young Hegelians: An Antology,* ed. L. Stepelevich (Cambridge: Cambridge University Press, 1973), p. 163.

128. Karl Marx and Friedrich Engels, *Collected Works,* 50 vols. (New York, 1975–2002), 3: 175–176, 182; 4: 119.

129. *Pravda,* October 28, 1921.

130. For an authoritative critique of naturalism by the head of Soviet medicine see N. Semashko, "Nevezhestvo i pornografiia pod maskoi prosveshcheniia, nauki i literatury," *Izvestiia,* April 8, 1927.

131. Velikovskii, "Pobeda materializma," p. 188; Vasil'ev, "K kharakteristike mekhanicheskogo materializma," pp. 46–47.

132. Val'gard, *O psikhologii polovoi zhizni,* p. 20.

133. Savich, *Osnovy povedeniia cheloveka,* pp. 86, 126, 142.

134. A. Stoliarov, *Dialekticheskii materializm i mekhanisty* (Moscow: Priboi, 1928); A. Emery, "Dialectics vs. Mechanics: A Communist Debate on Scientific Method," *Philosophy of Science,* no. 1 (1935); Bauer, *New Man in Soviet Psychology,* pp. 24–33; Sarab'ianov argued that complete denial of the existence of psychological states such as "feelings," "perceptions" etc. does not resolve

the contradiction between subject and object but only explains it away. V. Sarab'ianov, "O fizicheskom i psikhicheskom," *Sputnik kommunista*, no. 24 (1923), 329; For the argument that unless a self-generating energy in the brain is posited man will fall from a lofty position as the subject of nature to just one of its objects see Lazarev, *Ionnaia teoriia vozbuzhdeniia* (1923, n.p.), p. 149.

135. For a tally of such futuristic projects see *Zhizn' i tekhnika budushchego (sotsial'nye i nauchno-tekhnicheskie utopii)* (Moscow, 1928).

136. Bobryshev, "Pereulki i tupiki," pp. 51–52.

137. L. Tsyrlin, "Mekhanizm ili marksizm?" *Na literaturnom postu*, no. 3 (1929), 49–51.

138. D. Joravsky, *Russian Psychology: A Critical History* (Oxford: Basil Blackwell, 1989), pp. 162–163.

139. Bauer, *New Man in Soviet Psychology*, p. 97.

140. Raionov, "Otchuzhdenie deistviia," *Vestnik kommunisticheskoi akademii*, no. 13 (1925), 163.

141. Cheskis, "Neproizvoditel'nyi trud," p. 14.

142. Rigorously materialist scholars pointed out, however, that this Cartesian formulation was clearly "dualist," thus undermining Bukharin's self-professed "materialistic monism"; P. Sapozhnikov, "Ocherednoe izvrashchenie marksizma: O teorii enchmena," *Pod znamenem marksizma*, no. 8–9 (1924), 297; N. Bukharin, "Enchmeniada," in *Ataka* (Moscow, 1924), p. 341.

143. *Pravda*, December 14, 1923; Arkad'ev, "Vospominaniia profkursnika," in *X let. 1918–1928. Kommunisticheskii universitet imeni Ia. M. Sverdlova* (Moscow, 1928), p. 317; TsGIA IPD, f. 138, op. 1, d.2, l. 9.

144. P. Sapozhnikov, "Ocherednoe izvrashchenie marksizma: O teorii Enchmena," *Pod znamenem marksizma*, no. 8–9 (1924), p. 295; Kopp, "O neslykhanykh otkrytiiakh tovarishcha Enchmena," p. 97; Cheskis, "Neproizvoditel'nyi trud," p. 16.

145. *Pravda*, April 12, 1926.

146. Bauer, *New Man in Soviet Psychology*, pp. 97, 132–133.

147. Reisner, *Problemy sotsial'noi psikhologii*, p. 17.

148. Val'gard, *O psikhologii polovoi zhizni*, pp. 17–18.

149. N. Semashko, "O biologicheskom podkhode k postanovke polovogo vospitaniia," *Zvezda*, no. 5 (1924), 150–151.

150. L. Vygotskii, "Soznanie kak problema psikhologii povedeniia," in *Psikhologiia i marksizm*, p. 175.

151. Reisner, *Problemy sotsial'noi psikhologii*, pp. 30–32. See also his important disccussion in "Uslovnaia simvolika kak sotsial'nyi razdrazhitel'," *Vestnik sotsialisticheskoi akademii*, no. 9 (1924).

152. A. Luriia, "Vnimanie," in *BSE*, 30: 737–739.

153. A. Zalkind, "Tseleustremlennost'," *Krasnaia nov'*, no. 6 (1927), 170–171.

154. A. Ukhtomskii, "Dominanta kak rabochii printsyp nervnykh tsentrov," *Russkii fiziologicheskii zhurnal*, no. 6 (1923); L. Vygotskii, "Problema dominantnykh reaktsii," in *Problemy sovremennoi psikhologii* (Leningrad: Gos. izd, 1926).

155. A. Ukhtomskii, "Dominanta," in *BSE*, 23: 140. On the debt to Avenarius see idem, *Izbrannye psikhologicheskie issledovaniia* (Moscow, 1956), p. 9.

156. Zalkind, "Tseleustremlennost'," pp. 178–179; Gredeskul understood the Revolution as "reconditioning," that is, modification of the stock of conditioned reflexes in the proletariat; "Uslovnye refleksy i revoliutsiia," pp. 163–164. How such reconditioning could be induced was shown in L. Vygotskii, *Pedagogicheskaia psikhologiia* (Moscow, 1926).

157. Zalkind, "Tseleustremlennost'," pp. 179–185.

158. Kashkadamov, "Gigiena umstvennogo truda," p. 141.

159. V. Vagner, *Biopsikhologiia i smezhnye nauki* (Petrograd, 1923), p. 45.

160. G. Iakubovskii, "Psichologicheskii neorealizm Sergeia Malashkina," *Zvezda*, no. 1 (1927), 153.

161. M. Basov, "Volia," in *BSE*, 13: 106–108, 110.

162. Semashko, "O biologicheskom," p. 153. See also idem, "Polovoe vospitanie i zdorov'e," *Komsomol'skaia pravda*, August 15, 1925.

163. Gradovskii, "Polovoi vopros," p. 286.

164. M. Postnikov, "Polovoi vopros v srede sovremennoi uchashcheisia molodezhi," *Omskii rabfakovets*, no. 2 (1928), 50–51, 62.

165. Gradovskii, "Polovoi vopros," p. 286.

166. Lass, *Sovremennoe studenchestvo*, p. 53.

167. Gordon, *Gigiena umstvennogo truda*, pp. 54–58.

168. N. Antonova, ed., *Neizvestnyi Bogdanov: Stat'i, doklady, pis'ma i vospominaniia, 1901–1928*, vol. 1 (Moscow: Its—"AIRO XX," 1995), p. 23.

169. Lepeshinskii, "V vol'no-diskussionnom klube," pp. 113–129.

170. *Smena*, July 14, 1926.

171. Gel'man, *Polovaia zhizn' sovremennoi molodezhi*, p. 127.

172. M. Reisner, "Sotsial'naia organizatsiia lichnosti," *Krasnaia nov'*, no. 3 (1927), 149, 140–141. Through their call for the enhancement of consciousness and personality, Marxist psychologists returned to the project of their prerevolutionary counterparts, that is, to curb "spontaneity" and master the "elemental forces of rebellion." Compare L. Engelstein, *The Keys to Happiness: Sex and the Search for Modernity in Fin-de-Siècle Russia* (Ithaca: Cornell University Press, 1992), p. 255.

173. K. Kornilov, *Sovremennaia psikhologiia i Marksizm* (Leningrad, 1925).

174. Reisner, "Sotsial'naia," p. 141.

175. A. Ukhtomskii, *Izbrannye trudy* (Leningrad, 1978), p. 76.

176. A. Vladimirskii, "Lichnots' v obshchei tsepi iavlenii," *Put' prosveshcheniia*, no. 4 (1922), 48–51.

177. Ibid., pp. 41, 54.

178. A. Makarov, "Vospitanie voli i sotsialisticheskaia shkola," *Put' prosveshchenia*, no. 6 (1922), 66.

179. Semashko, "O biologicheskom," pp. 151–152.

180. The result of this critique was not the complete demise of reflexology but a number of methodological revisions. See V. Protopopov, *Vvedenie v izuchenie refleksologii* (Kharkov, 1924); idem, *Psikhologiia, refleksologiia, uchenie o povedenii* (Kharkov, 1929); *Refleksologiia ili psikhologiia* (Leningrad, 1929); *Refleksologiia i smezhnyie napravleniia* (Leningrad, 1930); A. Shirman, "O predmete i metode refleksologii kak nauki o sootnositel'nosti deiatel'nosti," in *Voprosy izucheniia i vospitaniia lichnosti*, ed. V. Osipov, no. 1–2 (Moscow: Gosmedizdat, 1930); M. Mogendovich, "Problema refleksa v psikhologii," *Sovetskaia psikhonevrologiia*, no. 4–5 (1933).

181. S. Sem'kovskyi, "Refleksolohiia, psikholohiia i dialektychnyi materiializm," *Student revoliutsii*, no. 6 (1927), 73. For a heated discussion of these issues see Iu. Frankfurt, "G. V. Plekhanov o psikhofizicheskoi probleme," *Pod znamenem marksizma*, no. 4–5 (1926); G. Astaf'ev, "Otnoshenie myshleniia i bytiia s tochki zreniia dialekticheskogo materializma," *Studencheskii zhurnal*, no. 2 (1927).

182. Sem'kovskyi, "Refleksolohiia, psikholohiia i dialektychnyi materiializm," p. 74. For a critique of reductionism and the reintroduction of "consciousness" as an independent factor in determining behavior see Vygotskii, "Soznanie kak problema psikhologii povedeniia," p. 177; R. Cheranovskii, "Refleksologiia i psikhologiia," *Pod znamenem marksizma*, no. 9–10 (1928); Struminskii, "Marksizm v sovremennoi psikhologii," *Pod znamenem marksizma*, no. 4–5 (1926).

183. N. Kazanskii, "Kollektivisticheskoe tuskneet, kogda raspukhaet liubov," *Krasnyi student*, no. 4–5 (1924), 42.

184. G. Bergman, "Za zdorovuiu zhizn'," in *Komsomol'skii byt*, p. 254; Liadov, *Voprosy byta*, p. 34.

185. L. Faingol'd, *Onanizm: Ego prichiny, posledstviia, i mery bor'by s nim* (Krasnodar, 1927), p. 25; P. Fridlender, *Polovoi vopros, gosudarstvo i kul'tura* (n.p., 1920), p. 17.

186. S. Nikulin, "Onanizm, ego prichiny i bor'ba s nim," in Kalmanson, *Polovoi vopros*, p. 166.

187. K. Geiger, *The Family in Soviet Russia* (Cambridge, Mass.: Harvard University Press, 1968), p. 63.

188. Liadov, *Voprosy byta*, pp. 35–37.

189. Lass, *Sovremennoe studenchestvo*, p. 198. One student at Leningrad State Uni-

versity stated that "love is something I do not recognize. Sexual sensations to me are everyting that matters"; TsGIA IPD, fl. 984, op. 1, d. 244, l. 21.

190. Gel'man, *Polovaia zhizn' sovremennoi molodezhi*, p. 75.

191. Sigal, *Polovoi vopros*, p. 56.

192. Postnikov, "Polovoi vopros v srede," p. 53.

193. One sexologist defined love as a "conditional reflex to an object which produces pleasure"; Val'gard, *O psikhologii polovoi zhizni*, pp. 67–69.

194. A. Lents, "Ob osnovakh fiziologicheskoi teorii chelovecheskogo povedeniia," *Priroda*, no. 6–7 (1922), 16–17.

195. N. Velt', "Otkrytoe pis'mo tovarishchu Smidovich," in *Komsomol'skii byt*, p. 181.

196. Kuz'min, "O 'molodoi starosti,'" p. 206.

197. Zalkind, *Polovoi vopros*, p. 53.

198. Gel'man, *Polovaia zhizn' sovremennoi molodezhi*, p. 75. Gel'man could not tell whether love in the future would be monogamous or polygamous. "We have to admit," he noted, however, "that monogamy is more adequate to the interests of race and society"; p. 130.

199. Ibid., pp. 65, 79–80, 129.

200. In the early 1920s, eugenics was an integral part of the curriculum. Bushmakin, the rector of the Irkutsk State University, for example, contended that the "nation that is the first to use the findings of eugenics will become the strongest"; *Trudy Pervogo Sibirskogo kraevogo nauchno-issledovatel'skogo s"ezda*, vol. 5 (Novosibirsk, 1928), p. 57. On "race improvement" see "Uluchshenie chelovecheskoi porody," *Biulleten' literatury i zhizni*, no. 2 (1924), 85–88; N. Volotskoi, "Spornye voprosy evgeniki," *Vestnik kommunisticheskoi akademii*, no. 20 (1927).

201. Zalkind, *Polovoi vopros*, p. 56; E. Preobrazhenskii, *O morale i klassovykh normakh* (Moscow, 1923), pp. 3–5; L. Vasetskii, *K zdorovomu polovomu bytu* (Moscow, 1926), pp. 21–22.

202. Zalkind, *Polovoi vopros*, pp. 39, 45–46, 56. See Vasilevskii's review of Zalkind in *Krasnaia molodezh'*, no. 1 (1925).

203. Zalkind, *Polovoi vopros*, pp. 40, 56; idem, "Tseleustremlennost'," p. 189; G. Batkis, "Polovoe vospitanie i prosveshchenie v usloviiakh sovetskogo stroiia," in *Osnovy obshchestvennoi venerologii*, ed. L. Bliashko (Moscow, 1926), p. 188.

204. R. Roman, "Novyi byt," *Komsomol'skii byt*, pp. 316–317.

205. Vasetskii, *K zdorovomu polovomu bytu*, pp. 25–26.

206. A. Deborin, "Freidizm i sotsiologiia," *Voinstvuiushchii materialist*, no. 4 (1925), p. 17.

207. Zalkind, *Polovoi vopros*, p. 14.

208. Ibid., p. 54.

209. A. Zalkind, "Freidizm," *Krasnaia nov'*, no. 4 (1924), 171.

210. A. Zalkind, *Zhizn' organisma i vnushenie* (Moscow, 1927), pp. 58–59.

211. Merel'zon, *Gigiena nervno-bol'nogo*, p. 8.

212. Kliachkin, "Polovaia anketa sredi Omskogo studenchestva," p. 128.

213. Gel'man, *Polovaia zhizn' sovremennoi molodezhi*, pp. 60–61.

214. N. Belov, *Lichnost' i vneshnost'* (Petrograd, ca. 1922), pp. 2–4, 10.

215. Maslov, *Uchenie o konstitutsiiakh* (Leningrad, 1925), p. 15; Lifshits, *Uchenie o konstitutsiiakh cheloveka* (Kharkov, 1924), p. 18.

216. E. Krechmer (Kretschmer), *Stroenie tela i kharakter* (Moscow, 1924), p. 118; A. Lazurskii, *Klassifikatsiia lichnostei*, 3d ed. (Leningrad, 1924); Petrova, *Psikhologicheskaia klassifikatsiia lichnostei* (Moscow, 1927); V. Vagner, *Psikhologicheskie tipy i kollektivnaia psikhologiia: Po dannym biologicheskikh nauk* (Leningrad, 1929).

217. Belov, *Lichnost' i vneshnost'*, pp. 26–28.

218. Kenneth M. Pinnow, "Making Suicide Soviet: Medicine, Moral Statistics, and the Politics of Social Science in Bolshevik Russia, 1920–1930" (Ph.D. diss., Columbia University, 1998); M. Miller and Y. Miller, "Suicide and Suicidology in the Soviet Union," *Suicide and Life-Threatening Behavior* 18 (1987), 442–447.

219. George M. Beard, "Neurasthenia or Nervous Exhaustion," *Boston Medical and Surgical Journal* 3 (1869), 217–221.

220. L. Merel'zon, *Nevrasteniia: Ee istochniki, preduprezhdenie i lechenie* (Krasnodar, 1927), pp. 8–10; A. Kholetskii, *Polovaia zhizn' i nevrasteniia* (Krasnodar, 1927), pp. 3–5.

221. R. Nye, *Crime, Madness, and Politics: The Medical Concept of National Decline* (Princeton: Princeton Univeristy Press, 1984), pp. 148–149.

222. Merel'zon, *Nevrasteniia*, pp. 14, 23–24.

223. The fundamental text on the question of heredity was Iu. Filipchenko, *Nasledstvennost'* (Moscow, 1917). On the preoccupation with heredity in the 1920s see M. Zavadovskii, "Darvinizm, Lamarkizm i problema nasledovaniia priobretennykh priznakov," *Pod znamenem marksizma*, no. 10–11 (1925); V. Slepkov, "Nasledstvennost' i otbor u cheloveka: Po povodu teoreticheskikh predposylok evgeniki," ibid. For an attempt to synthesize Darwin's theory of hereditary features with Marx's theory of features that are socially acquired see G. Gurev, *Darvinizm i marksizm* (Moscow, 1925); M. Ravich-Cherkasskii, *Darvinizm, Marksizm: Sbornik statei* (Kiev: Gos. izd. Ukrainy, 1925).

224. Lass, *Sovremennoe studenchestvo*, p. 45.

225. Faingol'd, *Onanizm*, p. 9.

226. Vasetskii, *K zdorovomu polovomu bytu*, p. 22; Postnikov, "Polovoi vopros v srede," p. 49. See also G. Sorokin, "Polovoe vospitanie detei v plane marksistkoi pedagogiki," in *Polovoi vopros v shkole i zhizni*, ed. I. S. Smirnov

(Moscow, 1925); A. Nevskii, *Razvitie rastushchego organizma i ego osobennosti*, (Moscow, 1927).

227. Lass, *Sovremennoe studenchestvo*, pp. 90–91.

228. Gushchin, *Rezul'taty*, p. 45.

229. Sigal, *Polovoi vopros*, p. 25.

230. Platovskii, *Polovaia zhizn' sovremennogo studenchestva*, p. 18.

231. Lass, *Sovremennoe studenchestvo*, pp. 110, 81–83.

232. P. Bakaleinikov, *Polovoe znanie* (Leningrad, 1927), p. 6.

233. L. Iakobson, "Onanizm s sovremennoi tochki zreniia i mery bor'by s nim," *Pedagogicheskaia mysl'*, no. 9–12 (1921), 29–30; I. Galant, "Masturbatsiia i avtokastratsiia v kartine shizofrenicheski-paranoidnogo zabolevaniia: K psikhologii paranoidnoi formy dementia praecox," *Zhurnal nevropatologii i psikhiatrii* 3 (1928), 307–315.

234. Merel'zon, *Nevrasteniia*, p. 18.

235. Faingol'd, *Onanizm*, pp. 18–19.

236. Merel'zon, *Nevrasteniia*, pp. 18–19.

237. Faingol'd, *Polovoe bessilie*, p. 14. For a similar argument see S. Nikulin, "Onanizm, ego prichiny i bor'ba s nim," in Kalmanson, *Polovoi vopros*, p. 171; Kholetskii, *Polovaia zhizn' i nevrasteniia*, p. 11.

238. Faingol'd, *Onanizm*, p. 16; idem, *Polovoe bessilie*, p. 25.

239. Grosser, "Onanizm," *Student revoliutsii*, no. 4 (1927), 35. The distinction between "outside sexual excitation" and "autoeroticizm" is elaborated in Val'gard, *O psikhologii polovoi zhizni*, pp. 24–26.

240. Gel'man, *Polovaia zhizn' sovremennoi molodezhi*, p. 39.

241. Ibid.

242. Kliachkin, "Polovaia anketa sredi Omskogo studenchestva," p. 127; Sigal, *Polovoi vopros*, pp. 36–37; Grosser, "Onanizm," p. 38; Lass, *Sovremennoe studenchestvo*, pp. 177–182; Vasetskii, *K zdorovomu polovomu bytu*, pp. 26–30; G. Sorokhtin, "Polovoe vospitanie detei v plane marksistkoi pedagogii," in *Polovoi vopros v shkole i zhizni*, ed. I. Simonov (Leningrad, 1925), p. 81. On the waste of physical and nervous energy due to masturbation see also M. Mikhailov, *Bor'ba s onanizmom v sem'e i shkole*, 2d ed. (Leningrad, 1925), pp. 7–10, 18–20; Ia. Golomb, *Polovaia zhizn'. Normal'naia i nenormal'naia* (Odessa: Chernomorskii meditsinsko-sanitarnyi otdel, 1926), pp. 19–20. For the medical conceptualization of the link between masturbation and degeneration see E. Hare, "Masturbatory Insanity: The History of an Idea," *Journal of Mental Science*, no. 108 (1962). For the Soviet expert discussion see L. Iakobson, *Onanizm u mushchin i zhenshchin* (n.p., 1923), p. 158; M. Mikhailov, *Bor'ba s onanizmom v sem'e i v shkole* (Leningrad, 1925), pp. 17–27; V. Bekhterev, "Ob izvrashchenii i uklonenii polovogo vlecheniia s refleksologicheskoi tochki zreniia," in *Polovoi vopros v svete nauchnogo znaniia*.

243. Gel'man, *Polovaia zhizn' sovremennoi molodezhi*, p. 30; Lass, *Sovremennoe studenchestvo*, p. 183.
244. M. Volotskii, "O polovoi sterilizatsii nasledstvenno defektivnykh," *Russkii evgenicheskii zhurnal*, 1923, 203–204.
245. Kliachkin, "Polovaia anketa sredi Omskogo studenchestva," p. 127.
246. Stratonitskii, *Voprosy byta v komsomole*, p. 32.
247. "Polovaia zhizn' studenchestva," *Student-proletarii*, no. 6–7 (1924), 67; PANO, f. 288, op. 1, d. 394, l. 14.
248. A. Platovskii, *Polovaia zhizn' sovremennogo studenchestva*, pp. 8, 14–15; Gel'man, *Polovaia zhizn' sovremennoi molodezhi*, p. 10.
249. R. Feuleop-Miller, *The Mind and Face of Bolshevism*, trans. F. Flint and D. Fait (London, 1929), p. 214.

5. Looking into the Oppositionist Soul

1. In terms of Bolshevik political theory, a "discussion" was a period preceding a Party congress when the Central Committee majority and the Opposition advanced their policy suggestions and the rank and file deliberated their pros and cons.
2. *KPSS: Spravochnik* (Moscow, 1963), p. 193; V. Mezenov, "Bor'ba kommunisticheskoi partii protiv Trotskizma na zavershaiushchem etape vosstanovitel'nogo perioda (Osen' 1923-Ianvar' 1925gg.)," in *Istoricheskii opyt bor'by KPSS protiv Trotskizma* (Moscow: Mysl', 1975), p. 376; V. Ivanov, *Iz istorii bor'by partii protiv levogo opportunizma* (Leningrad: Lenizdat, 1965), p. 55.
3. A. Leikin, "Iz istorii bor'by za preodalenie vliianiia melkoburzhuaznykh partii na studenchestvo, 1921–1925," in *Intelligentsiia i sotsialisticheskaia kul'turnaia revoliutsiia* (Leningrad, 1975), p. 50.
4. L. Trotsky, *K istorii Russkoi revoliutsii* (Moscow, 1990), p. 176.
5. I. Stalin, "O partstroitel'stve," *Pod znamemen kommunizma*, no. 1 (1924), 103; N. Akimov, "Oppozitsiia v vuzakh," *Krasnoe studenchestvo*, no. 6 (1927–28), 47.
6. *Pravda*, December 11, 1923; M. Shvedov, "Bor'ba moskovskoi partiinoi organizatsii protiv trotskizma v 1923–1924 gg.," in *Iz istorii bor'by KPSS za pobedu sotsializma i kommunizma* (Moscow, 1972), pp. 202–205.
7. *Pravda*, February 5, 1924; *Moskovskie bol'sheviki v bor'be s pravym i levym opportunizmom, 1921–29* (Moscow: Moskovskii rabochii, 1969), p. 83.
8. *Biulleten' XIX konferentsii petrogradskoi gubernskoi organizatsii RKP(b)*, no. 1 (Petrograd, 1923), 92–94; *Sbornik materialov Leningradskogo komiteta RKP*, vyp.7 (Leningrad, 1924), p. 121; *Pod znamenem kommunizma*, no. 1 (1924), 175.

9. *Petrogradskaia pravda*, December 28, 1923; TsGA IPD, f. 984, op. 1, d. 36, ll. 51–51; f. 16, op. 9, d. 9402, ll. 1–3.

10. *Sbornik materialov Leningradskogo komiteta RKP(b)*, vyp. 7 (Leningrad, 1924), p. 228; TsGA IPD, f. 16, op. 9, d. 9274, ll. 11, 35.

11. *Na piatom godu: Rabfak Leningradskogo gosudarstvennogo universiteta* (Leningrad, 1924), p. 55.

12. V. Ivanov, *Missia ordena: Mekhanizm massovykh repressii v sovetskoi Rossii v kontse 20kh—40kh gg. (na materialakh Severo-Zapada RSFSR)* (St. Petersburg: Liss, 1997), p. 54.

13. *Petrogradskaia pravda*, January 10, 1924.

14. TsGA IPD, f. 1085, op. 1, d. 27, l. 25; *Itogi proverki chlenov i kandidatov RKP(b) neproizvodstvennykh iacheek* (Moscow: Krasnyi Pechatnik, 1925), p. 87.

15. TsGA IPD, f. 138, op. 1, d. 38, ll. 1–2.

16. *Sbornik materialov Leningradskogo komiteta RKP(b)*, vyp. 7 (Leningrad, 1924), pp. 86–87.

17. *Izvestiia TsK RKP(b)*, no. 10 (1925), 5.

18. G. Zinov'ev, "O vuzovtsakh," *Iunyi kommunist*, no. 3 (1924).

19. I. Stalin, *Sochineniia*, 13 vols. (Moscow, 1946–1957), 6 : 45.

20. "Sovremennye zadachi propagandy Leninizma," *Pod znamemen kommunizma*, no. 2 (1924), 117–118; Stalin, "O partstroitel'stve," pp. 104–105.

21. *O rabote iacheek RKP(b) vysshikh uchebnykh zavedenii* (Moscow, 1925), pp. 6–7.

22. *Pravda*, March 27, 1924; *Sotsialisticheskii vestnik*, no. 11 (1924), 8–14; V. Feigin, "Vyvody iz opyta proverki vuzovskikh iacheek," *Student-proletarii*, no. 3 (1924), 14–15.

23. *Itogi proverki chlenov i kandidatov*, p. 39; A. Trebelev, "Likvidatsiia likvidatorstva?" *Krasnaia molodezh'*, no. 4 (1924), 83–84.

24. *Na piatom godu*, p. 56.

25. *Sbornik materialov Leningradskogo komiteta RKP*, vyp. 8 (Leningrad, 1925), p. 74; *Itogi proverki chlenov i kandidatov*, pp. 3–25; TsGA IPD, f. 6, op. 1, d. 224, l. 173; Gosudarstvennyi arkhiv Novosibirskoi oblasti, f. 288, op. 1, d. 104, l. 100.

26. A. Kurepin, "Iz istorii bor'by partii protiv vliianiia Trotskizma na kommunisticheskoe studenchestvo, 1923–24 gg," in *Istoricheskii opyt bor'by KPSS protiv burzhuaznoi ideologii, opportunizma i sovremennost'* (Leningrad, 1979), p. 43; V. Fortunatov, "Sistema partiinogo rukovodstva vuzami v Petrograde-Leningrade v vosstanovitel'nyi period (1921–25)," in *Voprosy razvitiia sotsialisticheskoi kul'tury* (Leningrad, 1977), pp. 102–103; TsGA IPD, f. 6, op. 1., d. 224, l. 22.

27. TsGA IPD, f. 984, op. 1, d. 55, l. 16.

28. TsGA IPD, f. 138, op. 1, d. 2, ll. 2, 6, 9.

29. TsGA IPD, f. 984, op. 1, d. 55, l. 17.
30. V. Mavrodin and V. Okun', eds., *Istoriia Leningradskogo universiteta, 1819–1969* (Leningrad: Izd. Leningradskogo univ., 1969), p. 255; V. Mavrodin, ed., *Na shturm nauki: Vospominaniia byvshikh studentov fak. obshchestvennykh nauk Leningradskogo universiteta* (Leningrad: Izd. Leninigradskogo univ., 1971), pp. 38–39; *Na piatom godu,* p. 56; *Sbornik materialov Leningradskogo komiteta RKP,* vyp. 8 (Leningrad, 1925), pp. 78–79; TsGA IPD, f. 984, op. 1, d. 176, l. 44; f. 6, op. 1, d. 99, ll. 227–230.
31. TsGA IPD, f. 16, op. 1, d. 176, l. 2.
32. TsGA IPD, f. 984, op. 1, d. 55, l. 26.
33. Ibid., d. 12, l. 31. Moscow authorities stressed that in the Institute of Red Professors 45 percent of the Oppositionists were former members of petit-bourgeois parties, whereas among the loyalists there were only 20 percent; *Izvestiia TsK RKP(b),* no. 2 (1924), 32.
34. *Trinadtsataia konferentsiia Rossiiskoi kommunisticheskoi partii (bol'shevikov). Biulleten'* (Moscow: Kransnaia nov', 1924), p. 147.
35. *Pravda,* April 30, 1924.
36. N. Babenkova, "Ukreplenie partiacheek vuzov v pervyi period nepa," in *Studenchestvo v obshchestvenno-politicheskoi zhizni* (Moscow, 1979), p. 64; Shvedov, "Bor'ba Moskovskoi partiinoi organizatsii," pp. 217–218.
37. TsaGA IPD, f. 138, op. 1, d. 2, l. 9.
38. R. Daniels, *The Conscience of the Revolution: Communist Opposition in Soviet Russia* (Cambridge, Mass.: Harvard University Press, 1960), p. 309.
39. *Izvestiia TsK VKP(b),* no. 42–43 (1927), 1–2; *Pravda,* November 15, 1927; Iu. Fel'shtinskii, ed., *Arkhiv Trotskogo,* vol. 4 (Moscow, 1990), pp. 225–231.
40. *Piat'nadtsatyi s''ezd VKP(b). Stenograficheskii otchet* (Moscow, 1928), pp. 68–82.
41. *Biulleten' TsK VKP(b)—NK RKI SSSR i RSFSR,* no. 6 (1928), 31; *Bol'shevik,* no. 4 (1929), 28; *Shesnadtsatyi s''ezd VKP(b)* (Moscow, 1930), p. 323.
42. PATO, f. 17, op. 1, d. 1065, l. 26ob.
43. TsGA IPD, f. 197, op. 1., d. 723, ll. 93ob.–94, 108.
44. TsGA IPD, f. 408, op. 1, d. 1175, ll. 51–60.
45. TsGA IPD, f. 197, op. 1., d. 723, ll. 97–98.
46. PATO, f. 17, op. 1, d. 1065, l. 4; TsGA IPD, f. 408, op. 1, d. 1175, l. 59.
47. *Krasnoe znamia,* January 17, 1928; PATO, f. 320, op. 1, d. 20, ll. 33–37; d. 883, ll. 10ob.–11; f. 76, op. 1, d. 512, ll. 115–129; d. 749, 1. 152ob; f. 17, op. 1, d. 749, ll. 151–151ob., 159.
48. PATO, f. 17, op. 1, d. 1076, l. 25.
49. Ibid., ll. 68–70.
50. Ibid., d. 1065, ll. 33–37.
51. Ibid., l. 9.

52. Ibid., ll. 8–13, 60–62.

53. Ibid., ll. 33–37.

54. Ibid., ll. 4, 33–37.

55. Ibid., ll. 8–13.

56. Ibid., ll. 26–29, 60–62.

57. G. Bykov, "Piatnadtstat' let kuznitse bol'shevitskikh kadrov," in *XV let Vsesoiuznogo Kommunisticheskogo sel'sko-khoziaistvennogo universiteta imeni I. V. Stalina* (Leningrad, 1933), pp. 47–48.

58. TsGA IPD, f. 197, op. 1, d. 732, ll. 7, 18.

59. Ibid., l. 11.

60. Ibid., ll. 20, 22.

61. TsGA IPD, f. 566, op. 1, d. 271, l. 99.

62. Ibid., d. 267, ll. 15–16.

63. Ibid., d. 271, ll. 97–98.

64. A. Zalkind, "Psikhonevrologicheskie nauki i sotsialisticheskoe stroitel'stvo," *Pedologiia,* no. 9 (1930), 308–324; "Itogi diskussii po reaktologicheskoi psikhologii," *Psikhologiia,* no. 4 (1931), 1–2; T. Kogan, "Na povorote," ibid., pp. 15, 22; V. Kolbanovskii, "Pshikhologiiu—na sluzhbu promyshlennosti," *Psikhologiia,* no. 3 (1932), 3.

65. Kolbanovskii, "Pshikhologiiu," pp. 5–6; "Marksizm i psikhologiia," *Psikhologiia,* no. 5 (1931), 182; "Itogi diskussii po reaktologicheskoi psikhologii," *Psikhologiia,* no. 4 (1931), 8. On the usefulness of "psychohygiene" to socialist construction see L. Rozenshtein, "Sotsial'no-profilakticheskoe napravlenie v psikhiatrii," *Zhurnal nevropatologii i psikhiatrii,* no. 4 (1930); S. Subbotnik, "Za bol'shevitskoe nastuplenie na teoreticheskom fronte psikhonevrologii," ibid., no. 2 (1931).

66. A. Verenov, "Psikhologiia i politprosvetrabota," *Psikhologiia,* no. 5 (1931), 188.

67. M. Gel'mont, "Pedologo-pedagogicheskoe izuchenie kollektivizirovannogo truda i byta," *Pedologiia,* no. 13 (1931), 17.

68. M. Feofanov, "Pedologiia i problemy stroitel'stva," *Pedologiia,* no. 13 (1931), 13–14.

69. "Itogi diskussii po reaktologicheskoi psikhologii," 7.

70. P. Rudnik, "K voprosu o burzhuaznykh vliianiiakh v izmerenii intellekta," *Psikhologiia,* no. 3 (1932), 24.

71. "Itogi diskussii po reaktologicheskoi psikhologii," pp. 1–2, 5. The theory of reflexes in the early 1930s was accused of upholding "a reactionary view of balance between the organism and the environment, thus pulling the carpet under any hopes to build socialist society"; N. Deborin, "O refleksologii," *Psikhologiia,* no. 4 (1931), 109; F. Shemiakin and P. Gershonovich, "Kak Trotskii i Kautskii revizuiut marksizm v voprosakh psikhologii," ibid., pp. 5–9; A. Zalkind, "'O polovom vospitanii,'" *Pedologiia,* no. 1–2 (1932), 14; K.

Kornilov, "Vozzreniia sovremennykh mekhanistov na zakon sokhraneniia energii i psikhiku," *Psikhologiia,* no. 2 (1929), 21.

72. A. Zalkind, "Diferentsirovka na pedologicheskom fronte," *Pedologiia,* no. 2 (1931), 8.

73. M. Turbina, "K voprosu o razvitii pedologii," *Pedologiia,* no. 4 (1932), 8–10.

74. A. Zalkind, "O metodologii tselostnogo izucheniia v pedologii," *Pedologiia,* no. 2 (1931), 4.

75. *Sovetskaia nevropatologiia, psikhiatriia i psikhogigiena,* no. 2 (1935), 168.

76. Turbina, "K voprosu o razvitii pedologii," pp. 8–9.

77. Rudnik, "K voprosu," p. 24.

78. Zalkind, "O metodologii," p. 3.

79. Rudnik, "K voprosu," p. 15.

80. Quoted in A. Zaluzhnyi, *Lzhenauka pedologiia v "trudakh" Zalkinda* (Moscow, 1937), pp. 27–28.

81. Zalkind, "O metodologii," pp. 1–2.

82. V. Kolbanovskii, "O znachenii i zadachakh sravnitel'noi psikhologii," in *Refleksy, instinkty i navyki* (Moscow: Gos. sotsial'no-ekonomicheskoe izd. 1935), p. 9.

83. N. Rybnikov, *Iunoshestvovedenie v plane pedologicheskoi piatiletki* (Moscow, 1929); A. Etkind, "L'Essor et l'echec du mouvement 'paidologue,'" *Cahiers du monde russe et sovietique* 33 (1992), 387–418. For a short history of pedology in the Soviet Union see E. Etkind, *Eros nevozmozhnogo: Istoriia psikhoanaliza v Rossii* (St. Petersburg, 1993), pp. 321–341.

84. A. Zalkind, *Osnovnye voprosy pedologi* (Moscow, 1930), p. 158; Zaluzhnyi, *Lzhenauka pedologiia v "trudakh" Zalkinda,* p. 13.

85. S. Molozhavyi, "Voprosy dialektiki i pedologii," in *Otchet 1go vsesoiuznogo s"ezda po izucheniiu povedeniia cheloveka,* ed. A. Zalkind (Moscow, 1931), p. 291.

86. M. Levina and D. El'konin, "V bor'be za marksistko-leninskuiu pedologiiu," *Pedologiia,* no. 5–6 (1931), 30–32.

87. *Pedologiia,* no. 2 (1928), 4–5.

88. "Za marksistsko-leniniskuiu pedologiiu," *Pedologiia,* no. 5–6 (1931), 4.

89. A. Zalkind, ed., *Pedologiia i vospitanie* (Moscow, 1928), p. 137.

90. A. Zalkind, *Pedologiia v SSSR* (Moscow, 1929), p. 41; *V bor'be za marksistko-leninskuiu pedologiiu* (Moscow, 1932), p. 109.

91. P. Blonskii, *Pedologiia v massovoi shkole pervoi stupeni* (Moscow: Rabotnik prosveshcheniia, 1930) and *Pedologiia: Uchebnik dlia vysshikh pedagogicheskikh uchebnykh zavedenii* (Moscow: Uchebno-pedagogicheskoe izdatel'stvo, 1934).

92. *Pedologiia,* no. 1 (1929), 5.

93. Zalkind, *Osnovnye voprosy pedologii,* p. 161.

94. F. Bekhler, *Matematika v detskom sadu i nulevoi gruppe* (Moscow, 1934), pp. 45–46.

95. See, for example, V. Smirnov, *Psikhologiia iunosheskogo vozrasta* (Moscow-Leningrad, 1929); P. Zagorskii, *Vtoroe shkol'noe detstvo i osobennosti ego sotsial'nogo povedeniia* (Voronezh, 1929); I. Arianov, *Osobennosti myshleniia sovetskogo podrostka i iunoshi* (Moscow, 1931).

96. A. Zalkind, "Eshche o zadachakh pedologii," *Pedologiia*, no. 2 (1931), 14; M. Bernshtein, *Pedologiia—nauka o detiakh* (Moscow, 1928), pp. 20, 32.

97. *Psikhologiia*, no. 2 (1931), 203–204.

98. *Krasnaia niva*, no. 7 (1935), 215; as well as V. Kolbanovskii, "O razvitii kombinatornykh sposobnostei u doshkol'nikov," *Trudy mediko-biologicheskogo instituta* 3 (1934).

99. For the Soviet concept of human development, see K. Koffka, *Osnovy psikhicheskogo razvitiia* (Moscow, 1934); K. Megrelidze, "Ot zhivotnogo soznaniia k chelovecheskomu," *Iazyk i myshlenie*, no. 5 (1935).

100. Y. Slezkine, "The Fall of Soviet Ethnography, 1928–1938," *Current Antropology* 32 (1991).

101. Rudnik, "K voprosu," p. 17.

102. V. Vnukov, "Psikhiatriia v sisteme sovremennoi meditsiny," *Sovetskaia nevropatologiia, psikhiatriia i psikhogigiena*, no. 1 (1935), 6.

103. On early attempts to treat youth as a specific category and to develop a "child psychology" and a "child anthropology" in the Soviet Union, see Iu. Portogalov, *Detskaia psikhologiia i antropologiia* (Samara, 1925); N. Rybnikov, *Iazyk rebenka* (Moscow, 1926); L. Vygotskii, *Voobrazhenie i tvorchestvo v detskom vozraste* (Moscow, 1930); R. Vilenkina, "K kharakteristike nastroeniia rabochego podrostka," *Pedologiia*, no. 1 (1930). For developmental psychologists discussing the problem of "backward children" in the 1920s, see L. Sakharov, "Obrazovanie poniatii u umstvenno otstalykh detei," *Voprosy defektologii*, no. 2 (1928). Soviet psychoanalysts worked in the same direction. A. Griboedov, a professor at the State Medical Institute in Leningrad argued that crime-prone children suffered from unsuccessful resolution of the Oedipal complex and failed sublimation. Freudism, he argued, was a necessary guide to the understanding of juvenile delinquency. Such views were, of course, anathema to the Soviet psychology of the mid-1930s. A. Griboedov, "Trudnovospituemye deti i psikhoanaliz," *Voprosy izucheniia i vospitaniia lichnosti*, no. 1–2 (1926), 60–62.

104. *Psikhologiia*, no. 2 (1931), 182.

105. "Osnovy patogeneza obshchei patomorfologii i opyt klassifikatsii nevroinfektsii," *Sovetskaia nevropatologiia, psikhiatriia i psikhogigiena*, no. 2 (1935), 1; A. Zalkind, *Voprosy sovetskoi pedagogiki* (Moscow, 1930), p. 18.

106. A. Zalkind, *Zhizn' cheloveka i vnushenie* (Moscow, 1929), p. 130.

107. *Sovetskaia nevropatologiia, psikhiatriia i psikhogigiena,* no. 9–10 (1935), 167.

108. See, for example, V. Giliarovskii, "Urbanizatsiia i zabolevaniia nervno-psikhicheskoi sredy," in *Psikhonevrologicheskie nauki v SSSR,* ed. Aron Zalkind (Moscow: Gos. Izd., 1930); L. Prozorov, "Obzor polozheniia dela psikhiatricheskoi pomoshchi v RSFSR," *Zhurnal nevropatologii i psikhiatrii,* no. 3–4 (1930); *Sovremennye problemy shizofrenii* (Moscow, 1933).

109. E. Ruzer, "Rol' eksperemental'no-psikhologicheskogo issledovaniia v psikhologicheskoi rabote v vuzakh," *Sovetskaia nevropatologiia, psikhiatriia i psikhogigiena,* no. 2 (1935), 127–132.

110. V. Bronner, "Zadachi venerologicheskoi organizatsii," *Sovetskii vestnik venerologii i dermotologii,* no. 1 (1935), 1.

111. "O zadachakh vserosiiskogo obshchestva nevropatologov i psikhiatrov," *Sovetskaia nevropatologiia, psikhiatriia i psikhogigiena,* no. 1 (1935), 187. See also Bronner, "Zadachi venerologicheskoi organizatsii," 1.

112. I. Kolubovskii, "Problema 'povedeniia cheloveka' v svete burzhuaznoi i sovetskoi mysli," *Chelovek i priroda,* no. 4 (1930), 15–20. See also V. Vnukov, "Povedenie cheloveka i ego izuchenie," *Revoliutsiia i kul'tura,* no. 2 (1930).

113. M. Basov, *Obshchie zakony pedologii* (Moscow, 1928), p. 124.

114. S. Molozhavyi, "Printsip tselostnogo izucheniia rebenka," in Zalkind, *Pedologiia i vospitanie,* p. 121; *Pedologiia,* no. 3 (1929), 315, 317.

115. Molozhavyi, "Printsip tselostnogo izucheniia rebenka," p. 121.

116. S. Molozhavyi, "Dialektika v pedologii," *Pod znamenem marksizma,* no. 9–10 (1928), 237.

117. M. Shirvindt, "Psikhoanaliz," *Chelovek i priroda,* no. 4 (1930).

118. E. Kol'man, "Pis'mo tov. Stalina i zadachi fronta estestvoznaniia i meditsiny," *Pod znamenem marksizma,* no. 9–10 (1931), 169; *Psikhologiia,* no. 2 (1931), 227. Perepel dated Freud's demise in the Soviet Union to the early 1930s; E. Perepel, "The Psychoanalytic Movement in the U.S.S.R.," *Psychoanalytic Review* 26 (1939), 299.

119. K. Veidemiuller and A. Shcheglov, "Freidizm," in *BSE,* 59: 188–190. That Freudism was legitimate only as a branch of knowledge studying the ill (neurotics) in the late 1920s and early 1930s is evident from D. Ozeretskovskii, "K kritike psikhoanaliza: O novykh putiakh v lechenii nevrotikov," *Sovremennaia psikhonevrologiia* 8 (1929), 311–319; B. Birman, "Psikhoterapiia, kak sotsio-refleksoterapiia nevropaticheskoi lichnosti," in Zalkind, *Psikhonevrologicheskie nauki v SSSR,* pp. 321–322; and V. Vnukov, "Psikhoanaliz," *Meditsinskaia entsiklopediia* 27 (1933), 733.

120. A. Zalkind, "Psikhonevrologicheskii front i psikhologicheskaia diskussiia," *Pedologiia,* no. 2 (1931), 4–5, 18.

121. Zalkind, "O metodologii," pp. 4–5.

122. Zalkind, "Diferentsirovka na pedologicheskom fronte," pp. 10–11.

123. V. Buzin, "Psikhoanaliz v Soveteskom Soiuze: K istorii razgroma," in *Puti obnovleniia psikhiatrii*, ed. Iu. Savenko (Moscow: Intermechanics, 1991); M. Miller, *Freud and the Bolsheviks: Psychoanalysis in Imperial Russia and the Soviet Union* (New Haven: Yale University Press, 1998), pp. 88–92..

124. *Za kommunisticheskoe prosveshchenie*, July 6, 1936.

125. A. Bubnov, "Vosstanovit' polnost'iu v pravakh pedagogiku i pedagogov," *Pod znamenem marksizma*, no. 10 (1936), 58; *Nachal'naia shkola*, no. 9 (1936), 9–14; *Sredniaia shkola*, no. 8 (1936), 1–8; I. Kogan, ed., *Dobit' do kontsa pedologiiu: Materialy o pedologicheskikh izvrashcheniiakh v sisteme Narkomprosov* (Leningrad, 1936).

126. *Sovetskaia pedagogika*, no. 1 (1937), 11; I. Sh., "Lzhenauka pedologiia i ee 'metodologiia,'" *Pod znamenem marksizma*, no. 10 (1936), 154.

127. B. Anane'v, "O glavnom 'zakone' pedologii," *Sovetskaia pedagogika*, no. 1 (1937), 14, 20. See also M. Malyshev, "Tak nazyvaemaia pedologiia," *Izvestiia*, July 11, 1936; A. Fomichev, "Iskorenit' lzhenauku do kontsa," *Izvestiia*, September 28, 1936.

128. P. Plotnikov, "Do kontsa razoblachit' lzhenauku pedologiiu i ee adeptov," *Sovetskaia pedagogika*, no. 1 (1937), 49.

129. Bubnov, "Vosstanovit' polnost'iu v pravakh pedagogiku i pedagogov," p. 60; Fomichev, "Iskorenit' lzhenauku do kontsa"; E. Rudneva, "K voprosu o pedologicheskikh izvrashcheniiakh v teorii obucheniia," *Pedagogicheskoe obrazovanie*, no. 1 (1937), 66–76; S. Satserdotov, "Potrebovat' uchebniki po psikhologii," *Za kommunisticheskoe prosveshchenie*, June 22, 1936.

130. *Psikhologiia*, no. 1–2 (1931), 171. See also M. Mitin, "Nekotorye itogi i zadachi raboty na filosofskom fronte," *Pod znamenem marksizma*, no. 1 (1936), 43.

131. I. Sh., "Lzhenauka pedologiia i ee 'metodologiia,'" p. 153.

132. A. Fomichev, "Pedologiia," in *BSE*, 44: 512.

133. Kolbanovskii's statement appeared in *Refleksy, instinkty i navyki*, p. 10.

134. I. Sh., "Lzhenauka pedologiia i ee 'metodologiia,'" p. 154.

135. L. Vladimirov, "Chemu uchili pedologi molodykh uchetelei," *V pomoshch' uchiteliu*, no. 3 (1936), 18–20; N. Semashko, "Teoriia i praktika pedologii," *Pravda*, July 11, 1936; V. Giliarovskii, "Ne toropites' s diagnozom," *Izvestiia*, October 2, 1936; Dvorkin, "Kleveta s kafedry pedagogiki," *Za kommunisticheskoe prosveshchenie*, October 24, 1936.

136. Anane'v, "O glavnom 'zakone' pedologii," p. 22.

137. *Sbornik prikazov i rasporiazhenii po Narkomprosu RSFSR* (Moscow: Gos. uchebno-pedagogicheskoe izd-vo, 1936), p. 4.

138. TsGIA IPD, f. 408, op. 1, d. 161, ll. 73–74.

139. *Pravda*, July 5, 1936.

140. *Leningradskaia pravda*, July 10, 1936.

141. Anane'v, "O glavnom 'zakone' pedologii," p. 15.

142. E. Kol'man, "Protiv lzhenauki," *Sovetskaia nauka* 1 (1938), 43.

143. Anane'v, "O glavnom 'zakone' pedologii," pp. 17–18.

144. A. Luria, *The Nature of Human Conflicts* (New York, 1932). Luriia's work from the early 1930s is summarized in *Ob istoricheskom razvitii poznavatel'nykh protsessov: Eksperimental'no-psikhologicheskoe issledovanie* (Moscow, 1974), pp. 112–113. The collaboration between Luriia and Vygotskii is examined in L. Radzikhovskii and D. Khomskaia, "A. R. Luria and L. S. Vygotsky: Early Years of Their Collaboration," *Soviet Review* 23 (1982).

145. Y. Slezkine, *Arctic Mirrors: Russia and the Small Peoples of the North* (Ithaca: Cornell University Press, 1994), pp. 286, 291.

146. Vnukov, "Psikhiatriia v sisteme sovremennoi meditsiny," p. 6.

147. I. Sh., "Lzhenauka pedologiia i ee 'metodologiia,'" p. 153.

148. A. Griboedov, *Novoe v defektologii* (n.p., 1938).

149. M. Zaretskii, "Kritika printsipov testovykh izmerenii," *Sovetskaia pedagogika*, no. 1 (1937), 35.

150. Besides *Pedology*—the main tribune of the pedological movement—*Psychology, Journal of Neurapathology and Psychiatry, Man and Nature, Soviet Neuropathology, Psychiatry and Psycho Hygiene, Instincts and Habits*, and many other journals were discontinued. By contrast, the first issue of *Soviet Pedagogic* came out in 1937 and of *Soviet Science* in 1938.

151. I. Sh., "Lzhenauka pedologiia i ee 'metodologiia,'" p. 151.

152. Anane'v, "O glavnom 'zakone' pedologii," p. 19.

153. Veidemiuller and Shcheglov, "Freidizm," pp. 189–190.

154. A. Luriia, "Psikhoanaliz," in *BSE*, vol. 47, s.v.

155. Bubnov, "Vosstanovit' polnost'iu v pravakh pedagogiku i pedagogov," p. 58; V. Skosyrev and T. Chuguev, "Lzhenauchnye otkrytiia pedologa Zalkinda," *Knigi i proletarskaia revoliutsiia*, no. 10 (1936), 21–33.

156. Zaretskii, "Kritika printsipov testovykh izmerenii," p. 39.

157. Zaluzhnyi, *Lzhenauka pedologiia v "trudakh" Zalkinda*, pp. 6–8, 12, 16, 19–21, 30.

158. Plotnikov, "Do kontsa razoblachit' lzhenauku pedologiiu," p. 49.

159. "O sostoianii i zadachakh psikhologicheskoi nauki v SSSR," *Pod znamenem marksizma*, no. 9 (1936), 88.

160. A. Luriia and A. Leontiev, "Psikhologiia," in *BSE*, 47: 512.

161. *Pravda*, August 31, 1936.

162. M. Odintsev, "K voprosu o vospityvaiushchem obuchenii v sovetskoi shkole," *Sovetskaia pedagogika*, no. 2 (1937), 23.

163. F. Georgiev, "Protiv bikheivorizma i reaktologii," *Pod znamemem marksizma*, no. 1 (1937), 168.

164. K. Fedorovskii, "Individual'nyi podkhod k uchashchimusia v sovetskoi shkole," *Sovetskaia pedagogika*, no. 3 (1937), 117–119.

165. Odintsev, "K voprosu o vospityvaiushchem obuchenii," p. 22. See also Zaretskii, "Kritika printsipov testovykh izmerenii," p. 34; Anane'v, "O glavnom 'zakone' pedologii," p. 21.

166. "Psikhofizicheskii parallelizm," in *BSE*, vol. 47 s.v.

167. Luriia and Leontiev, "Psikhologiia," pp. 512, 546.

168. K. Kornilov, *Psikhologiia* (Moscow, 1935), p. 131.

169. Georgiev, "Protiv bikheivorizma i reaktologii," p. 168.

170. "O pedagogicheskikh izvrashcheniiakh v sisteme narkomprosov," *Pedagogika*, no. 1 (1937), 10.

171. *Za kommunisticheskoe prosveshchenie*, October 14, 1936.

172. Fomichev, "Pedalogika."

173. A. F. Sukhanov, "Ustav vysshei shkoly SSSR," *Sovetskaia nauka*, no. 2 (1938), 82–83.

174. A. Iakovlev, ed., *Reabilitatsiia: Politicheskie protsessy 30kh–50kh godov* (Moscow: Izdatel'stvo politicheskoi literatury, 1991), pp. 169–170, 175.

175. *Leningradskaia pravda*, December 18, 1934.

176. Iakovlev, *Reabilitatsiia*, p. 142.

177. Ibid., pp. 191–192, 154.

178. *Vestnik verkhovnogo suda SSSR*, no. 5 (1991), 18; Iu. Stetsovskii, *Istoriia sovetskikh repressii*, vol. 2 (St. Petersburg, 1997), p. 58.

179. *Vestnik Verkhovnogo suda SSSR*, p. 15.

180. Iakovlev, *Reabilitatsiia*, pp. 194–195.

181. R. Prede, "Luchshii borets za kommunizm," *Zapiski kommunisticheskogo sel'sko khoziaistvennogo universiteta im. I. V. Stalina* (Leningrad, 1935), p. 4.

182. Ivanov, *Missia ordena*, p. 72.

183. TsGA IPD, f. 1816, op. 2, d.5091, l. 75.

184. H. Kuromiya, *Freedom and Terror in the Donnas: A Ukrainian-Russian Borderland, 1870s–1990s* (Cambridge: Cambridge University Press, 1998), pp. 208–209; Stetsovskii, *Istoriia sovetskikh repressii*, p. 166.

185. TsGA IPD, f. 1816, op. 2, d. 5091, l. 110; d. 5095, l. 31.

186. Ibid., l. 131.

187. N. Kuz'minov and I. Motaev, "Oruzhenostsy Zinovievshchiny," *Stalinets*, no. 176, January 27, 1935.

188. TsGA IPD, f. 197, op. 1, d. 1448, ll. 21–23; d. 725, l. 272; d. 1448, l. 17.

189. A. Zviagintsev and Iu. Orlov, *Raspiatye revoliutsiei: Rossiiskie i sovetskie prokurory, XX vek, 1922–1936* (Moscow: ROSSPEN, 1998), p. 48.

190. TsGA IPD, f. 1816, op. 2, d. 5091, ll. 31–32; Ivanov, *Missia ordena*, pp. 73, 123, and 368, n. 19.

191. *Leningradskaia pravda*, January 14, 1935.

192. TsGA IPD, f. 24, op. 2b, d. 1200, ll. 24–30.

193. TsGA IPD, f. 1816, op. 2, d. 5091, l. 132.

194. Ibid., ll. 75–76.

195. TsGA IPD, f. 197, op. 1, d. 725, l. 238; d. 1448, l. 14.

196. *Pravda,* March 18, 1936.

197. *Leningradskaia pravda,* March 17, 1936.

198. Ibid.

199. *Izvestiia TsK KPSS,* no. 8 (1989), 84, 100–115; no. 9 (1989), 39.

200. *Stalinskoe Politbiuro v 30-e gody: Sbornik dokumentov* (Moscow: ROSSPEN, 1995), pp. 149–150; *Izvestiia TsK KPSS,* no. 3 (1989), 138; *Sovetskaia kul'tura,* February 25, 1989.

201. *Izvestiia TsK KPSS,* no. 8 (1989), 100–115. It is from late 1936 and not from late 1934 that the number of "counterrevolutionaries" began to swell dramatically; A. Getty, G. Rittersporn, and V. Zemkov, "Victims of the Soviet Penal System in the Prewar Years," *American Historical Review* 98 (1993), 1036.

202. M. Mitin, "O likvidatsii klassov v SSSR i sotsialisticheskom, vsenarodnom gosudarstve," *Pod znamenem marksizma,* no. 5 (1936), 18.

203. *Sovetskoe studenchestvo,* no. 6 (1936), 1; *Leningradskaia pravda,* June 5, 6, and 11, 1936. The full text of the new constitution first appeared in the Leningrad press on June 12, 1936.

204. TsGA IPD, f. 566, op. 1, d. 277, l. 22.

205. R. Siming, "Sotsializm i kommunizm," *Pod znamenem marksizma,* no. 1 (1936), 89.

206. TsGA IPD, f. 197, op. 1, d. 982, ll. 52–55.

207. *Leningradskaia pravda,* November 20, 1936.

208. TsGA IPD, f. 197, op. 1, d. 983, l. 210.

209. V. Khaustov, "Politicheskii rozysk v SSSR vo vtoroi polovine 30kh godov," in *Politicheskii sysk v Rossii: istoriia i sovremennost'* (St. Petersburg, 1997), p. 44.

210. TsGA IPD, f. 197, op. 1, d. 1132, ll. 31, 34 (July 4, 1936).

211. Ibid., d. 982, ll. 303–213.

212. TsGA IPD, f. 408, op. 1, d. 52, l. 41.

213. TsGA IPD, f. 566, op. 1, d. 276, ll. 40–41.

214. Ibid., d. 254, ll. 65–67 (July 25, 1936).

215. A. Getty, *Origins of the Great Purges: The Soviet Communist Party Reconsidered, 1933–1938* (Cambridge: Cambridge University Press, 1985), p. 144.

216. *Stalinets,* no. 234, June 17, 1936.

217. TsGA IPD, f. 566, op. 1, d. 21b, ll. 30–31.

218. *Stalinets,* no. 236, June 25, 1936; no. 634, April 1, 1937.

219. TsGA IPD, f. 1816, op. 2, d. 4922, ll. 3–17.

220. TsGA IPD, f. 197, op. 1, d. 983, ll. 276–277; f. 566, op. 1, d. 276, l. 112.

221. A. Leont'ev, "Chelovekopredmety," *Sovetskoe studenchestvo,* no. 9 (1937), 43.

222. TsGA IPD, f. 24, op. 2b, d. 1200, l. 143; emphasis in original.

223. TsGA IPD, f. 566, op. 1, d. 288, ll. 68–69 (December 27, 1937).

224. *Voprosy istorii,* no. 6 (1994), 11.

225. *Voprosy istorii,* no. 5 (1990), 50.

226. *Voprosy istorii,* no. 9 (1993), 26.

227. *Partiinoe stroitel'stvo,* no. 22 (1936), 48–52; no. 23–24 (1935), 77–80; *Leningradskaia pravda,* April 27, May 21, and July 7, 1936.

228. *Stalinets,* no. 231, May 25, 1936.

229. *Leningradskaia pravda,* October 30, 1936.

230. TsGA IPD, f. 408, op. 1, d. 18, ll. 6, 14.

231. TsGA IPD, f. 197, op. 1, d. 983, ll. 141, 152; d. 986, ll. 22–24.

232. Ibid., d. 982, ll. 161, 169, 178, 184, 191.

233. Ibid., d. 331, l. 19.

234. Ibid., d. 269, ll. 33–34.

235. Ibid., d. 1737, l. 6.

236. Ibid., d. 986, ll. 62–67.

237. Ibid., l. 68.

238. TsGA IPD, f. 566, d. 274, ll. 33–34.

239. "Stalinskaia konstitutsiia i kommunisticheskoe vospitanie podrastaiushchego pokoleniia," *Sovetskaia pedagogika,* no. 4 (1937), 4.

240. Stalin, *Sochineniia,* 12: 10–11, quoted in E. Naiman, "Discourse Made Flesh: Healing and Terror in the Construction of Soviet Subjectivity," in *Language and Revolution,* ed. Igal Halfin (London: Frank Cass, 2002), pp. 19–20.

241. Stetsovskii, *Istoriia sovetskikh repressii,* p. 76.

242. TsGA IPD, f. 566, op. 1, d. 288, l. 49.

243. N. Perl, *Zakon sokhraneniia* (St. Petersburg: Borei, 1994), pp. 102–103.

244. TsGA IPD, f. 566, op. 1, d. 208, ll. 146–151.

245. V. Rogovin, *Partiia rasstreliannykh* (Moscow: Novosti, 1997), p. 283.

246. *Bol'shevik,* no. 16 (1937), 62–63.

247. TsGA IPD, f. 566, op. 1, d. 280, ll. 90–91.

248. A. Voitlovskaia, "Sud nad sledovatelem," in *Zven'ia,* vol. 1 (Moscow, 1991), pp. 403–407.

249. Iakovlev, *Reabilitatsiia,* p. 183.

250. *Obshchestvo i vlast',* p. 183.

251. For the typical injunction of the recent Russian press, "Do not blame the victims!" see L. Fink, "Nel'zia vinit' zhertvy!" *Nedelia,* no. 46 (1988).

252. A. Vyshinskii, *Sudebnye rechi* (Moscow, 1955), p. 560.

Epilogue

1. TsGA IPD, f. 984, op. 1, d. 126, ll. 38–39.

2. Victor Serge, *The Year One of the Russian Revolution* (Oxford: Oxford University Press, 1963), pp. 228–229.

3. Ibid., p. 229.

4. E. Iaroskavskii, "Filosofiia upadochnichestva," *Bol'shevik,* no. 23–24 (1927), 135–138.

5. *Izvestiia TsK KPSS,* no. 5 (1989), 71.

6. Quoted in O. Khlevniuk, *1937-i, Stalin, NKVD i sovetskoe obshchestvo* (Moscow, 1992), p. 201; V. Rogovin, *1937-i* (Moscow: Novosti, 1997), pp. 110–111.

7. *Voprosy istorii,* no. 6–7 (1992), 23–24.

8. *Kommunist,* no. 17 (1990), 73.

9. *Voprosy istorii,* no. 5 (1990), 53–54.

10. TsGA IPD, f. 197, op. 1, d. 982, ll. 209–211.

11. Quoted in Rogovin, *1937,* p. 108.

12. V. Denisov and Iu. Murin, *Iosif Stalin v ob"iatiiakh sem'i: Iz lichnogo arkhiva* (Moscow: Rodina, 1993), p. 22.

13. Quoted in Khlevniuk, *1937-i,* pp. 202–203.

14. Arch Getty and Oleg Naumov, *The Road to Terror: Stalin and the Self-Destruction of the Bolsheviks, 1932–1939* (New Haven: Yale University Press, 1999), p. 218.

15. *Pravda,* June 1, 1937.

16. Khlevniuk, *1937-i,* pp. 204–205, 201–202.

17. N. Lebina, *Povsednevnaia zhizn' sovetskogo goroda, 1920–1930 gody* (St. Petersburg: "Letnii sad," 1999), p. 115.

18. Getty and Naumov, *The Road to Terror,* pp. 216–217.

19. *Izvestiia TsK KPSS,* no. 8 (1989), 90.

20. *Izvestiia,* September 2, 1992.

21. *The Anti-Stalin Campaign and International Communism* (New York: Columbia University Press, 1956), pp. 22–23.

22. G. Haupt and M. Jean Jacques, eds., *Makers of the Russian Revolution: Biographies of Bolshevik Leaders* (Ithaca: Cornell University Press, 1974), p. 120.

23. A. Iakovlev, ed., *Reabilitatsiia: Politicheskie protsessy 30kh–50kh godov* (Moscow: Izdatel'stvo politicheskoi literatury, 1991), pp. 162–164, 184–185.

24. N. Bukharin, "Vsiudu i vezde ia budu nastaivat' na svoei polnoi i absoliutnoi nevinovnosti," *Istochnik,* no. 2 (1993), 25.

25. *Izvestiia,* September 2, 1992.

26. I. Berger-Barzilai, *Ha-tragedyah shel ha-makhpekhah ha-Sovyetit* (The Tragedy of the Soviet Revolution) (Tel Aviv: Am Oved, 1968), p. 147.

27. A. Larina, "Vsegda verila chto pravda vostorzhestvuet," in *Bukharin: Chelovek, politik, uchenyi,* ed. V. Zhuravlev (Moscow: izd. polit. lit, 1990), p. 398.

28. Marx's 1844 Paris Manuscripts are quoted in A. Walicki, *Marxism and the Leap to the Kindgdom of Freedom: The Rise and Fall of the Communist Utopia* (Stanford: Stanford University Press, 1995), p. 48.

29. Quoted in Igor Golomstock, *Totalitarian Art in the Soviet Union, Fascist Italy, and the People's Republic of China* (London: Collins Harvill, 1990), p. 27.

30. L. Trotsky, "Ikh moral' i nasha," *Biulleten' oppozitsii,* no. 68–69 (1938), 19.

31. This quotation, often repeated during World War II, was apparently first voiced during the battles at the Khasan Lake; *Krasnaia zvezda,* September 4, 1938.

32. Orlando Figes and Boris Kolonitskii, *Interpreting the Russian Revolution: The Language and Symbols of 1917* (New Haven: Yale University Press, 1999), p. 75.

33. N. Bukharin, *Tiuremnye tetradi,* vol. 1 (Moscow, 1996), p. 5.

34. Arthur Klinghoffer, *Red Apocalypse* (New York: University Press of America 1996), p. 82.

35. V. Demidov and V. Kutuzov, eds., *"Leningradsoe Delo"* (Leningrad: Lenizdat, 1990), p. 117.

36. Katerina Clark, *The Soviet Novel: History as Ritual* (Chicago: University of Chicago Press, 1985), pp. 49, 176, 179–182.

Index